Contentious Terrains: Boglands, Ireland, Postcolonial Gothic

Contentious Terrains

Boglands, Ireland, Postcolonial Gothic

DEREK GLADWIN

First published in 2016 by
Cork University Press
Youngline Industrial Estate
Pouladuff Road, Togher
Cork
T12 HT6V
Ireland

British Library Cataloguing in Publication Data
A CIP record for this book is available from the British Library.

ISBN: 978-1-78205-204-3

Printed in Malta by Gutenberg Press.
Print origination & design by Carrigboy Typesetting Services,
www.carrigboy.com

www.corkuniversitypress.com

Contents

List of Figures

Acknowledgements

Mike Collins and Maria O'Donovan, as well as the support staff, at Cork University Press deserve the deepest thanks for supporting this project and administering the publishing process with such care. I am also grateful to both peer reviewers for their incisive comments, many of which significantly improved the final product of this book. Thanks also go to the editorial board at CUP for final approval of the book.

I have been fortunate along the way to have so many quality readers who have offered comments and suggestions – some of which are currently on the cutting room floor, but which helped create the 'bones' of this book. At the University of Alberta, I wish to thank Garry Watson, Stephen Slemon, Jeremy Caradonna, and particularly Rob Brazeau for their diligent feedback in early stages of this research. At University College Cork, I wish to thank Claire Connolly, Heather Laird, Patricia Coughlan, and Maureen O'Connor, all of whom aided this book in various ways and at different stages. At Memorial University Newfoundland, I am indebted to Danine Farquharson for her continual encouragement and editorial assistance along the way. At DePaul University, I want to thank Jim Fairhall, who was an early proponent of my work on bogs and offered continual backing of this book; I am also grateful, at the bequest of Jim, to present some of this work at DePaul University's Earth Day event in 2015. At National University Ireland, Galway, I want to recognise Nessa Cronin and Tadhg Foley, both of whom regaled me with stories about bog-lore in Ireland. At National University Ireland, Maynooth, I am grateful for Moynagh Sullivan's feedback and ongoing cheer. At Seton Hill University, I am indebted to Christine Cusick, one of the few careful readers and scholars of Irish boglands and culture. There are numerous others not listed here who in some way or another were influential coordinates on the larger mental map of this book.

It should also be noted that I spent a few summers at the Irish Seminar held at the O'Connell House in Dublin, organised and funded by the Keough-Naughton Institute for Irish Studies at University of Notre Dame, where the seeds of this book began to take root. Thanks to the Director, Kevin Whelan, for early discussions about the importance of bogs and culture in Ireland. Two journals additionally helped me crystallise some of my ideas in early stages of development: *Irish Studies Review* and *Gothic Studies*. I am also grateful for the Vanier Scholarship of Canada, and other travel and academic awards received at the University of Alberta, which funded travel for various research trips to Ireland.

In addition, I am lucky to have been able to obtain the rights and gain permissions to reproduce the images in this book from various museums, archives, publishers, organisations, and individuals. Thanks to Kelly Sullivan for allowing me to use (again) such wonderful photographs of Irish landscapes, and to her other assistance along the way with concepts and approaches in the book; to Angie Shanahan for a beautiful drawing of a turf bank; to Anthony Haughey for capturing some bog footings in Donegal; to the Irish Peatland Conservation Council for a bog-map of Ireland; to the National Museum of Ireland Bog Bodies Research Project for reproductions of bog bodies; to Rachel Brown for the use of her photos from *The Donegal Pictures* (1987), as well as unpublished photos of bogs, one of which serves as the cover; to the John Hinde Estate for a Hinde photo; to the Seamus Heaney Estate, Faber & Faber, and Farrar, Straus and Giroux, LLC, for granting permissions to reprint (through Fair Use guidelines) sections from Heaney's *Preoccupations: Selected Prose, 1968-1978* (1980) and *Opened Ground: Selected Poems, 1966–1996* (1998); to Remco de Fouw and Christine Bond for a photo of earth-art in bogs; to The Tollund Man exhibit at the Silkeborg Museum in Denmark for a photo of Tollund Man; to Deirdre Kinahan, Pat Redmond, and Tall Tales Theatre Company in Ireland for photos of 2010 productions of *Bog Boy*; to the Tim Robinson Archive, Hardiman Library, NUI Galway for a map; to Pat Collins and Colm Hogan for a film still of Connemara bogland; and, finally, to the Bobbie Hanvey photographic archives, John J. Burns Library, Boston College for photos of Heaney.

Lastly, a colossal thanks goes to Patricia Barkaskas for her tireless support and encouragement. She not only read versions of this book, at various stages, but she also spent (probably too much) time traipsing across wet bogs during my empirical research sessions in Ireland. And, thanks to BMK and QM for their gentle and soft inspiration in the wee hours of the morning.

Foreword

Wetlands without Walls

In Maria Edgeworth's 1809 novel, *Ennui*, the well-intentioned Lord Glenthorn builds a new house for his old nurse, Ellinor: an 'ornamented farm-house' that provides such modern conveniences as a slated roof. The internal partitions are however 'built with turf or peat, instead of bricks', in what Glenthorn believes to be an act of 'wise economy'. Ellinor fails to appreciate these luxuries and the 'dirt, rubbish, and confusion' of her cottage becomes a shocking scene of misused resources: the slated roof is replaced with a thatched one, she dismantles the staircase for firewood and the walls are 'pulled down to get at the turf'.

What are we to make of this image of an elderly peasant woman burning the walls of her own home? Readers familiar with conventional English housing built by craftsmen who invested time and skills in the fabric of a stone structure are likely to understand this scene in terms of ignorance and vandalism. Edgeworth makes such a reading available but she does not simply endorse it. Rather, *Ennui* opens a perspective onto everyday Irish life on the edge of an upland bog, where many houses were built in a matter of days and made from the materials that were found closest to hand. Such routine environmental hazards as wet summers might mean fuel shortages and could result in a situation whereby the walls of the house became more valuable as fuel than as partitions. In a different reading, Edgeworth might be helping us to see the contours of a self-sustaining rural economy under threat from hasty modernization. Later in the same novel, Lord Glenthorn confesses that a sight he first understood in terms of Irish absurdity – turf-cutters working beside bonfires on a hot summer's day – actually has its own persuasive cultural logic, given the power of the smoke 'to drive away or destroy those myriad of tiny insects, called *midges*' by which the workers are 'tormented'.

As with Edgeworth's novel, uncertainty is central to *Contentious Terrains*. Boglands, argues Derek Gladwin, are 'visually deceptive, physically volatile, and conceptually elusive'. Edgeworth allows us to see (if we can look past the fire smoke) not only the central role of role of turf within the moral economy of pre-Famine Ireland but also the complex resonances of peat bogs in Irish culture and the difficulty of getting at their meanings. Bogs are everywhere present in Irish culture yet never straightforward in their associations: a liquid topography that is easily mistaken for solid ground and a metaphor that tends to misunderstanding and uncertainty. For Edgeworth, boglands speak to Enlightenment debates about knowledge and cultural difference and register the realities of an extractive colonial economy. They are also places of human habitation and contain and support lives and folkways no less mysterious and complex than the bog itself.

As befits a book about bogs and their many meanings within Irish culture, *Contentious Terrains* draws on a wide range of scholarly disciplines to advance its argument: cultural geography, history, Gothic and postcolonial studies. Its real energy though comes from the imaginative writing in which the book's argument is so productively immersed. Despite its impressive marshaling of the science of wetland environments, the book knows bogs best via their nuanced inscription in literature and culture. In contrast to the threatened ecology of peat bogs, the resources of literature are limitless, open-ended and generative – without walls.

Edgeworth's bog house finds an uncanny resonance in a contemporary short story that concerns itself with the bog both as concept and as lived reality. 'Dark Lies the Island', the title story of Kevin Barry's 2012 collection, depicts a depressed young woman who is spending time in the family holiday home that her father designed. Trying to resist the urge to cut or hurt herself, she ponders the house, built on a bog and overlooking Clew Bay in County Mayo. Her own damage is echoed in that of the landscape: '"Wounded," her father would call the bog', reminding readers of the cuts that scar industrialized peatlands but also referencing the traditional use of sphagnum moss for healing. The young woman's father, 'a radical architect who had reinterrogated the concept of walls', has created a house porous to the bog in which it sits. A bog stream runs through the open plan space, and the house resounds to the 'low constant murmuring of its brown tarry waters'. It as if Ellinor's cottage had found postcolonial expression: a lost tradition born from poverty, found again in an era of prosperity and second homes and made new within a glass and steel frame. The ability of wetland environments to preserve matter over time is key to such a drama of submersion and retrieval.

The scholarly power of *Contentious Terrains* lies in its attention to creative remaking of the meanings of bogland. Derek Gladwin performs his own act of remembering via compelling close readings of literary and cultural representations of mire, fens, swamp, morasses and other kinds of sodden topographies. The final chapter poses challenging questions derived from the current imperilled state of wetland environments: these act as a call to readers to generate their own readings and discover new critical ground. Perhaps the most powerful moment in this important book comes in its conclusion, with the suggestion that the science and culture of bogs should be brought into closer relationship. We can also appreciate their differences: where the specialised language of science can alienate, cultural representations of bogs retain a compelling power to throw down walls and open up paths to understanding. The power of literature to realize bog topographies in compelling ways remains a vital resource in efforts to preserve our peatland heritage and avert ecological disaster.

CLAIRE CONNOLLY
University College Cork

Indeterminate Boglands and the Irish Postcolonial Gothic

> Bogland is an obstructive, argumentative, quibbling, contentious terrain; it demands step-by-step negotiations.[1]
> – Tim Robinson, *Connemara: Listening to the Wind*

> Viscous landscapes evince a dangerously mesmeric attraction.[2]
> – Catherine Wynne, *The Colonial Conan Doyle*

Conceptualising the Bogginess of the Bog

This book is about boglands and how they are exceptionally numinous and representational terrains in Irish literature and culture. Boglands/ bogland, or 'bogs' as a shorthand name for a type of wetland (mires, morasses, swamps, lagoons, fens, and sloughs), are squishy, moss-covered topographies that function as a 'halfway world', neither exclusively water nor land and yet 'part of both'.[3] Part liquid, part gas, and part solid material composed of decomposed plant and animal remains thousands of years old, bogs challenge our notions of reality by creating imagined worlds through common material spaces. As unformed landmasses, bogs stretch across many parts of Ireland and are often associated with culture, politics, and history as much as they are with geography and geology.

On the surface, a bog appears to be firm land (see Fig. 0.1), and yet, it does not provide solid footing and historically accounts for untimely deaths through drowning and asphyxiation. Bogs also shift without warning, almost like avalanches, squashing and suffocating anyone or anything in their paths. Covered in mist, bogs produce a miasma effect, clouding reality and fiction. They are visually deceptive, physically volatile, and conceptually elusive. The doubling quality of the bog – paradoxically both

1

0.1 Bogland topography in Connemara (photo by Kelly Sullivan)

solid and liquid – resists obvious categorisation and therefore management, organisation, and control. Bogs are simultaneously limited and limitless, yielding and unyielding, canny and uncanny, stable and unstable, ordered and disordered, known and unknown, political and apolitical, spatial and indeterminate, and temporal and atemporal. In the Iron Age, a period in which Irish bogs saw rapid geological development and became the predominant landmass on the island, bogs were considered to be gateways to other worlds and therefore places of communication with spirits.[4] The related metaphor of bogs as doors or gateways signals their transitional and interstitial qualities, linking two worlds as one, even as these worlds are thought to coexist as separate spaces. As the epigraphs from Tim Robinson and Catherine Wynne intimate, boglands are both attractive and also dangerous because of their viscous qualities, distinct and yet integrated. They are also, as I will demonstrate throughout this book, contentious terrains that demand sustained critical attention.

When they are included in Irish literature and culture, bogs often evoke Gothic associations through the mysterious, mesmerising, and macabre. A considerable amount of Gothic fiction is located on opaque landscapes with unclear demarcations between the known and unknown.

In *Gothic* (1996), Fred Botting acknowledges, 'Gothic landscapes are desolate, alienating and full of menace.'[5] Lizabeth Paravisini-Gebert similarly remarks that the Gothic is continually 'linked to colonial settings, characters, and realities as frequent embodiments of the forbidding and frightening'.[6] It is the unity of the real (or biological) and the imagined (or symbolic) qualities of the bog that attract writers to its multi-dimensional viscous goo. Such a dynamic creates unclear, menacing, and forbidding qualities that associate the bog with Gothic literary themes. Over the years, Gothic scholars have to some extent identified these swampy and 'undefined zones' in British and Irish literature. Some notable examples – with what we would now call 'wetlands' as a central image – include the Yorkshire moors in Emily Brontë's *Wuthering Heights* (1847), Egdon Heath in Thomas Hardy's *Return of the Native* (1887), Dartmoor in Arthur Conan Doyle's *Hound of the Baskervilles* (1902), the morass-like no-place in Samuel Beckett's *Waiting for Godot* (1953), East Anglian fens in Graham Swift's *Waterland* (1982), and the marshes of north-eastern England in Susan Hill's *The Woman in Black* (1983).[7] While these works exemplify the contradictory qualities of wetlands and the way they are depicted in the Gothic literary form, they are not set in Ireland nor do they exclusively focus on bogs in Irish literature and culture.

The decision to write about how geography influences Irish culture and socio-political histories originated from a curiosity as to why the bog topography continually allures and seduces writers to its marshy depths. On the surface, one could deduce that recurring macabre descriptions of bogs were popularised in culture, but uncanny qualities associated with bogs – supernatural, ambiguous, eerie – do more than merely invite popular attention.[8] The images of bogs enable creative representation that compels sustained critical attention in Irish Studies. Because of their liminal states, bogs are also difficult to write about or discuss in definitive terms. How, then, do we critically frame a study about bogs when they are so conceptually and physically deceptive? More specifically, why are bogs in Ireland often associated with both Gothic themes and the politics of colonisation? Does writing about bogs and their ghosts make a writer 'Gothic' or do Gothic writers simply share a fascination with bogs and their symbolic and empirical union? How do writers use the bog and the Gothic form to conceal socio-political agendas in their work?

Bogs are considered to be Gothic because they haunt other forms of political or historical literary representation. According to the Gothic scholar Jarlath Killeen, 'What is peculiarly "Irish" about the Gothic tradition is that it emerged from a geographical zone which was defined as weird and bizarre. Indeed, Ireland as a whole was identified as a Gothic space'[9] (see Fig. 0.2). Killeen's description provides a productive beginning for my own point of departure because he identifies historical links between Gothic production and geographical spaces represented in certain works. Moving away from a totalising view that Ireland represents a certain kind of definable 'Gothic space', this book investigates how the bog elucidates this 'bizarre' geographical and Gothic zone through literature and culture.

Various modern and contemporary Irish writers are stimulated to write about bogs as they explore political ruptures in Irish history. As a result, I want to approach the politics of colonisation by way of the Gothic form through this specific geographical terrain that elicits both postcolonial and Gothic associations for Irish writers. The reason for this is because representations of bogs allow for certain slippages, or purposeful confusions, to occur – between memory and history or modernisation and tradition, for example – by writers who interrogate Irish socio-political history. Bogs are, as the geographer Diane Meredith points out, 'profoundly ambiguous landscapes',[10] and their ambiguity is what makes them so compelling. Due to their uncanny natures, bogs destabilise a sense of historical and spatial order, and this effect of disruption resounds throughout Irish politics and history.[11] Bogs consequently provide the ideal interplay between the empirical and symbolic in literary culture, especially given that bogs have all too often been simply considered in metaphorical or symbolic terms.

The larger aim of the book is to focus on specific Irish literary works in the modern and contemporary periods, from the 1880s to the present, through the ubiquitous and recognisable landform of the bog. Drawing on a range of writers, including Bram Stoker, Frank O'Connor, Sean O'Faolain, Daniel Corkery, Seamus Heaney, Marina Carr, Deirdre Kinahan, Patrick McCabe, Patrick McGinley, Erin Hart, and Tim Robinson, *Contentious Terrains* argues that the destabilising capacities of the bog provide a space to explore historical colonial tensions and social struggles through the postcolonial Gothic form. Bogs open the way toward transcending strict dualisms, and I refer to this process throughout the book as unions or simultaneities of opposites. Because the properties of bogs concurrently challenge and create oppositions, Irish writers use bogs as both terrestrial (real and earthly) and also symbolic (imaginative and conceptual) spaces to explore fissures in colonial politics. These

0.2 Gothic spaces in Irish bogland, Co. Cork (photo by Kelly Sullivan)

seemingly contrary representational spaces of opposites also let writers address the complexity of political narratives through the temporally and spatially flexible Gothic form. This book serves as an interface between two important issues in Irish Studies: modern and contemporary literary geographic histories of bogs and the literary and cultural dimensions of the postcolonial Gothic as a response to them. The bog not only represents a highly significant landform in Irish geography and culture; it also generates conversations about Irish literary histories related to colonisation through Gothic conventions. As such, this introduction underscores some of the geographical and postcolonial Gothic theories that foreground the larger study.

The bog, as explained more specifically in Chapter 1, is ultimately a loaded symbol/image/vector to examine in light of other slippery and multilayered topics related to postcolonial and Gothic literature. Some of these topics include modernisation and the environment (Chapter 2), nationalism and haunting (Chapter 3), mapping and bog bodies (Chapter 4), neocolonialism and gender (Chapter 5), and crime and ecology (Chapter 6). Ultimately, bogs are sites of both interplay and disjunction and demand a multifaceted and intertextual way of approaching how they are represented in literature and culture. The imaginative and biological qualities of the bog – both contradictory and also complementary – are what attract or seduce writers to incorporate them in important works. The bog is resonant for many reasons, but what produces its energy and what underscores its prevalence is also what makes sure that it never quite collapses into a single, definitive meaning. The anomalous phenomenon of the bog challenges clear representations of it in literature because it undermines many binaries that are prevalent in culture.[12]

Theorising the interplay between the material and symbolic qualities of bogs a bit further, I want to emphasise how they are not oppositional sites in terms of traditional either/or binaries. Rather, bogs function as sites that both terrestrially and imaginatively create what Edward Soja has called 'Thirdspace', a flexible way of thinking about fluctuating ideas, events, appearances and representations, and how these affect the material and perceptual ways geographical spaces change.[13] If Firstspace is the 'real' material world, and Secondspace is the 'imagined' world, then Thirdspace is the multiplicity of the 'real-and-imagined' world. Soja's notion of 'both/and also logic', as he explains in his book *Thirdspace* (1996), offers an alternative way to view space beyond the closed logic of either/or, and it does so without privileging one over the other, with the 'also' reverberating back to disrupt the implicit closure in two-dimensional either/or logic.[14]

Rather than adopting reductionist epistemologies of 'master narratives' or 'totalising discourses' (producing an either/or choice) often drawn from imperialist ideologies, the 'both/and also' logic associated with Thirdspace (or whatever term one chooses to use) draws from postmodern theories of knowledge formation that seek to alleviate deep divisions within spatial and historical analysis by creating simultaneous possibilities.[15] Soja's articulation of both/and also logic – which I instead refer to as unions/fusions/simultaneities of opposites – helps to conceptualise the spatial, in addition to the temporal and social, qualities of the bog in order to demonstrate that there is a critical exchange that moves beyond a limited one- or two-dimensionality to a limitless multi-dimensionality of geographical and social spaces.[16]

Thirdspace serves as a useful introductory paradigm for understanding bogs in pluralistic and multifocal ways, instead of through a singular or dualistic totalising analysis. This concept helps us conceive of a changing geography with imaginative as well as physical qualities, which does not ignore the obvious temporal or social dimensions, but also stresses the spatial elements as part of a 'three-sided sensibility' that is trans-disciplinary in scope.[17] In *Spatial Ecologies* (2012), Verena Andermatt Conley similarly notes: 'space is variously seen as a production, an invention, and opening, an area in-between, intermediary, a continuum in perpetual transition'.[18] With the bog there is a special privileging of a certain image/structure of an 'intermediary' metaphoric association in 'transition', a space that is socially produced, but this association comes about through its seemingly contradictory biological qualities as a wetland and cultural space. The space of the bog functions in an almost alternative 'third' or 'in-between' space that can be an opening, an invention, and a place of constant transition for writers. Bogs have not, heretofore, been associated with the notion of Thirdspace, but Soja's theory nevertheless offers a useful preliminary remark to help conceive of the both/and also unification of apparent opposites underpinning my own conceptualisation of the bog represented in literary culture.[19] Irish writers often draw on, consciously or unconsciously, the both/and also relationships inherent in the bog to syncretise discrete or opposite ideas and images to produce a complex and uneasy unity.

Looking at bogs from another geographical and Gothic reference point, they may be understood as what Yi-Fu Tuan calls 'landscapes of fear'. Although framed as a study in human geography, *Landscapes of Fear* (1979) draws useful parallels with Gothic spaces, which might include scenes represented in texts, imaginative conceptions, or physical locations that create anthropomorphic reactions to them. For Tuan, landscapes are both metaphorical and literal; they produce subjective feelings of fear and anxiety and objective analysis as biological or material spaces. Tuan has, throughout his work, examined the human individual and society in relation to various physical and cultural geographies. This has been evident, for example, in his formative book, *Topophilia* (1974), which assessed humans' sensorial relationship with space and place.[20] Writers and artists in the humanities often use the same topophilic approach – exploring affective ties with material environments through characters, senses, values, perception, and narrative – while developing the polymorphous nature of human experience in the world.

Building on the idea of narrative, which Tuan argues resolves contradictory or binary thinking, he writes:

In every study of the human individual and of human society, fear is a theme – either covert as in stories of courage and success, or explicit as in works on phobias and human conflict. Yet no one (so far as we know) has attempted to take 'landscapes of fear' as a topic worthy of systematic exploration in its own right and for the light it may shed on questions of perennial interest ... seeking in particular to trace links and resonances between various landscapes of fear.[21]

Landscapes of fear draw on the polymorphous experiences that transcend strict dualisms related to perception. Fear, marked by alarm (external forces of threat) and anxiety (self-induced dread from within), underscores our universally experienced and affective relationship with specific environments, even if not consciously recognised. Tuan adds to the human dimension the characteristics of 'landscape', which since the seventeenth century was construed as both a 'physical and measurable entity', culturally infused and yet geographically measured.[22] Indeed, landscape, like 'culture' and 'nature', remains a complicated and multivalent term.

For the cultural geographer John Wylie, in his roundly praised book *Landscape* (2007), landscapes capture a range of our everyday perceptions and are highly phenomenological as much as they are controversial, and therefore difficult to reduce into a single definition. In other words, landscapes are imagined culturally as much as they are physical or material. Moreover, landscapes exist in constant 'tension', creating what we might describe as a both/and also relationship 'between proximity and distance, body and mind, sensuous immersion and detached observation'.[23] Does the concept of landscape facilitate, as Wylie queries, an 'interconnectivity of self, body, knowledge and land' or a culturally constructed concept used by artists to create proximity and distance?[24] The answer to this rhetorical question might simply be that landscapes can be framed through both/and also logic because they are cultural as much as they are biological. Viewing bogs as *both* landscapes *and also* specific material landforms provides some flexibility in how they might be represented in cultural forms like literature and geography, while not negating their unique biodiversity and ecological agency as important ecosystems.

The anthropologist Stuart McLean, who has previously written some influential essays about bogs and wetlands in the cultural imagination, introduces the concept of 'interstitial landscapes', those existing 'between clearly differentiated states of matter, specifically liquid and solid'. He goes on to argue that such 'landscapes', seen as 'spaces' in 'cultural imaginaries', are 'distinctively, perhaps uniquely revealing of a materiality in which human cultural expression necessarily participates but which, at the same time forever exceeds their determinations'.[25] McLean critically draws on Gaston Bachelard's *Water and Dreams* (1942), which deftly explores the elemental substance of water and the role it serves in the cultural and material imagination through poetics, psychoanalysis, and materialism. For Bachelard, 'the union of water and earth produces an admixture', where matter contains an elemental experience before becoming form or a 'shape' that is 'supplanted, effaced, dissolved'.[26] Wetlands are themselves a combination of water and earth that forge a both/and also connection as both separate and also unified, material and also imaginative, formed and also formless.

Instead of framing my own approach as a strictly 'materialist' or 'physicalist' study – traditionally supporting a monist ontology where matter is the fundamental substance governing existence – I want to adopt a pluralist approach that draws on the material elements of bogs as much as the imagined and cultural ones. As Gothic studies fundamentally challenge, not all phenomena are linked to matter and the physical world, and even the essence of matter continues to be highly contested in scientific communities. Regardless, both McLean and Bachelard provide an additional means of conceptualising the material and imagined characteristics of bogs as wetlands. Such a spatio-historical ontology – cognisant of our being both/and also in space and time in the world – combines cultural and material elements drawn from the interstitial landscapes of bogs.

It should also be noted that the structure of bogs, like landscapes, complicate the oversimplified nature/culture binary often applied to them. 'Nature' is itself a highly constructed concept throughout social history, and the term remains infused with cultural layers and utilitarian agendas sustained by social and technological development. Rather than reduce 'nature' to a form of environmental determinism, environmental scholars either apply inverted commas to distinguish the term in usage, as I do here, or use a more specific term like 'ecologies' or 'built' and 'non-built environments', which explain the perceptions and uses of 'nature' instead of its own being in the world. These are part of the inherent 'tensions', as Wylie points out, that surround discussions about and interpretations of landscapes, either described as geographies or how they are represented in a cultural and human practice such as painting or literature.

At the same time, such tensions also provide additional 'third' spaces to engage with both terrestrial and imagined interpretations of bogs in literature, enhancing human perception in a literary form that in turn encompasses a political dimension. Both 'nature' and 'culture' intersect and overlap, providing an *in-between* space to explore. With this in mind, my efforts here are not to privilege either as independent or separate, but to draw on the ways in which they come together in literary practice through examples of human engagement with bogs, an attempt to express the elusiveness of these natural spaces in Ireland infused with culture and history.

In these ways specific landscapes trigger the macabre and uncanny that are developed as tropes and stylistic approaches in Gothic fiction. As Tuan argues, 'Awareness of preternatural evil, unique to the human species, enables a person to see and live in phantasmagorial [*sic*] worlds of witches, ghosts, and monsters.'[27] Feelings of fear are induced by various surroundings that draw on our polymorphous natures as human. Landscapes of fear manifest both natural and also human chaos (that is, fear of death or the end of the world), which are largely subjective reactions to specific material and imagined spaces. For Tuan, '"landscapes of fear" refers both to psychological states and to tangible environments'.[28] By deploying Gothic conventions in literature, writers enhance the already fear-inducing landscapes of bogs, creating both/and also interconnected epistemologies about humans and environments, which in turn place texts and audiences in a type of Thirdspace, between reality and fiction or real and imagined.[29]

Even in postcolonial contexts or in previous colonies within extant residues of imperialism, fear and geography forge similar links as they relate to human struggle, violence, and suffering. As the postcolonial scholar Edward Said famously wrote about imperialism, it is 'an act of geographical violence through which virtually every space in the world is explored, charted, and finally brought under control'.[30] The geographer Derek Gregory, known for his own approach to postcolonial and human geography, considers Said's postcolonial criticism to be a specific type of 'imagined geography' through the way in which places, peoples, or landscapes have consistently been culturally framed by their inventors. Gregory argues that Said 'describes landscapes and cultures being drawn into abstract grids of colonial and imperial power, literally displaced and replaced, and illuminates the ways in which these constellations become sites of appropriation, domination, and contestation'.[31]

Said's 'geography of violence', through the imagination as well as through physical violence and domination, serves as another way of approaching Tuan's 'landscapes of fear'. Fear, and fear in a particular relation to space, remains a fundamental tool used by imperial policy. It largely plays on the imagination as much as the actual occupation of physical territories. Such imaginative tools also leave residues in their aftermath that often emerge from the same spaces of conquest; writers then confront these imaginative and geographical spaces in their own creative social form. If geography is considered a type of 'earth-writing',[32] then literature focused on certain geographies (like bogs) could be considered a type of 'writing the earth'. Both expressions evoke the imaginative elements related to political histories of conflict and displacement as much as they describe elements of the actual spaces where these conflicts took place, often shrouded in the emotional trauma and haunting terror. This introductory discussion of critical geographical theory emphasises the interplay of geographical and social processes that construct underlying conceptions of space in this book, and how these constructs can reflect, reinforce, and destabilise the social and cultural relations that structure them.

Returning to the literary, representations of bogs included in some Irish literature provides a way of exploring some of the oppositions related to both circumstances of colonisation and the Gothic form, such as themes of political instabilities, transgressions, hauntings of the returning past, or even perceptions of history and memory. As I outline in this Introduction, a 'postcolonial Gothic' approach offers a pluralist, multi-temporal, and interdisciplinary field of critical thought, and one that mirrors similar qualities of the bog. Literary critic Catherine Wynne acknowledges that the 'sodden grounds' of the bog 'mirror the colonial landscape'.[33] Wynne briefly discusses these 'landscapes' within the context of the late nineteenth century in connection with the writings of Arthur Conan Doyle, but wetlands also remain associated with the colonial project and its aftermath into the twentieth and twenty-first centuries in Ireland. Investigating the bog as a Gothic and fear-inducing landscape used as a setting and symbol in literature highlights the relationships among landforms, national identity, and culture, and therefore contributes to an understanding of a multitudinous space that enables writers and readers another way to conceive of political histories tied to specific geographies.

Bogs serve as much as a pre-modern and pre-colonial archive as they do a postmodern and postcolonial one.

Some previous studies have partially examined how bogs relate to colonisation, literature, and culture. Wynne identifies bogs as 'colonial topographies' in nineteenth-century literature, though the moors in England are often treated as synonymous with bogs in Ireland. Wynne contends that 'the figure of the bog' is a common theme in nineteenth-century literature.[34] Terry Eagleton recognises that 'Objects preserved in bogs are caught in a kind of living death, and this sense of death as part of life has been a theme of traditional Irish culture.'[35] Eagleton implicitly underscores the union of death and life as part of the uncanny qualities of the bog. While he only briefly remarks on how bogs have become infused in Irish culture, Eagleton focuses on their relationship with popular culture through folklore. The archaeologist Karin Sanders acknowledges in her impressive book *Bodies in the Bog* (2009) that 'There is something fundamentally contradictory about bogs. They are solid *and* soft, firm *and* malleable, wet *and* dry; they are deep, dark, and dangerous; but they are also mysterious, alluring, and seductive.'[36] While Sanders alludes here to the bog's simultaneity of opposites, her otherwise incisive study on the 'archaeological imagination' is specifically concerned with 'bog bodies' in Europe, as archaeo-corporeal subjects through art, history, and culture, not the significance of representations of bogs in Irish literature and culture. Rod Giblett's *Postmodern Wetlands* (1996) also examines wetland environments more broadly and across many disciplines and geographies through postmodern and psychoanalytic theory. Throughout Giblett's wide analysis, he at times references bogs in literature and their persistent relevance in culture, but as a scholar of environmental humanities he mostly focuses on the interconnections among wetlands and many forms of culture around the world. Despite their appeal and importance in the field, these works do not focus exclusively on literary representations of bogs in Ireland or how Irish writers use bogs to decode recurrent connections they have with colonial politics. In fact, most research on Irish bogs remains concentrated on geographical, biological, anthropological, or archaeological elements, as opposed to literary features.[37]

Contentious Terrains combines disciplines to introduce geographical and literary research on the most well-known topography in Ireland, and in so doing brings together two other widely recognisable forms of theoretical enquiry – Gothic and postcolonial studies – as a critical lens. A study of bogs in Irish colonial literature and culture could conceivably begin in

1596 with Edmund Spenser's essay *A View of the State of Ireland*, in 1652 with Gerard Boate's natural history *Irelands Naturall History*, or in 1806 with Sydney Owenson's novel *The Wild Irish Girl*. Indeed, the eighteenth and nineteenth centuries offer many literary examples of bogs in Ireland (a history clarified in Chapter 1).

This book begins in the late nineteenth century because it is a transitional period in modern Irish history. On the one hand, this period concludes decisive issues in the eighteenth and nineteenth centuries, such as imbalanced land ownership and Anglo-Irish legitimacy; on the other hand, anticipation and subsequent action provoking shifts in political power occur, which drastically redefine national concerns leading to the revolutionary period of independence in the early twentieth century. The late nineteenth century also serves as a historical period where the scornful and discriminating perceptions of bogs and the people who live on or near them ultimately shift moving in to the twentieth century, when bogs are viewed as symbols of national identity and cultural spaces, and later as spaces of ecological diversity and importance into the contemporary period. The Gothic, to add another dimension, often appears at historical and social junctures to contest traditional ways of being; its apogee remains in crisis or traumatic transition, juxtaposing traditional knowledge or behaviours with modernity and forms of 'progress'. Characters and events in Gothic literature, for instance, confront monstrous representations of traditional epistemologies and mores through specific historical transitions and ruptures.[38] As a result, it makes sense that Gothic tropes continue to be deployed by writers throughout the modern and contemporary period amidst the residues of colonisation.

Much of the scholarship on the Irish Gothic tends to begin in the seventeenth century and end in the late nineteenth century, focusing on previous historical transitions and crises that pertain to the differences between Irish and Anglo-Irish identity and the changing power structures during colonisation. One case in point is a recently published collection, *Irish Gothics* (2014), which spans the years 1760–1890. My own intervention effectively takes up where this collection ends, framed as literary and cultural geographic history, and examining works concentrating on bogs in four tumultuous periods between 1890 and the present. It surveys this timeframe of Irish geo-history through various literary works that appropriate and re-appropriate one of the most familiar terrains in Ireland. Writings featuring bogs uncover some of the underlying questions during and after colonisation, showing how bogs relate to larger social issues in the development of modern Irish literary history, particularly after the Land Wars of the 1880s; during the Irish War of Independence (1919–1921) and post-Independence in the 1930s; in the sectarian conflicts of Northern Ireland in the 1960s and 1970s; and during and after the 'Celtic Tiger' cultural and economic phenomenon in the 1990s and 2000s. Continuities between and larger circumstances around modern and contemporary histories, although contextualised to some extent in each chapter, are less instrumental to my analysis than the immediate occurrences surrounding each specific literary work that represents the bog. Each work featured within these four periods utilises the bog to address historical moments, but these have only recently passed for each writer. Thus, each literary work exerts a controlling force on an unfolding present moment, while it also draws from the past and looks to the future, subverting temporal linearity.

The historical logic of this book somewhat defies an obvious periodisation of Irish literary history in the modern and contemporary periods. Typically, this literary history includes Irish Modernism, Revivalism, Big House novels, Irish language literature, and the literature of Northern Ireland, and is often separated into specific literary genres like modern Irish theatre, the Irish novel, or contemporary Irish poetry. The bog does not somehow disappear from 1900 to the revolutionary period starting in 1916 or later during the 1940s and 1950s.[39] Rather, the four periods selected for this study – with two additional bookending chapters describing the morphology of the bog and the expanding trends in contemporary bog literature – underscore sustained intervals of political and social struggle that also happen to offer many representational literary works incorporating the bog and employing Gothic tropes, particularly in how they highlight issues about geography, identity, and colonial history.

Accordingly, this book offers diverse historical and cultural scope that examines men and women, Catholics and Protestants, nationalists and non-nationalists, and canonical and non-canonical writers in multiple literary genres representing the novel, short fiction, drama, poetry, and non-fiction prose. Such a wide range of perspectives not only speak to the pervasiveness, range, and tenacity of bogs' allure, but also allows many different literary voices to partake in the conversation, some of which have not previously been associated with Gothic or postcolonial literature. By way of introduction, I ultimately explore how the physical and imaginative topography of the bog is an overlooked element in understanding why and how writers have responded in the Gothic form to specific political ruptures of Irish history.

Irish Postcolonial Gothic

Because the bog for Irish writers evinces a recurring set of concerns, one of the more effective ways to elucidate these concerns is through the critical lens of the postcolonial Gothic. For Irish writers, exploring aspects of the bog and its intimate link with Irish culture and history serves as one way to answer some of the unsettled questions about colonial relations – answering through the Gothic mode as a way of speaking back to the colonial encounter and also disrupting a sense of contemporary stability, thereby obliquely engaging with certain geographical characteristics related to bogs. In order to provide some methodological form to this otherwise mutable topic, I draw from two critical approaches that are distinct from each other and yet also surprisingly compatible. Similar to the seemingly contradictory qualities of bogs, both postcolonial and Gothic studies generate critical responses to opposing and yet complementary elements in cultural and historical texts. These two critical approaches question assumptions about historical accuracy, determinate thinking, and power structures related to diverse epistemologies about ecology, national identity, corporeal subjects, gender, law, and justice in Irish literature.

Postcolonial and Gothic scholars alike are concerned with cultural and literary histories. According to William Hughes and Andrew Smith, the literary Gothic tradition shares an intimate history with colonial projects, namely through representations of the self and other, the controllers and the repressed, and the subaltern and dominant outsider relationship.[40] For instance, the Gothic novel was immensely popular during the decade of the French Revolution because writers responded to forms of resistance in other destabilised and occupied zones.[41] Julian Moynahan maintains that the 'Gothic seems to flourish in disrupted, oppressed, or underdeveloped societies, to give a voice to the powerless and disenfranchised, and even, at times, to subvert the official best intentions of its creators'.[42] Gothic scholars, like postcolonial ones, identify political and cultural debates surrounding territories and people of colonial occupation. Gothic studies also attempts to rework, develop, and then challenge new forms of representation and readings to address the subaltern and dominant outsider relationship.[43] Broadening the critical scope by overlapping

Gothic and postcolonial criticism into one mode of examination enhances both the professedly generic study of the Gothic and the continual development of the postcolonial theoretical movement, thereby allowing for more specific forms of analysis drawn from commonalities in both critical applications.[44]

In the literary and cultural Gothic form, writers have the flexibility to work with the convention of paired opposites or doubling, specifically in how they centralise the interplay and confusion between and around material and also imaginative spaces. For example, landscapes, houses, churches, nations, and bodies all double as real and imagined constructs in Gothic fiction. In *The Architectural Uncanny* (1992), art historian Anthony Vidler discusses how haunted houses, much like the features of bogs, combine 'that mingling of mental projection and spatial characteristics associated with the uncanny'. The doubling of the 'real and unreal', adds Vidler, provokes 'a disturbing ambiguity, a slippage between waking and dreaming'.[45] Chris Baldick, in his Introduction to *The Oxford Book of Gothic Tales* (2009), provides one of the more compelling definitions of the Gothic, a concept notoriously difficult to reduce into a single definition. For Baldick, a Gothic text contains 'a fearful sense of inheritance in time with a claustrophobic sense of enclosure in space, these two dimensions reinforcing one another to produce an impression of sickening descent into disintegration'.[46] Baldick goes on to argue that writers of the literary Gothic remain obsessed with old buildings and sites of human decay, such as ancient houses or decomposing bogland. These 'Gothic' sites, '[d]oubling as both fictional setting and as dominant symbol', he continues, 'are simultaneously psychological and historical'.[47] Both Vidler's and Baldick's explanations suggest on some level why Irish writers turn to the bog as a fictional setting and prevailing Gothic symbol: the bog functions as a zone of enclosure and openness that dismantles spatio-temporal certainty. The tensions of opposites or non-binary forms of 'doubling' are largely why Irish writers are continually drawn to the bog.

The Gothic form typically concentrates on themes of transgression and transition couched in ambiguity and instability. Such topics present effective ways to rewrite history, question familial and political legitimacy, and excavate the hidden secrets from the vaults of society.[48] Consequently, the notion of the Gothic – as theoretical lens as well as a literary and cultural form – works as an interrogative or intransitive form of critical analysis.[49] The Gothic, functioning as both a proper noun and an adjective, encompasses a wide range of cultural output across several centuries and arguably begins with Horace Walpole's *The Castle of Otranto* (1764).

Yael Shapira reasons that the 'notorious difficulty of defining the Gothic genre lies in its being at once highly formulaic and subject to great variability'.[50] Such 'variability' could be classified as 'ambivalence', which David Punter, in his formative two-volume study of the Gothic, *The Literature of Terror* (1980), claims to be one of the fundamental terms of the Gothic tradition.[51] In this way, the ambiguities of the Gothic help to conceal other possible political motives for writers when addressing the effects of colonisation. Bogs function both biologically and metaphorically as ambiguous and continually misunderstood landforms – paralleling the Gothic's formulaic and variable tendencies – and because of this effect bogs serve as a space for Gothic writers to explore and contest traditional forms of political histories. Drawing from this critical background, I want to suggest that depictions of the indeterminate bog effectively serve Irish writers using elements of the Gothic form as a response to the uncertainties and disjunctures associated with past and present colonial conditions.

The broader literary and cultural directions of the postcolonial Gothic remain a relatively new critical territory. Prior to any cohesive formation of a body of criticism known as 'postcolonial Gothic' emerging in 2003, some scholars heretofore considered ways of engaging with imperialism and the Gothic in literature. The most notable example would be the 'imperial Gothic', coined by Patrick Brantlinger in *Rule of Darkness* (1988), which is a subset of Gothic literature that focuses on geographical explorations of empire between 1880 and 1914, and which are typically written within the imperial peripheries and as the apparatuses of the colonisers.[52] The term 'postcolonial Gothic' most likely originated in Judie Newman's larger study *The Ballistic Bard: Postcolonial Fictions* (1995). In it, she defines the 'postcolonial Gothic' as 'Janus-faced', drawing from the binary and doubling qualities in both critical methods. Newman goes on to write: 'At its heart lies the unresolved conflict between imperial power and the former colony, which the mystery at the centre of the plot both figures and conceals. Its discourse therefore established a dynamic between the unspoken and the "spoken for".'[53]

Despite some gestures toward its development by Brantlinger and Newman, the postcolonial Gothic only gained momentum as a specific critical field in the early to mid-2000s. William Hughes and Andrew Smith, editors of *Empire and the Gothic: The Politics of Genre* (2003), recognised in a larger study that 'postcolonialism explains the Gothic's instabilities by other means'.[54] In *The Gothic* (2003), David Punter and Glennis Byron maintain that some of the revealing characteristics of the postcolonial Gothic include: obfuscations of desire, oppression and confinement of the marginalised (especially through gender and race), revenants of imperialism, dislocation and disorientation, hauntings of ineradicable paths not taken, and impossible hybridities.[55] A special issue on the postcolonial Gothic in the journal *Gothic Studies* (also published in 2003) represents another one of the important studies to conflate these two interpretive paradigms. In their 'Introduction', editors Hughes and Smith write:

> There is a sense, though, in which the Gothic is, and has always been, *post*-colonial, and this is where, in the Gothic text, disruption accelerates into change, where the colonial encounter – or the encounter which may be read or interpreted through the colonial filter – proves a catalyst to corrupt, to confuse or to redefine the boundaries of power, knowledge and ownership.[56]

Gothic writers speak back to the colonial encounter by disrupting and redefining relationships of self and other, confinement and openness, control and repression, or even identifying the subaltern milieu and ubiquitous outsider culture.[57] By unsettling the grand narratives of empire wrapped in discourses of mastery and degeneration, as James Procter and Angela Smith argue in 'Gothic and Empire' in 2006, 'postcolonial Gothic' texts reframe the horror or ghosts from the colonised back to the abusers of the empire.[58] This type of reading can be located in many pre-existing Gothic or postcolonial works in the imperial peripheries of Caribbean, American, and Indian cultures, such as in Jean Rhys' *Wide Sargasso Sea* (1966), Toni Morrison's *Beloved* (1987), and Arundhati Roy's *The God of Small Things* (1997), among other literary works.

Gothic scholars investigate disruptions and fractures in the social sphere, thereby explaining instability by other means, but they also appear less interested in rewriting history than in probing ruptures in history. These less-defined Gothic narratives do not rewrite or reform existing histories into other master narratives or totalising accounts. Although exploring the unknown is as important as understanding the known in literary forms such as realism or naturalism, the union of the known/unknown – epitomised by the uncanny qualities of the bog – illuminates such a range of concerns. By the same token, there remains a tendency by writers to expose moments of Irish colonial histories through literary Gothic representations of the bog.

Luke Gibbons claims that the literary Gothic provides a more reliable template for rewriting Irish history than other recognised literary forms, such as classical realism, because it attempts to explain what has already been considered unknown or indefinable.[59] Gothicism in Ireland, similar to representations of the bog, provides a site for exploration about marginalised and repressed/suppressed histories that continually haunt the present.[60] The literary and cultural texts examined in this book present the bog as both an unstable and stable topography of power and knowledge that further elucidates such concerns. In this regard, the imbrication of the 'postcolonial' and the 'Gothic' serves as an effective way to address some historical layers and apparent contradictions in literary representations of bogs in Ireland.

A larger question, what I ultimately explore throughout the book, is how do Irish writers engage with the current and residual politics of colonisation through the Gothic form? With such an expansive history of both Irish Gothic and postcolonial literature, there have been only a handful of book-length studies on the subject. Applying a postcolonial Gothic framework to the Irish context brings together the critical work emerging from the 'Gothic turn' in the 1970s and the 'postcolonial turn' in the 1980s. The Irish Gothic as a critical mode of study is relatively contemporary and continues to garner more attention as the appeal of Gothic studies rapidly expands internationally. Only in the last forty years or so have critics revisited the Gothic in Ireland and labelled it with the distinctive national marker 'Irish Gothic'. The term Irish Gothic likely originated in 1972 when John Cronin described Somerville and Ross's *An Irish Cousin* (1903) as an 'overlay of Irish Gothic'. Although Cronin's distinction eventually became a specific subfield within the popular rise of Gothic studies during this same decade, the Irish Gothic, through recurring themes associated with Gothic literature more generally, had been less formally recognised as a mode of writing since the eighteenth century.[61]

Previous critical work on Irish Gothic literature and its association with British expansionism in Ireland has largely concentrated on eighteenth- and nineteenth-century literature and culture. As John Paul Riquelme recognises, 'Critics have yet to explore extensively the way in which elements of the Gothic tradition have become disseminated in the writings of the long twentieth century, from 1880 to the present.[62] Twentieth-century Gothic studies is considered to be, according to Catherine Spooner, a 'counter-narrative' to some of the 'high' cultural movements in the century.[63] The Irish Gothic tradition remains relevant in the 'long twentieth century', coupling both the modern and contemporary periods, precisely because some of the historical residues of British colonisation have yet to be resolved. Seamus Deane has noted that the 'territory of Ireland, with all its Gothic and all its nationalist graves, with all its estates and farms, its Land Acts and its history of confiscations, was in need of redefinition by the early years of the [twentieth] century'.[64] Colonial administrations in the eighteenth and nineteenth centuries left Ireland in an uncertain position by the 1890s, without a secure direction.

There are two recent and notable publications marking some new directions in Irish Gothic studies, but both concentrate on literature and culture prior to the twentieth century. Killeen's *The Emergence of Irish Gothic Fiction* (2014), which is his second book on the subject of Gothic Ireland, masterfully traces the histories, origins, and theories of the Irish Gothic. Despite a brief reference to contemporary trends of the Irish Gothic in the introduction and conclusion, it largely surveys the seventeenth and eighteenth centuries, with some tangential analysis focused on the nineteenth century.[65] Killeen's historical scope, while still proffering an essential and contemporary study of the origins of the Irish Gothic, indirectly (through their absence) reinforces the need to address modern and contemporary concerns in Irish Gothic literature.

In the previously mentioned publication *Irish Gothics: Genres, Forms, Modes, and Traditions, 1760–1890*, editors Christina Morin and Niall Gillespie, as well as the contributors to the volume, engage with various Irish Gothic 'forms' in similar historical periods as Killeen's book. The major difference is that Morin and Gillespie's volume of essays offers an updated and necessary discussion of the term 'the Irish Gothic'. Is it, for example, a 'tradition', 'genre', or 'mode'? This volume challenges some of the 'fundamental terminological confusion' that has led to various debates regarding the ways in which the term 'Gothic' might be framed in the last thirty years and calls for an end to using the Irish Gothic as a restrictive 'tradition'. Rather than continually refer to the Irish Gothic as an extended literary tradition traceable back to Protestant writers of the Anglo-Irish Gothic, *Irish Gothics* proposes multiple descriptors – such as 'mode' or 'register' – thereby circumnavigating the thorny issue of supporting a 'canon' or 'tradition' that marks a specific type of Irish Gothic.[66]

Contentious Terrains adopts a similar approach by using the Irish Gothic in a multiplicity of ways. It explores, as it mirrors the changeability and murkiness of the bog, the Gothic as a genre, mode, and form, all of which can be used interchangeably in modern and contemporary conceptions of the Irish Gothic. In Chapter 6, for instance, I focus on three specific classifications or sub-genres of Gothic literary modes focused on the bog. As Killeen puts it, '"Gothic" is notoriously the most slippery term in the literary critical dictionary, and has been defined in very many ways.'[67] The form has been 'a mess' from the start.[68] Its malleable nature is the one major reason forms of Irish literature have adopted various 'Gothic' conventions to address the politics of colonisation.[69] This is also partly why some writers discussed in this book – such as O'Connor, O'Faolain, and Heaney – do not fall under the traditional rubric of 'Gothic', yet can still be discussed in such terms. The Gothic functions as a mixture of elements, absorbing and assimilating other genres, disciplines, themes, devices, terminologies, and theories,[70] providing an ideal technique to survey and dislocate forms of colonisation associated with the bog as another unstable and unclassifiable geographical space in Irish literature.

Despite some of the postcolonial Gothic critical output in the early 2000s from Punter, Byron, Smith, and Hughes, among others like Newman and Brantlinger a specific form of the 'Irish postcolonial Gothic' has yet to be significantly charted as a critical medium.[71] It has, however, appeared in some books and essays but without this specific distinction. Jim Hansen's *Terror and Irish Modernism: The Gothic Tradition from Burke to Beckett* (2009) serves as perhaps the most recent and extensive study of the Irish Gothic within a postcolonial framework. *Terror and Irish Modernism* informs my own approach here because of its association with twentieth-century Ireland and its use of 'doubleness' found in Irish postcolonial Gothic writings. The 'structurally bipolar' identities Hansen discusses are similar to the union of opposites that characterise and explain the phenomenon of the bog.[72] However, even though his study ends in the twentieth century, many of Hansen's concerns remain rooted in the nineteenth. With such Gothic writers as Charles Robert Maturin and Oscar Wilde, who all create male characters that are simultaneously characterised as both the masculine terrorist and feminine terrorised, *Terror and Irish Modernism* draws on the popular female Gothic convention employed after the Acts of Union in the early nineteenth century.

Hansen also locates the beginning of the Irish postcolonial Gothic (although he does not actually use the phrase) with the 1990 publication of Stephen Arata's 'The Occidental Tourist: *Dracula* and the Anxiety of Reverse Colonization', which, while focusing mainly on *Dracula* (1897), also partly addresses the colonial dimensions of *The Snake's Pass*, among other Stoker writings. For Arata, according to Hansen, Stoker's *Dracula* offers an original study of the political and cultural complexities in colonised Ireland.[73] Arata asserts that Stoker's oeuvre provides underlying 'narratives of invasion and colonization'.[74] In *Dracula's Crypt: Bram Stoker, Irishness, and the Question of Blood* (2002) – conceivably another Irish postcolonial Gothic study, though again not explicitly acknowledged as such – Joseph Valente scrutinises Stoker's association with Ascendancy Protestants and his simultaneous support of cultural nationalism. Valente's book is as much a response to the Irish Gothic as it is a response to the postcolonial debates in Irish Studies during the 1990s about Stoker (largely initiated by Arata). In order to perform a specifically 'Irish' interpretation of *Dracula*, Valente insists that we must look beyond the novel itself and make some 'radically different deductions about its racial and national politics'.[75] Arata's and Valente's publications serve as two important examples that bookend the debates about *Dracula* by investigating connections between colonisation and the Irish Gothic at the end of the nineteenth century.

In addition to Hansen, Arata, and Valente, there are two other influential book-length studies that have helped to pave the way for what we now might call the 'Irish postcolonial Gothic' as a critical approach in twentieth- and twenty-first-century literature. In *The Gothic Family Romance: Heterosexuality, Child Sacrifice, and the Anglo-Irish Colonial Order* (1999), Margot Gayle Backus sketches perhaps the earliest book version of an identifiable Irish postcolonial Gothic, impressively spanning the fourteenth century to the present, using the emerging British and Anglo-Irish colonial family in literature as the central narrative. Backus underscores the 'interrelations between history and narrative' in 'colonial and postcolonial politics' where 'colonial rule … requires the production of children', while also exploring the 'gothic trope of the return of the repressed'.[76]

Luke Gibbons' *Gaelic Gothic: Race, Colonialism and Irish Culture* (2004) focuses entirely on the 'Gaelo-Catholic' Gothic as a subversive form of resistance. Gibbons turns to early forms of the Gothic all the way up to Stoker's *Dracula*, ranging between the sixteenth and nineteenth centuries, to investigate the racialisation that dominated colonial representations of Irish culture.[77] Gibbons' book leaves us at Stoker as the transitional colonial/postcolonial Gothic writer moving into the twentieth century, much like other scholarly works on the Irish Gothic. Arata, Valente,

Hansen, Gibbons, and Backus all convincingly pinpoint how certain writers locate some of the disruptions and inconsistencies that directly relate to the combination between postcolonial and Gothic approaches in Irish literary culture, and they provide a foundation for future work on the subject in the twentieth and twenty-first centuries.

Sites of Struggle, Conflict, and Resolution

Expanding the critical discussion of the Irish postcolonial Gothic further, the following chapters examine how modern and contemporary Irish writers have responded to colonisation both implicitly and explicitly through the marginal space of the bog within the historically peripheral 'Celtic Fringe', a space that is considered outside of the English centre, while at the same time part of the Gothic.[78] The English viewed Celtic landscapes, according to Killeen, as 'zones of the weird', or 'repositories of all that which England wished to deny and banish (the irrational, the superstitious, the perverse, the Catholic, the cannibal)'. They were places of the 'primitive and the atavistic which the modern world had not yet touched'.[79] Bogs are zones of the ephemeral and repositories of culture and history where the past can be recovered as a reminder of colonial encounters. At the same time, bogs also resist this sort of definition by concealing or obfuscating such histories through their simultaneous inaccessible and preservative qualities. An unacknowledged feature of the Irish postcolonial Gothic is how literary and cultural representations of bogs can be used to explore some of the lingering questions and assumptions about an ever-changing postcolonial milieu in the twentieth and twenty-first centuries. The following chapters examine how Irish writers explore the bog as both a geographical and cultural site of struggle, conflict, and, at times, resolution.

Chapter 1, 'The Protean Nature of Bogs', provides an overview of the biological makeup and morphology of bogs, along with their literary and cultural associations in Ireland. Understanding the imaginative qualities of the bog in literary works requires an understanding of the physical elements, such as biological formation, chemical qualities that lead to preservation, and utilitarian uses as an energy source. The chapter then links some artistic work in literature and photography to the physical properties, thereby underscoring the overlap between culture and geography that underpins the entire book. The second part of the chapter sketches a brief literary and cultural history of bogs as it relates to Irish identity, which is also partly addressed in Chapter 2. This is done by surveying the earlier writings of Giraldus Cambrensis, Edmund Spenser, Gerard Boate, William King, Maria Edgeworth, Sydney Owenson, and Robert Lloyd Praeger, and then moving briefly into the modern and contemporary period through James Joyce, Seamus Heaney, and Máirtín Ó Cadhain. The perceptions of bogs as wastelands in earlier writings by Spenser, Boate, and King, in particular, to the increased nationalistic tendency in writings by Owenson and Stoker, transition toward the latter half of the nineteenth century and extend into the twentieth and twenty-first centuries. These perceptions parallel the politics of colonisation and are infused with a Gothic aesthetic. Thus, the aim of this opening chapter is to discuss the foundation of this study as an abbreviated scientific, literary, and cultural history.

Chapter 2, 'Environments of Empire', examines the ecological effects that colonisation had on bogs in Ireland as they are shown in Bram Stoker's second novel, the only one set in Ireland, *The Snake's Pass* (1890). Colonial and environmental themes underpinning Gothic writings provide a productive way to see the bog as a location where British industrialisation threatens and ultimately destroys much of it. Gothic themes, such as aspects of the uncanny, haunted landscapes, and transgression, explain some of the anxieties about land ownership and land-use within colonial models of administration, ambivalent ethnic and cultural identity, and the political milieu of Ireland at the time. Stoker's ideology of nationalism, as it is portrayed in the novel through the protagonist Arthur Severn, can be understood as a union of opposites; he mourns the loss of the bog as a part of Irish identity, while at the same time he justifies its elimination for the economic and political sovereignty of the country. In this sense, the chapter is as much about Stoker's relationship with Ireland and Irish natural history surrounding land-use of the bog in the nineteenth century as it is about *The Snake's Pass*. The bog serves as a tool for understanding colonial politics and Stoker's vision of nationalism, but I approach this somewhat obliquely by emphasising that what we would now call the 'ecological' significance of boglands in Ireland remains pivotal to this understanding.

Chapter 3, 'Spectral Histories of Nationalism', investigates how in 1920s' and 1930s' post-Independence Ireland Frank O'Connor, Sean O'Faolain, and in part, Daniel Corkery, use the bog in their writings as a specific site of haunting to address some of the uncertain histories of social violence during the Irish War of Independence/Anglo-Irish War (1919–1921). Ghosts materialise after this tumultuous and historically unresolved period as a way of dissolving linear time and challenging previous conceptions of the nation.[80] O'Connor and O'Faolain use the bog in their representative short stories 'Guests of the Nation' (1931) and 'A Meeting' (1937) not as a space representing the nation – as it is for Corkery in *Synge and Anglo-Irish Literature* (1931) – but one that both confuses and illuminates the slippages in history, memory, and identity that have occurred since the period of nation formation. Despite their labels as literary realists, O'Connor and O'Faolain surprisingly draw on Gothic conventions and use the bog as a haunting symbol and setting of a past that, for them, has not resolved itself in the present and perhaps never will. For O'Connor and O'Faolain in the 1930s, earlier national identities formed during the revolutionary period are treated in both stories as unsettled ghosts that are bound by the bog. The bog, then, serves as an ideal location for O'Connor and O'Faolain to consider unresolved moments in and feelings about the post-Independence era of Irish history, where traces of power, violence, and oppression subtly remain. These writers draw from and employ what we can now call postcolonial Gothic conventions – entailing hauntings associated with anti-colonial struggles – and the bog is central to these political encounters.

Chapter 4, 'Mapping Gothic Bog Bodies', demonstrates how bodies symbolically and physically function as literary maps in Seamus Heaney's bog poems and prose written between 1966 and 1978. The practice of literary cartography provides a means of examining creative works as maps through actual physical features and metaphorical images. Literary maps, similar to bogs, function as fusions of opposites because they are both real and imagined spaces rife with contradictions and commonalities. Mapping and bodies are significantly linked to both postcolonialism and the Gothic; the body can be mapped and colonised, while it also conjures Gothic themes and images. This chapter claims that bog bodies – drawing them into conversation together as a constellation of symbols and physical objects – serve as maps that can be charted and interpreted in Heaney's poetry and prose. When examining the mapped bodies unearthed from bogs, I specifically explore five of Heaney's bog poems: 'Digging', 'Bogland', 'The Tollund Man', 'The Grauballe Man', and 'Punishment', as well as some of his earlier non-fiction prose about bogs in *Preoccupations* (1980), interviews, and later talks given in Demark at bog symposiums in the 1990s.

Chapter 5, 'Gendered Boglands', recognises the recurring penchant for feminising rural nature in Ireland. It also explores how Irish women in Carr's *By the Bog of Cats...* (1998) and Kinahan's *Bog Boy* (2010), among other contemporary Irish works, resist the neocolonial Celtic Tiger years by embracing the bog as a space of both struggle and liberation. As notoriously represented in W.B. Yeats' play, *Cathleen Ni Houlihan* (1902), an ongoing cultural perception remains in Ireland that antiquated concepts of 'feminine' and 'nature' are interchangeable. Although Carr and Kinahan place women in rural settings, they quickly subvert how representations of femininity function in relation to a common rural landscape like the bog. Carr and Kinahan use the bog as a gendered terrain not as a symbol or metaphor of feminised male nationalism, but of women's autonomy from and resistance to a neocolonial society that emerged out of a patriarchal national history. The bog can serve as a place of refuge and liberation for Irish women precisely because it is non-domestic and not already inscribed with nationalist gender narratives of 'home' and 'motherhood'.

Chapter 6, 'Bog Gothic, Bog Noir, and Eco-Bog Writing', considers some ways this topic has already developed into sub- 'modes' or 'genres' of Irish literature from the 1970s to the present. This chapter begins by explaining this in Patrick McCabe's novel *The Butcher Boy* (1992). Various critics and scholars have labelled McCabe's writing 'Bog Gothic'. However, I want to problematise this term a bit more by arguing that McCabe's literary form creates a 'bog affect', conjuring metaphors of a regressive and supernatural rural Ireland that align with long-lasting stereotypes of boglands. Bogs are also increasingly employed in the popular genre of Irish crime writing. Patrick McGinley's and Erin Hart's detective fiction serve as examples of a sub-genre we might call 'Bog Noir', which uses the bog as a primary motif in Irish crime writing. The third section of this chapter examines Tim Robinson's topographic or 'landscape' non-fiction writings and how they address environmental threats to bogs in Ireland. Robinson's prose and forms of activism serve as the most contemporary examples of 'Eco-bog' writings that discuss the ecological deterioration of bogs and promote their environmental sustainability in the present and future. Despite the different approaches in the writings of McCabe, McGinley, Hart, and Robinson, these authors' works all contain political and Gothic undercurrents that challenge us to think about the status of bogs in contemporary and future Irish literary and cultural works.

The intention of this book is to explore why the bog continually resonates in modern and contemporary Irish literature and culture with

Gothic and political overtones, rather than to limit or prescribe the ways in which we approach writings about the bog. Bogs in literary, historical, and cultural depictions tend to be for the most part over-determined sites or signifiers and this is precisely why so many writers approach them as an effective place to accentuate issues related to postcolonial politics. There are many more questions than clear answers in the murky waters of bogs, much like in Irish postcolonial history. The difficulty in writing about bogs, and the issues that surround them in literary and cultural works, is that they defy definitive meaning. The bog is a kind of narrative that reveals some of the potentially unanswered questions in Irish literary geo-history. Bogs, and the lore that surrounds them, according to Robinson, are 'like patches of mist, sometimes merging and becoming indistinguishable, sometimes fading into thin air for a time and then re-forming themselves out of nothing'.[81]

In an attempt to bring some meaning and structure to a subject that defies linear definition, I have an overarching critical approach: the bog for certain Irish writers provides an effective means to analyse colonisation, in its various iterations of prefixes (post-, anti-, de-, and neo-), through Gothic conventions and during four major political junctures from the 1880s to the present. As Gregory maintains, the goal of critical geography is to 'uncover the underlying multivocal codes which make landscapes cultural creations, to show the politics of design and interpretation, and to situate landscape at the heart of the study of social process'.[82] Literary writings featuring bogs do in fact 'uncover' some of the underlying questions both during and after periods of colonisation in Ireland, and show how they relate to larger social processes in the development of modern and contemporary Irish literary history.

1

The Protean Nature of Bogs

Bogs provide us with a palimpsest of Ireland's cultural development
stretching back to the first inhabitants of this island.[1]
> – Barry Raftery, 'The Archaeology of Irish Bogs'

A bog is in fact a giant inefficient compost heap, which, left to its own
devices, can never complete its rotting process because it is super-
saturated with water. It is a gigantic store of energy and chemicals
that can be an investment for all our futures and a repository of
information relating to all our pasts.[2]
> – David Bellamy, *The Wild Boglands*

In the observed world of rationality and logic, largely influenced by the
Enlightenment, bogs have refreshingly provided a sense of irregularity,
fear, and the unexplainable, what Tadhg Foley insightfully describes as
their 'protean nature' that harnesses 'terror' because of their formlessness
and 'lack of identity'.[3] This perceived shapelessness is, however, largely
because of their biological makeup and origins on a geologic scale. It
is necessary, then, before specifically examining in subsequent chapters
how some modern and contemporary Irish writers represent bogs, to
first overview the bog's biological or physical attributes – their formation,
vegetation, and morphology – in order to provide a useful foundation for
their place in Irish cultural and literary history.

As the epigraphs from Bellamy and Raftery suggest, bogs hold a
unique cultural, aesthetic, and scientific position within Irish history. Not
only are they perpetually decomposing compost heaps and thus seemingly
utter waste, but they also contain tangible and intangible properties –
vacillating between being natural resources and existing as historical
records – that provide ecological and cultural narratives for thousands of

years. This chapter first explores the scientific and utilitarian properties of bogs, which as each epigraphs indicates are relevant to the cultural and imaginative properties that attract writers and audiences to their murky waters. The chapter then briefly outlines some of the influential writings on bogs in Irish history leading up to the nineteenth century (Chapter 2 will expand upon land-use policies and reclamation practices in the late nineteenth century through Stoker's novel *The Snake's Pass*), as well as some of the literary and visual works that have captured the essence of the protean nature of boglands to the present.

Formation and Utilisation

Bogs, consisting of an absorbent spongiform surface, remain an important factor in the climate and vegetation of Ireland. The word 'bog' is defined as 'soft ground' and is derived from the Irish word *bogach*.[4] Bog is shorthand for a type of biological product of peatlands, which are a specific type of wetland; the bog therefore shares similarities with the moor and fen. Covering approximately 400–500 million hectares of the world's surface (about 8 per cent), though largely found in northern latitudes, peatlands are as significant to the world's landmass as are tropical forests or deserts in terms of surface area, and yet they receive much less critical attention in the humanities.[5] Even though they often appear to be solid ground, bogs can be comprised of anywhere between 85 and 98 per cent water.[6] Over a period of years and even decades the wet bog can become dry, only to then become wet again because of the continual buildup of rainwater. One of the many enticements of bogs is their 'slow' or 'deep' geologic time, spanning thousands of years. The micro-geography of bogs is constantly in flux, but the change is too slow for the human eye to observe the constant and intricate rearrangement of textures and colours over time and space.[7] Such a spatio-temporal existence, often outside of immediate human perception, is what contributes to the protean nature of the bog.

There are two general types of peatlands: fens and bogs (also called peat bogs or boglands). Fens are nutrient-rich and somewhat fertile peatlands, whereas bogs have higher acidity and tend to be nutrient-deficient.[8] While fens are more prevalent in eastern England – as in East Anglia where Swift locates his novel *Waterland* – bogs are found more often in Ireland, Denmark, and Finland. Bogs currently cover one-

1.1 Close-up of a bog in Connemara, Co. Galway
(photo by Derek Gladwin)

sixth (1.34 million hectares) of the total land area in Ireland, which is
unparalleled in any other country in Europe, except for Finland.[9] Bogs
also contain a medley of animal (including insects and invertebrates) and
plant life, the latter changing colour over seasons and providing the bog

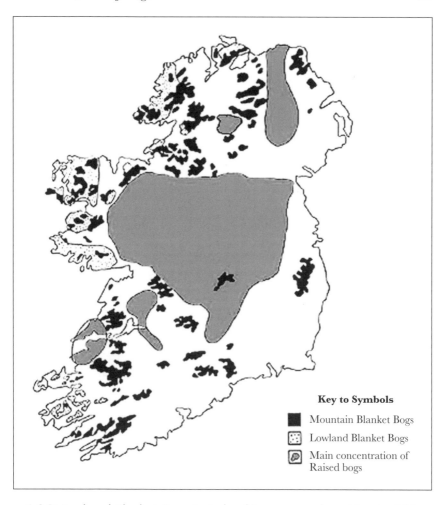

Key to Symbols

■ Mountain Blanket Bogs

▦ Lowland Blanket Bogs

▣ Main concentration of Raised bogs

1.2 Raised and Blanket Bogs in Ireland (image produced by the Irish Peatland Conservation Council, IPCC)

walker, should one look closely enough, with a dazzling display of visual complexity (see Fig. 1.1).

Two specific types of bogs are found in Ireland: raised and blanket (see Fig. 1.2). Raised bogs are found mainly in lower, non-coastal elevations where there is less drainage. The middle part of the country known as the Midlands (Offaly, Westmeath, Longford, and Laois) contains the most raised bogs due to its flat, treeless, and low-lying topography. One of the characteristics of raised bogs is their dome-shaped centre, hence the origin of the term 'raised'. Raised bogs originally began as post-glacial lakes, but then gave way to fen vegetation about 9,000 years ago, and finally turned into bogs about 7,000 years ago. This is why the depths of raised bogs usually far exceed the lowest point of blanket bogs. The average raised bog is about seven metres deep because of the pre-existing post-glacial lakebeds underneath, but they can be well over twelve metres deep in some places. Raised bogs in Ireland are also located in areas that receive between 800 and 1,100 mm of rainfall per year.[10] Because of their accessibility and depths, the majority of industrial turf removal for fuel occurs on raised bogs.

Blanket bogs, in contrast, are located along the west coast of Ireland, where there is poor drainage and large amounts rainfall throughout the year.[11] Blanket bogs, which are typically treeless with flat to undulating vistas, are littered with rock formations (granite and limestone) and accentuated with mountain ridges, often dotting the landscape in between small pools of water and larger lakes. In Ireland, there are two kinds of blanket bogs: lowland Atlantic (sea level to 200 m) and upland Mountain (above 200 m). Roundstone Bog, located in Connemara (County Galway), serves as the most preserved of the Atlantic blanket bogs in Ireland, largely because of constraints on turf-cutting and forestry.[12] Blanket bogs are located in the counties of Kerry, Clare, Galway, Mayo, Sligo, and Donegal, where there is higher rainfall (average 1,200 mm per year).

Bogs, or peatlands, are a special type of terrestrial wetland ecosystem; they are distinguishable from other wetlands by annual accumulation of peat. Peat consists of the remains of plants, trees, and animals that once flourished on the surface of peatlands but have since decayed. After they die and eventually decompose, they become part of the composition of peatlands because of the waterlogged, anaerobic environment. Because the production of animal and plant matter exceeds decomposition capabilities, partially decomposed organic matter called 'peat' builds up over time.[13] This plant and animal material accumulates over thousands of years, due to the bacteria and fungi breakdown in the anaerobic zones, eventually forming layers of peat with preservative properties. The accumulation of peat is dominated by *sphagnum* (bog moss), which excretes antibiotics and hydrogen ions over time, a process that increases the acidity in the water of bogs, thereby slowing the process of decay.[14] Very little life can exist in anaerobic zones, a characteristic producing a Gothic world of the decomposed un-dead, with much hidden from the scope of society. As the famed bogland biologist David Bellamy writes, the decomposition process of bogs is a product of 'the dank, dark world

1.3 Hand of Oldcroghan Man, Co. Offaly. National Museum of Ireland Bog Bodies Research Project.

of the anaerobic layer, a glimpse of what life was like on earth some three billion years ago', before life as we know it existed.[15]

The chemical process at work in bogs preserves many objects found in them, including ancient butter, oaks, gold, bronze, cultural artefacts (weapons and valuables), bodies, and even entire Stone Age villages such as the Céide Fields in County Mayo (discovered by Seamus Caulfield in the mid-1980s). 'As the living bog grows,' the scientists Peter Foss and Catherine O'Connell explain, 'it buries and conserves anything in its path, including the early pine woodland and "bog oaks" often exposed by turf cutters at the cut-edge of bogs.'[16] In the bog bodies exhibit at the National Museum of Ireland in Dublin, for instance, one can see how hair and fingerprints are still preserved on corpses over 2,000 years old (see Fig. 1.3). In another of many examples, an ancient book of psalms was dug up in an Irish bog by a backhoe during turf removal in 2006. Irish archaeologists have dated the book to between 800 to 1,000 CE, and compare the find to the Book of Kells.

In this way, artefacts found in bogs reveal histories that generate conflicting memories for peoples and cultures through both material reality and symbol. But unlike customary archaeological digs, the wetland environments of bogs preserve these artefacts with a greater accuracy in terms of their origins, thereby containing and producing cultural memory, a way of accessing multiple and often conflicting forms of history through society and culture. Particular artefacts – such as the bog bodies represented in Heaney's poems and non-fiction (see Chapter 4) – are both material and imaginative. Sanders maintains that in multiple ways bog bodies 'negotiate the liminality that comes with having to travel between their material reality as archaeological artifacts (mummies) and the temporality that comes with their humanness'.[17] In this sense, bogs collect and record memories of the material and cultural human past, thereby serving as useful tools for writers to account for re-visitations of certain histories, such as how bog bodies reveal the purposeful extermination of certain peoples before their bodies were deposited in bogs. The archaeologist Barry Raftery claims that 'in the waterlogged recesses of the dark and silent peat, because of the anaerobic conditions, the story of Ireland's past is preserved for us, often in startling detail, a detail which has long since vanished on dryland sites'.[18] The history of social struggle in Ireland is so strongly preserved in the anaerobic environment of bogs – through metaphor, symbol, and material objects (like bog bodies and relics of battles) – that layers continue to unfold, much like a palimpsest, even to the present day.

One of the most common uses for bogs throughout recorded Irish history has been peat production, a process that transforms the wetland into a fuel and energy source called 'turf'. Bogs remain an energy source, as well as a cultural landscape, even though the European Union (EU) has prohibited peat production in areas protected for environmental preservation. Hand extraction of peat reached its apex in the nineteenth century, after which mechanised peat removal appeared. Despite the level of industrialised production over the last 200 years, around 3,000 people still cut turf by hand. Turf-cutting remains a contentious issue in traditional peat harvesting areas.

Historically, patches of bogs around the country would be personalised – simply called Seamus' bog or Kevin's bog – and maintained by individuals and their families for generations. Families would work the bog each year in order to produce enough fuel for cooking and heating. To retrieve the decomposed peat material of the bog by hand, workers would use a long-bladed four-inch-wide spade called a *sleán* in Irish (anglicised as 'slane'). Interestingly, *sleáns* differed in various parts of the

1.4 Stacks of footings (*gróigíní*) in a bog, Glenveagh, Co. Donegal
(photo by Anthony Haughey)

country; in County Kerry it had a foothold that allowed for larger turf pieces, whereas in County Galway smaller *sleáns* were used. Before slicing into the bog, however, the surface layer called the 'scraw' – consisting of vegetation with roots of sedge, ferns, furze, rushes, bog cotton, and heather, depending upon the bog's location – must be removed. Once the scraw material of about six inches to one foot deep is discarded (also called 'paring'), largely because scraw is not conducive to burning, the *sleán* slices into peat about eighteen inches deep, which is a layer called the 'spit' of the bog. There can be three to four spits in one 'bog-hollow' (*lagphortach*), which is a turf lane cut from the bank (see Figs. 1.5 and 1.6). The removed peat, or chunks of turf called 'sod', is then arranged using a 'pike' (turf-fork) and dried in the oxygen-rich air on the banks of the bog-hollow for a few days to develop a hard enough outer layer so that the sod does not crumble. Eventually the sod pieces are placed in small pyramid stacks known as 'footings' (*gróigíní*) (see Fig. 1.4). If a larger machine is used to harvest the peat, then the turf appears in horizontal symmetrical rows. After about ten days, the turf is 'refooted' (*athgróigthe*) into larger heaps about twice as large as the *gróigíní*, with the most damp sod pieces located on the outside of the stack to dry more quickly. In one of the last stages of drying, the stacks of sod then increase into a large mound with a four-foot base called a *dúchán*. After the turf has dried over several cycles in various-sized footings, it is moved by wheelbarrows or baskets via human or donkey, stored indoors, and eventually sold or used as fuel to burn and cook in Irish households or public houses.[19]

This painstaking process of peat harvesting demonstrates the intimate, humanised relationship between Irish culture and this multifaceted landform. However, the traditional practice of cutting turf continues to dwindle, for a few reasons. First, a belated electrification process in mid-twentieth-century Ireland lessened the need for families to harvest turf from the bog each year in order to cook food and heat homes. Second, mechanised peat extraction (with the use of large tractors) has become the predominant method for corporate operations, producing larger quantities in a much shorter period. Much of the mechanised peat extraction, still legal in Ireland and in other places with bogland such as Scotland and Denmark, is sold on international markets rather than made available in the place of extraction. Third, the EU has largely outlawed turf-cutting in much of Ireland and elsewhere in Europe to preserve the remaining bogland habitat, which has been systematically destroyed by up to 40 per cent between 1995 and 2012. Bogs are also carbon sequestration 'sinks', which help to prevent climate acceleration due to global warming (see Chapter 6 for more on bog ecologies and climate change).

Moratoriums on cutting turf by hand in designated protected areas have remained a divisive issue, with many turf-cutters being arrested for not adhering to these laws. Some politicians, such as Luke 'Ming' Flanagan (former mayor of Roscommon, TD, and currently MEP), have publicly supported campaigns opposed to turf-cutting restrictions.[20] In addition, the process of harvesting peat remains prohibitive in terms of both time and labour in today's modernised society. One piece of sod reduces by half its original size once it is dried and produces only about one-third the heating value of a piece of coal. It would also take a week's worth of work to supply a family for enough fuel to last a year.[21]

The process of turf-cutting by hand remains a complex operation and one that has been etched in Irish society and culture for centuries, paralleling various forms of artistic production in literature and visual culture. For example, Rachel Giese's book of photography, *The Donegal Pictures* (1987), contains some exemplary images capturing the cultural and utilitarian dialectic of turf-cutting in visual culture.[22] The photograph, 'Cutting Turf/*Ag Baint Mónadh*', pictures the two brothers Charles and John

1.5 'Cutting Turf' (photo by Rachel Giese Brown)

1.6 'Taking Out the Turf' (photo by Rachel Giese Brown)

McHugh cutting and stacking pieces of turf in Donegal (see Fig. 1.5). One has a *sleán* and the other is picking up and subsequently throwing the sod on the side of the bog-hollow next to where they are presently standing. The turf is, as previously described, placed in footings next to the long ditches so it can dry. The turf lanes run parallel to each other like rows of corn, except they are much wider apart. The preceding picture to 'Cutting Turf' in *The Donegal Pictures* is entitled 'Taking Out the Turf/ *Ag Cur as Poll*' and demonstrates a close-up of the turf removal with the *sleán* cutting into the turf, while another man's hands pull the sod free in order to throw it on the side of the turf bank (see Fig. 1.6). Three-quarters of the frame in 'Cutting Turf' focus on the two men cutting turf. Where the diagonal lines of the turf ditches stop, there begins the rest of the bog, which appears to be preserved all the way up to the adjoining mountains. Bogs here stand at the crossroads between civilisation and 'nature', where policies and inhabitants often pursue separate ends. Giese Brown's photo also echoes what Irish environmentalist Michael Viney has recognised about the Irish countryside: 'utility remains the benchmark of Irish rural attitudes to nature'.[23] These two photographs of bogland, similar to other literary examples surveyed in this book, demonstrate the ongoing link (and also opposition) between the natural utility embedded in the Irish rural ethos and the aesthetic appreciation of the cultural artefact of the photograph.

In 'Collecting Turf from the Bog', which is probably one of the most famous landscape photographs of twentieth-century rural Ireland, John Hinde represents the bog as a symbol of rural Irish nostalgia by foregrounding two children in front of a donkey-cart full of sod pieces (see Fig. 1.7). The crossover between culture and practical agriculture remains evident in Hinde's image. Hinde employs what Roland Barthes has referred to as the 'rhetoric of the image', a visual persuasion strategy to lure the viewer into the 'rustic' imagination of Ireland.[24] As a result, Hinde's postcard photography is reduced to a commodity because it produces visual texts for consumption and then exploits the idea of Irish landscape for marketing tourism. Admittedly, postcards are commodities for consumption, whereas a collection of photography functions as art for public appreciation in an exhibition. As W.J.T. Mitchell has noted (similar to Wylie's and Tuan's understanding of landscape in the Introduction), a landscape is not 'an object to be seen or a text to be read', as a postcard would seem to suggest, but 'a process by which social and subjective identities are formed'.[25] Instances of turf-cutting in visual culture – either

1.7 'Collecting Turf from the Bog', Connemara, Co. Galway
(photo © John Hinde Ireland Ltd).

in Hinde's popularised 1950s' postcard photography or contrastingly in
Giese Brown's realist photography, or even in the pages of a literary text
as this book demonstrates – signal larger issues that can be examined in
culture and society as much as in the formation of a bog.[26]

Moreover, the vegetative and chemical properties of bogs help
explain Irish culture's penchant to classify them as Gothicised sites,
where the union of the scientific and supernatural merge to create eerie
atmospherics. Mountain blanket bogs swell from prolonged amounts of
rainfall and eventually start to 'shift' or move in large sheets. To the human
mind, this otherworldly effect could signal some sort of spirit possession
from beneath the earth. In geological terms, however, the swelling bog
eventually subsides from the lower granite or limestone base and slides
in various directions depending upon the gravitational pull of the bog
location. Also, according to Irish mythology, the 'pooka' (*púca*) – a shape-
shifter capable of morphing into various frightening or desirable forms:

black horses, goats, rabbits, and cats, as well as humans – purportedly materialises on bogs. The pooka can be either malevolent (blood-thirsty killers) or benevolent (spirit guides). Another Irish Gothic tale attempts to explain the distant lights that spontaneously appear in uninhabited locations on bogs. These lights represent a spirit known as the 'Bog Sprite' or 'Water Sheerie' who entices the wayward traveller to an untimely death on the bog.[27] Myth credits this phenomenon to the 'will-o'-the-wisps' (*ignis fatuus*), which are flickering lights that dance on the bog signalling the appearance of malevolent spirits. Scientists, in contrast, have shown that the layer just below the surface of the bog produces several gases that assist in the decomposition process. Two of these specific gases – methane (marsh gas) and phosphine – when exposed to oxygen can be highly flammable, and they often spontaneously combust on the surface of bogs.[28]

In addition to spirits, moving bogs, and the gaseous-induced combustion effect, which all induce a rich mythology involving ghosts and hauntings, the bogs of Ireland contain over eleven species of carnivorous plants, including sundews, butterworts, bladderworts, and pitcher plants.[29] Sundews, in particular, are a commonly seen species of carnivorous plant that contain around 200 pin-shaped red tentacles called 'stalked glands', that respond immediately to touch. Trapping up to five insects per month, the sundew plant uses mucilaginous secretion to entrap its prey, a veritable feast consisting of flies, beetles, ants, and sometimes damselflies.[30] Both literally and metaphorically, bogs are undoubtedly mysterious and multifarious terrains; they are also territories of fear-inducing phenomena, consumption, and death. As a result, writers use these inexplicable horrors and imaginative virtues of the bog to support their own literary and political ends.

A Brief Literary and Cultural History

The bog continues to be etched in Irish history as both a geographical and human record more than in any other European country except perhaps Denmark (mostly due to the prevalence of bog bodies).[31] Incidentally, the word *bog* in Danish is linguistically associated with the word 'book',[32] which explains the multitudinous ways in which the bog can be interpreted or imagined through narrative in literary culture. This history spans back centuries, and is laced with colonial agendas that draw on Gothic conventions, bringing us to the modern and contemporary period.

The longer cultural and literary history of bogs in Ireland could arguably begin with Giraldus Cambrensis (Gerald of Wales), who attempted an early technical account of Ireland's topographies after the Norman invasion during the Middle Ages. In *Topographia Hibernia* (*c.*1185). Giraldus' observations are arranged in three sections: a) the physical topography (with naturalist observations); b) the spiritual essence of place; c) the cultural aspects of the landscape. Originally written in Latin, *Topographia* is a type of bestiary, a collection of animal observations framed through Christian morality.[33] Regardless, 'bogs' are mentioned by name in the third section, 'Of the inhabitants of Ireland', wherein the claim is made that Irish people do not have an affinity with castles as a means of defence; instead, 'they make the woods their stronghold, and the bogs their trenches', which is an observation later reiterated in the writings of Boate and King.[34] *Topographia* nevertheless provides an early form of natural history which included boglands, along with other topographies and zoologies (for example, Giraldus also wrote extensively about birds).

Edmund Spenser, the first English poet to use Ireland's topographies within a literary work, *The Faerie Queene* (1596), is infamous in the history of England's colonisation for castigating Ireland in *A View of the Present State of Ireland* (1596). *View* is a semi-fictional story about a conversation between two people, Irenius and Eudoxus, who discuss the management and ultimate outcome of Ireland. Spenser depicts Ireland as a 'wasteland' in need of improvement and promotes displacing the population by transforming topographies that are 'flat, empty and inscribable', extended metaphorically of course to the Irish people.[35] The implied topography here is that of the bog. At the time Spenser was writing *View*, Ireland was covered in many bogs and forests. In it, Irenius extols the virtues of the Irish landscape, a 'sweete Country as any is under heaven', and one that contains 'excellent commodities'.[36] This Protestant view tended to paint 'nature' as a binary: as a prelapsarian space (and therefore undeserved Eden) opposing its other characteristics as a sinful or fallen wasteland.[37]

Spenser remains a complex and controversial figure in Irish history, but his purely economic interests, usually at the expense of disenfranchising local populations, might be considered as much a product of his time as an act of hostility toward the Irish. 'Civilising' was synonymous with colonising, both of which had cultural and economic implications. The resources of Ireland, mainly bogs and forests, were available commodities for the empire; they also happened to house troublesome wolves and 'woodkerne' (Irish soldiers), both regarded in the same light – Irenius recalls that the Irish (like the Scythians) turn into wolves once a year.[38] The Elizabethan view of 'nature' persisted in being hierarchical and taxonomic because it was largely derived from Renaissance cosmology of the Great Chain of Being, and therefore lacked much scientific grounding (hence the misunderstanding about animals/wolves). The same division of divine superiority with the natural world also existed between peoples.[39]

As a result, Spenser's discussion of boglands as synonymous with Ireland (resources and commodities for England) centred entirely on its economic value for England, a view that continues to develop throughout other writings over the next few centuries and one that justified conquest through plantations. The economic value, however, stems from cultural perceptions rather than scientific or rational evidence. John Wilson Foster has aptly called Spenser's literary approach a form of 'commodity pastoralism'.[40] Many literary historians have already documented Spenser's infamous disdain for Ireland, but the point in mentioning *View* here is to identify one of the early links between colonial administrators and the demonisation of boglands/wetlands (a point expanded upon in Chapter 2).

Although Giraldus and Spenser address bogs in Ireland on some level, the two most influential pre-modern historical and geographical studies of bogs are by Gerard Boate and William King. Boate's *Irelands Naturall History* (1652) includes two extensive chapters on the taxonomy of bogs, which represent the most detailed accounts recorded in print at that time. He not only provides scientific classifications of bogs – describing both correctly and incorrectly the various types, colours, and textures – but he also alludes to the traditional rural practice of turf-cutting before going on to explain the process by which bogs are drained. He opens Chapter 13, 'Of the Heaths and Moores, or Bogs in Ireland', by describing the 'Boggy-heaths' across various parts of the country. He catalogues them as 'dry' (or 'red') and 'wet', which are now called 'blanket' and 'raised' in contemporary terminology, and are found across 'the whole Kingdom' in the mountains, hills, and 'Plain-countries'.[41] He recognises the early peat extraction methods: 'fit for to dig Turf out, to the great commodity of the inhabitants, in places where other fuel is wanting'.[42] His next chapter explains how bogs differ in various parts of Ireland, providing labels that are now antiquated vernacular: 'Watery-', 'Miry-', 'Grassie-', 'Hassocky-' bogs.

In Chapter 14, 'Originall of the Bogs in Ireland; and the manner of Draining them, pacified there by the English Inhabitants', he offers more insight into land-use issues that eventually bring us to Stoker's *The Snake's Pass* in Chapter 2 of this book. Boate first sketches the preservative elements of bogs, particularly bog oak found by turf-cutters, which leads to draining or reclamation practices of bogs and criticism of the Irish in their use of them. His analysis is, however, not without some prejudice toward Irish culture. Boate, in an abrasive change in tone and direction from scientific to racial, maintains:

> But as the Irish have been extreme carless in this, so the English, introducers of all good things in Ireland (for which that brutish nation from time to time hath rewarded them with unthankfulness, hatred, and envy, and lately with a horrible and bloody conspiracie, tending to their utter destruction) have let their industrie at work for to remedy it, and having considered the nature of the Bogs, and how possible it was to reduce many of them unto good land.[43]

Boate equates the 'wet', 'red', and 'dry' quagmires associated with the previous chapter with the Irish and the industrious practice of bog drainage with the English. The discourses of colonisation underline the discussion of 'draining of the Bogs' as a remedy 'to the general good of the whole land'. Boate's descriptions of bogs are remarkably accurate for having allegedly never set foot in Ireland; he wrote reports while in England based upon first-hand accounts.[44] Like Spenser, profit and utility (with a large dose of justifying English colonisation) remains for Boate, who was a physician for Cromwell, the key purpose, whereas William King's approach adds another layer of what Liam Heneghan appropriately calls 'the epistemology of hatred'.[45]

King built upon Boate's study of Irish natural history with his own paper entitled 'Of the Bogs and Loughs of Ireland', which was originally presented to the Royal Society in 1685. King referred to the bog in Boate's language as 'red' and 'quaking'. What is unusual about King's background and interest in bogs is that he was initially Bishop of Derry and later named Archbishop of Dublin (1703–29) and Lord Justice; he was not a natural scientist. His interest in controlling and colonising boglands went so far that he proposed that an 'act of Parliament should be made' in order to 'make some progress in draining their [Ireland's] Bogs', thereby bringing bogs as a point of national interest into conversation for the first time.[46] The subject of bogs in this speech (resulting in the subsequent paper) fulfils two functions: utilising the immense space of

the bog for utility and profit (like Spenser and Boate) and demonising
the Irish character through the metaphor of this 'barbarous' wasteland.
Consequently, King's attention to bogs focuses as much on the cultural
and historical connections to Irish identity, as it does on profit and
industry through peat cultivation for 'iron work', 'char-coal', and
harvesting of trees found in the bog.[47] King identifies bogs, with explicit
overtones of imperial ideology, as the hallmark of 'every barbarous ill-
inhabited country'. Bogs inherently attract industry and it is, he goes on to
argue, 'no wonder if a Country, famous for laziness, as *Ireland* is, abound
with them'.[48] According to King, bogs are 'a shelter and refuge to Torys
[dispossessed Irish who became outlaws], and Thieves, who can hardly
live without them'.[49] Indeed, the term 'bog trotter' – a Pan-like trickster
character considered to be mischievous, untrustworthy, and often drunk
– later developed an association with the Irish peasantry. King continues:

> The Natives heretofore had nevertheless some advantage by the
> woods, and Bogs; by them they were preserved from the conquest
> of the *English*, and I believe it is a little remembrance of this, makes
> them still build near *Bogs*: it was an advantage then to them to have
> their country unpassable, and the fewer strangers came near them,
> they lived the easyer; for they had no inns, every house where you
> came, was your inn; and you said no more, but put off your broges
> & sate down by the fire; & since the natural *Irish* hate to mend high
> ways, and will frequently shut them up, and change them, (being
> unwilling strangers should come and burthen them;) Tho' they
> [bogs] are very inconvenient to us, yet they are of some use;[50]

Originally from Antrim in the north of Ireland, King continually
resisted the Catholic Jacobites and supported the Protestant William of
Orange in the decisive Battle of the Boyne of 1690. As a supporter of
colonial policy, bogs were obstacles as much as they were a source of
fascination and terror for King. Perhaps this is also why King was so
obsessed with Gothic occurrences marked specifically by the Catholic
affiliation of the Irish; he was constantly claiming to see Catholic ghosts
and monsters hiding in the darkness and haunting him.[51] Here again the
bog serves as a colonial space with Gothic qualities. Notwithstanding
the racial overtones in King's paper, it became quite accidentally an
influential work on the ecological dynamics of bogs for later conservation
biologists in both Ireland and America. Even King admitted that he lived

in 'an Island almost infamous for Bogs, and yet, I do not remember, that any one has attempted much concerning them'.[52] As discussed in Chapter 2, Stoker references King as a pioneer of bog utilisation and industry through his biologist character; Stoker even goes so far as to centre the novel's narrative on the very 'quaking bog' that King analyses in his paper.

While these aforementioned writings about boglands that span from Giraldus to King are not necessarily exhaustive, they represent the bog as both a symbol and also a material space that conjures colonial and Gothic associations. This is arguably why Stoker references these writers in his own literary account of boglands in *The Snake's Pass* rather than referencing other objective studies in the nineteenth century. Moreover, these early writings ultimately contribute to the construction of a depreciatory historical and cultural narrative of bogs, one that many writers in the nineteenth and twentieth centuries eventually dispute and then reclaim in the social order.

Two other notable studies of bogs in Ireland were conducted in the nineteenth century. One was a series of reports by engineers published between 1810 and 1914, *Report of the Commissioners Appointed to Enquire into the Nature and Extent of Several Bogs in Ireland: and the Practicability of Draining and Cultivating them*. This survey, unlike Boate's and King's more subjective accounts, charted all of Ireland's bogs in the most comprehensive study to that point.[53] Because engineers conducted the surveys, examinations of bog ecologies had yet to be completed. The other series of studies was guided by the famed Irish botanist Robert Lloyd Praeger, who is also known for extensively researching Roundstone Bog (also a source of focus for contemporary eco-bog writer Tim Robinson (see Chapter 6)). Praeger's 'Irish Topographical Botany' (1901) examined bog vegetation, in addition to other geographies and ecologies of the Irish flora; the paper was later expanded into *The Botanist in Ireland* (1934).[54] Both the *Report* and 'Irish Topographical Botany' expanded scientific understandings of bogs, among other geologic landforms and botany in Ireland, but they remain largely objective and less tied to the cultural dimensions that influenced the pejorative associations with bogs, which largely existed between the sixteenth and nineteenth centuries, and to a lesser extent into the twentieth century.

With the increased attention in the social sphere, literary production in the nineteenth century utilised boglands as both settings and symbolic spaces to underscore Irish identity. This was particularly true in the 'national tales' or novels of the early nineteenth century that focused on national landscapes and their simultaneous historical characterisations of plentitude and loss within a colonial framework, the result of which included narratives about national issues and detailed descriptions of the Irish landscape.[55] Maria Edgeworth's *Castle Rackrent* (1800), published close to the Act of Union, depicts a new type of Spenserian political economy, but from the perspective of the returning absentee landlord. Such landlords re-inhabit their estates and slowly begin to 'improve' the land. In *Rackrent*, however, the bogs are not drained or reclaimed for 'improvement'. The landlord's English bride, who is unfamiliar with a 'turf stack', calls the bog near the property a bizarre 'black swamp out yonder'.[56] She questions the reason for keeping the bog as opposed to planting more civilised scenery such as 'trees'. Sir Kit, the landlord and husband, scoffs at the idea and claims the bog has been in the family hundreds of years and 'we would not part' with it.

Edgeworth's novel examines the highly dysfunctional landlord system in Ireland, a system that eventually disintegrates because of the Land Wars later in the 1870s and 1880s. The novel contains Gothic overtones in its depiction of supernatural phenomena lurking outside of the estate, such as the 'fairy-mounts' (hills where fairies would appear) and 'Banshees' (an aristocratic fairy signalling someone will soon die), as well as the bog.[57] In this regard, the bog surfaces often more as a cultural signifier associated with what lies beyond the estate – a zone of imperial safety – than as a physical part of 'nature' as described in depth in Boate and King, or even later in Stoker.[58] The bog reinforces the different English and Irish perceptions of 'nature' more than it does a justification for development.

Published shortly after *Castle Rackrent*, Sydney Owenson's *The Wild Irish Girl* (1806) is set in the West of Ireland (County Mayo) amidst vast hills of Atlantic blanket bogs. The protagonist, although somewhat marooned in this location because of debt, eventually learns to value Irish culture and history. Although framed as an epistolary novel, it is also a polemic for Irish society. The novel marks a subtle transition in the role of the bog in Irish society, particularly in how it is no longer perceived as a wasteland or a product for commodification, a trend that Edgeworth began with Kit's refusal to remove the bog. Owenson's novel also functions as a type of colonial Gothic tale, with crumbling castles dotting the rugged mountain bog terrain that have been neglected since the conquest of the Gaelic nobility during Cromwell's reign. Throughout Owenson's and Edgeworth's nationalistic tales, among others, there are indicators that although the bog was once considered a loathsome nuisance, it manifests into a site of national importance. 'For nationalist commentators,' as Katie Trumpener argues, 'the bog is important as both a material site and a discursive one, as the locus of a long-running struggle between improvers and nationalists, beginning already with the Elizabethan colonization and settlement of Ireland.'[59] There is a noticeable contrast between Spenser, Boate, and King, and Edgeworth and Owenson. Stoker, as well as other writers, film-makers, and photographers in the twentieth century, extends the national importance of the bog that arguably began with these national tales in the early nineteenth century.

Moving into the modern and contemporary periods (1890 to present), which will be the focus of the remainder of this book, areas in Ireland that still contain bogs are not only used as settings, but utilised more often as cultural barometers during periods of sectarian struggle and are imbued with Gothic conventions. For example, the fictional setting for Stoker's *The Snake's Pass* is actually located in County Mayo, a region home to some of the largest areas of mountain blanket bogs in Ireland and, like Owenson's *The Wild Irish Girl*, replete with Gothic structures framed in divisive colonial histories of land ownership. Marina Carr's *By the Bog of Cats...* and Deirdre Kinahan's *Bog Boy* are both set on opposite ends of the Irish Midlands, an economically depleted rural setting containing Ireland's largest area of raised bogs, including the famous Bog of Allen. The Bog of Allen still resonates in the Irish modernist literary archive because of the closing lines of James Joyce's short story 'The Dead' in *Dubliners* (1914), describing the 'softly falling' snow on 'the dark central plain' of the vast bog.[60] Although not a focus of this book, Joyce's incredibly brief depiction of the Bog of Allen in 'The Dead' underscores the postcolonial Gothic, as Michael Furey's ghost remains stranded somewhere between the past and the present, continually haunting Gabriel and Gretta's relationship. Joyce's use of the bog in 'The Dead' serves as a bifurcated reminder of two Irelands: the independent Ireland that Gabriel advocates throughout the story and the Ireland that remains locked to the past. The Bog of Allen conjures up a repressed and colonised past, which, as Jonathan Swift wrote, swallows up moments of Irish history:

> Great Bog of Allen swallow down
> That heap of muck called Philipstoun
> And if thy mor can swallow more
> Then take and relish Tullamore.[61]

In poetic verse Heaney's bog poems allude to some of the raised bogs in County Derry in Northern Ireland; they serve as political and cultural metaphors deep within Irish history as much as they reveal the uncanny and aesthetic characteristics of the physical bog. The poems ascribe historical agency to the bog, plunging deep into the amorphous time-scale of the peat and subsequently histories.[62] Heaney explains the biological construction of bogs in his poem 'Kinship', a poem whose form visually pierces each page in short three- or four-word lines, like a *sleán* into the 'spit' layers of the turf bank:

> This centre holds
> and spreads,
> sump and seedbed,
> a bag of waters

The poem discusses the 'sour and sink' in 'heather unseeds' of the bog and then recognises the personal relationship between the speaker and the bog:

> I grew out of all this
> like a weeping willow
> inclined to
> the appetites of gravity.[63]

The closing stanza specifically reveals how the speaker of the poem 'grew out of all this' boggy setting, forging a cultural connection with the previous five stanzas that describe the physical qualities of bogs and the cultural mapping humans graft onto the bog (see Fig. 1.8).

In addition to writers, poets, and photographers, Irish artists have turned to the multiplicities of the bog. In 1990, *Boglands: A Sculptors' Symposium* was held in the Wicklow mountains; artists from Ireland, the UK, the Netherlands, and Japan gathered for three weeks to produce sculptures constructed entirely out of bogs. Inspired by other 'land art' or 'earthworks' – similar to Richard Long and Andy Goldsworthy, among others – *Boglands* celebrated the phenomenological elements of the bog, accentuating its shapes, textures, and cultures through sensorial experience and artistic practice.[64] Dutch sculptor Remco de Fouw, who was a contributing artist and lives in Ireland, explains his own experiences of probing the depths of the bog through land art and culture:

1.8 Heaney sitting on turf stacks in Bellaghy Bog, Co. Derry, Northern Ireland (photo by Bobbie Hanvey)

> To me it's a place that has a terrific presence by itself – this black primordial goo … There's a tremendous history there too. I suppose because the vegetation has been deposited over thousands of years … like a little store-house of history … The bog is such a black soup – almost like a metaphor for the subconscious … so I'm trying to make a connection between the sleeping bog and an aspect of ourselves possibly.[65]

The physical qualities described here by de Fouw, as much as the imaginative or symbolic, inform how and why Irish writers and artists use bogs in their works. De Fouw demonstrates how aesthetic and material elements blend together as an overarching conception of the numinous, historic, and subconscious appeal of bogs in Irish culture. He goes on to explain that 'the wilderness of the bog' can be viewed as a 'metaphor for a journey of mind', where 'layers of years upon years of its own sleeping memories, consciousness turned to matter'.[66] The earthworks created by de Fouw also draw on Gothic elements associated with the bog (he created a series of human heads of various sizes, shapes, and expressions that were sculpted out of peat). In one example, *Let Sleeping Bogs Lie* (1990), de Fouw carves the face of a man in the bog, demonstrating how materiality and consciousness form a complex unity in the bog (see Fig. 1.9). Once the three weeks ended, the land art was left *in situ*, waiting for the natural breakdown of the elements through changing seasons and climate cycles.[67]

The literary and cultural scholar Terry Eagleton also offers some insightful remarks about how bogs associate with the Irish cultural imagination. In *The Truth About the Irish* (2002), a comically playful book published during the Celtic Tiger and thus mainly aimed at tourists and mass audiences, Eagleton comments in one section devoted to 'Bogs':

> If bogs have haunted the Irish imagination, it may be partly because they reveal the past as still present. With a bog, and its buried contents, the past is no longer behind you, but palpably beneath your feet. A secret history is stacked just a few feet below the modern world in which you're standing. This, in fact, has been one way in which the history-plagued Irish have sometimes conceived of their past – not as a set of events over and done with, but as something still alive in the present.[68]

Bogs have indeed 'haunted the Irish imagination' through their uncanny ability to address and redress history in the present. Eagleton goes on to make the connection between the prevalence of bogs in Ireland and the 'Irish love of the ghost story, in which the shades of the dead slip into the living present'.[69] Gibbons conceives of the bog similarly to Eagleton when he contends that the 'secret disclosed at the bottom of the bog represents indeed the return of the repressed for colonial rule'.[70] Such psychoanalytic readings also follow the theoretical trajectory of the Irish Gothic in the 1990s, focusing on 'fictional representation' and 'repressed fears and anxieties' about not only the Anglo-Irish populations as Moynahan and Backus suggest,[71] but also about land rights and ownership. While part of the allure, it is not only Eagleton's allusion to or Gibbons' direct association with Sigmund Freud's psychoanalytic idea of the 'return of the repressed', as it connects to Irish colonial history, that induces writers to engage with the bog in their works. It is the bog's ability to conceal and reveal both real and imaginative elements of history that offers writers a

1.9 *Let Sleeping Bogs Lie* (1990), Remco de Fouw
(photo by Christine Bond)

fitting literary image for exploration. The morphology of the bog and its status as a ubiquitous landform in Ireland, in addition to any metaphorical renditions, lead to psychological and realist renderings of traumatic pasts and presents.

Máirtín Ó Cadhain's 'The Edge of the Bog/Ciumhais an Chriathraigh', in the collection *Cois Caoláire/Beside the Bay* (1953), is an excellent psychological realist short story that does not fit into the historical and thematic trajectory of the subsequent chapters, but is worth discussing briefly here. In it, Ó Cadhain underscores the fear of repression and ultimately death of the people who reside on the peripheries of society, on the literal and metaphoric bog. For the protagonist, Muiréad, a woman in her late thirties, the psychological fear of loneliness and repressed sexuality (awoken by a brief encounter with a drunken soldier at a wedding) are mirrored by the stagnating sterility of the anaerobic bog – both a symbol and literal place of infertility.[72] For Muiréad, whose encounter with the soldier triggered the haunting memory of her five stillborn babies, such sterility reflects simultaneous utilisation and the lack of production the bog represents. Muiréad and characters like her, portrayed as living in economically depressed and socially repressed areas near bogs, represent those at the margins of society who are also symbolically living reminders of a disenfranchised and traumatic past in Irish history. In this story, the bog simultaneously serves as a symbol of a modernised and pre-modern Ireland where past/present ghosts haunt the living, like Muiréad, who are forced to society's margins.

Even beyond Ó Cadhain's sympathies for Muiréad's difficult position as a single, middle-aged woman living in Connacht (an Irish-speaking region), the short story invokes the anxiety of alienation resulting from living on the edge – of sexual liberation, personal freedom, and economic prosperity. The bog appears to repress these symbols of modernity. Looming on the edge of Muiréad's life, the bog manifests conspicuously on the one hand as a space that devours people into its historical repository of nothingness: 'there was a cloud, a dark, shapeless cloud, lying over the bog'.[73] On the other hand, it ushers in modernity for rural populations by providing an economic and pragmatic resource. To this end, the fear of being devoured by the 'shithole of the bog',[74] which here signals a persistent anxiety about the haunting of the present by the past as demonstrated through Muiréad's own life and that of Connacht more generally, is the overarching thematic in Ó Cadhain's story and other literary examples like it.

Images and the structure of the bog provide ways to access simultaneous and contradictory versions of history (as well as the present and future). Not only can this be as an awakening to a repressed state or awareness of a sterile future, like it is in 'The Edge of the Bog', but also as a way to address previously unexamined aspects of history. In other words, it is not simply a way to decode history that compels one to explore the bog; rather, it is the bog's ability to function as an atemporal and non-teleological space, while at the same time allowing the opposite to occur – through stratified layers of peat – that empowers researchers to explore the historical record through material artefacts. Accounts of Western history usually move from A to B in a linear fashion. Bogs automatically disrupt such linearity by forging opposites in unity, both distinct from one another and yet occurring simultaneously as a type of Thirdspace, and thereby creating a multifocal space that disturbs the accepted norms of temporality. This effect creates the slippages in history and memory that writers often use as formal tools in their works, such as changing narrative structures. Time and history can even be proven by carbon-dating the organic matter in bogs, such as the bog oaks or DNA of bog bodies. But time, in a cultural context, becomes much less precise or even unnecessary. The return of the repressed cannot simply be found 'at the bottom of the bog', as Gibbons alludes, because the bog is bottomless and has no centre. As a spatio-temporal amorphous terrain, the bog challenges any single definable ontology. In his poem 'Bogland', Heaney astutely reminds us that 'the wet centre is bottomless', and his meaning is metaphorical as much as it is geological ('bogholes' as 'Atlantic seepage').[75] Centre, as viewed by imperial systemisation, implies periphery, which then suggests that a totalising binary structure exists. The bog resists this totalising structuring of a centre by functioning as another type of formless space utilised in literary culture – as a fusion of opposites that emerges in various ways through the literary works explored in the following chapters.

The specific formation and morphology of bogs through their composition and positioning across Ireland often leads to greater understanding of how they are used as images in cultural and literary works. Like many other topographies in Ireland, bogs have changed over time through conflicting land-use systems and cultural practices surrounding them. As this chapter demonstrates, there are three qualities giving rise to the bog's characterisation as both a terrestrial and imaginative Gothic site: anaerobic composition, fuel source, and gaseous state. The scientifically physical and culturally symbolic elements of bogs enhance each other.

For example, the lack of oxygen in bogs induces biological preservation, which in turn generates conceptions about time, history, space, and memory. Bogs, as a fuel source, are consumed for heating and cooking and invoke hospitable or homely qualities (features that are fundamental to the Freudian Uncanny, which are further analysed in Chapter 2). Lastly, bogs emit gases, contributing to supernatural interpretations of how they harbour malevolent or ghostly manifestations. These three overlapping correlations between the physical and imaginative attributes of bogs exemplify some of the core reasons why Irish writers have used bogs as representational spaces throughout the country's cultural and political histories, in addition to postcolonial Gothic contexts in modern and contemporary periods. To this end, writers who engage with bogs often employ ghosts and hauntings as Gothic conventions because they too exist in zones that resist and redefine time and space and yet are integral to our everyday lives.

2

Environments of Empire

Mapping the un-consciousness of the island, the bog is established as the emblem of colonial politics.[1]

– Catherine Wynne, 'The Bog as a Colonial Topography'

A Foreigner, having come to a land by the accidents of history, he has succeeded not merely in creating a place for himself but also in taking away that of the inhabitant, granting himself astounding privileges to the detriment of those rightfully entitled to them.[2]

– Albert Memmi, *The Colonizer and the Colonized*

The Cultural 'Seedbed' of 1880s and 1890s Ireland

This chapter considers the environmental effects of colonisation in relation to the bog in *The Snake's Pass*, Bram Stoker's second novel and the only one set in Ireland. In it, Stoker relies on the ambiguities and contradictions inherent in the literary Gothic form to work out his conflicting views of Irish nationalism and land development. We locate our literary history of the bog at the end of the nineteenth century with *The Snake's Pass* because this transitional period in Ireland marks a shift from when physical landscapes were recurrently defined through somewhat inefficient modes of colonial administration, politics, and economics, and through cultural appropriation by the colonisers.[3] Through a shift of political power this period also attempts to finally address the vexing question rooted in colonial history of who owns the land in Ireland. Moving into the twentieth century, progress and modernisation appear to be the answer to Ireland's economic stability and political independence.

Any study of land, geography, or landscape in twentieth-century Ireland must first recognise the entangled land-use policies administered in the preceding century. In this context, Stoker's novel provides an ideal historical and geographical setting – on a preternatural bog in the culturally and politically tumultuous west of Ireland in the 1870s and 1880s – during a period and in a location that historian Roy Foster calls 'the seedbed of cultural revolution'.[4] Devoting an entire chapter to a Stoker novel other than the famed *Dracula* may seem too exhaustive, but *The Snake's Pass* is not only a postcolonial Gothic literary work focused entirely on a bog in Ireland; it more broadly serves as a point of departure for discussing other concerns pertaining to Irish literary culture and the cultural history of bogs leading up to the twentieth century, particularly in earlier works by Cambrensis, Spenser, Boate, King, and Arthur Young. To this end, Stoker's depiction of bogs as Gothic spaces reveals some of the larger underlying colonial tensions surrounding land-use and ownership that underscore the relationship between environments and the colonial administration of the British Empire in Ireland at the end of the nineteenth century.

Land has long been a focal point of geopolitical strife in Ireland. Land can be viewed as an economic, political, and ethnic category, as well as a geographical one.[5] Unequal distribution and ownership of land existed for several centuries under colonial administrations. In the eighteenth and nineteenth centuries, the battle for land ownership, which equated to political legitimisation, reached its peak around the time of Prime Minister William Gladstone's second Land Act of 1881 (first was in 1870). Paralleling Gladstone's Acts were the Land Wars of the 1870s and 1880s. During these Land Wars, disenfranchised Catholic tenants fought the Protestant Anglo-Irish landowners for land rights, including the right of ownership, to create an 'owner-occupying farming class'.[6] County Mayo, in the west of Ireland (arguably the setting of *The Snake's Pass*), was one of the most tumultuous zones during the Land Wars. Mayo was home to Michael Davitt who, along with Charles Stewart Parnell, led the Irish National Land League. The Land War of the 1880s drastically diminished the power of the Anglo-Irish as a dominant class, both in terms of land wealth and cultural legitimacy, and consequently signalled a serious threat to the future of colonial rule.[7]

The Land Acts and Wars caused significant shifts in ownership and power during this turbulent period and ultimately provide the historical, political, and geographical backdrop for *The Snake's Pass*. Land and legitimacy not only represent palpable anxieties continually expressed in the Anglo-Irish Gothic literary tradition, but they also become increasingly important leading up to and through the Irish revolutionary period between 1916 and 1923. Between 1870 and 1923, land ownership shifted considerably to the Catholic middle class. In 1870, for example, only 3 per cent of Irish householders owned land, most of which were Anglo-Irish, but by the 1916 Easter Rising as many as 63.9 per cent of householders owned land.[8]

Stoker's novel illuminates some of the contested rural spaces that are home to the bog and that are central to understanding Irish land identity both in the past and moving into the twentieth century. While Stoker does not specifically refer to the Land Wars in the novel, he was clearly preoccupied with the issues surrounding the land struggle since he sent both Gladstone and Davitt copies of *The Snake's Pass* upon its publication.[9] In fact, Stoker's protagonist, Arthur Severn, travels from England by way of Co. Mayo as a detour to Co. Clare so that he could 'improve' his 'knowledge of Irish affairs'.[10] Mayo, after all, was a 'seedbed' of such affairs at the end of the nineteenth century. *The Snake's Pass* is set on the uncanny and unstable bog-covered mountain of Knockcalltecrore (*Cnoch cailte cróin óir* / Hill of the Lost Golden Crown), the rocky pass of Shleenanaher (*Slí na nathair* / The Snake's Pass), and Knockcalltore (*Cnoch cailte óir* / Hill of Lost Gold) all located in the scenic west of Ireland. While the novel is set in the ambiguously fictitious town of Carnaclif, it clearly resembles Connemara – a region in the west comprising Co. Galway and Mayo – particularly in terms of the overarching land politics and topographical descriptions.

The Snake's Pass is considered a Gothic novel because of its intersecting themes of romance, usurpation, and murder, all of which are accompanied by a sense of foreboding that hints at the supernatural. In addition to the constructed romance plot, the novel reveals an incongruity between what we would now call the conservationist views of Irish tenant farmers and the commercialisation or modernising efforts of bog reclamation by Anglo-Irish Protestant landowners. Indeed, Stoker refers to the shifting bog as a 'carpet of death', where 'scientific and executive man exerts his dominance' over it at the peril of those who happen to be near (55).

The Snake's Pass specifically tells the story of a wealthy English tourist (Arthur) who has received a substantial inheritance from his aunt. While travelling from Co. Mayo to Clare to visit some friends, Arthur's coach is caught in a storm that delays his trip for a few days. During his stay at a local public house, he witnesses a contentious meeting between Phelim Joyce, a local farmer, and Murtagh 'Black' Murdock, over a land leasing and ownership dispute. Murdock has taken Phelim's farm as restitution for late payments. Murdock is known as 'the village gombeen man', a nineteenth-century term that describes people conducting shrewd practices of money-lending as an 'agent or middleman' for absentee landlords.[11] As the novel progresses, Arthur falls in love with a woman on the mountain bog whose identity remains unknown to him until later in the novel (she is Norah Joyce, the daughter of Phelim). Arthur quickly immerses himself in local politics about land ownership and it almost results in his own death. As Arthur pursues Norah romantically, he also finds himself in conflict, both attracted to and repelled by the bog on Knockcalltecrore (or the 'Hill'). Arthur purchases the entire mountain of Knockcalltecrore to protect Norah and the land she and her father, Phelim, have temporarily lost to Murdock. Simultaneously and coincidentally Murdock hires Richard (Dick) Sutherland – a geologist and old university friend of Arthur's who is originally from Ireland – to help him locate an alleged lost treasure of French gold in the bog. Murdock's meddling with the bog terrain ultimately results in death; the shifting bog slides off the mountain into the sea and takes him with it.

Two key issues arise that question the relevance of *The Snake's Pass* as an important literary text. One is that the novel contains standard, and at times hackneyed, Gothic themes of romance, adventure, treasure-hunting, and horror not too dissimilar to other imperial Gothic novels and stories of the same period written by H. Rider Haggard, Rudyard Kipling, and Arthur Conan Doyle. The other is character-based in that the characters never move beyond stale two-dimensionality, often reminiscent of popular nineteenth-century fiction. We might explain the brittle characters as a shortcoming attributable to the fact that this is Stoker's second novel. One might even argue that the early work appears unbalanced, with the bog receiving far too much attention in the text, robbing human characters of dimension.

However, I shall propose that the bog serves as a multidimensional character – not just a physical terrain – and is central to the novel's action in every way. The overabundant narrative of the bog, couched in a turbulent period of Irish colonial history where the problem of land and ownership has dominated politics for centuries, is precisely why *The Snake's Pass* provides an ideal starting point for a critical analysis of other twentieth-century Gothic writings about the bog. The topography of the bog – simultaneously centralised and marginalised in the text – serves as an important link in understanding colonial politics in this period. Stoker focuses on the bog, with its union of opposites that help explain *both* the symbolic *and also* physical characteristics, to synthesise dominant themes of colonisation, industrialisation, nationalism, and supernatural folklore, which can all be examined through the critical lens of the postcolonial Gothic. Stoker also incorporates the writings of Cambrensis, Spenser, Boate, and King, all of which have discussed the bog in Irish history to varying degrees, as pointed out in Chapter 1. In this sense, the novel serves as both a starting point and a bridge, referencing Irish land concerns in previous centuries and providing an abbreviated natural history of the bog (more than any other Irish literary work to this point), while also anticipating similar issues in the twentieth century.

Despite it being such a substantial literary work about the Irish bog, *The Snake's Pass* had received relatively little critical attention until the mid-1990s. Nicholas Daly concentrated the most scrutiny on *The Snake's Pass* in his book *Modernism, Romance, and the Fin de Siècle* (1999).[12] Primarily focusing his reading of the novel on the 'imperial' marriage plot in the larger genre of the imperial adventure novel, Daly considers Stoker's story to be an allegory of English imperialism because it presents uneasy parallels with the treasure-hunt genre in an 'imaginary imperial space'.[13] Daly analyses the novel as an imperial adventure romance that provides colonial discourses outside of the typical imperial romance genre, which is usually set far away from the epicentre of Britain. However, Daly's analysis centres more on imperial relations with Britain, particularly the allegory of the treasure hunt and the imperial marriage, than on the bog and its relationship to Ireland. The bog receives attention inasmuch as it supports Daly's argument about spaces in the imperial imaginary – a colonial landscape that becomes 'domesticated' in Stoker's novel – and therefore remains an ideal backdrop for the colonial wedding between Arthur and Norah. Daly's chapter on Stoker's novel nevertheless initiates critical conversations focused on the bog even if the bog merely represents one of 'the blank spaces' of the colonial 'map' of the adventure novel, and one that generates colonial memory.[14]

Luke Gibbons also briefly discusses *The Snake's Pass* to show the conflicting structures of a colonial economy within a system with deep roots in the older Gaelic order.[15] While Gibbons' perspective is worth noting here because of its focus on the bog, it is largely based on the Gothic notion, drawing on psychoanalysis, of the return of the repressed, which reveals how people who were subordinated through colonial projects in the past will eventually haunt the present. Gibbons examines how plunging into the bog unintentionally 'reactivates' the past, as opposed to 'repudiating' it, which is the coloniser's goal.[16] It could also be argued, however, that Stoker's use of the bog questions the contemporary moment (in the 1880s and 1890s) in Irish and English relations, anticipating the future rather than repressing the past. It is important to consider the bog as a symbol of repression in Stoker's novel, as Gibbons suggests, but the bog also undergoes conflicts and challenges to it from the omnipresent narratives of progress and modernisation based upon projections of the future.

William Hughes' position on *The Snake's Pass* resembles claims made by Daly and Gibbons, insofar as the colonial connections to Ireland that appear in the novel highlight the tensions between English capitalism and rural Ireland in the late nineteenth century. Hughes maintains that Stoker's 'ambiguous relationship to Ireland' is clearly outlined in *The Snake's Pass* in that it serves as a 'fable of reconstruction' that identifies 'representative Irish problems'.[17] Hughes' argument largely aims at readers who are not already familiar with *The Snake's Pass*, or those who have yet to fully realise its importance in Irish Gothic literature, and he provides an overview of the novel's place in Irish Gothic history and supports its critical relevance. Hughes challenges W.J. McCormack's claim in *The Field Day Anthology of Irish Writing* (1991) that Stoker's second novel offers little critical relevance (McCormack essentially argues that *The Snake's Pass* should not be considered a key text in the Irish Gothic tradition). Hughes responds to McCormack's claim by arguing that 'Stoker does not sit comfortably within the Irish canon of *The Field Day Anthology*' because he does not sit comfortably within the Irish Literary Revival.[18] For Hughes, more than any other novel written by Stoker, *The Snake's Pass* investigates the ambiguous relationship between Ireland and England. The bog, again, only receives limited exposure in Hughes' overview of the novel and its relationship to Ireland. More than any other aspect of *The Snake's Pass*, the bog serves as a concrete and recognisable landform in Ireland for understanding this ambiguous relationship through its own misunderstood classification and indeterminate qualities.

The bog remains important not only because of what it reveals in the novel, but also because it is an important and ubiquitous terrain in Ireland, and one compelling enough to warrant such sustained attention by a Gothic writer. *The Snake's Pass* discloses some of the key oppositional qualities of the bog, emphasising the relevance of the bog in debates about the land as a natural resource in Ireland's economic future. For

Daly, Gibbons, and Hughes, the bog is subordinate to the colonial politics that it underpins and functions as one of many factors in the novel relating to larger colonial concerns. In contrast, Catherine Wynne considers the bog to be an allegory for nineteenth-century colonial politics: 'the colonial condition of nineteenth-century Ireland is evidenced in the anomalous and unstable depiction of bog and moor'.[19] Wynne's argument locates bogs and moors as keys to understanding a range of colonial issues in nineteenth-century British and Irish writings, one of which includes *The Snake's Pass*. For Wynne, the '[s]odden grounds' of a 'primeval past' function 'as sites of agrarian and political strife'.[20]

One issue with these critical examinations of *The Snake's Pass* is that they all tend to align the bog with the past rather than view it as foregrounding the future.[21] The associations with the past remain crucial to examine and build upon, but the novel reveals a looming threat pointing the reader forward as much as to the past. The bog in late nineteenth-century literature serves not only as a nexus for shifting histories in rural areas associated with colonisation, it also points to future encounters (as we will see in the following four chapters), serving as a non-linear temporal space that swings throughout history. The elimination of the bog through reclamation in Stoker's novel, and the depleting consequence of these actions in Ireland, anticipates a future in the twentieth century where the bog continues to be affected by political fissures created by colonisation, industrialisation, and nationalism.

Stoker acknowledges how the bog can ameliorate Ireland's economic independence from Britain; however, Stoker also recognises that such independence might result in complete exploitation of the 'natural' environment. Previous criticism has addressed issues of land ownership and nationalism, but the environmental impacts of the bog subtly discussed in the novel remain unexamined. This chapter aims to demonstrate that the bog serves as a tool for understanding colonial politics, particularly through Stoker's vision of nationalism, but I approach this somewhat circuitously by emphasising that what we would now call the 'ecological' significance of bogs in Ireland is vital to this understanding. *The Snake's Pass* reveals historical undercurrents about the preservation of bogs, even if they appear peripheral to predominant arguments in support of bog reclamation during the nineteenth century.

In the novel, the bog serves as a representative terrain related to Irish colonial politics. At the same time, such politics are couched in Gothic aesthetics used by Stoker to explain some of the limited and limitless qualities of the bog. The bog is a nexus for these concerns. It is not strictly the 'ecological' or 'environmental' history of the bog that conjures up these associations, but also the socio-economic, cultural, and ethno-religious histories in relation to a specific topography. In other words, there is a bifurcated environmental history of the bog: on the one hand, a scientific history frames the bog as a specific ecosystem; on the other hand, a disputed political history remains associated with ownership of the bog. The bog has been simultaneously a colonised space and one that resists colonisation because of its symbolic and biological qualities, both of which clearly appear in *The Snake's Pass*. I partly approach this chapter through environmental criticism (ecocriticism) – a way of theorising the intersections among literature, culture, and the environment – to the extent that the bog, framed through the devices of the Gothic tradition, is subordinate to British land management and industrialisation and therefore exploitable both as a capital resource and as a symbol of Ireland.

While this chapter focuses on what could be considered a postcolonial examination of Stoker's novel, it builds upon and at times challenges these earlier critical perspectives by exclusively surveying Stoker's representation of the bog. As both an imaginary and terrestrial topography used in the novel, the bog reflects some of the perceptions regarding land and natural resources in late nineteenth-century Ireland. Environmental manipulations of the bog, seen as both a Gothic and colonised space, underscore the contradictions and instabilities of its sodden grounds. Colonial and environmental themes underpinning Gothic fiction provide a productive way to see the bog as a place where British industrialisation – imported through the protagonist Arthur – threatens and ultimately destroys the bog. Gothic conventions, such as aspects of the uncanny, materiality, or transgression, help to explain anxieties about land ownership and land-use within colonial models of administration in *The Snake's Pass*. In this way, the influence is reciprocal: Gothic themes uncover land-use questions in colonial Ireland and environmental readings expand our understanding of the Gothic.

Thus, it is beneficial to analyse *The Snake's Pass* and the period of literary history surrounding it through the lens of the postcolonial Gothic because it offers another way of examining the damaging environmental practices of British imperialism, as well as other similar forms of historical imperialism. We see this process unfold through the English character Arthur, in addition to Stoker's own hybrid relationship with Ireland and

England in a synthesis of biography, history, and fiction that all inform and intertwine in the novel. Stoker, through his protagonist, reflects on the larger consequences and confusions of colonisation as it relates to natural resources in Ireland. This approach, resembling the anomalous state of the bog itself, offers no identifiable or totalising conclusions. Instead, it opens up other ways of considering Stoker's theory of modernisation as both conflicting and complementary in combination with acknowledging the bog as a threatened environment. Stoker's ideology of nationalism portrayed in the novel can be understood as one of the primary fusions of opposites framing the bog: he both mourns the loss of the bog as part of Irish identity and also justifies its elimination to assist economic and political sovereignty from England. *The Snake's Pass* ultimately raises the question: should Ireland embrace modernisation despite its potential effects on the environment and culture? Critical approaches to the novel have focused on notions of British industrialism, colonial consciousness, and the way the bog serves as an allegory for Ireland; however, focusing on environmental destruction of the biological bog, in combination with its symbolic significance, takes a different direction.

The following two sections examine how the novel addresses what are ultimately unanswered questions about the ecological and cultural impacts of the bog that also reflect some of the changing land-use policies of the time. The first section provides an historical account of the tensions surrounding land-use and bog reclamation, particularly in how they intersect with colonisation, culture, and Stoker's own 'Anglo' and 'Celtic' background embedded in the novel. Stoker's noticeable biographical interjection generates one of the simultaneous oppositions between modernisation and preservation; he both supports and resists the bog's destruction. Drawing on earlier writings by Spenser, Boate, and King, among others, Stoker's novel raises the contradictory question: should we protect bogs from elimination or use them as natural resources to promote economic independence from England? The second section further explores the elements of the first section as they specifically relate to the text. In doing so, I look at how the environmental composition of the bog connects to industrialisation and commercialisation by examining Gothic themes of opposition, the uncanny, material ecocriticism, and ecological transgression. Viewing the bog as a threatened environment through an Irish Gothic novel reveals other ways of understanding colonial politics and land-use practices in the late nineteenth century.

Reclamation and Demonisation of Bogs

Critical approaches to land ownership and tenant anxieties concerning
the Anglo-Irish and Catholics in Irish Gothic literature frequently address
the gap between the economic practices of land-use and management.
Land, for instance, was not only a politically charged space; it was also a
repository of culture where tenuous lines between history and memory
were drawn. Uses for the material environment were based on the division
among Irish Catholic labourers (tenants who worked or leased the land
without much economic or political benefit), Protestant Anglo-Irish
landowners (those who held on to political power due to landholdings),
and English tourists (those who wanted to enjoy the landscape as an
aesthetic commodity in the empire). Cultural nationalists wanted to
preserve the bog as a place of cultural identity. Indeed, the bog served as
a repository of culture with its ability to localise forms of history through
the layers of stratification in the bog, often revealing relics and artefacts.
For cultural nationalists, bogs needed to remain a physical and symbolic
presence in order to reinforce a supposedly once-stronger national identity
and Irish tradition prior to colonial occupation.[22]

The literary historian Katie Trumpener specifies that bogs in Romantic
novels are 'a place where outlines of the past can still be glimpsed' and
where there are 'visible marks of many centuries of continuous human
presence, the scars of military battles, and the traces of occupation'.[23]
Even for the Anglo-Irish landowners in the eighteenth and nineteenth
centuries, the bog was under threat as part of a colonial imperative to
increase the amount of usable agricultural land. According to Trumpener,
bogs served as an 'emblem for Ireland's intractable national character'.[24]
Ethno-religious tensions surrounding the land debates contained cultural,
economic, and environmental implications. In this context, a disputed
association existed between conservation and modernisation. Such an
opposition of simultaneity – the bog as commodity and yet the bog as
land of fertile arability – underpins these tensions in *The Snake's Pass*.
While Trumpener's remarks primarily elucidate the relationship between
bogs and Ireland in the eighteenth and early nineteenth centuries, they
also point to a conservationist trend embedded in the land debates during
the latter half of the nineteenth century.

The English, as seen explicitly in Boate and King, often perceived
bogs throughout Irish history as wasted space and zones of decay. As a
result of the pejorative association with bogs, policies were put in place

to reclaim them through drainage projects, with the intention of increase agricultural production for the Protestant and Anglo-Irish landowners and the larger British Empire. This process mostly dispossessed Catholic peasants who lived near or on bogs for socio-economic reasons. Reclamation projects were a new land reform that attempted to 'beautify' the sublime qualities of bogs. The government-appointed Bogs Commission, established in 1809 to research bogs and their commercial uses, remains a primary example of these bog-reclamation projects. The commissioner's reports, published between 1810 and 1814, outlined the formation and composition of bogs, while also including maps, drawings, and advice on drainage. The report estimated that 1.4 million acres could be reclaimed for tillage and 2.3 million for pasture.[25] By this calculation, the elimination of bogs would result in agricultural improvement and further displacement for the Catholic majority living in rural areas. In the context of *The Snake's Pass*, Daly surmises that the 'bog suggests that what is really at stake in the murkiness of the past is the violence of colonial history'.[26] But what is really at stake in the murkiness of history in the novel is systematic bog eradication.

In addition to the economic benefits, the process of bog reclamation conveniently justified cultural and religious discrimination against those who lived on or near them. Anglo-Irish landowners imposed a darker, ominous, and therefore Gothicised view of bogs in Ireland in order to justify the exploitation and elimination of them in the eighteenth and nineteenth centuries. Demonising bogs and the people who lived on or near them advanced a larger aim of the reclamation project: to dispossess the Irish peasants and generate profit from bogs. Just as the Anglo-Irish literary Gothic form became an expression of cultural anxieties in response to an increasingly minority status, the perceptions of bogs conveniently served as a way to marginalise topographies while also buttressing the interests of the status quo.

As part of a pre-existing English prejudice, bogs were, according to Hughes, 'an overt signifier of Irish topography, and the source of derogatory racial stereotypes'.[27] Donal Clarke, a recent President of the International Peat Society, cites an anonymous nineteenth-century account in his article about bogs, which describes people who lived near them as 'miserable and half-starved spectres who inhabited the dreary waste'.[28] In a literary example, George Moore's *Parnell and His Island* (1887) describes the Irish peasant class in Co. Mayo as a race 'that has been forgotten and left behind in a bog hole; it smells of the wet earth, its face seems as if made of it, and its ideas are moist and dull, and as sterile as peat'.[29] These examples demonstrate how the Irish peasants were often discriminated against because of their association with bog topographies.

Disparaging characterisations of bogs through rhetoric of reclamation and demonisation also signal the Gothic aesthetic often associated with them. In *Empire and the Gothic*, Smith and Hughes argue:

> One of the defining ambivalences of the Gothic is that its labeling of otherness is often employed in the service of supporting, rather than questioning, the status quo. This is perhaps the central complexity of the form because it debates the existence of otherness and alterity, often in order to demonise such otherness.[30]

Bogs and the people who lived on or near them were collectively marginalised in order to reinforce their subordinated 'otherness' status, as not only peasants and Irish Catholics, but also colonial subjects. In the eighteenth century, bogs were considered to be sources of 'sin and sloth, a site of social and moral darkness', where 'drainage takes on the status of an exorcism'.[31] Thus, bog reclamation achieved two important aims for the Anglo-Irish in their relationship with the Irish Catholics: it increased economic revenue for the Anglo-Irish landowners and it eliminated the iniquities of the bogs and the people who lived on them (namely Catholic peasants). Rhetorically framing bog reclamation through proselytisation – saving Irish Catholics from sin and eternal damnation – generates another form of religious and economic conversion through the materiality of the bogs. These accounts of discrimination, coupled with a history of land reclamation leading up to the Land Wars and Acts, all contextualise the dominant issues underpinning the narrative of *The Snake's Pass*, as well as the environmental history of bogs in Ireland as a whole.

Arthur, the novel's landowning English character, views the bog on two opposing levels. On one level, Arthur takes more interest in the Hill (consisting of bog) than the local Irish do because of his desire to possess and transform it as part of a larger commercial project. On another level, Arthur wants to preserve the beauty of the landscape for his own visual pleasure as an English tourist. When looking at the blanket bog on the mountain, Arthur remarks, 'The sight of the Hill filled me with glad emotion' (206). Ireland's scenic and sublime landscapes in the west function as places of refuge for the nineteenth-century English traveller because of their close proximity yet distance from England's polluting coal factories. The novel begins with Arthur representing such a traveller, who immediately becomes 'arrested' by the beauty of Ireland's landscapes (8). Maintaining what we would now call ecological balance through preservation policy was paradoxically more important to the gaze of the privileged English traveller – often desiring an aesthetic escape or picturesque experience of rustic landscapes distinct from increasingly industrialised England – than it was for the local Irish tenant farmers who were a labour force ultimately resigned to work for Anglo-Irish landowners.

At the opening of the novel, Arthur's description of the Irish topography provides an example of aestheticising the land:

> Between two great mountains of grey and green, as the rock cropped out between the tufts of emerald verdure, the valley, almost as narrow as a gorge, ran due west towards the sea … The whole west was a gorgeous mass of violet and sulphur and gold – great masses of storm-cloud piling up and up till the very heavens seemed weighed with burden too great to bear. Clouds of violet, whose centres were almost black, and whose outer edges were tinged with living gold … The view was the most beautiful that I had ever seen; and accustomed as I had been only to the quiet pastoral beauty of grass country, with occasional visits to my great aunt's well-wooded estate in the south of England, it was no wonder that it arrested my attention and absorbed my imagination. (7–8)

Arthur appears in the novel as the English gentleman traveller who eventually purchases 'the whole mountain' so that he can save Norah's Cliff Fields and then Phelim Joyce's farm from Black Murdock's economic and psychological oppression (180). Despite these chivalrous intentions, Arthur concurrently wants to profit from the land's productivity, aligning him more with an Anglo-Irish landowner than an English tourist.

Understanding Stoker's contradictory ethno-national identity, reflected largely in Arthur's character, remains crucial when reading *The Snake's Pass* and understanding the treatment of the bog. Despite his English birth and upbringing, Arthur appears to be more Anglo-Irish than English because of his divergent identities. For example, he becomes a landowner in rural Ireland and eventually a land developer even though he begins the story as an English tourist. Daly has previously questioned Arthur's identity, complicating the purely English association:

While Arthur is English, to the extent that he is also Stoker's most obvious representative in the text, he may also be seen as having Irish roots. He is an orphan, his parents 'lost in a fog when crossing the Channel' (11). His father 'had been pretty well cut off by his family on account of his marriage with what they considered his inferior' (11). The doubled sense of isolation – his father's disinheritance and his own orphanhood – as well as the suggestion of inferior blood on the mother's side, make Arthur an appropriate figure for a class whose identity might well seem to have been lost overboard, albeit somewhere in the waters between Ireland and England.[32]

This 'doubled sense of isolation' further explains the pervading opposition in the novel. Daly's description of Arthur provides a tragic tone and draws attention to some of the Gothic elements, with references to inheritance, 'orphanhood', and inferior blood lineage. In fact, Arthur's ambivalent ethnic identity, both English and Irish (the 'inferior blood' on his mother's side), parallels Stoker's own conflicted background.

Declan Kiberd maintains Stoker had produced a sort of 'Catholicized Protestantism' that was later featured in Irish modernism from Augusta Gregory and W.B. Yeats to Bernard Shaw.[33] Kiberd's simultaneous and yet oppositional phrase partly provides insight into why Stoker initiated the practice of using occult symbolism and supernaturalism drawn from the Catholic peasantry in *The Snake's Pass*. Stoker's similar and yet differing Catholicised Protestantism position also informs his other novels, such as *Dracula* and *The Lair of the White Worm* (1911), in how he reconstructs Irish politics around land that symbolically and imaginatively represent Ireland.[34] These ties to both Protestant and Catholic traditions suggest sympathy for the difficult position of the Catholic tenant class. Anglo-Irish writers like Yeats, Gregory, and Synge equally took up support for Irish nationalist politics, often in the form of a particularly Catholicised Protestantism, by blending together an odd mix of ideas from pre-colonial Gaelic mythologies in pseudo-Gothic forms of the occult and supernatural, with colonial notions of landowning elites.

Valente most convincingly examines Stoker's ambivalent 'ethno-national' identity and concludes that despite previous assertions, Stoker is not Anglo-Irish but 'Anglo-Celtic', a combination of Irish and British/Anglo-Saxon ancestry.[35] Valente explains that Stoker's father claims an Anglo-Saxon or British descent while his mother is originally from the rural west of Ireland in Co. Galway, hence the injection of Irish myth and folklore in the semi-fictionalised setting of *The Snake's Pass*. Stoker's own 'metrocolonial immixture' identity, what Valente argues to be the opposition and yet simultaneity of the metropolitan (Anglo) centre shadowed by the connection with the colonial (Celtic) fringe, serves as a more convincing way to reimagine Arthur, a character in which Stoker discloses some of his own anxieties about Irish and Anglo identity in a novel about land ownership and bogs.[36]

Regardless of Stoker's perceived identity as an Anglo-Celt rather than traditionally Anglo-Irish, the tension and anxiety surrounding his ethno-national identity remains the same. Stoker's identification as a 'philosophical Home Ruler' – in that he supported an independent Ireland but also repeatedly voted against the devolution of British imperial rule in Historical Society debates – might exemplify the contradiction he experienced through his Anglo and Celtic ethno-nationalities.[37] David Glover also writes about this tension underpinning the novel: 'From the outset his [Stoker's] encounter with Ireland promises to reveal to him a new truth about himself, a truth that is necessitated by his confused sense of disappointment with his own origins.'[38] Despite living in Dublin for much of his early life and university years (at Trinity College), Stoker gave up a promising civil service career and relocated to London to become a writer. Such an ambivalent ethno-nationality reveals his own 'doubled sense of isolation' (a characteristic also ascribed to Arthur) because this anxiety exists in many of Stoker's writings, but it is particularly evident and explicit in his only Irish novel that pertains to a quintessential Irish terrain of the bog.

Stoker thought Ireland's landowning practices needed to be eliminated, or at least significantly reformed, and because of this stance he supported contradictory positions: he supported both Irish Home Rule and British imperial rule.[39] The dysfunctional landlord system in Ireland at the time, which disenfranchised too many people, largely fuelled this belief. Stoker observed the harsh realities in rural Ireland when travelling the country as Inspector of Petty Sessions during part of his civil service job between 1868 and 1878 and, among the many abuses, 'witnessed how farmers in the countryside suffered under the English landlord system'.[40] Because of these first-hand experiences, Stoker sympathised with the plight of the tenants and the land on which they worked. These earlier experiences imbued Stoker with a profound sense of compassion for the Irish peasantry, along with an increased awareness of the debilitating poverty that many of them faced. Stoker believed that scientific and technological solutions might help their situation, while they also might lift Ireland out of poverty as a whole.[41] But, as one of the many oppositions through the novel associated with the bog, technology and modernity continue to be challenged by the supernatural and uncanny, suggesting that the idea of 'progress' has its own reproductions.

Such biographical details provide critical insight, adding new and compelling layers to *The Snake's Pass* that might not be as apparent in the superficial conventions of the romance plot. Paul Murray, Stoker's most notable biographer, has argued that all of Stoker's fiction should be read with an autobiographical lens.[42] Stoker's conflicted ethno-national identity underlines the treatment of the bog for both Anglo-Irish and Catholic histories, as well as for Ireland's interests as a whole, which plays out in the novel. Arthur, under Dick's engineering guidance, decides to drain the bog in order to extract limestone for mass profit. After seeing the streaks of limestone buried in the bog, Dick tells Arthur this 'is what we have wanted all along' (243). By framing Arthur's character as a prototypical Anglo-Irish industrialist who initiates bog reclamation through his economic and landowning privilege, Stoker manifests a colonial preoccupation dating back to the Tudor period where the 'wild Irish landscape', according to archaeologist Aidan O'Sullivan, transforms 'into a model of English settlement' designed 'to exploit in a much more organized and entrepreneurial way its rich resources of woodland, river and land'.[43]

The Anglo-Irish landowners traditionally managed the land through utility, organisation, and commodity, thereby reproducing policies established by the Tudors. In contrast, early Gaelic and later Catholic Irish predominantly practised subsistence farming. Trumpener acknowledges some of the Anglo-Irish views of land utilisation surfacing in the eighteenth and nineteenth centuries that combined values of progress and redemption:

> Anglo-Irish landowners secure their right to the land they occupy by molding the surface of the country in their own image, bringing new Irelands into being out of the void. Here colonialism and expansionism appear as progress and as the incontrovertible economic salvation of the whole country, Irish peasantry and all.[44]

The Snake's Pass, however, simultaneously supports and rejects this notion. Arthur's application of imperial land-use ideology – although initially motivated by chivalrous actions designed to protect Norah and her father against Murdock (striking another parallel with the conflated feminisation of the land and the colonised, as we will see more of in Chapter 5) – mirrors an environmental history of bog reclamation in the eighteenth and nineteenth centuries. The novel concurrently challenges and maintains such policies. Stoker, while supporting a future of Irish self-subsistence through natural resource extraction by way of technology and science, also questions the consequences of this action on the very terrain extolled by the cultural nationalists. While the novel promotes capitalist ideas of progress and growth, it also confronts and resists them, particularly by framing the narrative through literary Gothic conventions that typically revisit the past instead of projecting into the future.

Throughout the novel this conflict centres on Arthur's purchase of the land and subsequent strategies for commercialising it. Arthur's plans have haunting repercussions for him, and the Gothic form deployed in the novel uses dreams as a platform to explore his inexplicable paranoia. Arthur's nightmares repeatedly assault him with worry and dread about the dangers of the shifting bog, the threat of Black Murdock, and his own precarious hybrid position in rural Ireland. The first instance of these fears appears in a dream that occurs right after he finalises 'the purchase of the whole mountain' with the solicitor from Galway, Mr Caicy (182). Arthur notes, 'I did not sleep very well', and 'there seemed to grow a fear – some dim, haunting dread of a change – something which would reverse the existing order of things' (182).

Arthur's fears indicate a colonial unconsciousness brought into consciousness by unearthing the bog, a symbol of Irish conflict and resistance in a colonial space. The French treasure Murdock attempts to locate, for instance, signals an alternative history also buried in the bog, from the time when the allied French troops, under the direction of General Humbert, attempted to liberate Ireland from British colonial rule in the 1798 Rebellion. Arthur's subsequent trepidation acts, in part, as an unconscious reminder of the colonial history that recurs in his dreams. He refers to these nightmares as 'a sort of Mazeppa in the world of dreams' (221). *Mazeppa* is an opera written by Pyotr Ilyich Tchaikovsky (based on Pushkin's poem *Poltava*), written seven years before *The Snake's Pass* and essentially telling the tale of love, political persecution, vengeance, murder, and madness.[45] Arthur recalls:

> Again and again the fatal Hill and all its mystic and terrible associations haunted me; again the snakes writhed around and

took terrible forms; again she I loved was in peril; again Murdock seemed to arise in new forms of terror and wickedness; again the lost treasure was sought under terrible conditions; and once again I seemed to sit on the table rock with Norah, and to see the whole mountain rush down on us in a dread avalanche, and turn to myriad snakes as it came. (221)

For Arthur, the bog represents personal danger as much as it does commercial investment. The more Arthur visits the bog and makes plans to reclaim it, the more his unconscious fears generate these terrifying dreams. The recurrent symbol of the snake in his dreams – often considered in dream analysis to signify the unconscious or warn of upcoming transitions in one's life – portends something unknown and unsettling in Arthur's future.

Dreams, as a frequent theme in Gothic writings, often contain symbols and warnings for characters, and are implemented as a literary device of foreshadowing.[46] Dreams appear in *The Snake's Pass* to foretell a death on the bog, but they also predict possible consequences of Arthur's plans to reclaim the bog. In another dream, Arthur recalls:

That night again I kept dreaming – dreaming in the same nightmare fashion as before. But although the working of my imagination centred round Knockcalltecrore and all it contained, and although I suffered dismal tortures from the hideous dreams of ruin and disasters which afflicted me, I did not on this occasion arouse the household. (218)

Arthur continues to be haunted for two primary reasons: his wishes to develop the bog on Knockcalltecrore for his personal aesthetic luxury and to reclaim the bog to generate a return on his investments. In this regard, industrialisation – in the form of reclamation and drainage for wealth accumulation – underscores the lingering colonial ethos of reclaiming bogs for agriculture. However, both reclamation schemes – for agriculture and for industrialised projects – environmentally and culturally affect bogs. Instead of recalling the past, as in many Gothic narratives, Arthur's dreams disclose possible futures and challenge the idea of progress as it relates to the Anglo-Irish understanding of land-use.

In his multivolume *Tour of Ireland* (1780), the agriculturalist and economist Arthur Young identifies earlier accounts of bog reclamation and emphasises that supporting large-scale reclamation projects advantaged Anglo-Irish landowners and provided an economic union with Britain.[47] Since bogs were seen as unused space, policy administrators proposed they should be drained to produce higher profit yield for landowners and resource development for the British Empire. Irish bog reclamation projects mostly began in the mid-eighteenth century when clearing bogs for agricultural land followed the 1731 Act (initiated by King) entitled 'Encourage the Improvement of Barren and Waste Land, and Boggs'.[48] Later, during the transitional years between the nineteenth and twentieth centuries, peat from bogs became an increasing priority in fuel production. At the time, reclamation for agriculture and peat extraction for fuel were both considered beneficial as they would rid Ireland of these cesspools of 'unused' and 'wasted' space. Yet these actions primarily benefited the landowning classes. References to wasted space appear in these opposing and yet overlapping positions about the bog. In one scene Dick explains to Arthur how bogs can be an economic drain on the landowner and tenant:

> [Joyce's] farm is almost an ideal one for this part of the world; it has good soil, water, shelter, trees, everything that makes a farm pretty and comfortable, as well as being good for farming purposes; and he has to change it for a piece of land which is irregular in shape as the other is compact; without shelter, and partly taken up with this very bog and the utter waste and chaos which, when it shifted in former times, it left behind. (53)

Through his more industrious characters, Arthur and Dick, Stoker implies that bogs can contribute to Ireland's economic enhancement, and therefore lead to possible independence, if some form of reclamation and drainage can be implemented successfully.

Stoker undoubtedly researched early writings about bogs in Ireland. Through his character Dick, for instance, Stoker introduces several of these texts (as discussed in Chapter 1), which promoted industrialising these so-called wasted spaces for economic gain within the British Empire. In addition to Young, Boate also discusses the 'opportunity' of draining the bogs for the land.[49] Dick references writings from Boate, as well as from Cambrensis and Spenser, as precursors to his current research on bogs. Arthur recalls how Dick described the importance of boglands through the project of reclamation: 'He told me of the extent and nature of the bog-lands, of the means taken to reclaim them, and of his hopes of some heroic measures being ultimately taken by Government to reclaim the vast Bog of Allen, which remains as great evidence of official ineptitude' (55). Dick claims that one of the most important writings about Ireland's bogs is by King, who ardently promoted bog reclamation. Dick's reference to 'evidence of official ineptitude' indicates Ireland's inability to reclaim the Bog of Allen, which echoes King's earlier assertions that bogs are 'barbarous'. After explaining this somewhat political and literary history of bogs, Dick offers some suggestions about how to drain and reclaim bogs for their own economic gain.

Stoker incorporates these earlier writings to acknowledge a longer history, where the Irish boglands were viewed as a resource for the British Empire, as well as to mark the discriminatory language embedded in these writings. He does this even though such a move inhibits the literary structure of the novel's romance plot by focusing more on the natural history of bogs than on Norah. What these earlier English writings indicate through their tone and language is that bogs were not only desirable for economic gain; their ongoing existence also impedes further control of the local Irish population and therefore must be removed. In fact, Gibbons' argument about *The Snake's Pass* partly examines the sordid relationship between commercialisation and the past:

> The bog, in fact, stands for those aspects of the Irish past which will not go away, but whose threats to the social order are actively reproduced by the forces of modernisation which consigned the poorest of the peasantry to these outlying areas … This dysfunctional form of modernisation, which reactivates rather than repudiates the past, was bound up with the anomalies of the landlord system, a caste which, while aspiring to anachronistic pretensions of aristocracy, yet presided over the unrestrained commercialisation of the Irish economy. The affront which this presented to the philosophy of progress is amply illustrated in the complex relation of Black Murdock to modernity in *The Snake's Pass*.[50]

It is not only that modernisation 'reactivates the past', as Gibbons argues. It also challenges the future where bogs – anomalous and uncanny symbols of Ireland – are eliminated through resource extraction for certain types of nationalist interests to gain economic independence from Britain. For Gibbons, these interests are bound up in the landlord system enabled by the Anglo-Irish.

Stoker's nationalism that emerges in the novel might appear only to serve the interests of the Anglo-Irish, or what Gibbons goes on to identify as 'the full-scale commercialisation of land, and its disenchantment through the scientific discourse of geology'.[51] However, the novel presents a more ambiguous outcome in the oblique way it promotes bog reclamation, while also simultaneously questioning the efficacy of commercialising the land for the Irish. Discourses about geology are also contradictory in the novel; science is used both as a justification to industrialise and as a way to underscore the intrinsic or ecological value of Irish bogs. Stoker offers these opposing outcomes of progress to query which might be more beneficial to Ireland. In this regard, progress has a two-pronged effect: modernisation provides economic prosperity for Ireland, not Britain, securing independence through Home Rule; modernisation eliminates some of the topographies that are essential to Irish culture and identity.

Modernisation, in addition to reactivating the past, also ignores the material history of the actual bog as an important landform. The effects of industrial and economic progress have consequences for Ireland even beyond the dynamics of the ruling classes. Even Stoker, who remains on one level a supporter of commercialising the Irish economy through resource extraction, presents an equally compelling contradictory position. The novel implicitly asks the questions: what happens when Ireland utilises its natural resources for political or economic gain? Does this development only react to or repudiate the past? Or, in addition to reviving the past, does it question the integrity of the land and its role in the future? Stoker's novel may not be an early form of what we might now call an ecologically focused activist novel, but it serves as a warning by subtly questioning the problems associated with exploiting and then developing boglands for profit rather than subsistence, an issue that still resonates in economic and social debates in Ireland.

The Snake's Pass raises the possibility that Stoker also laments the necessary loss of bogs in support of economic independence from Britain. The novel reinforces the historical reality that bogs, although often misunderstood and shrouded in mysteries of the occult through folklore, are fundamentally part of the Irish consciousness. Eliminating bogs might provide immediate economic gain, but it would also cause greater ecological damage in the future, depleting local populations both culturally and numerically. *The Snake's Pass* presents an argument about the complexities of industrialisation in a modernising Ireland during the 1880s and 1890s and shows how these ideas of cultural nationalism contrast with other views of conservation. Stoker's novel provokes the reader to engage with these opposing positions and uncovers how they reflect the qualities of the bog as a union of opposites. In this sense, both the structure of the novel and the imaginative and material qualities of the bog match each other, reflecting the inherent oppositions in Irish colonial politics.

Through various micro-fissures of Irish politics, bogs become contentious terrains where anxieties about legitimacy can be worked out. By the end of the novel, Stoker never fully resolves the question about whether to embrace reclamation or conserve the bog. Even though the bog tumbles into the ocean after a heavy storm, thereby exposing the limestone on the mountain, the reader is left with a sense of ambivalence about the outcome. Arthur and Dick never have to make the decision whether to reclaim the bog because the heavy rains, in combination with Murdock's digging and prodding, alter their plans for commercial development. Arthur clearly wants and expects to embrace industrialisation because of his financial position. But the novel suggests, particularly through Arthur's dreams, that legitimate concern remains about the cost of destroying the bogs. This is why the bog retains so much emphasis in the novel; it draws attention to the importance of this landform in Ireland as both a material resource and a cultural symbol. *The Snake's Pass* explores the tensions between possible economic salvation and the consequences of drying the bog, bringing into awareness cultural anxieties about a commercialised economy based largely on resource extraction. Stoker cloaks industrialisation in the cultural construction of the subordinate, whether it is the land, Norah, or what will be explored in the next section as the inherent oppositions in bogs' supernatural and terrestrial qualities.

Environmental Opposition, Materiality, and Transgression

As discussed in the Introduction, overlapping oppositions are a central feature of bogs and one of the main reasons they remain attractive to writers and artists. Oppositions are also part of the Gothic form, where relations among the supernatural and natural, modern and atavistic, civilised and barbaric, and the rational and fantastic remain in constant connection.[52] Some of the more noticeable intersecting oppositions in *The Snake's Pass* include Ireland/Britain, Anglo (masculine)/Celtic (feminine), Norah/Bog, landowner/tenant, past/future, conservation/ commercialisation, and supernatural/material. Many of these oppositions are revealed through the local Irish storytellers (Andy Sullivan, Bat Moynahan, and Jerry Scanlan), who orally convey the myth of the King of the Snakes and the mysteries of Knockcalltecrore, and through Dick, who investigates what he calls 'the correlation of bog and special geological formations' (64). This section demonstrates how oppositions are used as a method of constructing unity in *The Snake's Pass* through the uncanny, material ecocriticism, and ecological transgression, which all underscore threats to the environmental integrity of the bog.

Hughes claims that Murdock 'functions as a negative Other', who stays in constant opposition to Arthur and all of the elements that constitute Arthur's identity as the coloniser.[53] A more subtle opposition exists between Dick and Murdock, both of whom seek a sort of treasure in the Irish bog. Geological exploration and excavation motivate Dick's actions. Dick explains:

> The main feature of the geological formation of all this part of the country is the vast amount of slate and granite, either isolated patches or lying side by side. And as there are instances of limestone found in quaint ways, I am not without hope that we may yet find the same phenomenon. (64)

In contrast, superstition and lore about the treasure continue to compel Murdock. Stoker switches the implied distinction and contrasts antiquated land-use practices as employed by Murdock with theories of English industrial capitalism as articulated by Dick. This difference between pursuing and exploiting natural resources (Dick) and the nineteenth-century method of absentee landlordism (Murdock) contributes to the novel's dramatic arc and influences how each character attempts to locate the various treasures in the bog.

Three divergent and yet complementary visions can be seen through the treasures buried in the bog on Knockcalltecrore: the jewelled crown of the King of the Snakes, the French chest of gold, and the layer of limestone submerged under the bog. These three treasures serve a greater purpose than simply to move the narrative forward. They indicate an imbricated history of paganism, supernaturalism, colonialism, and industrialism, all of which are linked through the bog.

First, the pre-Christian pagan story serves as an obvious reminder of a time before colonisation. According to the legend, the King of the

Snakes resided over the bog on the Hill and insisted he receive a sacrificed infant once a year. Eventually St Patrick expelled the King to the sea, but ostensibly the King left his crown buried somewhere underneath the bog on the mountain before banishment. When Arthur and Dick do finally locate the crown on the bed of limestone after the bog shifts off of the mountain, they also find ancient *ogham* writing, dating back to medieval Ireland, as early as the fourth century. The symbolic link between pre-Christian and Catholic Ireland is obvious; however, the correlation between the bog and buried treasure links the other two treasures. Second, the treasure chest of gold bullion highlights a particularly contentious period of imperial history when a French expeditionary force had allegedly delivered gold to Ireland via Killala, Co. Mayo, to facilitate Irish resistance to Britain during the 1798 Rebellion. As it turns out, the soldiers were never seen again after they headed out on the bog carrying the chest of gold. It remains unclear at the beginning of the novel whether the soldiers purloined the gold or sunk into the bog with it, but these uncertain accounts of colonial history continually linger in the bog. Lastly, the actual bog remains the most significant treasure in the novel, with its deposits of limestone that are hypothesised to be quite large.

This third and most important treasure propels the narrative and the historical context in which the novel is situated. 'Limestone,' as Hughes notes, 'becomes a metonym for the changes that will take place consequent to Arthur's possession of the land and draining of the bog.'[54] By dividing the 'productive from the commercial' in British capitalism,[55] Arthur and Dick challenge Irish methods of subsistence farming and quickly realise that the real treasure is not in the mythic or supernatural traditions buried in the past, but in the economic capital obtainable in the present and future. Dick agrees that it 'will be a fine investment for you' as Arthur prepares to 'buy the whole of the mountain' (179). If and when Arthur and Dick 'find the limestone', they would be 'the most prosperous set of people to be found in the country' (205).

After realising the resource potential of Knockcalltecrore, Dick acknowledges, 'With limestone we could reclaim the bogs cheaply all over the neighbourhood – in fact a limekiln there would be worth a small fortune. We could build walls in the right places; I can see how a lovely little harbour could be made there at a small expense' (64). For Dick and Arthur, an underlying expectation is that they 'could fathom the secret of the Shifting Bog, and perhaps abolish or reclaim it' (64). This outcome would allow them to develop the purchased land at the expense of the surrounding bogland to access the limestone, slate, and granite. Dick imagines:

> A limestone quarry here would be pretty well as valuable as a gold mine. Nearly all these promontories on the western coast of Ireland are of slate or granite, and here we have not got lime within thirty miles. With a quarry on the spot, we can not only build cheap and reclaim our own bog, but we can supply five hundred square miles of country with the rudiments of prosperity, and at a nominal price compared with what they pay now. (205)

But, in opposition to the modern explanation of commercial progress, the novel provides a mythic explanation bordering on the supernatural: the bog also conceals the crown of the King of the Snakes.

In this context Arthur mentions that the 'remarkable mountain must have been a solid mass of gnomes, fairies, pixies, leprechauns, and all genii, species and varieties of the same' (107). Such supernatural histories provide a ready-made location in which to set a Gothic novel of such proportions. Stoker's engagement with supernatural elements serves as an effective way to use Gothic themes in order to emphasise divergent perspectives of the bog and recognise how they overlap and also oppose each other. These supernatural elements, as a counterpoint to the scientific explanations purported by Dick, relate to the uncanny characteristics of the bog and are essential in setting up some of the oppositions that mirror the qualities of the bog.

In his essay 'The Uncanny', Freud investigates under what conditions the simultaneous 'familiar' (*heimlich* or homely) and 'unfamiliar' (*unheimlich* or unhomely) can become 'uncanny and frightening'. He continues to explain 'that the uncanny is that species of the frightening that goes back to what was once well known and had long been familier'.[56] Instead of assuming that the unfamiliar solely evokes fear, Freud argues it is the simultaneity of the unfamiliar coupled with the familiar that creates an almost inexplicable feeling of the uncanny. Freud's uncanny unites both familiar and unfamiliar elements as both the same and separate; it unites two oppositions as both connected and opposite. When applying the uncanny more directly to *The Snake's Pass*, the bog can be viewed as a familiar terrain in the west of Ireland, where people live and depend on it, as well as look at it daily. And yet, despite this familiarity, it continually contains unknown and inexplicable qualities. In this sense, the bog remains uncanny because of its simultaneously familiar/known and unfamiliar/unknown oppositions.

When Arthur arrives in the west of Ireland he does not appear to have any fear of the bog, although he immediately witnesses its uncanny elements: 'From the first moment that my eyes lit on it [the bog], it seemed to me to be a very remarkable spot, and quite worthy of being taken as the scene of strange stories, for it certainly had something "uncanny" about it' (56). He often walks on the bog, particularly when he frequently (although under clandestine circumstances) meets Norah on the other mountain called Knockcalltore. One might think that the unfamiliarity of the bog should evoke some element of terror in Arthur, but the fear lies within the community that knows about the terrorising qualities of the bog – the way it can shift, engulf, and threaten any human or non-human. The familiar might evoke more fear than the unfamiliar or, as Freud claims, 'not everything new and unfamiliar is frightening'.[57] Fear can be experienced on two levels: the familiarity of the bog frightens people because of its known qualities and the unfamiliarity of the bog frightens people because of its unknown qualities. What is specifically useful about investigating the bog, particularly in Stoker's novel, is that several of the taxonomies of the uncanny exist in varying registers, from non-human agency and anthropomorphism to the fear of being buried alive and fear of repetition.[58] One way of explaining the uncanny in Gothic works is that it animates terrestrial objects, calling into question the notion of material identity.

In order to explain why the bog in *The Snake's Pass* is described as oppositional (terrestrial/supernatural) and imbued with a form of non-human identity, I want to briefly draw from the critical concept of 'material ecocriticism', which is a way of examining matter as a non-anthropomorphic interaction between text and world in literary studies. The 'more-than-human' materiality of landforms, as well as cities, toxicity, animals or bodies (both inanimate and animate matter), serve as complex ecologies and inform humans about the world they inhabit. At the same time, material phenomena in the world provide ways to interpret various narratives. In other words, matter can be read as text. Material ecocriticism underscores elements of the non-human and post-human world by considering how human agency exists as one category of a much larger material world.[59] We are now in contemporary society able to decipher Stoker's explanation of the bog as containing some form of ecological importance. Even though it is merely a material landform, it serves as one of the main characters in the novel and both controls the narrative and functions as a non-human text to decipher. In this sense, then, material ecocriticism is a form of environmental criticism used to interpret the distinctiveness of matter in two different ways. First, the non-human capacities of matter imbued with some form of identity can be described or represented in various narrative works, such as literary, cultural, or visual. Second, the narrative power of matter creates meanings and substances that enter into and interact with human lives 'into a field of co-emerging interactions'.[60]

There are many examples of how material environments contain forms of non-human identity in literature and culture. However, two specific wetland spaces are excellent examples to cite in this chapter, one of which is the unnamed bog in *The Snake's Pass*, and the other, a brief but poignant non-Irish example, is Egdon Heath in Thomas Hardy's *The Return of the Native* (1878). The topography of Egdon Heath has a powerful non-human distinctiveness that resists any attempts to control its forces; it also functions as its own text in the novel, providing a controlling force upon the narrative. In the opening chapter of the novel, aptly titled 'A Face on Which Time Makes But Little Impression', Hardy writes that Egdon Heath 'was at present a place perfectly accordant with man's nature – neither ghastly, hateful, nor ugly; neither commonplace, unmeaning, nor tame; but, like man, slighted and enduring; and withal singularly colossal and mysterious in its swarthy monotony'.[61] Likewise, Stoker writes of the bog,

> a long, low gurgle, with something of a sucking sound – something terrible, resistless, and with a sort of hiss in it, as of seething waters striving to be free. Then the convulsion of the bog grew greater; it almost seemed as if some monstrous living thing was deep under the surface and writhing to escape. (233)

In both novels, the entire action takes place in and around the bog and heath, both of which serve as the main characters that remain feared and as narratives that control the story. The bog and heath are also essential to everyone's existence in some way.

In these two excerpts, Stoker and Hardy assign the bog and the heath meaning as non-human characters with distinctive identity. The bog and heath appear to be entities with some level of autonomy in the text, much like a human character. When matter shows non-human identity, it is capable of producing its own meaning and provides an exchange between human and non-human agents.[62] Instead of subordinating landforms to an inferior position, Stoker and Hardy depict the bog and heath as both containing non-human identity, even if such relevance becomes menacing and dangerous at times to the humans interacting with each unpredictable terrain. The echo of the phrase 'the mountain holds, and it holds tight' reverberates in Arthur's head as he thinks about trying to leave the dangers of the bog at one point in the novel (207). *The Snake's Pass* demonstrates the complexity of the bog's non-human identity, which then forces the reader to question its destruction as a resource.

Material ecocriticism also enables us to further understand some of the interpretations of the uncanny. The familiar material object and the unfamiliar image of a landform that assumes identity are used to both repel and draw the reader closer to the bog. Dick, for example, refers to the bog as a 'carpet of death' that resembles both human and non-human qualities, simultaneously repelling and attracting people:

> What you see is simply a film or skin of vegetation of a very low kind, mixed with the mould of decayed vegetable fibre and grit and rubbish of all kinds, which have somehow got mixed into it, floating on a sea of ooze and slime – of something half liquid, half solid, and of an unknown depth. It will bear up a certain weight, for there is a degree of cohesion in it; but it is not all of equal cohesive power, and if one were to step on the wrong spot – (58)

Dick's definition brings together corporeal and scientific understandings of this terrain, while it also invokes a Gothic tone in the context of land in an extant colonial Ireland. Placing somatic characteristics on terrains like the bog personifies haunting and horrific actions, and portrays them as living creatures waiting to devour intruders. Dick references the corporeal qualities of bogs in connection with medical science when he states:

> we cure bog by both a surgical and a medical process. We drain it so that its mechanical action as a sponge may be stopped, and we put in lime to kill the vital principle of its growth. Without the other, neither process is sufficient; but together, scientific and executive man asserts his dominance. (55)

The bog, then, serves as non-human matter with corporeal characteristics that becomes at times in the novel subordinate to the 'executive man' who decides to assert dominance in the name of science or, more specifically, capital and political gain.

Stoker's representation of the bog alludes to the possible benefits of industrialisation, as proposed by Arthur and Dick, where the bog exists solely as a resource to increase capital through production. And yet, Stoker writes about the bog in the novel to explore his ideas about whether exploiting the natural resources will help Ireland with its own economic position in the British Empire. In his article from *The World's Work*, published in 1907, Stoker contends that Ireland should exploit its natural advantages in agriculture, fishing, and mineral possibilities. He maintains that the vast areas of the bog if used as a fuel source could be 'sufficient alone for national wealth'.[63] While Stoker supported such industrial practices, he did so to partly propose that Ireland could function without British economic support during the series of Home Rule debates in the British parliament. Stoker's ostensible support of commercialising bogs, as exhibited in *The Snake's Pass*, could be a metaphor for industrialising Ireland to escape the economic and colonial yoke of Britain. This seemingly contradictory stance raises another question for consideration in relation to the novel: is there ultimately a choice between the ecological balance and the people existing under colonial rule or can both concerns be addressed in tandem?

According to Serenella Iovino and Serpil Oppermann, material ecocriticism allows for an understanding of 'the corporeal dimensions of human and nonhuman agencies, their literary and cultural representations are inseparable from the very material world within which they intra-act'.[64] The bog can be viewed as a terrestrial object that has non-human identity, especially through its cultural and literary representations, and as a possible resource for economic independence from Britain. There are concurrent uses and perspectives for colonial topographies, and this opposition pervades the novel, leaving the reader questioning the value of the bog in the context of Ireland and its future. Arthur queries, 'Is it a quagmire, then, or like a quicksand?' Dick responds, 'Like either, or both' (58). The conflict and cohesion of the bog's elements overshadow the novel's narrative about land-use options and political oppositions. The bog – both real and imagined – challenges such fixed positioning and mirrors the mutable political and economic circumstances facing Ireland at the time.

By focusing directly on the bog, we can recognise the significance of cultural and material landforms in Ireland. But Stoker also establishes it as a central character and asks us to distinguish its identity not in categories of living or non-living, but human or non-human, both of which contain

physical and symbolic distinctiveness. This opens the possibility that once
an object becomes animated, assuming living characteristics, it complicates
any actions toward its elimination or oppression. As a terrestrial non-
human agent, the bog projects itself as a textual form of matter through
the material imagination of its human counterparts.[65] For example,
the folklore surrounding the bog animates what is already present as a
biological reality; it is a 'carpet of death' because it shifts and suffocates
humans. Despite Stoker's complicated position on commercialising
rural areas of Ireland, he also considers the bog important and multi-
dimensional enough to frame it as a character with unique non-human
identity. In this respect, *The Snake's Pass* serves as an earlier text that
actively engages with environmental materiality as a central literary
concern; it establishes a way of imbuing matter with non-human identity
that can also interact with human agents, especially as its own character,
in the primary narrative of the novel. After all, 'executive man', despite
many efforts to subdue the bog, never completely controls it in the novel
because the bog eventually slides off of the mountain during a rainstorm.

In addition to animating the bog through oppositions of the material
and uncanny, the Gothic motif of transgression plays a significant role in
The Snake's Pass. Murdock's transgression of the environment – particularly
his disruption of the bog – culminates in his horrific demise. He is sucked
into the pit of the shifting bog as it slithers toward the ocean during a
torrential storm. Since transgression serves as another literary Gothic
trope, *The Snake's Pass* can be viewed as an environmental parable of sorts
wherein violating the ecological 'law of nature' will result in retributive
consequences on the transgressor. In relation to the nineteenth-century
Gothic, Botting remarks:

> In an age that developed philosophical, scientific and psychological
> systems to define and classify the nature of the external world, the
> parameters of human organization and their relation to the working
> of the mind, transgression is important not only as an interrogation
> of received rules and values, but in the identification, reconstitution
> or transformation of limits.[66]

The function of transgression in the late nineteenth-century Gothic
novel moves between traditional notions of virtue, estate takeovers,
and lineage disputes, to more contemporary concerns of race, political
sovereignty, and modernity. What I refer to here as 'environmental' or

'ecological transgression' associated with Murdock's obsessive treasure hunt is reminiscent of earlier Gothic writings where greed and selfishness result in retributive consequences. The pursuit of excess is certainly one of the markers of transgression in Gothic writings.[67] In Murdock's case, transgression against the environment results in his untimely and gruesome death, caused by the very landform he seeks to destroy, which occurs because of his obsessive desire to obtain the gold at any cost. Murdock's actions reinforce violations of not only moral, but also ecological codes in society.

Murdock initially hires Dick to locate metal deposits (the treasure of gold) in the bog. On several occasions, Dick warns Murdock of the dangers of the shifting bog, cautioning him that his plan to dam the bog in order to find the gold will ultimately lead to ecological catastrophe. While the desired effect is to limit the water content in the bog so that Murdock can dig, the actual effect is that the bog itself continues to rise to dangerous levels, where it could at any point shift or slide off its rock base because of the rise in the water table between the *sphagnum* moss (bog moss) surface and lower solid layer of limestone. Murdock's resistance to Dick's warnings about the bog results in a judgement that accentuates the limits of the human in relation to the external world. Murdock transgresses against the environment, despite ongoing warnings, by attempting to manipulate and control the bog.

As the cataclysmic ending of the novel demonstrates, reconfiguring the bog's ecological integrity in order to extract the buried treasure proves fatal for Murdock. Transgression is frequently employed as a motif in Gothic writing to reinforce social values and tradition. Botting contends that the 'terrors and horrors of transgression in Gothic writing become a powerful means to reassert the values of society'.[68] *The Snake's Pass* reveals what happens to transgressors of social mores and environmental balance through the horror of Murdock's demise as he is 'sucked below the surface of the heaving mass' of the bog, and all that could be heard is his 'wild cry' (233).

Values in the novel draw attention to how individual characters transgress environmental codes through forms of excess for monetary and political gain. These transgressions occur against the backdrop of the system of landownership established in eighteenth- and nineteenth-century Ireland. Such excesses underpin the limits and boundaries of the bog as a representative terrain in the novel. A character's internal pathologies and irrationality, as forms of excess, manifest themselves outwardly and affect the treatment of the bog. Murdock, Dick, and Arthur all transgress against the bog; their actions follow the model of a tortuous Gothic tale of how social behaviours or rules are neglected through vice, corruption, and depravity.[69] Set in a colonial milieu of late nineteenth-century Ireland, the vices presented in the novel do not result in some absolute retribution or a clear moral direction. Instead, their vices signal, as they do in many Gothic writings, the ambiguities and oppositions inherent in socio-cultural notions of the period. In the case of *The Snake's Pass*, the socio-cultural dilemma concentrates on whether to industrialise or conserve rural landscapes in Ireland or, perhaps, some combination of the two, as Stoker suggests throughout the action of the novel.

In contrast to Murdock, Arthur and Dick transgress the environment by persisting with their plans to commercialise the bog through natural resource development, thereby enhancing economic production for their own investment. They spend most of their days researching the bog as part of Dick's scientific enquiries. But after Arthur purchases all of Shleenanaher and Knockcalltecrore, he prioritises resource development over any other possible research projects that involve the bog. Arthur initially plans to build his future estate there, but then focuses on the more lucrative possibilities of reclaiming the land. Dick tells Arthur:

> Let us once be able to find the springs that feed the bog, and get them in hand, and we can make the place a paradise. The springs are evidently high up on the Hill, so that we can not only get water for irrigating and ornamental purposes, but we can get power also! (179)

Dick first envisions how Knockcalltecrore will provide all of the necessary elements to live quite comfortably. He then contradicts himself when he predicts, 'I suspect, that there is a streak of limestone in the Hill, the place might be a positive mine of wealth as well!' He continues, 'We can build a harbor on the south side, which would be the loveliest place to keep a yacht in that ever was known – quite big enough for anything in these parts – as safe as Portsmouth, and of fathomless depth' (179). Propelled by the potential of development for both personal and capital gain, Arthur insists, 'Dick, this has all to be done; and it needs someone to do it' (179). Arthur ultimately decides to be the person to do it, and makes plans to 'buy the mountain' in an area where 'land is literally going a-begging' (180).

Modernity supplants previous notions of subsistence living as Arthur and Dick plan a development project that will ultimately produce extensive ecological changes on the mountain and surrounding terrain. In this respect, the novel invites the reader to reimagine time and space. To recognise such an environmental manipulation is to enter into a suspension of time, which robs the colonial project's strategic timeline of cultural and topographical disruption. But it does so differently from the writers in the Irish Literary Revival, a cultural movement that attempted to manufacture a pre-colonial utopia of Celticism in the late nineteenth and early twentieth centuries. Such a colonial ideology hinges on the assumption that there are limitless resources in the colonies and that such spaces are rife for economic exploitation executed in an efficient and timely manner. In *Postcolonial Ecocriticism* (2010), Graham Huggan and Helen Tiffin maintain that doctrines of resource exploitation are central to colonial projects: 'Such places, after all, were apparently untamed, unowned and above all, *unused*; and, accordingly, settlers set about rendering them productive and profitable through imported methods rather than by accommodating them to local circumstances.'[70] The bog serves as both a limited and limitless space in the novel, challenging the slippages between time and history as much as resource management and exploitation; it does so as a warning to the future, as much as a recognition of past resource exploitation. The novel not only reactivates the past, as Gibbons argues, but it more directly engages with the future.

Arthur never intends to stay on Knockcalltecrore until his courtship with Norah begins, and only then does he decide to settle permanently in the west of Ireland. At this point, Arthur acknowledges the economic potential of the bog. Instead of viewing the bog as a tourist enjoying the natural sublime aesthetic, he exploits the untamed, unowned, and unused space that the bog inconveniently occupies. Arthur attempts to justify his transgressions against the bog through modern theories of innovation and science that were pervasive in the 1880s and 1890s. In nineteenth-century Gothic writing, for example, scientific theory and technological innovation were often used to validate various forms of excess and social decadence. Knowledge, as Smith observes, is a subject that Stoker keeps returning to in all of his writings, particularly in terms of 'knowledge of the national and/or the racial Other'.[71] Certainly the nomenclatures of knowledge pervasive in the nineteenth century influence expansions of scientific theory. In Arthur's case, bogs were simply unowned and unused landscapes waiting to be exploited. Dick and Arthur draw from the scientific and technological innovations in their plan to industrialise the bog, but ultimately create an unintended consequence; they alienate themselves from their surroundings through a knowledge laced with objects of fear and anxiety.[72]

There is a sense, however, that Arthur's actions will affect not only the future of the bog, but also the futures of both himself and Norah. He realises: 'There was a curse on the Hill!' (206). The Hill's curse relates to Arthur's transgressions, which are continually manifested in his nightmares. After a spate of these nightmares, Arthur reflects that the 'terrible dreams, whencesoever they came, must not have come in vain; the grim warning must not be despised' (222). Although he is consciously referring to Norah, the dreams indicate that such grim warnings are also about the bog. Norah, like the bog, is also referred to as 'Unknown' (126). Arthur speaks about going to the 'bog', by which he means seeing Norah. This occurs before he realises that Joyce's daughter and the mysterious 'Unknown' woman he meets on the bog are the same person. In addition, Andy consistently chides Arthur about his infatuation with Norah by comparing her to the bog: 'Begor, a bit of bog to put your arum around while ye're lukin' at it' (57). Andy continues the bog/Norah parallel throughout the novel: 'I'm not the man to go back on a young gintelman goin' to luk at a bog. Sure doesn't all young min do the same? I've been there meself times out iv mind! There's nothin' in the wurrld foreninst it! Lukin' at bogs is the most intherestin' thin' I knows' (49).

Ultimately, Arthur's purchase of Knockcalltecrore is also an acquisition of Norah, who symbolises both the bog and Ireland for Arthur. This ownership of the land reinforces Arthur's intention to also reclaim Norah. For instance, he sends her to become educated at finishing schools in England, Dresden, and Paris, an act that ultimately drains her of any Irish cultural identity but increases her capacity to enhance Arthur's wealth and status in Ireland. Nora and the bog are interchangeable and synonymous throughout the novel, underlining an allegory of not only the 'imperial marriage' between Ireland and England or the 'metropolitan marriage' between the hyper-masculine John Bull and the feminine Erin, as Daly and Valente have posited,[73] but also an allegory of the land and commercialisation practices through subordination. In this respect, Arthur's transgression against the environment can be compared to his union with Norah; as an allegory for his relationship with Ireland and the bog, it holds the significance of the past while it inevitably foreshadows the future.

Looking Forward

Bogs function in Bram Stoker's *The Snake's Pass* as contested and peripheral spaces, and as significant cultural markers they have nevertheless been treated as zones of waste that are ready for exploitation. Gothic motifs of opposition, materiality, and transgression appear in the background of a story about landownership and reclamation, and through these themes we can investigate the threatened ecology of the bog. Previous arguments have been made that suggest the Irish Gothic represents certain colonial anxieties,[74] but this chapter argues that landforms, particularly the bog, present one of the underdeveloped elements of this argument. 'For the native,' as Edward Said points out, 'the history of colonial servitude is inaugurated by loss of the locality to the outsider; its geographical identity must thereafter be searched for and somehow restored. Because of the presence of the colonizing outsider, the land is recoverable at first only through the imagination.'[75] In *The Snake's Pass*, Stoker provides such an imaginative reclamation by re-establishing the geographical identity of the land, not by looking backward through the crumbling codes of the Anglo-Irish Gothic, but by questioning progress and modernity related to Ireland's independence in the immediate future. We can mourn the status of the bog through Stoker's deployment of the Gothic mode within a colonial context, thereby recognising the political and environmental legitimacy of the land. If, as Gibbons states, the 'bog ... stands for those aspects of the Irish past which will not go away',[76] then despite its near extinction the bog will haunt the imagination of those who continually explore its cultural and environmental depths in the twentieth century.

At the same time, *The Snake's Pass* leaves us with a contradictory question: should Ireland commercialise in the name of progress to seek economic independence from England or should Ireland preserve some of its culturally and environmentally significant landforms? Although the novel (and narrative within it) provides an ambiguous and shifting answer to this enquiry, it nevertheless raises such a question about a contentious terrain that has largely been overlooked in literary and cultural criticism. Stoker introduces bogs to an audience beyond Ireland to show the potential importance of this indefinite and mysterious landform. In this sense, the novel reclaims the bog in the narrative of the social order. In one of the most telling lines Dick states that:

although the subject [of bogs] is one of vital interest to thousands
of persons in our own country – one in which national prosperity is
mixed up to a large extent – one which touches deeply the happiness
and material prosperity of a large section of Irish people, and so
helps to mould their political action, there are hardly any works on
the subject in existence. (54)

As Dick suggests, the importance of bogs should not be understated
in Irish history. Bogs, which are mixed up among issues of national
prosperity, cultural identity, and geopolitics, serve as a 'seedbed of
activity', referring back to Foster's opening comment, not only in the west
(as showcased in *The Snake's Pass*), but also in other parts of Ireland and
through other literary works.

Examining bogs may not provide clear answers, but, like their limited
and limitless qualities, it can offer important questions about the future,
as much as about the past and present. To this end, *The Snake's Pass* is
an important forerunner of later twentieth- and twenty-first-century
Irish writing that deals with bogs and the effects of colonisation, whether
confronting environmental issues (as in this chapter) or social hauntings in
the revolutionary and post-revolutionary periods (as examined in the next
chapter). Contradictory links between the supernatural and nationalism
in narratives about bogs continue to emerge in literary and cultural
narratives about postcolonial Ireland in the twentieth and twenty-first
centuries.

3

Spectral Histories of Nationalism

Haunting is one way in which abusive systems of power make
themselves known and their impacts felt in everyday life.[1]

– Avery Gordon, Ghostly Matters

Ghosts of Post-Independence Ireland

Ghosts, like bogs, unite opposites because they simultaneously appear
visible and invisible, dead and alive, material and immaterial, and are both
feared and welcomed.[2] As discussed in the previous chapter, ghosts and
bogs share a similar relationship with mythical, irrational, and mystical
powers in culture, especially in how they are often associated with social
disruptions related to colonial histories.[3] This chapter looks at how two
writers in post-independence Ireland of the 1930s use the bog as a specific
site of haunting – sometimes directly and at times obliquely – in order
to address some of 'the unresolved social violence' and social decay from
the Irish War of Independence/Anglo-Irish War and subsequent Irish
Civil War period.[4] Irish writers employ ghosts and hauntings in literary
and cultural narratives to offer another way of explaining ruptures in
postcolonial history, challenging both past and current political histories.
'What is distinctive about haunting,' argues Avery Gordon, 'is that it is
an animated state in which a repressed or unresolved social violence is
making itself known, sometimes very directly, sometimes more obliquely.'[5]
Sometimes ghosts are conjured up as spirits of the past to clarify the
present, but sometimes ghosts appear in times of chaos and disorder as
connectors between an unresolved past and the present.

The discussion to follow looks at two short stories by Frank O'Connor
and Sean O'Faolain (sometimes referred to in Irish as *Seán Ó Faoláin*),
along with prevalent cultural and historical narratives surrounding this

period, but it also considers Daniel Corkery's influence on both writers and his comment about the Irish bog in his book *Synge and Anglo-Irish Literature*. Through O'Connor's 'Guests of the Nation' and O'Faolain's 'A Meeting', haunting is used as a theme to challenge and disrupt nationalist histories in the revolutionary period between 1919 and 1923. These two stories, albeit in different ways, explore how ghosts materialise in and around bogs and challenge previous conceptions of the Irish nation. This chapter also refers to other writings by O'Connor and O'Faolain in order to contextualise how each story responds to the larger historical movements in this revolutionary period.

Language and ideas about hauntings, ghosts, and bogs would usually stem from Gothic studies, and while I draw from Gothic critics in this chapter, Gordon's study of social theory, *Ghostly Matters: Haunting and the Sociological Imagination* (2008), most effectively underscores some of the collective consequences of ghosts and hauntings in national discourses.[6] For Gordon, the notion of haunting is more complicated than social or cultural critics might assume because it interrogates the evidence of ghostly traces or inexplicable phenomena and what this might clarify about exchanges of power, knowledge, and experience in the contexts of slavery, torture, or other forms of oppression. *Ghostly Matters* assists in theorising my own argument because it provides a way of viewing ghosts, spectres, and revenants in a historical, cultural, and sociological context.[7]

While Gordon's book focuses on racism and capitalism within certain power structures of the United States, her formulations about haunting are equally relevant to Irish nationalism. Haunting, for example, confuses and complicates linear perceptions of spatio-temporal histories. Gordon argues: 'Haunting raises specters, and it alerts the experience of being in time, the way we separate the past, the present, and the future.'[8] While haunting disrupts time, as Gordon suggests, it does so not by merely separating the temporal nomenclatures of a historical record, but by creating simultaneity of time, thereby rendering it non-linear. O'Connor's and O'Faolain's characters, for instance, relate to and reminisce about an actual time in Irish history that is fraught with unresolved outcomes. The ghosts of Irish history materialise on bogs in O'Connor's and O'Faolain's short ghost stories, particularly in how spectres of the nation haunt fragmented memories of the present and past.

'Guests' and 'A Meeting' are both ghost stories, but there are many ghosts throughout each story. Ghosts do not have a positive definition (in the positivistic sense), so I am approaching them not simply as a materialisation of the dead, but that which haunts. In this regard, ghosts are hauntings of an uncertain national identity in Ireland over a decade after both O'Connor and O'Faolain experienced these events. According to Gothic scholar Andrew Smith, 'In its unsettling of the relationship between the living and the dead the ghost story ostensibly raises some radical, putatively metaphysical questions about identity.'[9] The ghosts of the nation materialise in 'Guests' and 'A Meeting', thereby raising questions about how identity is established through acts of violence. O'Connor and O'Faolain re-examine a turbulent period of Irish history to question and at times challenge ideas of nationalism and national identity.

Exploring this historical material within the convention of the ghost story forces certain issues to the forefront in each of O'Connor's and O'Faolain's realist literary work, neither of which have previously been associated with the Gothic. For example, both stories present relationships between dead and living, national and personal identities, and temporality and atemporality. In each story, the bog complicates ideas of home and hostility connected to the nation because it functions as a space of confusion and uncertainty. We have already seen similar uncertainties explored in *The Snake's Pass* when Arthur feels both connection to and dislocation from the bog through his own developing identity with Ireland. So, in this sense, the bog serves as the instrument and the ghost is its amplification; the subject of ghosts and haunting does not displace the underpinning topic of the bog. The focus on ghosts illuminates bogs, not the respective parallel ideas and themes that they embody, and O'Connor's and O'Faolain's stories are two unexpected examples of this occurring in Irish literature.

Ultimately, then, this chapter explores how ghosts in 'Guests' and 'A Meeting' are projections of a haunted nation. They appear not simply as visible bodies of energy, but they emerge in various forms and affect the characters on the bog in different ways, namely through narratives of identity, decay, and violence. Indeed, images of hauntings and spectres were often used in nationalist propaganda campaigns to give shape and form to debatable and formless histories.[10] If the Irish landscape is, as Deane argues, an archetypal marker of Irish nationalism,[11] then we can approach O'Connor and O'Faolain's use of the bog not only as a space representing the nation, but also as a space that both confuses and illuminates the slippages in history, memory, and identity that have occurred since the Irish War of Independence. The idea of nation itself serves as a type of ghost that relies on the imagined consciousness of the collective through colonial histories. Richard Kearney maintains that the 'spectre of Irish nationalism might be said to represent Britain's return of the repressed'.[12]

In national ghost narratives, the idea of nation is often viewed as a spectre because its form and existence derives from the imagined collective consciousness of individuals and groups that rely on an interpretation of the past. Nationalism is often haunted by history, which is both perceived and read by people who are also haunted by history. 'Nation' serves as the 'big idea', whereas 'nationalism' represents the smaller ideological fragments that people believe in – real and imagined – and which they perform, act out, or live in to achieve the larger idea of 'nation'. Nationalism is built around a range of concepts, such as freedom, culture, and ideological life, which ultimately support the specific needs of the nation in colonised, decolonised, and postcolonial contexts.[13] Whether through religion, language, economics, or culture, as Kearney suggests, Irish nationalism has remained versatile and 'extremely variegated'.[14] Irish nationalism, like many other global forms of nationalism, is also a totalising concept, even in its various manifestations. And the bog, with its oppositional and yet simultaneously bonding qualities, is used in these two stories to resist such certainty about the nation. Benedict Anderson claims in his famous study on nationalism, *Imagined Communities* (1983), that concepts of the national, nationality, and nationalism are all difficult to define and analyse, but they ultimately cohere around the idea of the nation as an 'imagined political community – imagined as both inherently limited and sovereign'.[15]

With these definitions in mind, ghosts and haunting are perhaps an ideal form used by O'Connor and O'Faolain, on a bog no less, to explore these otherwise ethereal concepts of the nation as both real and imagined. O'Connor and O'Faolain use the bog as a haunting symbol and setting of a past that has not resolved itself in the present for them and perhaps never will. Also used as a specific *site* of haunting, the bog defies, confuses, and even at times reinforces the definite meanings often associated with ideas of the nation. National identities formed between 1916 and 1923 are treated as unsettled ghosts in both stories and are bound by the bog for O'Connor and O'Faolain in the 1930s. But before taking up the main subject of this chapter, it is necessary to outline some of the historical background of the Irish Literary Revival – a period marked by cultural nationalism that affected both O'Connor and O'Faolain and ultimately shaped their response to Irish nationalism – and overview each story and the related criticism supporting my own argument about hauntings.

The transition from the late nineteenth century into the first third of the twentieth century serves as one of the more turbulent periods in modern Irish history. Monumental political events occurred in the early half of the twentieth century, which significantly changed Ireland and subsequently triggered more impassioned literary responses from writers. The 1916 Easter Rising was staged during this period, even though many people in Ireland at the time did not support it because of its overlap with the First World War.[16] After the British state indiscriminately executed some of the leaders of the Rising, the nationalist movement garnered more support in Ireland; the people even elected Sinn Féin (Irish nationalist party) to a majority of parliamentary seats for the first time. This turning point in Irish support and sentiment initiated the guerrilla-style Irish War of Independence (1919–21), which resulted in the Anglo-Irish Treaty of 1921. The Treaty separated the new state into Northern Ireland (six Irish counties still governed by Britain), and the Republic, or Irish Free State, consisting of the remaining twenty-six counties in the south. Due to substantial opposition to the Treaty, Ireland broke out in civil war from 1922 to 1923, a war fought between the Free State Pro-Treaty and the Republican Anti-Treaty sides. As a result of this 'Revolutionary period' of political history in the modern era (essentially lasting from 1880 to 1930), when Ireland transformed from part of the British state into a modern independent state, notions of society and stability were far from normal in the Irish experience, and this had a particularly profound effect on literature and culture.

The modern Irish literary movement in the early twentieth century largely responded to British imperialism by redefining, reimagining, and reconstituting the idea of an Irish nation. This cultural movement is commonly referred to as the Irish Literary Revival – a period also known as the Irish Literary Renaissance, Celtic Revival (second one), or the Celtic Twilight – and celebrated Irish culture, literature, and art supporting an independent Irish nation. Before, during, and after the events of 1916, as well as during the tumult of two wars, writers of the Revival responded to British occupation by re-engaging with earlier forms of Irish cultural nationalism of the nineteenth century. Irish nationalism of the Revival, argues Deane, 'was and is so imbued with the sense of the past as a support for action in the present that it has never looked beyond that'.[17] If colonisation attempted to destroy national culture, then national legitimacy depended upon rehabilitating the cultural past.[18]

In an attempt to rehabilitate the past, writers of the Revival focused specifically on casting current cultural and political events in pre-modern mythologies, what David Lloyd has called a 'mythopoeic space', from Celtic to Nordic and Greek myth.[19] Many writers in the economically depressed post-independence period of the 1930s, like O'Connor and O'Faolain, revisited historical moments and often depicted them with piercing realism instead of relying on abstract myth far removed from the current political moment. Another reason O'Connor's and O'Faolain's stories are biting and realistic is because both writers were involved in the wars, and history for them remains personal as well as political.[20] The Revival intended to focus on a pre-colonial and pre-modern Ireland where Gaelic culture, language, and myth flourished. The problem was that such an idyllic reimagining of historical Ireland was largely constructed by cultural nationalists and resulted in another form of hegemonic nationalism.

O'Connor and O'Faolain, both of whom came to be known as masters of the modern short story, were too inexperienced during the Revival to fully participate in the national literary movement. However, when they were in their prime – publishing in the 1930s to the 1950s – they rejected Revivalist writers and associated topics of mysticism and nostalgia, despite the fact that Irish nationalism continued to flourish in this period. Joe Cleary defines this 1930's era of modern Irish writing as the 'field of counter-Revivalist realism', which contained other notable writers of the movement including the novelists Liam O'Flaherty and Elizabeth Bowen, the dramatist Seán O'Casey, and, to a lesser extent, the poet and novelist Patrick Kavanagh.[21] Indeed, this realist period of modern Irish literature still remains in the shadow of earlier and often more 'canonised' writers of the Revival, such as W.B. Yeats, George Moore, Douglas Hyde, Lady Gregory, J.M. Synge, and James Joyce.[22]

Post-Revival writers like O'Connor and O'Faolain responded to the Revival by raising concerns about nationalism and ideas of nation-building in this earlier period, from a now distant and retrospective vantage point. One of Cleary's critiques of the post-Revival naturalism that O'Connor and O'Faolain exhibit in their own writing is that it fails to offer 'its own informing criteria of evaluation and assessment'. 'For O'Faolain and O'Connor,' he goes on to argue, 'literature is conceived as an instrument capable of changing society, yet the mechanics of social change seem scarcely ever to be an object of serious reflection in their own fiction.'[23] Cleary largely critiques the post-Revival generation for its failure to exhibit the literary complexity, structural vigour, and political forcefulness that are characteristic of Revivalist writings. Michael Neary, in contrast, views O'Faolain – and we could extend this to O'Connor as well – as working in the nebulous area of opposition and ambiguity in his fiction. 'For O'Faolain,' argues Neary, 'withholding the center, the "telling detail", does fictional justice to the murky, painful, "in between" moments of life, leaving the imagination with the task of ordering those moments.'[24] O'Connor and O'Faolain write in a difficult period of nation formation in the 1930s, and although they attempt new ways to probe the past in the very 'productive dialectical relationship' that Cleary supports, they do so through gripping forms of realism as a counter to the aesthetic and structurally rigorous writings of the Revivalists. In the two short stories discussed here, O'Connor and O'Faolain do indeed offer serious reflection and address the 'mechanics of social change' by confronting the catastrophic consequences of romanticising the nation in a sparse and sobering form of realist fiction while set on a haunted bog.

While 'Guests' and 'A Meeting' are not typically characterised as Gothic literature, largely because they are realist stories, they nevertheless evoke themes associated with ghosts, histories, violence, and hauntings. Even though literary realism remained a popular form in the Irish Free State period of the 1920s and 1930s, literature and culture that deployed ghosts and hauntings also began to surface. These writings were, however, predominantly pro-republican and nationalist in scope and often referred to the nation as a 'phantom Republic'.[25] Gothic conventions allow writers to explore 'a spectre of unfinished historical business' where 'ghosts demand redress and destabilize the certainties of the living'.[26] Franco Moretti famously reminds us in *Signs Taken for Wonders* (1983) that the 'literature of terror is born precisely *out of the terror of a split society*, and out of the desire to heal it'.[27] O'Connor and O'Faolain challenge rather than support ideas of nationalism that erupt out of their own 'split society' through realist fiction using Gothic conventions.

O'Connor's 'Guests', first published in the eponymous collection *Guests of the Nation* (1931), resonates in Irish literature as one of the starkest, most poignant, and non-romanticised depictions of violence related to war and decolonisation. Set at some point during the Irish War of Independence, 'Guests' tells a disturbing tale about two Irish Republican Army (IRA) soldiers (Bonaparte and Noble) ordered to execute two British soldiers (Belcher and Hawkins) in reprisal for the killing of four IRA men in British custody. The major tension in the story centres on the fact that the Irish and British soldiers have become 'chums' and are noticeably affected by the prospect of execution 'down towards the fatal bog'.[28] Jeremiah Donovan, the IRA commander, communicates to Bonaparte that the English 'hostages' are the 'enemy' despite their friendly disposition. He informs Bonaparte that the enemy has 'prisoners who belong' to us, and now they talk of shooting them. If they shoot our prisoners we'll shoot theirs, and serve them right' (6). This news comes as a shock to Bonaparte, who 'went back to the cottage, a miserable man' (6). After this clear foreshadowing, the story eventually leads to the executions of Belcher and Hawkins out on the bog. The bog enters the story as a prevailing metaphor for death, political violence, and the supernatural on both sides of the war. 'Guests' presents nationalism as a damaging and life-threatening discourse stitched into narratives similar to those rooted in the Revival. O'Connor's short story offers this critique by examining the complex relationship between the IRA and the British soldiers, but also by showcasing the fundamental human connections that can exist and flourish between some combatants. The story also explores in-between spaces, particularly through themes of absence and silence where the ghosts dwell on the bog.

The frequent adaptations of this evocative tale throughout the twentieth century have only increased its imposing status as one of the greatest short stories in the Irish literary canon.[29] Despite being such a canonical story, there has been surprisingly little critical attention devoted to it. Stanley Renner addresses the inherent 'hidden powers' that seem to propel and mystify the story. He argues that Bonaparte's and Noble's failure to recognise their own human responsibility, more than merely cosmic circumstance guided by fate, is largely responsible for their murderous actions. While the opposition between fate and human responsibility provides a productive way to scrutinise 'Guests', the bog remains fundamentally a place where these hidden powers appear. Renner explores almost every aspect of these powers, including referencing the final scene that takes place in 'vacant cosmic immensity',[30] without actually pinpointing the bog as a central topic and a possible way to confront a history of distressing human responsibility amidst anti-colonial circumstances.

Michael Storey, in contrast, recognises some of the links to anti-colonial struggle, while comparatively analysing O'Connor's 'Guests of the Nation' and Albert Camus' 'The Guest'. Storey relates colonial conditions in French-occupied Algeria and British-occupied Ireland in order to offer an analysis of the way O'Connor underscores colonial struggles relevant in other literary contexts. Storey provides a discerning point that connects to my own analysis in this chapter; he compares the setting in both stories and identifies a similar environment of desolation. In Camus' 'The Guest', the characters endure 'on the vast expanse of the high, deserted plateau … where nothing had any connection with man'.[31] The bog, too, is often perceived as a space disconnected from humanity, but for O'Connor it is the heart of the story, teeming with national ghosts shifting between the past and present.

Eugene O'Brien's more contemporary engagement with O'Connor does examine ghosts. O'Brien's perceptive argument focuses on the way in which Derrida's concept of 'hauntology' reveals ideas about guests and hospitality in the story. O'Brien contends:

> It is this movement – from guest of a nation to ghosts of a nation – that encapsulates the effect of violence and death on the perpetrators. These two men clearly affected all of the rest of Bonaparte's life: they fulfilled a ghostly function, physically absent, yet present and influential, changing his perspective about everything and about his future.[32]

For O'Brien, the haunting in 'Guests' is more 'open and emancipatory' than traditional forms of ghosts of the nation, who are hostile rather than hospitable.[33] While I agree with O'Brien's premise that guests become ghosts of the nation, I want to change direction a bit and identify how confusions about Irish nationalism reflect the oppositional qualities of the bog, and then explore why both O'Connor and O'Faolain locate the climactic scenes of their stories on the bog.[34]

O'Faolain's 'A Meeting', from the collection *A Purse of Coppers* (1937), describes a spontaneous encounter between two people who once knew each other during 'the Revolution'.[35] The unnamed protagonist, also the first-person narrator, meets Sally Dunn in the town of Burnt Hall, just outside Limerick. During the revolution, the narrator admired Sally for her unflinching commitment to the Irish cause. They decide to take a walk and reminisce. This walk takes them out to 'the fields' where the bog stretches for 'miles and miles' (275). Although the narrator begins their 'meeting' with enthusiasm, he becomes depressed when hearing about Sally's current life. He wants to revisit the 'good times' of the past, but for Sally, unlike the narrator, the past remains in the past and is no longer part of her current life. The story unfolds concurrently in two locations: the imaginative (the memories of the past and present moving back and forth) and the real (on the bog). The bog, in fact, generates the reveries of the past. Prior to arriving on the bog, the narrator appears elated at the sight of Sally. But once they arrive at the bog, the mood of the conversation, or perhaps the narrator's feelings about the conversation, dominate and darken the mood of the story.

The story raises questions about forms of decay: eroding buildings (houses and shops), places (the bog), people (the narrator), ideology (Irish nationalism), and history (nostalgic memories of the past). From the opening lines, O'Faolain indicates a sense of loss and decay emerging from and past and moving to the present. 'Many towns in Ireland,' writes O'Faolain, 'suddenly begin to decay; and "decay" is the word for it' (273). The story also raises questions about nationalism: the nationalist movement the two protagonists supported together twelve years ago as younger revolutionaries, and the decayed remains of that movement as viewed from the present. In this regard, the story moves back and forth temporally and spatially, while the setting of the bog triggers the contradictions and uncertainties occurring throughout the story. 'A Meeting' could serve as a microcosm of O'Faolain's entire body of work because it reflects upon the revolutionary period with both regret and reverie, concern and critique, thereby forging an 'in-between' or 'centre' space that similarly reflects the qualities of the bog.[36]

O'Faolain's short fiction has garnered significant attention among scholars, but the sheer volume of stories has limited the amount of critical attention devoted to the more peripheral ones.[37] As a result, previous criticism has yet to examine 'A Meeting' in any great detail. In one short article, however, Katherine Hanley briefly overviews three of O'Faolain's less 'frequently studied' short stories, one of which is 'A Meeting'.[38] Hanley describes the narrative technique as 'a progressive restraint, a movement from the carefully stated to the unsaid, from the simple to the elaborately cryptic'.[39] Hanley focuses on the writing technique rather than issues related to haunting and nationalism, and in particular how these relate to the bog.

Ghosts materialise in both 'Guests' and 'A Meeting' as a means of dissolving time and challenging previous conceptions of the nation. The bog, nationalism, and ghosts are all what Anderson might call 'anomalies' of the nation, because they resist classification despite their forceful presence in the stories themselves.[40] Nationalism may work on the social terrain in Ireland, but it has less sure 'footing' on the bog (to use Daniel Corkery's term, examined later in this chapter). Through the Gothic form, both O'Connor and O'Faolain are able to question some of the narratives that typify identity politics in Irish culture, particularly during the revolutionary and post-revolutionary periods of Irish history. Postcolonial Gothic theory partly addresses the 'after' of colonisation as a way of assessing and redressing hegemonic policies of the past where, according to Punter and Bryon,

> the attempt to make, for example, the nation in a new form is inevitably accompanied by traces of the past, by half-buried histories of exile, transportation, emigration, all the panoply of the removal and transplantation of peoples which has been throughout history the essence of the colonial endeavor.[41]

The bog allows O'Connor and O'Faolain to employ Gothic subjects in their stories about the nation, accompanied by traces of the past through its ambiguous doubling. But the bog also allows them to double the cultural and symbolic anomalies in the stories that we can now examine through a postcolonial Gothic lens that supports such an overlapping analysis.

In what follows, I track how the bog functions as a space where O'Connor and O'Faolain resolve anomalies of nationalist sentiment through the haunting narratives of violence and decay caused by nationalism. By using critical and social definitions of hauntings, I explain how residues of nationalism and ideas of the nation create haunting effects for the characters in each story. These hauntings emerge when the characters find 'footing' on the bog. The first section discusses how social violence and decay work in both stories as indicators of hauntings. The second section moves to a broader concept of national identity and narratives of nationalism through names and story titles. This second section also explores the contentious relationships among O'Connor, O'Faolain, and Daniel Corkery, and shows how all three writers use the bog differently as a symbol for Irish nationalism. Both stories confuse national identities through the real and imagined space of the bog. The bog serves as an ideal location for O'Connor and O'Faolain to address unresolved moments in and feelings about the post-independence era of Irish history, where traces of power, knowledge, and oppression subtly remain. These writers draw from and employ what we now would call postcolonial Gothic conventions – entailing how hauntings are associated with postcolonial struggles – and they use the bog as a central motif in these political encounters.

Hauntings of Violence and Decay

The complexity of the bog as a cultural landform functions like a heritage artefact; it is polyvocal, with many histories, and has the ability to express and represent multiple conflicting ideologies.[42] O'Connor uses the bog in 'Guests' as a site of execution for two British soldiers because of its contradictory qualities, as a site of both death and birth; two men are killed, idealisms are ended, friendships die but a man is born (it is also a coming of age story), eyes are opened, and realisms are found. The bog is the space of 'both/and also' that contests popular notions of 'either/or' nationalism in the story. O'Faolain's 'A Meeting' shows that the bog similarly hosts the ghosts of revolution, but these ghosts haunt the narrator when he attempts to conjure up the nationalist spirit he and Sally shared twelve years previously. O'Faolain and O'Connor use the bog to further refute the seemingly definite view of Irish nationalism through themes of social violence and decay that ultimately compress time and space through the idea of haunting.

The notion of the 'past' in the Gothic form, Killeen observes, never completely ends and 'it has a nasty habit of bursting through into the present, displacing the contemporary with the supposedly outdated'.[43] Pheng Cheah has also argued that the relationship between nationalism and the desire for an atavistic past 'suggests that nationalism destroys human life and whatever future we may have because its gaze is fixed on the frozen past'.[44] O'Connor's and O'Faolain's stories caution the present as much as they interrogate the past by demonstrating the flexibility and fluidity of the temporal, thereby intimating that ideology is ever-changing and complex. Ghost stories challenge seemingly stable worlds where the past represents a dangerous place that nevertheless must be visited, often at the initial desire or reluctance of the narrator or the characters in the narrative. Through the bog these ghost stories also inherently challenge the notion of the static, determinate, and unmovable often associated with national ideologies.

Fiction functions as a social and cultural method of exploring time, particularly since the form itself often defies time by creating an unreliable sense of action in an equally unreliable space in the text. Anderson points out that fiction remains a form of writing – along with newspapers – that helps to imagine the nation.[45] Fiction in general can be used as a device for what Anderson, referencing Walter Benjamin's notion of Messianic time, calls 'simultaneity in "homogenous, empty time", or a complex gloss upon the word "meanwhile"'.[46] Using the ghost story set on the bog to explore the compression of time and space in 'homogenous empty time' allows both writers to move freely between the notions of pasts and presents, thereby creating a haunting effect in their fiction. The collapsing of time, especially to recall moments of violence and decay, permits the writers to bring forth ghosts of unresolved pasts and grapple with the social and political confrontations from which these spectres emerge.

'A Meeting' most exemplifies the displacement of time through the notion of decay. O'Faolain sets the tone of the story in the first two paragraphs, talking about the past through decay, melancholia, dream, and emptiness.[47] Through the first-person narrator, O'Faolain writes:

> Many towns in Ireland, after fifty or sixty years of prosperity, suddenly begin to decay; and 'decay' is the word for it, because they become not so much old as, in literal truth, decayed. Houses fall idle. Then they fall down. The street becomes gapped like an old man's mouth. (273)

The opening paragraph foregrounds the tone and theme of the entire story and depicts the loss and demoralisation of the past that such spaces embody. This description also exposes the ghost towns that have been abandoned and yet still have some form of life. This town, however, is located on a bog, also considered a perpetually haunted space in Ireland. The ghosts of history in the opening lines invoke the notion of decay through past histories and linger as unrealised forces that remain unresolved and disconnected from the present.

Burnt Hall is a town where the 'English cavalry began to train', but after the war 'the English cavalry is gone' (273). The reference to burning in the name increases the sense of doubles; fire both destroys and purges in a process toward regrowth; fire is both dangerous and illumining. That the hall is 'burnt', however, makes it clear the fire itself has decayed the town and only the ghostly traces remain. Even the normally wet bog is described at one point as 'dry as dust' in the summer heat, indicating further signs of decay (275).

The spectral traces of war and violence in the town do not incite a celebrated post-revolutionary spirit as one might assume. Instead, the story portrays O'Faolain's own loss of enthusiasm after the revolutionary period in the 1930s, mainly because of national support in favour of staying predominantly, as Cheah phrases it, 'fixed on the frozen past'.[48] Burnt Hall is 'crumbling to pieces' and the people of the town are 'staring emptily at the mirror of their own future' (273). Irish nationalism, as a ghost of the past, shimmers through the town, through both real (decaying structures) and imagined (vestiges of the English military post) manifestations that haunt the narrator.

The decay does more than foreshadow the haunted nation through the ghostly town of Burnt Hall; it sets the scene for a moment on the bog when the narrator questions his own unyielding nationalist support. By the third paragraph, the unnamed narrator walks 'down this melancholy street one afternoon' in summer and decides 'to go for a walk on the bogs' (273). This walk leads him through the half-conscious, ghostly stares of some of the people in the town on the edge of the bogs: a 'man strolled out of the mossy gateway of the barracks and looked at me with suspicion', while the narrator 'smelled the dinner-bones burning in the cabins' (273). The smell of dinner-bones reinforces an already pervasive feeling of decay through a history that continues to haunt the present as a reminder of the rotting past without any hope of a future. Eventually, after moving through the ghost town of Burnt Hall, the narrator sees a woman who had been staring at him; it turns out to be Sally Dunn from the revolution days of twelve years earlier. The narrator describes Sally as she was in the past, not in her present state: 'When I first knew Sally she was up to her eyes in the Revolution. If there was a dangerous dispatch, or a bomb or two, or a gun to be carried through the British patrols, she was the safest girl in Limerick for the job' (273).

The physical and temporal setting of this reunion/meeting provides a clear sense of deterioration through descriptions of the physical buildings of the town, the people who still inhabit it, the colonial history haunting it, and the bog that looms over everything. Moreover, the emptiness of the town is largely due to the English cavalry leaving after the war. O'Faolain delivers an odd juxtaposition. In one respect, paralleling a renewed national identity through revolutionary activity decades earlier would seem also to be reflected in the current state of Burnt Hall. In another respect, Burnt Hall functions as an economically and culturally depressed ghost town chiefly because of Ireland's transformation into a nation. This concurrence shows not only the sobering reason Burnt Hall became a ghost town – because the English left – it also reveals O'Faolain's difficulty with the revolutionary period, when full support of the nation left Ireland dispensing with the spectres of the past in a decaying present.

What scholars of O'Faolain's work have previously referred to as fragmented memories are actually ghosts haunting the narrator in the present. In *Sean O'Faolain's Irish Vision* (1987), Richard Bonaccorso maintains: 'O'Faolain's fiction often evokes an opposing kind of hidden Ireland to Corkery's: one of cultural frustration rather than cultural integrity. He portrays Irish people who long for more than their indigenous past can provide, who seek self-realization in moral and intellectual experimentation.'[49] In the first issue of the literary and social magazine *The Bell*, published in 1940 under O'Faolain's editorial stewardship, O'Faolain describes how Ireland in the 1930s contains the traces of 'dead' symbols, such as 'Cathleen ni Houlihan' and 'the swords of light', both of which once resonated for Revivalists as pre-colonial symbols of the nation.[50] Although O'Faolain often employs realist conventions in his fiction, he also incorporates disjointed memories that conjure ghosts of the past. The Revival's 'dead' symbols mentioned in *The Bell* illustrate a similar decay and crumbling of reimagined visions to that of the degenerating histories of the revolutionary period portrayed in 'A Meeting'.

The description of O'Faolain's cultural decay resembles similar characteristics in O'Connor's 'Guests' because it revisits earlier periods when nationalist vitality resulted in haunting repercussions. In the words of Irish playwright and film director Denis Johnston, who adapted O'Connor's 'Guests' into a silent film in 1935, 'The birth of a nation is never an immaculate conception.'[51] As 'A Meeting' suggests, the 'birth of the nation' left Ireland with scars of decay rather than progressive momentum for the future. According to Donal McCartney, O'Faolain believed that the anachronistic but nevertheless pervasive nationalism, largely opposed to innovation and progressive nation-building, prevented positive development toward a dynamic industrial future.[52] Setting 'A Meeting' in the 1930s, as opposed to in the past (like 'Guests'), allows O'Faolain to introduce the ghosts of nationalism from the revolutionary period through the narrator's memories of fighting twelve years earlier, and through the current state of Burnt Hall. Setting the story in the 1930s and reflecting on the past enhances the power of haunting through the effect of decay because it suggests that Ireland's national narratives have not resulted in a dynamic industrial future; rather, the present or future continually looks backward because of nationalism's obsession with the past. In this sense, stories that centre on absence, exclusions, and invisibilities are ghost stories.[53]

In 'A Meeting', silence serves as another indicator of an absence or 'decay' related to nationalism. As the narrator and Sally talk, he quickly laments that Sally's life has shifted a little too comfortably into the domestic sphere. The narrator withdraws from the conversation the more Sally discusses her life with her husband, a dentist. As they walk along the bog and talk, the narrator becomes increasingly silent until the climactic moment when he finally ends the conversation. Before this the narrator admits Sally 'was draining' him. He goes on to reflect that 'Life – these few hours of it, anyway – was become like music in the distance, as quiet as the bees wandering near us into the thistle-flowers and the furze' (277).

Life becomes distant for the narrator because Sally, by mostly avoiding discussing the 'rebelly' days, engages with him in the present rather than musing on the past. He ponders:

> As we walked back our talk was like the dusty smell of the boreens – a musk – hardly a scent, something so faint and slight that it really hardly touched the senses. It was just pleasant, companionable talk – getting its meaning from old memories – nothing more. We might otherwise be strangers. (277)

For the narrator, the absence of Sally's nationalist support equates to the 'dusty smell of the boreens' that 'hardly touched the senses' (see Fig. 3.1).[54] The relationship between him and Sally might as well resemble that of strangers if the link of nation does not bind, motivate, or identify them. The 'music in the distance' recalls the sound of the past that only the narrator still hears and it too, like the town of Burnt Hall, decays into the recesses of a once vibrant and energised nationalist past. Now it only haunts the narrator; Sally has seemingly resolved her past and moved forward without the spirit of the nation guiding her.

The ghost town of Burnt Hall is used as an overt symbolic setting where the ghosts can manifest, but the 'dusty smell of the boreens' winding through the bog ultimately conjures the ghosts of the nation. When waking out on the bog, everything shifts for the narrator. The bog becomes the connector for the overlapping tensions in the story; the decay of the past is clearly extant in the present independent nation because of unresolved issues related to colonisation. The price of independence,

3.1 Boreen winding through a bog (photo by Kelly Sullivan)

according to the story, results in the decay of the nation. Since the reality of independence ultimately disappoints an idealised nation, because revolution always falls short of a projected idea, then the nation that decays is an imagined notion that could not come into being. The meeting with Sally on the bog inadvertently activates the confusion between the past and the present for the narrator and ultimately leads to his moment of clarity. The first three paragraphs of 'A Meeting' provide enough evidence to suggest that the ghosts of Burnt Hall, a rural town located in the middle of the bog, still haunt from the revolutionary past in the decaying political present. The ghosts emerging from the decay challenge the direction of the nation as a decaying ghost itself, much like that of Burnt Hall.

A violent nationalistic past also haunts O'Connor's 'Guests'. Hauntings and war often closely align as a way to explain some of the known and unknown motivations for justifying and supporting violence. 'Nationalism,' Cheah argues, 'has almost become the exemplary figure for death.'[55] Nationalism frequently relies on haunting narratives to garner military and public support in times of casualty and violence. But death seems too one-dimensional to properly frame nationalism in terms of violence and war. It is, rather, the simultaneity of life and death that constructs an equally potent idea of 'enemy' or 'other' constructed to justify national violence. The concept of the 'enemy', or the many 'others' used in O'Connor's story, could easily be reduced to us/them or either/or binaries, but social representations of spectres complicate what might initially seem like an easily split opposition. Gordon writes:

> What is this enemy if not a conjuring malevolent specter? It is not what it seems to the visible eye. It has extraordinary powers to take familiar shapes and to surreptitiously mess up boundaries and proper protocols. It travels across fields promiscuously. It shimmers through the walls of factories and schools. It emerges uninvited from plots of land.[56]

Gordon aptly describes the ephemeral ghost 'enemy' related to violent conflicts such as war. The spectres permeate throughout society not only in predictable forms of haunting, such as visible ghosts, but also psychically and emotionally for the people who remain in the destructive aftermath of war.

Since the concept of the 'enemy' relies on perpetually indistinguishable, unclear, and often changing forms, the enemy used in the story may not signify the British soldiers, who are clear markers of opposition in sectarian conflict, but rather the ghosts of the nation. In other words, nationalism conjures 'malevolent specters' of the past where the enemy is the ghost. Ghosts, much like bogs, can be difficult to pin down and discuss in concrete terms, as can be fiction itself – difficult to articulate or accept as real – and there, too, it is the 'not-quite' or 'in-between' which brings allure and artistry. Therefore, it is important to recognise how ghosts relate to nationalist histories: they contain 'extraordinary powers' and take many forms that ultimately disrupt boundaries; they 'shimmer' through the walls of state institutions; they constantly morph into new manifestations; and they emerge from 'plots of land', such as bogs. In this sense, then, the spirits materialising from nationalism represent the primary ghosts haunting Bonaparte and Noble in 'Guests' because they penetrate their psyches and possess them. Bonaparte is haunted for the rest of his life because, as he admits, 'I didn't want him [Hawkins] to be bumped off' (9). Thus, national spirits frighten them into allowing acts of unwitting violence against those who may be more like them than other supporters of the nation whom they are supposed to represent.

In 'Guests', hauntings related to violence correlate with the characters' ideas about nationalism and eventually manifest on the bog. Violence is often perpetuated through binary oppositions, such as the construction of 'enemy' or 'others'. O'Connor presents this ambiguous tension in the closing lines when Bonaparte describes saying 'good-bye to the others' before he and Noble leave 'along the desolate edge of the treacherous bog without a word' after they bury the corpses of the British soldiers, Hawkins and Belcher (12). Who are the uncertain 'others' that Bonaparte and Noble feel compelled to say good-bye to? Is it the dead men? Is it the other IRA soldiers? Is it other ghosts from the bog? The word 'other' is loaded with meaning and related to social violence, and unpacking it elucidates a key to understanding the story's connection to nationalism and haunting. According to Homi Bhabha, 'The "other" is never outside or beyond us; it emerges forcefully, within cultural discourse, when we think we speak most intimately and indigenously "between ourselves".'[57] The 'other' in 'Guests' is represented in many ways, all of which support the underlying 'cultural discourse' in the story. Thus, the use of 'other' complicates the relationships and presumed alliances in the story, as well as the Irish nationalism that O'Connor directly challenges.

First, the 'others' appear to be literally and functionally Donovan and Feeney, the two IRA soldiers at the execution site who dislike the relationship Bonaparte and Noble have forged with Belcher and Hawkins during their captivity. Second, 'others' invokes the idea of ghosts at the heart of this chapter. What is 'others' but a nondescript title for undefined spirits, whether they are the subordinated Other in postcolonial discourse, as Bhabha explains, or the ghosts that resist definite meaning in a national narrative. Although Belcher and Hawkins die at the end of the story, they remain both physically present (as warm corpses in the bog) and beyond the present (in memory and in spirit). The soldiers are two of the most obvious ghosts in the story; they challenge the temporal zone of activity on the bog and the imaginative space of knowledge related to the nation.[58] Belcher and Hawkins also represent the 'guests' in the story, an idea that challenges the concept of performing one's duty for the nation. Hawkins, for example, wants to join the IRA as opposed to die for his own nation. He claims, 'You won't come over to my side, so I'll come over to your side. Is that fair? Just you give me a rifle and I'll go with you wherever you want' (10). Sides or political positions within each nation are treated as formalities that rhetorically frame an often unwanted national identity and reinforce an either/or binary not well suited to either side. Hawkins goes on to proclaim, 'I'm through with it all' (10). For both Hawkins and Bonaparte, the loyalty to friendship supersedes any duty to nationalism. Their duty is not to promote violence or 'playing at soldiers', as Hawkins jests, but to support the 'guests' in the nation (9). In this regard, the story raises questions that directly challenge nationalism as a simple either/or binary. How can one kill one's guests? How hospitable is the nation if it murders its guests?

Third, and finally, the 'others' signify the collective (un)dead or generations of ghosts from national conflicts buried in the 'fatal bog', where the penetrating silence of their being and not being in the world triggers a ghostly response from Bonaparte and Noble (8). The bog poses as a silent, omniscient historical witness, both in the past and the present, for various acts of sectarian violence. As Noble muses, 'the boglands was like the pain of death in my heart' (9). At this point in the story, Bonaparte and Noble have reacted to the haunting by 'saying goodbye' to their idealistic and youthful support of the nation, to the guests they hosted, and to the generations of the dead in Ireland. The dead shimmer through the silence of the bog is a reminder of unresolved violence resulting from extreme forms of nationalism.

Some ghosts manifest explicitly in hauntings, while others do not. When ghosts are less explicit and serve as an unexplainable essence, such as an absence or deficiency, they provide a symptom of what is missing as much as what is known. In spectral theory, according to Gordon, 'the ghost or apparition is the principal form by which something lost or invisible or seemingly not there makes itself known or apparent to us'.[59] The ghost 'makes itself known' through the various processes of haunting, but the process by which one is haunted can also be unknown or interpreted as an absence or silence of a presence/energy/spirit known to be present. Moments of history can therefore haunt both stories as much as they haunt the characters themselves. For O'Connor's and O'Faolain's stories, the bog serves as a real topography and imagined symbol that supports and challenges narratives of nationalism. By framing such narratives as ghost stories, they scrutinise the certainty and loyalty attached to nationhood.

In 'Guests', silence signifies violence through the state of an unmarked grave out in the bog, one that exists without any language inscribed on a gravestone indicating individual identity. Silence culminates 'out in the middle of a blasted bog' (10), where the characters were forcibly still and 'silent in the boglands' (9). Belcher's silence mirrors the spirit of the bog. Belcher, the larger, more affable British soldier, is so reticent that Bonaparte calls him a 'ghost'. Bonaparte states, 'he had an uncommon shortness – or should I say lack – of speech. It took us some time to get used to him walking in and out like a ghost' (4). The others responded to Belcher's presence as they would to that of a spectre, appearing in both known visible and unknown invisible form. Likewise, Hawkins is called 'a fright to argue' with, which signals through pun another ghostly kind of being (5).

The story does not focus on the corpses after the killing; instead, it turns its attention to the setting of the ominous bog as a descriptive emotional reminder for Noble and Bonaparte. Bonaparte reflects, 'It was all mad lonely, with only a bit of lantern between ourselves and the pitch blackness, and birds hooting and screeching all round disturbed by the guns' (12). The bog, as an emblematic translator, transmits the feelings after the execution, with loneliness and blackness dominating the mood. The bog and the actions therein create an affective response for Bonaparte and Noble where their emotional states, not supporting the idea of the nation, are mirrored upon the bog. It functions as one large unmarked grave permeated with the collective spectral presence of violence compressed in the silent history of the peat. Bonaparte reflects on the killing of Belcher and Hawkins: 'I don't remember much about the burying, but that it was worse than all of the rest' (12). This particular bog contains the ghosts of Bonaparte's own past haunting him through an experiential, visceral association with this particular 'landscape of fear'.

The graveyard of the bog similarly relates to the 'others' that represent the generations who died to support nationalism. O'Connor enhances the scene by evoking sensorial details of the 'windy' bog and the aural sounds of the familiar birds collectively responding to the gunshots. 'A Meeting' contains similar sensory effects with the heat and smells of the burning boreens. These 'unmarked' graves are discernible through the spectral presences around the bog and partly felt through the senses. The markings appear through the absence of life and the silence hovering over the bog. Bonaparte laments, 'Then having smoothed all signs of the grave away, Noble and I collected our tools, said good-bye to the *others*, and went back along the desolate edge of the treacherous bog without a word' (12, my emphasis). Desolation and silence, which are interchangeable and equally penetrating in the story, infuse the graveyard of the bog.

O'Connor's story clearly comments upon the state of Ireland within a violent conflict, using the bog to portray nationalism as a confusing and ambiguous concept that cannot be celebrated, sentimentalised, or buried in Irish history. Whereas O'Faolain focuses on national decay, O'Connor emphasises the inherent social violence in nationalism. The impact of violence is certainly relevant to Bonaparte as he delivers the tormenting lines at the end of the story, while reflecting upon 'the little patch of black bog with the two Englishmen stiffening into it'. He states:

> But with me it was the other way, as though the patch of bog where the two Englishmen were was a thousand miles away from me, and even Noble mumbling just behind me and the old woman and the birds and the bloody stars were all far away, and I was somehow very small and very lonely. And anything that ever happened me after I never felt the same about again. (12)

Bonaparte copes with the immediate aftermath of his violent experience by distancing himself from the physical space that has resounded in his memory. The old woman, birds, stars, and bog serve as visceral reminders for Bonaparte of his friends, Belcher and Hawkins. While on the bog, Bonaparte's personal and national memories interweave. Here, space and time have become compressed; Bonaparte remains simultaneously 'a thousand miles away' while also minutes away from the bog grave. Bonaparte experiences haunting effects of not only his actions, but a longer history of violence supported by nationalism. The memories that will persistently haunt Bonaparte become a transformative experience activated by this sense of the bog, a space associated with killing not only Belcher and Hawkins, but also many others in support of the nation.

The ghosts of Belcher and Hawkins haunting Bonaparte do not allow forgetting or reimagining the events of the past with nationalist vigour. The ghosts, rather, highlight a doubled sense of *dis-ease* for Bonaparte; he is both traumatised and inoculated by his past. Bonaparte laments, 'I began to perceive in the dusk the desolate edges of the bog that was to their last earthly bed, and, so great a sadness overtook my mind' (9). Ghosts manifest as a result of abusive systems of power, and in so doing impact the everyday lives of people who have been a part of these power systems.[60] Bonaparte, Noble, Hawkins, and Belcher, as well as the unnamed 'others', are all people whose lives have been affected because of the abusive systems of power that continually emerge from various forms of nationalism. In the story, these systems of power haunt the characters immediately after the violence occurring on the bog, thereby questioning a national identity based upon this violent past.

Spectres of National Identity

O'Connor's and O'Faolain's subtle invocation of ghosts and nationalism also challenges notions of identity and names. Narratives of nationalism and identity are as elusive as ghosts and hauntings, and the one way to address such histories is through the similar ambiguities and complexities of the bog. Smith maintains that the Gothic has a tradition of focusing on complex models of identity.[61] Likewise, Bhabha observes that political histories are half made with the intention and process that they will fully be made in nationalist models through constructed (or narrated) forms of identity.[62] The larger question explored in this section focuses on how these two short stories reveal legitimate concerns about national identity, particularly in how hauntings on bogs, seen as spaces of the supernatural and irrational, dismantle and disrupt national identities.

'Guests' and 'A Meeting' fundamentally question the effectiveness of nationalism and imagining the Irish nation during a time when support for it ran high. O'Connor and O'Faolain shared histories steeped in Irish nationalism. Their positions, however, remained contradictory throughout their lives because they both opposed the extremes of Irish nationalism, while at the same time they remained supporters of it on some level.[63]

Daniel Corkery – an Irish writer, politician, and scholar – who at one point served as a mentor to O'Faolain and O'Connor as their professor at University College Cork, eventually shunned them because of their less fervent support for developing an Irish national literature. Corkery was, quite simply, a zealot of Irish nationalism and approached it with what O'Faolain recognised in a 1936 issue of the *Dublin Magazine* as an admiration for the 'masculine and belligerent'.[64] Both O'Connor and O'Faolain, as younger and more impressionable writers, shared Corkery's views. But by the time they had published 'Guests' and 'A Meeting', O'Connor and O'Faolain had moved away from Corkery's 'belligerent' forms of nationalism and turned to other liberatory ideas of individualism and universalism. This is why, in part, Corkery would not even acknowledge his support for their literary work. Corkery went so far as to refuse a signed copy of *Guests of the Nation* from O'Connor upon its publication.[65]

What links Corkery, O'Connor, and O'Faolain are not only their connections to the Revival, nationalism, and writing, but also their interest in bogs. In a famous quote, from his book *Synge and Anglo-Irish Literature* (1931), Corkery calls for a need to establish an exclusive form of Irish national literature. He does so through the curious metaphor of a 'sod' (or piece of bog):

> The difficulty is not alone a want of native mould; it is rather the want of a foundation upon which to establish them. Everywhere in the mentality of the Irish people are flux and uncertainty. Our national consciousness may be described, in a native phrase, as a quaking sod. It gives no footing. It is not English, nor Irish, nor Anglo-Irish.[66]

Corkery's frequently cited statement emphasises the need to return to a purportedly idyllic era of pre-colonial stability or a 'native mould' in Ireland, but one that can be built upon a more stable base. For Corkery, Irish national literature, as distinct from English literature, should contain three main ingredients: religious consciousness of the people, land, and Irish nationalism.[67] The 'quaking sod', or bog (connecting land, Catholic religion, and Irish nationalism), serves as a universal symbol of Irish identity to express his particularly dogmatic views about nationalism. The sod, like the national consciousness, does signal flux and uncertainty in Irish political history, but it also reflects the instability of nationalism and the ways in which writers like Corkery attempt to frame the nation. Corkery believes that there is something essentially 'Irish' about Ireland and it must be re-discovered through a national literature. But, as he suggests, national consciousness more readily resembles the 'quaking sod'; it moves, changes, and complicates fixed ideas that elude definition and determinate logic. Like other Revivalists, Corkery idealises earlier forms of Gaelic culture when the bog – often a symbol of the peasantry in the seventeenth and eighteenth centuries – served as an unusually stable icon of Irish identity. However, what both he and the Revivalists often overlook is that Irish identity, like all national identities, has always been as uncertain, unstable, and indefinable as the bog.

O'Connor and O'Faolain demonstrate how the ghosts of nationalism emerge when each story's action takes place on a bog for the very reason that it negates some easy definitions of the nation. Much of O'Faolain's social commentary during the 1930s and 1940s consciously responded to and refuted Corkery's earlier writings.[68] O'Faolain's book *The Irish* (1949) serves as a key example. In it, he argues that Irish literature and culture expands much further than the limitations of Corkery's paradigm. For O'Faolain, the taxonomy of branches include: the New Peasantry, the Anglo-Irish, the Rebels, the Priest, the Writers, and the Politicians. O'Faolain disagreed with Corkery's idealisation of an uneducated peasant culture as the model citizenry in a post-independence Ireland.[69] The bog for Corkery symbolises the peasants – his idealised symbol of the nation – which may be why O'Faolain returned to the bog in 'A Meeting' as a place of confusion and ultimately questioning for the nationalist narrator.

Cultural developments in Irish nationalism present more complexity than Corkery's absolutist position indicates. And as David Pierce reminds us, 'we need to bear in mind that from the outset the knife cuts both ways, that passionate realism frequently accompanied passionate idealism, and that Irishness, as Joyce, too, understood, was at once a natural feeling and a contestable concept'.[70] Both O'Connor and O'Faolain find balance between the realism and idealism suggested here by Pierce. In an era of intense national sympathies – particularly in the 1930s when Éamon de Valera with his recently formed Fianna Fáil party took power and cemented a socially and culturally conservative and reactionary state for decades to come in Ireland – it is no accident that both writers couch their oppositional political positions in literary narratives set on the bog.

As mentioned in the previous section, both stories speak to violence and decay through the physical and symbolic bog. O'Faolain and O'Connor uncover a relationship between the bog and language, and in particular, the narrative of the 'nation' or nationalism. In 'Guests', Bonaparte and Noble are fighting for the Irish nationalist cause in the midst of an anti-colonial war against the British over the tyrannies that are alleged to have lasted in Ireland for hundreds of years. Because they are part of the IRA, they are considered 'rebels' by the governing British state structure (until its dissolution in 1922). However, the language of nationalism, as well as national identity, decays for Bonaparte and Noble as they increasingly become entwined with what function as their Gothic doubles – Belcher and Hawkins.

The story blurs the divide between imperial soldiers and nationalist rebels through the cultural and linguistic 'chumming' between both sides. The four men not only become friends, they become almost indistinguishable. Neither pair, for example, supports either nationalist cause (Irish or British) in their dialogue or actions. Belcher and Hawkins could have easily taken on, in another circumstance, a 'native' Irish identity. At the beginning of the story, Bonaparte comments:

> I couldn't at the time see the point of me and Noble being with Belcher and 'Awkins at all, for it was and is my fixed belief you could have planted that pair in any untended spot from this to Claregalway and they'd have stayed put and flourished like a native weed. I never seen in my short experience two men that took to the country as they did. (3)

Such Irish identity is predicated on and imparted by the actual geography of Ireland. Bonaparte reflects, 'But little 'Awkins made us look right fools when he displayed he knew the countryside as well as we did and something more' (3). The term 'native weed' is particularly striking in reference to the knowledge Belcher and Hawkins have of Irish geography because it reinforces the rootedness of identity upon a geography, while also underscoring the intransigence of a weed, which can thrive anywhere upon 'native' soil. There is an implicit interchange of identity in this description of the two British soldiers; the implication is that Belcher and Hawkins could be as Irish as Noble and Bonaparte.

The scene infers the familiar notion in postcolonial theory that new incarnations of nationalism eventually replace the power structures that precede them. Kearney has argued that 'Irish and British nationalism are Siamese twins',[71] which implies a co-equal exchange of power and identity, creating both a subordinate and dependent interchange. Bonaparte and Noble become British in a sense because they replace the hegemonic power backing Belcher and Hawkins by executing them for the nation out on the bog. These exchanges of identity confuse the outcomes arising from duty or serving the nation.

O'Connor challenges specific strains of Irish nationalism dedicated to such a zealous blind duty beyond rationality. What we might call the Gothic double bind between the British (Belcher and Hawkins) and Irish (Noble and Bonaparte) in the cultural logic of the story is used to question the whole notion of identity. In *Terror and Irish Modernism*, Jim Hansen examines the concept of the 'Gothic double bind' that utilises a convention of doppelgängers by drawing out instances in Irish culture where the construction of an identity appears materially, psychically, and structurally doubled, producing definitions based upon their own disjunction in the social context. Bonaparte and Noble contain what Hansen refers to as their own 'dark doubles' through Belcher and Hawkins,[72] or 'Siamese twins' referring back to Kearney, further complicating the question of Irish identity in nationalist discourses.

However, these doubles then become the ghosts that haunt the nation because they are simultaneously guests and hosts of the nation. In fact, the words 'guest' and 'host' are etymologically linked to the Indo-European root *ghosti-*, similar to other words doubled in the story through the two sets of characters, including 'hospitable' and 'hostage'. The Latin words *hostis* (stranger or enemy) and *hospes* (hospitable stranger), which stem from *ghosti-*, confuse the distinction between guests and hosts and how they relate to national identity in 'Guests'.[73] The interplay of word choice and language around 'guest' and 'host' also provides a basis for ghost, or a 'stranger', 'enemy', or even the 'others' discussed in the previous section of this chapter. In other words, the identity between guests and hosts becomes blurred. When the hosts (Bonaparte and Noble) walk away in the end, and double as guests of the nation, it is because they question the very idea of nationalism through their role as hosts. This raises two larger questions in the story: Who were the guests of the nation? Are those who own the land also those who own the narratives of the nation?

O'Connor does indeed question the idea of who owns the rights to narrate the nation – whether it is the guests, hosts, or even ghosts. This ambiguous query – explored through both the anomalies of nationalism and the bog – serves as an ambiguous background marker to the stories. David Lloyd contends that nationalism and identities of 'Irishness' are built around a narrative, and controlling these narratives reinforces legitimacy within political and legal frameworks.[74] Even in the nineteenth century when the 'crisis of representation' affected the narrative modes in the novel,[75] or with Revivalists like Corkery who argued for a national literature in order to control the narrative, the question continually arises as to how the nation should be narrated. The action in 'Guests' scrutinises the relationship between nationalism and the presumed authority over narrative in Ireland. O'Connor does not explicitly address this overtly nationalist question, but through other morbid means it seems clear that he sympathises with the uncertainty of the answer. The question of 'who owns the right to narrate the nation?' has continually loomed over Irish history and, especially for O'Connor and O'Faolain, appears on the bog where the answers are as uncertain as the questions.

What O'Connor does do is to summon the ghosts of nationalism through some of the names used in the story, which provides a more concrete reading of hauntings in contrast with some of the themes of decay and absence explained in the last section. The names of characters are also ghosts of other nationalisms, all of which are directly or indirectly related to Irish history. The surnames of Bonaparte and Noble have cultural meanings rooted in revolution and nationalism, which invoke notions of fighting for land rights in the long nineteenth century (bookended by the 1798 Rebellion and the fourth Home Rule Act in 1920). Bonaparte's name harkens back to Napoleon Bonaparte, who haunts Irish history as a figure capable of transforming colonial dynamics in the late eighteenth century. Similar to the dormant French chest of gold in *The Snake's Pass*, Bonaparte's name signals the alternative course of history that might have followed if the French allies had provided the Irish with more support during the 1798 Rebellion and beyond. According to Thomas Bartlett in his book *Ireland: A History* (2010), Napoleon Bonaparte is hailed as the greatest hero in Irish Catholic folklore, other than 'The Liberator' Daniel O'Connell. This elevation existed despite the failed attempt on three separate occasions by the revolutionary Theobald Wolfe Tone to persuade Napoleon to help with the 1798 Rebellion. Napoleon's lack of support resulted in the Act of Union as a response to 1798, which significantly challenged progress toward Catholic sovereignty and reinforced Protestant landownership throughout the nineteenth century.[76] In short, the idea of land/nation and the name of Bonaparte share a revealing history in Ireland that underpins the ghosts in O'Connor's story.

Noble's name signifies loyalty without question to a political cause; the name is also synonymous with Donovan's nationalist call to 'duty' and 'obeying our superiors' (9). Noble is the one who carries the lantern in the middle of the bog during the execution, indicating his connection with Catholicism and carrying the 'light' of God for the group in the dark recesses of violence. Notwithstanding his brother is a priest, Noble engages in debates with Hawkins over Christian morality and whether there was a god, 'answering in his best canonical style that there was' (6). Hawkins even uses Christian reverse psychology on Noble as a way to extricate himself: 'What d'you think I'd do if I was in Noble's place and we were out in the middle of a blasted bog? I'd go with him wherever he was going. I'd share my last bob with him and stick by 'im through thick and thin' (10). If Bonaparte's name represents a national figure, then Noble's name signifies a balance to this position or a reminder that killing the 'guests' will only create ghosts that plague Irish history.

While Feeney and Donovan serve as minor characters in the story, their names invoke the most Irish nationalist connection, reflecting their own unrelenting support for the nation. Feeney invokes Fenian, which recalls the warrior bands in Gaelic Ireland denoting an early form of Irish nationalism, beginning with the Fianna, or Irish warriors in the second and third centuries, then to the Fenians or Irish Republican Brotherhood in the nineteenth century, and later the IRA in the twentieth century. Jeremiah Donovan's name refers to Jeremiah O'Donovan Rossa, mentioned by Patrick Pearse as one of the 'ghosts' of the Fenian dead.[77] In addition, O'Donovan is O'Connor's original surname. O'Connor took his mother's maiden name as a pen name, which ultimately stuck. O'Connor's pejorative depiction of Donovan as a dogmatic nationalist in 'Guests' might be explained by the fact that during a long stretch of his life he denounced his own O'Donovan lineage.[78]

Both Bonaparte and Noble challenge the cultural etymology of their names through their transformative experience on the bog where they emblematically bury their own nationalist identities as they submerge the still warm corpses of Belcher and Hawkins. For IRA combatants, questioning Irish nationalist duty typically led to dire consequences. Unlike the rigid codes of nationalism within the anti-colonial/revolutionary struggle, the bog functions as a witness to events rather than a rhetorical tool, conjuring moods and moments of history rather than dogmatic doctrine, and challenging definitions of identity. Bonaparte lays awake at night imagining ways he can 'prevent the Brigade from shooting 'Awkins and Belcher' (7). He hesitates in 'a cold sweat' because only one outcome to this course remains; he too would end up in the bog along with them. He reflects, 'Because there were men on the Brigade you daren't let nor hinder without a gun in your hand, and at any rate, in those days disunion between brothers seemed to me an awful crime. I knew better after' (7). This last thought, 'I knew better after', reveals that Bonaparte does not imagine his physical death, but a figurative one through participation in the executions. Bonaparte recognises that because of his reluctant support for the nation the ghost of Hawkins will haunt him hereafter, but he also understands that it is better to bury a constructed identity related to the nation rather than that of a 'brother'. In the end, both Noble and Bonaparte share a similar fate as Belcher and Hawkins; they lose a firm sense of national identity while out on the bog because of the violence they must commit on it. While they do not physically die, they execute a part of themselves by killing two 'chums', their Gothic 'dark doubles' or 'Siamese twins', whose only crime was a superficial commitment to England.

In 'A Meeting', unlike in 'Guests', names are almost non-existent, reflecting the absence and decay dominating the story. We never know the narrator's name or that of any of the characters except Sally. Even the fictional town name, Burnt Hall, sounds more like an abandoned community centre than a town in Ireland. O'Faolain uses the absence of traditional identity markers (such as names) as a determining narrative in the story. Distinct from O'Connor, who celebrated more apparent allusions and closure in stories, O'Faolain detested obvious symbolism and conclusions and strove for ambiguity and absence in his fiction.[79] In contrast to the explicit identities connected to nationalism in 'Guests', 'A Meeting' emphasises the ghosts of nationalism through the lack of names and an emptiness of story (there is very little plot or action), both of which parallel the vastness of the bog. The absence of distinct Irish identity and nation, as opposed to their overt markers in O'Connor's story, reveals another type of ghost: the impression of identity left lingering in memories and dreams.

The markers of nationalism peek through when the narrator and Sally discuss the past, but the past materialises as fragmented memories that function as dreams or even ghosts that convolute the histories unfolding in the story. O'Faolain reveals situations in Irish history by providing both material (bog) or imagined (memories) spaces where specific content suggests what Neary calls the elusive 'whispers' in the story.[80] 'A Meeting' ends by describing the geography of the 'little country town' where the story is set: 'the bog into which it all sank behind the train was already whispering and dim' (277). Rather than overtly narrate the nation, O'Faolain creates a sense of absence to indicate the ghosts 'whispering' out on the bog.

Even the titles of the stories evoke explicit connections to nationalism and ghosts. The 'guests' become the ghosts of the 'nation' and the 'meeting' implies a union with the ghost of nationalism. In his analysis of 'Guests', O'Brien incisively foregrounds the idea of the ghost in his article about Guests/*Geists* of the nation and argues that the fundamental notion of 'hauntology' in 'Guests' emerges from Derrida's idea of hospitality and hostility. For O'Brien, guests of the nation are really the ghosts or *Geists*, playing off Hegel's use of the German *Geist* (spirit) to conceive 'ghosts of the nation' as 'some sort of organic energizing force that shapes nations and individuals'.[81] O'Brien's observation and reference to Hegel supports his thesis that ghosts are the guests of an Irish nation (Belcher and Hawkins), but O'Brien inadvertently references a way of perceiving the bog as a national space with ghostly undertones by demonstrating the Hegelian sense of *Geist*.

Drawing from O'Brien's point here, bogs function in 'Guests' as an 'organic energizing force' shaping the nations, individuals, and memories that circulate around them. This 'force' is clearly illustrated through Bonaparte and Noble, whose actions on the bog are cataclysmic in response to their own nationalistic questioning through silence and absence. With the concept of 'chums' ringing 'painfully' in his 'memory', Bonaparte reflects prior to killing Hawkins, 'But why should Noble want to shoot him? Why should we want to shoot him? What had he done to us?' (9).

Bonaparte questions nationalism's *sine qua non* of duty in 'Guests'. A reluctance to embrace a nationalist identity rings true for Bonaparte and Noble who carry forth 'doing our duty' while also demonstrating an inner conflict prompted by these actions (9). Even Donovan, who lives by the nationalist code about 'duty and obeying our superiors' (9), begins to question this process himself prior to shooting Belcher in the head while out on the bog. 'You understand,' he claims, 'it's not so much our doing. It's our duty, so to speak' (11). O'Connor describes that Belcher raises his head 'like a real blind man's' because he wears an execution blindfold. Framing him in the tradition of sightless seers, Belcher admits, 'I never could make out what duty was myself' (11). The blind allegiance to the idea of duty appears to be as elusive as the apparitions in the story because duty is a concept that has severe personal impact while it also reinforces national identity.

This microcosmic scene about national loyalty frames the story as a whole; the spirit of nationalism confuses duty as much as it does identity and such obscurities appear out on the bog. Belcher responds to his own puzzlement about duty, 'but I think you're all good lads, if that's what you mean. I'm not complaining' (11–12). Blind and unjustly killed, Belcher provides a realistic glimpse of the world O'Connor so penetratingly paints regarding definitive forms of nationalism. The bog provides an enduring primordial place where the horror of a murky colonial history has been buried, even though this past is never actually forgotten and continues to haunt the present. The action in 'Guests' takes place in the midst of nation-formation where a sense of spirit manifests out on the 'fatal bog' (8).

The title of 'A Meeting' also invokes narratives of nationalism and ghosts tied to identity. The 'meeting' occurs in two co-existing places: the imaginative past and present of fragmented memories on the real bog that symbolises both the memory and the physical decay in the story. The meeting begins at the edge of the bog, moves to the streets of Burnt Hall where the two characters sit near Sally's little villa that was 'originally built by some English colonel' (275), and finally ends back on the boreens winding through the bog. At the moment when the narrator rests in front of Sally's villa, ironically built by the coloniser, he begins 'to feel a lack in her talk' (275). Sally then leaves to attend to her crying child and while away the narrator looks at her bookshelf: 'Only on the little book-shelf did I find any memories of the old days – pamphlets from Russia, poems by this rebel leader who was shot in action, and that one who died in a hunger-strike – and even they were down on the lowest shelf behind the armchair' (275). These memories, or ghosts of the revolutionary past, are as much buried in the past as are the generations of ghosts/bodies submerged in the bog from violence in 'Guests'. When Sally comes back and tells the narrator she is ready to walk 'in the fields', she notices him 'fiddling' with the relics of the nationalist past that bind them together in the current moment. Sally 'just laughed and lifted her eyes comically to the ceiling, and shook her head a little as if to say … I did not know what' (275; original ellipsis). In only a few sentences O'Faolain demonstrates the infrequency of linear time through fragmented memories.

Neary has argued that O'Faolain's writing 'is not his creation of large worlds from spare materials, but his location of these spare materials in characters' memories, in the dimly perceived personal and national histories characters must reconstruct if they are to establish identities'.[82] If we expand Neary's claim a bit further, it shows that ghosts of national histories continually haunt the narrator. Sally, in contrast, no longer feels haunted by the past because she has buried it. The past does not represent living memories haunting Sally, but decaying relics of the Revolutionary period stored in the 'lowest shelf behind the armchair' (275).

The climactic moment in the story transpires when the narrator attempts to excavate some of Sally's memories while they walk on the bog. Because she will not openly offer them to him, the narrator states, 'I promised myself to find out while we walked in the fields' (275). O'Faolain writes that the 'bog was dry as dust and in the heat it trembled like a mirage. For miles and miles it stretched across Ireland, dark purple with heather, and bright with furze' (275). The 'mirage' described in this scene parallels the mirage of the nation that continues to linger in the narrator's point of view, still visible but only reconstructed in the imagination. The mirage, like the bog, stretches across Ireland and appears as both dark and bright. Nationalism still burns brilliantly for the narrator, but for some like Sally, Bonaparte, and Noble, it remains an elusive spectre that now appears as haunting memories of the past rather than manifesting as something definable or comprehensible in the present. Gordon maintains that in instances of social hauntings the 'ghost is not simply a dead or missing person, but a social figure, and investigating it can lead to that dense site where history and subjectivity makes social life' (8). The bog in the story, a space where 'history and subjectivity makes social life', reflects this quality of contradiction and ambiguity that attracts writers to stage such poignant scenes on its topographic and imaginative contours.

The change in the narrator from quixotic nationalist to questioning brooder occurs at the point when he walks on the bog, and reflects the confusion and ambiguity coming over him while on this provoking terrain:

> But although it was lovely, not merely old but immemorable, not merely unchanged but unchangeable, it began to weigh heavily on me; and to that feeling, partly of the day, partly of doubt about my friend, was added a sense of other hidden lives when I saw the bog-cabins with the dark water lapping to their doors, just like arks, all sinking back into the mould. (275)

While it may initially appear that O'Faolain speaks here about Burnt Hall, or other decaying towns similar to it in post-revolutionary Ireland of the 1930s, or even Co. Limerick more generally, the description similarly resembles the union of opposites of the bog: unchanged but unchangeable; lovely and immemorable. The 'hidden lives' or ghosts that appear on the bog are part of the characters, the people in the town, or anyone else buried in history. On the one hand, there is the Sally he once knew (and his memory of her) versus the Sally he speaks to in the story while walking on the bog. Sally now values a different future without the nation as a central feature in her life. On the other hand, there are both the real and imagined 'hidden lives' buried in the bog (as a result of the violence realistically portrayed in a story like 'Guests') and in the historical past. Are the people living in the bog-cabins with the ominous 'dark' bog water lapping at their doors real or imagined? O'Faolain creates a significant amount of ambiguity in this sequence and raises doubts about their existence as spectres or 'real' people.

Nations are also simultaneously imagined, and real spaces. The moment the narrator starts to grow introspective he notices everything 'sinking back into the mould' (275). This clearly echoes Corkery's reference to the 'mould' of the Irish 'quaking sod'. Much to the lament of nationalists like Corkery, in the new post-revolutionary nation no homogenous national mould remains. In addition, O'Faolain's social commentary in the 1930s and 1940s, often embedded in his literary work, consciously attempted to respond to and refute much of Corkery's earlier writings.[83] In 'A Meeting', the word 'mould' could also indicate that the only thing sinking into the mould of the bog is the decaying nationalism that the narrator espouses.

The narrator's nationalism is also mirrored by the town's own dilapidation, instead of the optimism exhibited by Sally for her new life. The bog here serves as an uncanny space where the narrator recognises another world outside of his decayed nostalgia for the revolutionary days. 'If haunting describes how that which appears to be not there is often a seething presence, acting on and often meddling with taken-for-granted realities,' argues Gordon, 'the ghost is just the sign, or the empirical evidence if you like, that tells you haunting is taking place.'[84] In one particularly poignant paragraph set only on the bog, everything shifts in the story and the signs of the ghosts acting as a 'seething presence' suddenly become numerous: the people, memories, and fragmentation of time all confuse the narrator's current state of knowing about his national identity. In this sense, the narrator is haunted. The paragraph ends by describing one of the inhabitants of the bog: 'We saw a woman inside one door, her eyes as dark as bog-pools, and as patient and as still' (275). Not only does this woman resemble a spectre, obscuring the spaces between life and death, she also mirrors the fate of the nation in the eyes of the narrator, 'patient and as still' as the bog.

O'Faolain chooses to set the story and locate the climactic scene on the bog precisely because it defies logic and structural certainty and serves as a transformative space that invites hauntings. According to Neary, 'Many of O'Faolain's stories create the feeling of characters being haunted by something uncontrolled from the past, something that *cannot be grasped*, cannot be made sense of.'[85] What *can* be grasped, therefore, are the ghosts of nationalism that exhibit unexplainable contradictions and that appear to the narrator while on the bog. As they leave the bog, the narrator re-embraces his national identity and attempts to draw Sally back to discussing the 'old rebelly days and nights' (276). He quickly realises, after exchanging some meaningless banter, that at this point he and Sally 'might otherwise be strangers' because she chose to embrace her own personal identity over that of the nation (277). He laments, 'I felt like a person giving a transfusion of blood. She was draining me' (276–7). The narrator equates Sally's vampiric effect on him to what happens when national identity is lost and buried; it becomes a ghost. Being haunted, as in the example of the narrator, 'draws us affectively', often a bit magically and unwillingly, into the experience of 'transformative recognition'.[86] The narrator's transformative recognition of the past, more than the nostalgic reveries, percolates into consciousness while on the bog, only to then be lost again as he leaves Burnt Hall.

Confronting Ghosts on the Bog

'Guests' and 'A Meeting' function as ghost stories in which O'Connor and O'Faolain endeavour to revisit history in the post-revolutionary period through narratives of haunting. The bog in 'Guests' appears on the margins of social and political discourse because, at the time, 1930s Ireland was still confronting the nationalistic fervour of a past that once led to violent social disruptions. 'A Meeting' stages a moment of clarity on the bog when the ghosts of the past speak to the narrator and confront his present state of nostalgia. In this respect, both O'Faolain and O'Connor suggest that one way to approach these issues is to revisit the past by going on the bog and confronting the ghosts of the violent revolutionary struggles that continue to haunt the nation. Haunting can be a frightening experience because it reveals the social violence of the past in the present, which is surrounded by and steeped in the decaying idealism of that past. Regardless, Bonaparte and Noble, and the unnamed narrator in 'A Meeting', reflect upon the sites of their haunting experiences and revisit the past at the end of each story.

In both stories, a critique of Irish nationalism clearly emerges through the direct engagement of the bog. O'Connor and O'Faolain use the mutable and uncertain qualities of the bog to question the certainty and stability often associated with the idea of the nation. 'Guests' and 'A Meeting' are two literary examples that draw out the inherent contradiction of nationalism; the spirit of the nation can only materialise if oppressive powers are neutralised, but in doing so it is often replaced by similar oppressive and reactionary powers. O'Connor and O'Faolain challenge the idea of nation as a fixed and attainable space by casting it against the bog, an unfixed, uncertain, and Gothic space. The nebulous qualities of the bog reflect and refract the uncertain qualities of the real and imagined nation. O'Connor and O'Faolain use the ghost story as a narrative of the nation, but they do so in order to confront nationalist sentiment of people like Corkery, rather than support it.

Building on O'Connor's and O'Faolain's challenge to nationalism through narratives of haunting and ambiguity, the next chapter examines how the topographical and Gothic elements of the bog confuse and raise questions about some of the entrenched politics of colonisation in Northern Ireland during the Troubles. In the same ways bogs create congruent oppositions through ghosts, bog bodies in Heaney's early poems and prose challenge notions of the human and non-human, temporal and atemporal, and political and apolitical through how they mediate history and culture.

4

Mapping Gothic Bog Bodies

You can take the person from the bog, but you cannot take the bog
from the person.[1]

– old Irish proverb

The act of writing itself might be considered a form of mapping or
a cartographic activity.[2]

– Robert T. Tally Jr., *Spatiality*

Troubled Bog Bodies

From 1966 to 1978, Seamus Heaney compiled four volumes of poetry
and one collection of non-fiction prose that addressed, among other
things, the phenomenon of the bog and its role in Irish culture. Heaney
produced the bulk of his 'bog poems' after major political tensions and
sectarian violence erupted in 1969 during what is known as 'the Troubles'
in Northern Ireland.[3] This period of unrest serves as the third political
era related to colonisation under scrutiny here, after the Land Wars of
the 1870s and 1880s (Chapter 2) and the Irish War of Independence
from 1919 to 1921 (Chapter 3). Heaney turns to the bog in his literary
works, like Stoker, Corkery, O'Connor, and O'Faolain before him, to
explore some of the contestations of the period. However, the focus of
this chapter is not entirely about the Troubles, inasmuch as this period of
Irish history demands careful, step-by-step negotiations and is therefore
too broad to cover in one chapter.[4] The sectarian conflict in Northern
Ireland nevertheless serves as an important backdrop to Heaney's bog
poems and a way of understanding the use of the bog as a metaphoric
and material symbol to address his own troubled connection to Irish
politics and culture.

4.1 Heaney standing in turf rows in Bellaghy Bog, Co. Derry,
Northern Ireland (photo by Bobbie Hanvey)

In this chapter, I aim to show how Heaney's bog body poems function as a form of literary cartography. A traditional map provides lines, dots, and shapes that simulate the delineations of land and deploy names to classify and describe topographies, whereas literary maps are a way of plotting real and imagined spaces more clearly through literary works. Focusing mostly on bog bodies, originally made famous through P.V. Glob's book *The Bog People* (published in Danish in 1965 and translated into English in 1968), Heaney diagrams physical and imagined features of the bodies found in the bogs. Bog bodies, similar to the bogs from which they emerge, also elicit both postcolonial and Gothic associations (see Fig. 4.2). According to David Kennedy:

Reading terrorism in terms of ritual, sanctuary and the sacrifice highlights the particular role of the body. The body in the present both narrates and is narrated by acts of violence. Through this narrating and narration the body itself comes to function as a site and transcript of the recursive history exemplified in the origin myths.

Kennedy then concludes, 'the victims of violence become literal transcripts of this recursive history'.[5] Rather than survey Heaney's bog bodies as agents of terrorism mediated through sacrificial Iron Age bodies, a theme Kennedy and others have productively explored, this chapter focuses on how bog bodies are used as transcripts, not only 'narrated through acts of violence', but also mapped or charted by Heaney to provide connections between the bog and culture. Linkages between literary cartography and the body are sensorial and experiential as much as material. In some of Heaney's bog poems, for instance, bog bodies serve as real and symbolic maps for readers to navigate through notions of the haptic (tactile) and the Gothic body. Later in this chapter, after explaining Heaney's cartographic connection to the bog through his own body, we will look at the poem 'The Grauballe Man' through the notion of haptic visuality, which serves as a way of visualising images of the bog body through simultaneous senses of touch and sight, or seeing through touch. Also in 'Punishment', Heaney maps bodies in the bog poems as both human and non-human, or what Gothic scholar Kelly Hurley calls the 'abhuman', which is a type of cast-off object (or abject) in between human and non-human form, used in Gothic fiction to depict monsters or other unexplainable bodies dislocated from society.[6]

Reading bodies in the bog poems could help illuminate slippages of time, as Kennedy proposes, which allow comparisons between past ritual sacrifices and present-day acts of terrorism and violence. There are, however, other ways to understand Heaney's body maps that expose less examined areas, such as the haptic and abhuman body. Kennedy argues that the 'body as re-enactable and legitimating origin and as literal and historical transcript is central to Seamus Heaney's "bog poems"'.[7] While I agree with Kennedy's main assertion here – the body serves as something we can decode – I shall differ in my approach to the extent that instead of examining the body as transcript, based upon what he calls 'text and narration',[8] I investigate how these bog body poems create a type of literary cartography that draws from both physical and imaginative elements, ones quite similar to examinations made of the bog itself in previous chapters of this book. Bog bodies, viewed as maps, tell stories and can be deciphered in various ways. 'To ask for a map,' claims Peter Turchi in *Maps of the Imagination* (2004), 'is to say, "Tell me a story".'[9] Mapping the bodies draws out how they tell a different story about Heaney's bog poems. The bog and the bodies found in them are both able to be creatively mapped and charted, despite their distinctive differences; they are also part of the larger political and social circumstances of the Troubles that underpin some of the bog poems.

The ethno-religious or sectarian conflict commonly referred to as 'the Troubles' initially stemmed from some of the social injustices and political incongruities occurring in Northern Ireland between Protestants and Catholics in the 1960s. The modern Troubles, however, date back to when the Treaty of 1922 separated the six counties of Northern Ireland from the twenty-six counties in the south (originally the Irish Free State that later became the Republic of Ireland). The Protestant majority in Northern Ireland, still a part of Britain and yet separate from it, maintained political power from 1922 to the 1960s, when the Catholic minority began to speak out vociferously against an increasingly anti-democratic governance. As David Lloyd explains, this outcome created a 'self-governing enclave' with an 'artificially constructed majority of Protestant citizens'.[10]

The problems in Northern Ireland partly resulted from a Protestant majority holding 95 per cent of top public service positions, which not only created a system of income, civic, and legal inequality, but also allowed for systemic manipulation of voting systems (called gerrymandering), giving Protestants more elected candidates and therefore guaranteeing constant majority rule for over fifty years. The largely disenfranchised Catholic communities lived with lower wages, fewer jobs, inadequate housing, and other social inequalities compared to the Protestant communities. Many scholars have already marked and subsequently explained this history as a significant part of postcolonial Ireland, and I briefly introduce it here and focus on the Catholic position to contextualise Heaney's involvement as both an artist and individual who lived amidst the Troubles until he moved to Co. Wicklow in 1974.

4.2 Torso and head of Clonycavan Man, Co. Meath, demonstrating the Gothic or 'abhuman' qualities of the bog bodies. National Museum of Ireland Bog Bodies Research Project.

Heaney's bog poems remain linked to the sectarian conflicts on some level because of the turbulent history from which both he and they arose. Many Catholic nationalists from Northern Ireland were encouraged and in many ways expected to respond to the escalating conflict. Heaney chose to respond to the political violence partially through the unconventional and yet familiar landform of the bog because of its symbolic and real qualities that mark similar motifs of uncertainty in Heaney's own poetic voice. The bog serves as an ideal metaphor for Heaney's poetics of space and history, but it also highlights political connections to the actual geography in which Heaney lived, just forty miles from the city of Derry/Londonderry.[11] The west of the city, referred to as the Bogside, is where the majority of Catholics live. The name 'Bogside' disparagingly associates with the sinking, decomposing, and stagnant mire of peat bog. In addition, the Bogside is also where the events of 'Bloody Sunday' occurred on 30 January 1972, a day when the British army opened fire on civilians marching for civil rights, killing fourteen people.[12] The name Bogside also derives from the fact that many of the impoverished Catholics worked as labourers out on the bogs, just outside of Derry; in his poem 'Digging', for instance, Heaney shows how his family came from a line of farm and bog labourers (see Fig.4.1 of Heaney standing in Bellaghy Bog near where he grew up).

Heaney uses the bog as a general symbol and metaphor to address the politics of colonisation in Northern Ireland. However, the bog also serves as a terrestrial and symbolic space that draws writers to investigate the contradictions of political violence more than it serves as an attempt to speak with certainty about them. In an otherwise uncertain and unstable situation, Heaney uses the bog to explore issues he otherwise might not have been able to speak about as a Catholic from Derry in the 1960s and 1970s.[13] In this regard, the ways Heaney's poems represent bog bodies and the bogs in which they are found as creative maps (both connected to and separate from the Troubles) serve as a key to understanding some of the links to the postcolonial Gothic and the bog.

Heaney, as a cultural, political, literary, and international figure, has received a formidable amount of critical attention.[14] While many critics acknowledge bogs and bog bodies in Heaney's poetry, they tend to position them as purely mythic symbols or totalising concepts functioning as portholes into the Irish psyche or imagination. Most critics agree that the bog in Heaney's poetry and non-fiction prose serves as a loaded vector for fruitful interrogation. The disagreement largely exists in what specific subjects the bog stimulates and how Heaney arrives at such themes. Debates widely vary, of course, but the major arguments generally range from the ethno-religious conflicts in Northern Ireland, national 'soil' and Irish identity, and the feminisation of Irish land and bodies, to the aestheticisation of violence and archaeological metaphors between pre-history and the present.[15] Briefly outlining some of the criticism that directly examines the bog from literary, cultural, anthropological, archaeological, geographical, and postcolonial perspectives demonstrates the range of interdisciplinary approaches that foreground this chapter and Heaney's association with bogs.

In his first book on Heaney, literary scholar Eugene O'Brien asserts that the bog poems 'have formed a powerful symbol of the racial memory of the nationalist community, a memory which allowed violence to thrive in the thirty years of Northern Irish "troubles"'.[16] According to O'Brien, Heaney probes the past in the peat in order to explore the psychic history of Ireland and how such a past uncovers a 'nationalist-republican narrative of history'.[17] O'Brien claims Heaney's verb/metaphor of 'digging' examines the Irish past as it relates to the Irish present during the 1960s and 1970s in Northern Ireland. In *Seamus Heaney* (1998), Helen Vendler carefully considers that 'the bog poems are, for the poet, as much a replication of self as a symbolic representation of history'.[18] For Vendler, the shift between Heaney's collections *Door in the Dark* (1969) and *North* (1975) occurred when the quaint archaeologies of preserved objects in the bogs, such as butter or the elk in a poem like 'Bogland', became associated with sectarian violence. Vendler, like many other critics, argues that the poems in *North* respond directly to Northern Irish politics, whereas the earlier three volumes of poetry did not as much. Heaney represents a poetry of 'undoing, of dilution, of loss' that ultimately leads to 'the processes of unmaking',[19] a point I later argue that comes through in 'Punishment' as a disturbance and destabilisation of the persona/speaking subject itself. What is partly missing in these two accounts is Heaney's ability to chart and diagram meanings not only in the bogs, but also in the concurrent and yet opposing qualities that are grafted onto the Gothicised bodies found in the bogs. Both O'Brien's and Vendler's books, while illuminating and incisively argued, do not explicitly discuss some of the Gothic elements found in his poetry.

If Heaney's earlier work contains Gothic elements, it may be because it focused on the dead through the metaphor of national terror and sacrificed bodies, or what Vendler describes more obliquely as 'the appurtenances of archeology' that are 'blood-tinged and corpse-haunted'.[20] John Wilson Foster comparably remarks, 'Heaney's bog poems are a longer sequence in that horror film [of Northern Irish history].'[21] Both critics briefly allude to a Gothic aesthetic embedded in Heaney's bog poems, but they do so without drawing any further analysis to it. Functioning as a Gothic space or 'landscape of fear', Heaney also acknowledges the bog as a way to accentuate terrifying and macabre circumstances surrounding sectarian violence. The Gothic flourishes in zones of uncertainty and social upheaval, whether writers fixate on the actions of disorder or not.[22] While Heaney's work has not previously been correlated with Irish Gothic literature, his bog poems resonate in the Gothic archive because the bog remains a Gothic space with its contradictory qualities and unexplainable phenomena.

A case might even be made that the Gothic qualities of the bog are what initially attracted Heaney to them in his poetry and prose. In his first collection of selected prose, *Preoccupations* (1980), which was written between 1968 and 1978, he recalls the supernatural link to bogs:

> This was the realm of bogeys. We'd heard about a mystery man who haunted the fringes of the bog here, we talked about mankeepers and mosscheepers, creatures uncatalogued by any naturalist, but none the less real for that. What was a mosscheeper, anyway, if not the soft, malicious sound the word itself made, a siren of collapsing sibilants coaxing you out towards bog pools lidded with innocent grass, quicksands and quagmires?[23]

In *North*, Heaney again signals to his own Gothic impulse in the second part of the poem, 'Mossbawn: Two Poems in Dedication'. In 'The Seed Cutters', he references Renaissance landscape painter of the sixteenth century Pieter Brueghel the Elder. Many celebrate Brueghel not only for his depictions of peasants in rural settings, but also for his apocalyptic depictions of people in landscapes, such as *The Triumph of Death* (1562), that have continued to be recognised as part of the Gothic tradition in visual art. Heaney writes, 'They seem hundreds of years away. Brueghel, / You'll know them if I can get them true'.[24] Heaney indirectly references Brueghel's depictions of death and chaos, which may seem historically remote, as a parallel to the present sectarian conflicts in Northern Ireland. The Gothic elements that appear in some of the bog poems also reflect some of the actual scientific qualities of bogs that have attracted more than just literary and cultural scholars.

Many scholars outside of literary or cultural studies continue to examine Heaney's bog poems through geography, anthropology, and archaeology. The geographer Dianne Meredith argues that Heaney's poetic imagery of bogs actually provides insights into humanistic geography. She considers how 'place-creation' is subjective and based not only on cultural perceptions, but also on environmental factors. Rather than using the 'bog landscape as a metaphor for the Irish psyche' or an 'icon for Ireland', according to Meredith, Heaney uses the bog as a way into the bodies submerged in them to uncover other uncertainties.[25] This is not to say that an allegory does not exist between the bog and the Irish psyche, but that such a characterisation overstates his approach and reinstitutes some of the overdetermined criticism of his poetry – that is, Heaney + bog + Ireland = Irish imagination. Bogs, and the preserved bodies in them, create other worlds, some of which directly connect to Irish politics and some that do so more obliquely, as in the case of memory.

The anthropologist Stuart McLean argues that it is the transformative power of collective memory drawn from the bog bodies that enables both human and non-human understanding.[26] Memory is not limited to human understanding, but instead materialises from the bogs through a process of collecting these memories from bodies, whether they are through poetry (in the case of Heaney) or through technologies (CT scans and carbon dating of the corpses), philosophies, or geography. Similar to McLean's focus on bodies as collective memory holders, this chapter also underscores how bodies serve as markers to be mapped; in the poem 'The Grauballe Man' bog bodies can be read as a memory map, holding both collective and individual memories. Heaney's mapped bodies uncover the depths of memory as something that is more textured and nuanced than an overt political impulse.

In a short section on Heaney, the archaeologist Karin Sanders deduces in her book focused on bog bodies that the bog serves as a place of national Irish identity in Heaney's poetry.[27] Sanders' somewhat totalising archaeo-cultural analysis regarding Heaney's 'identity', resembling Meredith's geographical claim about the Irish psyche, examines more closely the impact bog bodies have had on what she calls the 'archeological uncanny', rather than providing an extensive literary analysis of the poems themselves.[28] Sanders maintains that Heaney aims 'to mend a conflicted present in Ireland by understanding the depth of the bog', and in so doing affirms 'the poet's love for his country' through 'ritual and process'.[29] What is neglected here is Heaney's ambivalence, or even a type of disturbance, about what 'love for his country' actually means. What is really at stake in terms of a political commitment to a nation? Instead of offering clear answers, Heaney uses the bog as a medium, mirroring his own destabilising position, to explore both national and personal incongruities and ambiguities further.

Lastly, Lloyd – who offers one of the more pointed and often-cited postcolonial critiques of Heaney's earlier poetry – upholds that Heaney continually returns to the intersection where 'place, identity and language mesh'.[30] For Lloyd, Heaney echoes previous articulations of cultural nationalism in the nineteenth century, but he avoids political specificity by concentrating on aesthetics. Lloyd argues that Heaney's poetry, despite his reliance on aesthetic representation, is in fact political and continues to raise the central question that Irish nationalist writers have been asking since at least the eighteenth century: what exactly is Irish identity?[31] Lloyd ultimately proposes that Heaney reduces 'history to myth', which has the effect, in addition to creating an identity of place, to aestheticise violence.[32] Lloyd's densely reasoned chapter understates the ambivalence in Heaney's poetry, what Deane identifies elsewhere as 'that note of uncertainty, of timorousness which recurs time and again both in his poetry and in his prose'.[33] Viewing Heaney's bog bodies as literary maps highlights such destabilising ambivalence, reflecting similar qualities of the bog, and offers ways to chart bogs in the postcolonial Gothic.

All of these critical readings offer important insights and form powerful responses to Heaney's bog poems from many disciplinary and theoretical perspectives. Building upon and challenging these critical approaches, as well as others in this chapter, I want to argue that bog bodies – drawing them into conversation together as a constellation of symbols and physical objects – serve as maps that can be charted and interpreted in Heaney's poetry and prose. In Heaney's bog poems there remains a fundamental reluctance in tone and meaning about his commitment to politics and the nation. The indeterminate elements of the bog in his work allow for this sort of slippage when national identities, histories, and memories are being re-examined in violent times. On one level, a slippage of time and certainty resembles qualities of bogs and bodies found in them. On another level, his poetry draws a map of the bog bodies that reveal some of their uncertain histories and features (through personal and collective memories). Maps are, after all, fundamentally flawed and subjective documents and body maps are doubly so. Heaney turns to bogs and bodies found in them to purposefully create such uncertainty about some of the polarising sectarian debates in the late 1960s and 1970s, a move that would seem to contradict the whole project of mapping.

Mapping the body through literature might be best approached through a process known as literary cartography, which examines written creative work as a type of map through actual physical features and metaphorical images. Literary cartographers plot certain points and draw various lines that result in a literary map, whether it is a poem, a play, or a novel. According to Graham Huggan, in his formative study *Territorial Disputes* (1994), the literary map is both a 'product and process: it represents both an encoded document of a specific environment and a network of perpetually recoded messages passing between the various mapmakers and map readers who participate in the event of cartographic communication'.[34] It seems for Heaney that the 'encoded document' is the body (or bog in certain cases) described in specific poems, where the 'product and process' is negotiated through the mapmaker (poet/writer), map (work), and audience (reader/decipherer). Literary maps, like bogs, create a Thirdspace because they are both real and also imagined spaces rife with contradictions and imbrications. The spatial theorist Robert Tally similarly explains that there is 'an almost simultaneous figurative and literal aspect of literary cartography'.[35] Bog bodies are equally simultaneously literal and figurative. For example, the bodies in the poems are concurrently human and non-human, liquid and solid, prehistoric and contemporary, temporal and atemporal, feminised and masculine, and political and apolitical.

Heaney's poetic maps describe the topographic contours of the bogs, but they also chart the anatomical and imagined features of the bog bodies that have been famously unearthed from the bogs and touted as archaeological discoveries. Moynagh Sullivan further contends the body of a poem (form), particularly in the case of Heaney, is also simultaneously the body of Ireland (metaphor).[36] Body maps are where individual and collective stories, as well as recollections, overlap and exist instantaneously. In this regard, body mapping is a process that recognises, through organic objects (bogs or bog bodies), the imagination associated with collective and individual stories.

Heaney flatly describes why the bog serves as an ideal vector for his poetry:

> I had been vaguely wishing to write a poem about bogland, chiefly because it is a landscape that has a strange assuaging effect on me, one with associations reaching back into early childhood ... So I began to get an idea of bog as the memory of the landscape, or as a landscape that remembered everything that happened in and to it.[37]

Mapping and bodies – drawing from memory, geography, and nation in Heaney's poetry – both remain significantly linked to colonial politics and a Gothic aesthetic. Bog bodies can be mapped and colonised, while they also conjure Gothic imagery of the tenuous line between living and dead.

This chapter principally looks at five bog poems. The first section begins with 'Digging' and 'Bogland'. Both poems are examples of earlier literary maps that stem from and reveal Heaney's own embodied experience and connection to the bog. Although neither poem technically has bog bodies *in* them, they each show bodies *on* bogs and reveal Heaney's synesthetic attraction to bodies and bogs. The following section illustrates how Heaney charts both the textual and physical bodies in his poetry. Heaney's poem 'The Tollund Man' offers a more journalistic approach to the body, which serves as a clearer model for body mapping that later becomes more complex and nuanced in other poems. Next I examine 'The Grauballe Man', which is probably considered Heaney's most famous bog poem. The quasi-optical feel of the poem provokes a visually haptic response (seeing through tactility) that serves as another form of body mapping. As Heaney's bog aesthetic develops, the haptic becomes more pronounced within it. Bodies/corpses can also be mapped in the poem through memory, what are called 'memory maps', which is a way to record subjective memories tied to specific political geographies. I conclude with the poem 'Punishment', which reveals the symbolic and physical mapping of a feminised abhuman Gothic body. The poem shows how disturbance and desire are used in oppositional ways to create an abhuman bog body, a body that is both human and non-human and yet neither. The process of literary cartography allows us to examine various mapped bodies in Heaney's poetry as both products and processes of real (physical, organic, corporeal) and imagined (symbol and memory) bogs.

Digging/Mapping/Writing

Heaney's interest in bogs formed early in his life and subsequently became a topic of artistic and cultural importance throughout his career (see Fig. 4.3). He and the Irish painter T.P. Flanagan, to whom he dedicated his poem 'Bogland', would travel to the neighbouring Co. Donegal in order to seek artistic inspiration in the countryside. Flanagan has noted, similarly to Heaney, that the bog is 'the fundamental Irish landscape' with connections to a pagan and supernatural past.[38] The bog hoards

4.3 Heaney standing in turf stacks in Bellaghy Bog, Co. Derry, Northern Ireland (photo by Bobbie Hanvey)

objects that hold culture, history, and memory, all of which are charted in Heaney's first ten years of published poetry. 'With the bog as a locus of preservation,' Heaney recalls, 'that guaranteed a link to a verifying history and culture.'[39]

By way of introduction to this section, I want to provide a citation from 'Kinship', a longer poem in *North* with six sections, because it plots a 'real' and physical bog. This particular poem also serves as a synecdoche for all of Heaney's bog poems, where the confusion of the physical and symbolic bog fold together and contain traces of Gothic and political markers. In the second section of the poem, Heaney paints a particularly vivid picture of bogs:

Quagmire, swampland, morass:
the slime kingdoms,
domains of the cold-blooded,
of mud pads and dirtied eggs.

But *bog*
meaning soft,
the fall of windless rain,
pupil of amber.

In the opening two quatrains, Heaney contrasts two perceptions of the bog, setting them apart and then talking about the aliveness, the soft fecundity, and fertility of memory grafted on the bog.

Ruminant ground,
digestion of mollusk
and seed-pod,
deep pollen bin.

Earth-pantry, bone-vault,
sun-bank, embalmer
of votive goods
and sabred fugitives.

Beginning with the word 'Quagmire' in the first stanza and then questioning 'But *bog*' with its 'Ruminant ground' in the second and third stanzas, the poet juxtaposes traditional notions of bogs as wastelands against the idea that bogs are revealers of memory, with 'votive goods' that provide ways to discover and explore their depths.

Insatiable bride.
Sword-swallower,
casket, midden,
floe of history.

Ground that will strip
its dark side,
nesting ground,
Outback of my mind. (121–2; original emphasis)

This poetic description demonstrates the seductive wetness of the bog that descends into the depths of time and space, a reason writers and readers alike are attracted to its muddy waters. Even the formal elements of the poem descend narrowly down and deep onto the page. In addition, these six stanzas demonstrate how bogs are living spaces where human history continually endures political conflicts in the 'domains of the cold-blooded' in the 'dark side' with 'sabred fugitives' and 'nesting ground'. The words demanding and dangerous might best characterise the bog, in what Heaney labels 'the slime kingdoms', but these adjectives also summon the political and horrific climate associated with bogs in Northern Ireland. These elements overshadow all of Heaney's bog poems in some way or another, but before moving to the mapped bog bodies, the poems 'Digging' and 'Bogland' lay the groundwork for later bog body poems through the speaker's own embodied relationship to the bog.

In 'Digging', from *Death of a Naturalist* (1966), Heaney creates an obvious analogy between digging potatoes or cutting turf in the bog and writing, another act of digging and foraging deep within. Although Foster notes that Heaney's early poetry 'startled with its physicality',[40] employing the term 'physicality' as a descriptive term limits the imagined qualities of the early poetry, particularly in how these poems foreground later poems about mapping bodies. But using the word 'physicality' to describe Heaney's poetry has another unintended consequence in how it signals corporeal features related to the body. Physicality can reflect a form of stasis, similar to superficial perceptions of bogs, whereas mapping entails the idea that the physical (whether topography or bodies) triggers many narratives through imaginative forms of expression. The verb 'digging' serves as a metaphor for anything that explores, disinters, or investigates. The verb indicates an obvious connection to 'physicality', but it also contains the real and imagined oppositions of unity; although digging is a physical action, it signals an imagined excavation into something unknown or unexplored deep within something.

While Heaney makes an explicit comparison with writing, he also establishes this relationship through mapping. Probing the depths of the bog provides an effective symbol for exploring our own inner unknown, the obscurity of our psyches. The bog poems attempt to locate and map geographies, histories, material objects, and memories for others to decipher meaning. As a way of doing this Heaney first attempts to dig them out with his spade/pen as he famously implies in 'Digging'. The metaphor bog/poem also extends to the idea of a map. Instead of just 'digging' in the bog, Heaney is also mapping the bog; in some cases the map locates artefacts (such as in the poems 'Bogland' and 'Relic of Memory') and the unconscious, and in other cases it finds bodies.

Mapping, like writing and digging, comprises both physical and imaginative terrains. The bog serves as an archaeological site of creation and inspiration in 'Digging'; the poem also imagines histories and genealogies threaded in the bog. Heaney admits that the poem 'Digging' was 'dug up' because it was 'laid down in me years before' as a child exploring bogs in Co. Derry.[41] The poem begins with Heaney's sensorial responses to digging, another foregrounding link to visual and haptic experience, where one can hear a 'clean rasping sound' where the 'spade sinks into gravelley ground' when the father is 'digging' (3). The digging action of the father attracts the speaker's attention through the body's sensation of movement. The act of digging is a process of excavation, particularly since the act of digging attempts to locate an object, such as potatoes for farmers or bodies for archaeologists. Digging generates body sensations – 'his straining rump' and 'Stooping in rhythm through potato drills' – and investigates the terrain through movement and feeling.[42]

The literal spade is an inadequate tool for the speaker's own form of cultural labour as a writer. He demonstrates a clear relationship between the spade and pen. Of the pen, the speaker claims, 'I'll dig with it' (4). Both are, in many ways, extensions of each other and interchangeable as textual metaphors. The pen and spade are essential tools for exploration and mapping because both provide the terrestrial (digging in the earth) and imaginative (digging in one's history and past) elements involved with the mapping process. Just as the 'curt cuts of an edge' of the bog provide a chart of the physical ground, the 'living roots' of the imagination 'waken' in the speaker's 'head' (4). The spade is one-dimensional and limited as a tool to explore the bog, whereas the symbolic pen contains multitudes of possibilities not limited to the terrestrial but expansive of memory and genealogies. Writing, then, is mapping. It is a means by which one structures personal experience; it is a way of conveying something to others just like the process and purpose of a map; and it functions as a process and product, always in flux and never exact.[43] Literary cartography remains both metaphorical (digging/writing process) and tangible (physical and textual product).

In 'Digging', as well as in other bog body poems, the body mediates this process as a digger/mapper/writer. Heaney archaeo-culturally excavates, or maps, as a writer: digging/writing with the body on the bog generates a way to articulate this as both product and process. It is the very presence of the body that generates inspiration for the poet in 'Digging', in addition to the sensorial details of the 'potato mould', the 'squelch and slap/Of soggy peat', or 'the curt cuts of an edge', all forging a connection as 'living roots awaken in my head' (4). By evoking the visual, aural, and olfactory senses, the poem suggests that the process and product of digging/mapping/ writing the bog comes first from the physical body, which digs the turf and becomes mapped onto the textual body of the poem. The tactile sensation of 'slicing', the visual depiction of 'heaving sods' above 'his shoulder', and the sounds of 'digging' all arouse multi-sensual embodied actions, whether it is digging, writing, or even mapping the bog (4).

Ending with the idea that the pen will serve as the digging implement instead of the gun at the beginning of the poem, or even a spade, does not simply prove what Lloyd claims is a common 'aesthetic resolution' found in Heaney's poetry.[44] Rather, the ending indicates an ambiguous structural metaphor of exploration; the process of digging is to disinter without any way of knowing the outcome or product. Digging/mapping/ writing all function as actions that investigate and probe rather than show certainty. Choosing the gun as opposed to the spade might appeal to nationalist militarism – one of the choices offered as a way forward – but the speaker of the poem instead chooses the pen as an instrument that confuses and surveys political violence more than it aestheticises or promotes it. Mappers/writers do not decipher their encoded documents; they create them.

If Heaney's formal impulse for mapping bogs appears in 'Digging', then his experiential and imaginative instincts develop further through his own body in 'Bogland', another poem about bogs in *Door in the Dark*. The speaker of the poem recalls some compelling cultural objects found in the bog, such as the 'skeleton' from the 'Great Irish Elk' and 'butter' in the peat over 'a hundred years' old (41). The relics that Heaney describes are actual memories from his childhood. Mappers, as people who literally make claims about land, subjectively chart symbolic co-ordinates as well. Literary maps are similarly subjective documents; in fact, they often materialise from real geographies but thrive in imaginative realms. As the speaker claims, 'The ground itself is kind, black butter' (41).

In *Sensuous Geographies* (1994), Paul Rodaway argues, 'Although maps depict what is actually visible, they also can "visualize" what is not visible in everyday experience, and through the selectivity of the map-maker certain elements are shown and given relative importance whilst others are not.'[45] Heaney infuses these sensorial evocations that develop through his own body experience into his literary maps. He recollects, 'As a child I used to imagine my helpless body whistling down a black shaft forever and ever: now I imagine the imagination itself sinking endlessly down and under that heathery expanse.'[46] Heaney subtly plots out this experience in 'Bogland', setting the foundation for later bog poems. The speaker states, 'Our pioneers keep striking/Inwards and downwards', with the result that 'Every layer they strip/Seems camped on before' (42). The visceral experience of seeing the elk and butter in the bog transitions to his ancestors who continually search to unearth deeper cultural experiences that have been 'camped on before'. The pioneers, like his family, use their bodies on the bog through both labour (farming) and culture (artefacts), exploring inwards and downwards. Heaney equally uses his body to map the bogs both inwardly (the personal and familial) and downwardly (the historical) through his own cultural labour as a writer.

Rodaway also maintains that geographical experience is fundamentally mediated in the body; it begins and ends there.[47] The combination of the bog (as a physical part of geography) and the body (as a mediator) allows Heaney to draw literary maps through personal experiences that might otherwise stay buried or unidentifiable. As a child labouring on bogs, Heaney comments on what he calls his 'genuine obsession' with them:

> It was an illiterate pleasure that I took in the landscape. The smell of turf smoke, for example, has a terrific nostalgic effect on me. It has to do with the script that's written into your senses from the minute you begin to breathe. Now for me, 'bogland' is an important word in that script and the first poem I ever wrote that seemed to me to have elements of the symbolic about it was 'Bogland'.[48]

Heaney's description and ultimate lure to the bog contains many sensuous and symbolic qualities related to the physical geography. The bog's essence was 'written' into his 'senses' at an early age and that enhanced his ability to understand the physical and imagined qualities that he was then able to chart specifically through bodies in his poems. Heaney recollects, 'I loved the textures of the bog banks after the spade had done its work in the turf-face'.[49] The process of mapping these memories through sense perception has a lasting effect for the reader, as well as the poet, and moves beyond other analyses of 'Bogland' that only relate to family or community.

In his essay 'Mossbawn', Heaney further describes how he used his own body to establish an early, and in many ways, embodied experience between the body and bog. When describing the 'wet corners, flooded wastes, soft rushy bottoms' of bogs, he recalls:

> It is as if I am betrothed to them, and I believe my betrothal happened one summer evening, thirty years ago, when another boy and myself stripped to the white country skin and bathed in a moss-hole, treading the liver-thick mud, unsettling a smoky muck off the bottom and coming out smeared and weedy and darkened.[50]

Here, Heaney partly became a living bog body through his experience of bathing in the bog waters. The word 'betrothal' underscores a recurring sensual desire rooted in his embodied experience of the bogs, a point further explored in 'Punishment'. In this sense, Heaney's ability to map the bodies in the bogs stems from his experience of mediating the sensual qualities of the bog through his own body. Rodaway's claim that the mapmaker selectively includes the elements that sustain greater importance underscores Heaney's mediated experiences displayed in this excerpt. For Heaney, this is the body.

'Bogland' additionally functions as a doorway to later bog poems. Since it is the only poem with the word bog in the title, it accentuates the importance of bogs and the ways in which they reveal multi-dimensions. 'When I called my second book *Door in the Dark*,' Heaney later discloses,

> I intended to gesture towards this idea of poetry as a point of entry into the buried life of the feelings or as a point of exit for it. Words themselves are doors; Janus is to a certain extent their deity, looking back to a ramification of roots and associations and forward to a clarification of sense and meaning.[51]

Although words refer to doors here, he also defines the appeal of the bog as a similar 'door' that looks backwards to the past as much as forward to the future to unearth buried lives and bring to light new futures. Bog bodies, for example, surface in the past but will continue to be mapped in future literary works through their own real and imagined timeless qualities. Hence, the invocation of Janus – the double-faced god of transitions and beginnings symbolising doors or passages – resembles the opposition and concurrent qualities of the bog, as well as the bodies in them. The bog poems remain productive vehicles to chart paths to the 'buried life of the feelings'. However, Heaney moves quickly from looking at bogs as doors to examining the bodies – equally uncanny and charged symbolic and physical objects – as other kinds of doors that establish continuities and discontinuities between time and space.

Jay Parini hails 'Bogland' to be 'a watershed poem in the Heaney corpus' because it 'refuses to go much beyond a literal representation until the last line: "the wet centre is bottomless"'.[52] Parini also acknowledges elements in 'Bogland' that develop further in later bog poems. 'Bogland' serves as a 'watershed poem' not only because of its obvious literal representation of the bog topography that ultimately affords his poetry international audiences, but also because it demonstrates the connection between the actual bogland, as a personal and collective geography for Heaney, and Heaney's body as a cultural digger/mapper/writer of it. In 'Bogland', Heaney entered 'into a place' that he 'knew already', a place that 'now promised to reveal still more'.[53] Instead of digging in the bogs, as he does in 'Bogland' and 'Digging', Heaney's later poems focus on specific objects – namely bodies – found in the bog that reveal complex, rich, and mysterious maps.

Bodies out of the Bog

Heaney's specific interest in bog bodies came about when reading *The Bog People*, written by Danish archaeologist Peter Vilhelm Glob. In fact, both of his poems 'The Tollund Man' and 'The Grauballe Man' focus on two real bog bodies located by turf-cutters in Denmark.[54] Glob's pioneering archaeological digs of bog bodies discovered the two male figures named in Heaney's poems. In his 1996 opening speech 'Face to Face with Your Past', for the exhibition of bog bodies at the Silkeborg Museum in Denmark, Heaney discussed his 'discovery' of Glob's book and the way he wrote 'so lovingly' about the 'boggy landscape', recalling that it 'was all completely familiar to me'.[55] He went on to point out that bogs could be physical, imaginative, and embodied. Upon first seeing bog bodies, Heaney admits to have experienced them in his 'very bones'.[56] Reciting the old Irish proverb, 'you can take the man from the bog, but you cannot take the bog from the man', Heaney suggests that the reason we are still discussing the relevance of bog bodies is precisely because you cannot 'take the bog from the man'.[57]

With Heaney's comments in mind, mapping the bodies is as important as describing the bog. 'If bogs are slippery,' Sanders reasons, 'the bodies in them are doubly so.'[58] Bodies themselves are bog-like; they are organic liquid and solid matter containing over 70 per cent water and exhibiting an accretion of layers of skin, muscle, bone, and organs. Scientists have been able to determine the date of death in each of the bodies found in the bogs through carbon dating the microscopic pollen grains preserved in the tissues, a process that can also be duplicated with other items found in bogs. The Grauballe Man's death, for instance, dates back to 310 CE.[59] But he was discovered much later, in 1952, during a peat-cutting operation at the Nebelgård Fen, just outside the village of Grauballe in Jutland, Denmark. After carbon-14 dating hair from the bog body in 1996, the date of death was pushed back even earlier to the European Iron Age, 290 BCE.[60] Heaney sets out in his poems to verify, explore, and map forms of history and culture through some of the bodies found in the bogs. The bog bodies, which, for Heaney, build upon his interest in how bodies mediate between the terrestrial and imagined, become one of the concentrations of his next two volumes of poetry.

'The Tollund Man', from *Wintering Out* (1972), serves as possibly the most objective and journalistic bog body poem. It contains a cautious structure and tone that the other poems do not. 'The Tollund Man' provides a blueprint for later, more controversial bog poems in *North* about conflicts and cultural accretions. For example, the poems 'The Grauballe Man', 'Bog Queen', 'Kinship', and 'Punishment' all present a more binocular view of past and present, archaeological and contemporary, and sexual and religious.[61] Elmer Andrews maintains that 'The Tollund Man' serves as a pilgrimage for the poet balancing 'sacrificial demands' and 'individual values'.[62] In his analysis of Heaney's work, Kennedy focuses on the body, what he calls 'corpses as sublime art objects', which Heaney takes from Glob and appropriates as a 'contemplative form of address'.[63] Andrews' and Kennedy's positions highlight important strains of collective ritual and aesthetic impulses in the poem.

These critical commentaries are helpful in understanding the links between the archaeological, sexual, and religious up to a point; the physical bodies tend to be an afterthought. The bog poems show the uncanny phenomenon of bodies in the bog that have been found through various turf-cutting operations in both Ireland and Denmark – what Heaney calls in 'The Tollund Man', 'Trove of the turfcutters'/Honeycombed workings' (64). Rather than view the Tollund Man body as an object of art or a symbol of religious ritual, Heaney maps the body with almost the precision of an investigative journalist, a process he eschews in 'The Grauballe Man' and 'Punishment'.

4.4 'The Tollund Man' (photo from Silkeborg Museum).

The poem is composed of three sections: the first contains five stanzas mapping the anatomical features of the body; the second includes three stanzas charting personal and familial relationships of the body; the third also incorporates three stanzas and draws a historical and geographical context for the body. In the opening stanza, the speaker indicates a spatial disconnect between him and the body; 'Some day' the speaker will travel to Aarhus to 'see' the bog body's 'peat-brown head', among other features (64). The opening line indicates that the speaker has not yet visited the body in Aarhus, Denmark. The words 'some day' imply spatial and temporal distance that must be traversed between the body and the poet. Heaney does, however, draw the lineaments of the body's head through shape ('pointed'), colour ('peat-brown'), anatomy ('eyes'), and imagination ('skin cap') (see Fig. 4.4).

The speaker goes on to describe the topography where the body rested in the bog, in a 'flat country' where he was 'dug' out (64). The 'flat country' describes the physical terrain of the bog; we later know this to be Jutland, the large peninsula where the town of Aarhus is located. Even though the Tollund Bog is not in Ireland, Heaney demonstrates an almost visceral understanding of bogs because of his own family background working on them, when he recalls they are 'all completely familiar to me'.[64] For the speaker, the bog embraces or envelops the body. Heaney's own mediated experience between the body and bog articulated in 'Digging' or 'Bogland' fills in some of the empty space of the 'flat country' where they 'dug him out' that substantiates the description of topography and a visceral understanding of bogs.

Heaney next maps the anatomical interiors of the body itself, where the 'gruel of winter seeds' was lined in 'his stomach' (64). The juxtaposition of the first two lines about geographical proximity and the second two lines about the contents of the stomach accomplishes two aims in the literary map. First, charting the stomach's food residue determines the importance of the overarching biology of the bog. Scientists were, for instance, able to identify some of the contents of the man's last ingested meal. It consisted of a vegetable gruel of clover, spelt rye, Yorkshire fog, rye-grass, goosefoot, buttercup, lady's mantle, black night-shade, yarrow, wild chamomile, and smooth hawksbeard.[65] Second, the quatrain contrasts the anatomical and the geographical body, indicating that the body not only comes from the bog, but also functions as a type of bog.

The poem curiously shifts from objective to subjective language when the speaker personifies the bog as a body: 'She tightened her torc on him/ And opened her fen, / Those dark juices working' (64). These lines animate the bog as a body, not only through overt sexual innuendo and gendering, but also in how it shifts to subjective experience in the poem. Poetically mapping the body topography equally provides insights into the bodies found in the bog. These descriptions all suggest that even in the science of retrieving bog bodies it views them as maps. Due to the preservative qualities of the anaerobic environment of bogs, bodies retrieved out of them still contain many distinguishable external features and internal organs, including hair, fingernails, fingerprints, lines on the soles of the feet, eyeballs, and even the brain (see Fig. 4.5).[66] These body maps allow archaeologists to examine histories, ages, environments, and diets, much like a forensic scientist would obtain clues after a suspicious death.

The physical descriptions of the body in the first section shifts to personal accounts in the second. This transition is also accompanied by a move from what has remained mostly a cultural analysis in 'Digging' and 'Bogland' to increasing political undertones in 'The Tollund Man'. Although a change occurs, the focus remains on mapping the bog body's experience. The purely physical and scientific features of the bodies mapped in verse now shift to the more personal and imaginative. Who were these people? What sort of lives did they live? The temporal element moves between the body of the Tollund Man, meticulously described, and to what Neil Corcoran refers to as the 'incorrupt bodies of Catholic hagiology'.[67] Beyond the ungratifying deaths of the 'labourers' who were 'scattered, ambushed', the last quatrain in the second section suggests a way of understanding these bodies not only through political metaphors but also through the poem's form. The lines of the poem lie next to each other, as do the bodies 'Laid out in the farmyards' that were 'For miles along the lines' (65). In addition, the hard consonant sounds of these two stanzas reflect the harshness of the subject. The violent alliterative sounds of 'Tell-tale skin and teeth' invoke embodied experiences of the way people died more than descriptions of the bodies themselves. The structure of the poem holds the map together not as an aesthetic escape from politics, but as a description of bodies used as markers of location and time. These other 'bog bodies', which are bodies the speaker claims 'germinate' into being, are victims of sectarian violence; they are also not actual or physical, but imagined. The format of the poem itself germinates into the bodies; the bodies lie 'along the lines' of the poem. The poem brings them to life as though it too were a bog.

The third section of 'The Tollund Man' provides an overview of the geographical region in order to contextualise the more local personal and physical features related to the actual bog bodies. The speaker of the poem lists the various bodies found in bogs, such as Tollund, Grauballe, and Nebelgård, almost like an invocation or a litany. In addition to being obvious town names, they also identify the names of the bodies. In this regard, bog bodies mediate geographies and cultures in another important way; they are named after the locations of the bogs in which they are found. The nomenclatures of bog bodies remain geographical in almost every way. They are part body and part bog; they are also a point on a map, such as a town or region, reflecting a real location with imaginative associations with history, culture, and literature. Therefore, the name of the body is the same name as the cartographic coordinate on a topographical map.

Even though Heaney attempts to map these bodies through knowledge and understanding of the bogs based upon his own family history and through studying Glob's *The Bog People*, he indicates some elements of unknowing and uncertainty in the penultimate quatrain, where these 'country people' do not know 'their tongue' (65). Maps do not provide

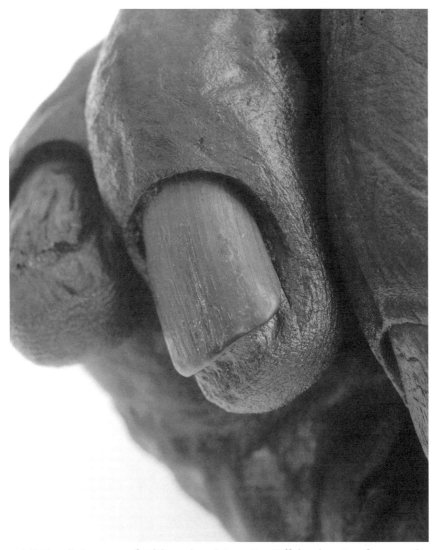

4.5 Hand close-up of Oldcroghan Man, Co. Offaly, showing fingernails and prints in detail. With kind permission of the National Museum of Ireland Bog Bodies Research Project.

accurate descriptions, but flawed, subjective ways to understand a geographical region that is entirely limited by what Huggan refers to as the 'process and product' in literary cartography.[68] The process of literary cartography matters as much, if not more, than the product because the process remains experiential and rooted in the body, much like the importance of 'digging' in Heaney's earlier poem.

Heaney's speaker begins 'The Tollund Man' excited to 'get to Aarhus' to see the 'peat-brown head' of the bog body. But after plotting the features of the body in the poem, his excitement fades into despair; he feels 'lost' out in Jutland and 'Unhappy and at home' (65). In the final line of the poem, the speaker feels 'at home' presumably because it is a similar bogscape to what he knows, but it is also a similar 'man-killing' parish, conjuring images from the sectarian violence in Northern Ireland.

There is some way in which this map merges the physical and the political (as all maps do) through a simultaneous opposition between homely and vanished people. The last quatrain foretells some of the themes of his later bog poems, such as loss, despair, death, violence, disturbance, desire, and dispossession. Indeed, all of these motifs underscore postcolonial and Gothic undercurrents that persist in these poems. The last quatrain returns to the beginning of the poem, coming full circle in order to complete the literary map, which both articulates the somatic contours of the body and the imaginative and personal elements that emerge out of Heaney's own objective and distinct perspective of the real Tollund Man. O'Brien maintains that 'The Tollund Man' should be viewed as 'an intellectual' response to the body, one read about and viewed through photography.[69] Rather than use the metaphor of photography, Heaney's description serves more as a distanced, technical literary map, one that becomes more nuanced and imaginative in his next volume of poetry, where he develops an inventive technique based on the personal and collective when charting bodies.

'The Grauballe Man', published in his fourth collection *North* (1975), exhibits another mapped bog body. Along with 'Punishment', it is perhaps the most discussed and controversial of Heaney's bog poems. In the poem, as Vendler points out, 'The poet overturns the objectivity of history by the insult of the actual, putting his contemplative power to aestheticize squarely in conflict with his political power to sympathize.'[70] Vendler then raises the question, 'Is it wrong to aestheticize?'[71] Anthony Purdy comparably suggests that a 'figural language' parallels the 'aesthetic preservation of the body' as it compares to the peat.[72] Sanders too remarks that Heaney's bog poems present 'a representational minefield' that challenges what the bog, bodies, or symbols therein represent in the larger context, whether it is political or aesthetic.[73]

The bog body in the poem serves as more than simply an aesthetic object employed with the intention to politicise the present through the discontinuities of time in the past; rather, it remains simultaneously a physical, organic object for archaeological examination and an imaginative object for cultural representation. Both lines of enquiry might be approached creatively through literary cartography, where the poet maps the physical and cultural contours of the body. The imbrication of both the organic and the imaginative body creates further contradiction in the poem, which moves beyond claims of aestheticising violence or reducing history to myth, as Lloyd contends,[74] and opens pluralistic readings of the body as a map of the senses and memory.

The first half of 'The Grauballe Man', consisting of six quatrains, meticulously diagrams the physical condition of the body. Through Heaney's visual mapping of the body in the poem, the reader *feels* the anatomical features of the bog body through the visual imagery. The speaker moves down the body as though the visual and tactile senses were aligned through both image and touch, from the 'ball of the heel', the 'instep', and the 'foot', up to the 'hips', 'spine', 'chin', and 'throat' that has been 'slashed' (115). Heaney's careful charting functions like a film camera slowly tracking up the body literally from heel to head.[75] Yet despite its physicality, the poem is surprisingly void of actual contact with the bog body.

The visual qualities in 'The Grauballe Man' produce a process of 'haptic visuality' – or what film scholar Laura Marks defines as a sense of touch (haptic) through the visual encounter in a film or photograph.[76] Through this tactile, quasi-visual experience the viewer develops a deeper relationship with the subject/object in the image, thereby bridging the separation of viewer and object in what media scholars have called 'embodied spectatorship', where the seemingly contradictory sense perception and cognition do not detach but work in tandem.[77] This haptic approach integrates images within our own embodied experience so that the visual can also become tactile (subjective and close) instead of remaining solely optical (objective and distant). For example, 'The Tollund Man' is more optical, whereas 'The Grauballe Man' is more tactile. The viewer can feel the visual image as though it were a part of them, contained within as a visceral experience.

Mapping the body through the senses, offering a deeper experience in the poem, evokes a type of haptic visuality. 'The Grauballe Man' opens with visual descriptions that are also highly tactile, invoking images of a body being 'poured / in tar' but actually laying on a bog resembling a restful 'pillow of turf' (115). The last line of the stanza, indicating that the bog appears to 'weep', produces great pathos from the image and directs the viewer to empathise with the body. The softness of the 'pillow of turf' contrasts with the sticky 'tar' in which the body lays, stressing the tactile sensation evoked through the visual image of a soft and yielding white pillow juxtaposed against the dark and sticky black tar. The Grauballe Man's body appears 'almost vegetative, almost bronze'.[78] The simultaneity of opposites also appears in the sensuously mapped body: preserved skin, hair, and fingernails mark traits of a living body even though the body remains dead. This description additionally charts the oppositional qualities of the bog. It appears to be squishy and soft to the touch on the surface, but once submerged in the bog, the viscous quicksand qualities of the goo hold the body in place like cement.

The real and imagined Grauballe Man appears in various mani-festations: in Heaney's poem, in a glass case in a museum, and in various forms of visual media (photographs, films, texts, and interactive digital displays).[79] The visual elements of the poem resemble other forms of the real Grauballe Man put on display, which Heaney observed many times when writing the poem. Even Heaney experiences haptic visuality on some level through his own embodied experience as the poet. He examines the various methods of displaying the real Grauballe Man while mapping his own poetic and imagined version of the bog body. Heaney recalls the power of the bog body photographs upon first seeing Glob's book: 'And the unforgettable photographs of these victims blended in my mind with photographs of atrocities, past and present, in the long rites of Irish political and religious struggles.'[80]

Likewise, Heaney reflects upon the photographic and visual elements of the bog bodies in 'The Grauballe Man' when he initially witnessed 'his twisted face' with his 'head' surfacing out of the peat, 'bruised' (116). The literary mapping that Heaney constructs here resulted from a visual process of looking at photographs, not the actual body of the Grauballe Man. This visual process assists Heaney in drawing a literary map that does more than deliver aesthetic pleasure; it provides a small glimpse into the bog's history through the delineations of the body itself. As Purdy comments, bog bodies 'allow us to *see* time' through the physicality of the body and the science of carbon dating.[81] Heaney articulates the contours of the body to accentuate visual elements through other senses.

Seeing the poem through the haptic brings the viewer closer to the body, while it also engenders compassion and empathy for the victim. The bog body has obvious parallels with the dead corpses of Northern Ireland. In an interview Heaney once stated, 'I've tried to make a connection lately between things that came to the surface in bogs … and the violence that was coming to the surface in the north of Ireland.'[82] Through provoking other senses, the poem draws personal connection to both victims in the poem, one that is physical (Grauballe Man) and one that is imagined (bodies from the Troubles). Rather than minimising violence as art in these lines, the poem elicits empathy for the victims of violence, whether they are from the Iron Age or Derry in the 1970s. Provoking an intense visual invokes knowledge of our own physical body as it relates to the dead bodies of victims of sectarian violence. Through haptic visuality we can *touch* the body by way of various iterations of it as charted in the poem and feel the corporeal qualities that confuse history. The visual qualities of the poem emit a haunting effect that compresses the time and space of the body through both the biological and imagined qualities, highlighting the ambiguities about death, time, memory, and violence. This body, similar to the bog, attracts a poet like Heaney because it works in a limited and limitless register where both opposing elements can be explored subtly without having to evoke overt political symbols.

In addition to the visual qualities of the poem, 'The Grauballe Man' raises some provoking questions about the notion of corpses compared to bodies, an idea that leads us to a form of mapping through memory. Years later in Denmark Heaney reflected on the bog bodies in his earlier poetry:

> Once upon a time, these heads and limbs existed in order to express and embody the needs and impulses of an individual human life. They were the vehicles of different biographies and they compelled singular attention, they proclaimed 'I am I'. Even when they were first dead, at the moment of sacrifice or atrocity, their bodies and their limbs manifested biography and conserved vestiges of personal identity: they were corpses. But when a corpse becomes a bog body, the personal identity drops away; the bog body does not proclaim 'I am I'; instead it says something like 'I am it' or 'I am you'. Like the work of art, the bog body asks to be contemplated.[83]

In this passage Heaney explains how these sites of memory in both the bog and the bodies diffuse contested identities and establish a collective memory where the 'I' transforms into a pronoun 'it' or 'you'. In this regard, individual identity attributed to a corpse transforms into collective identities of bog bodies. Bog bodies may well speak for the collective as an uncontrolled memory. Collective memory functions as a shared, less individualised approach because the public at large can access it without limitation; people see or feel or experience mapped identities at a distance in poems or through museum cases. These bodies, like the bogs from which they emerge, hold memories that can be examined publicly as memory maps, whether they are encased in a museum, viewed in a photograph, or read in a poem. Memory maps, according to Purdy, emerge out of a diverse interplay of photographs, drawings, texts, and excavated objects,[84] all of which could also relate to bog bodies. As the speaker recognises in the poem, the bog body 'asks to be contemplated', or investigated and mapped through these various cultural sites of interplay. The speaker in 'The Grauballe Man' observes how the body is 'perfected in my memory' (116). Similar to the visual elements in 'The Grauballe Man', the speaker's memories emerge when he follows the map of the body from the 'red horn' of the 'nails' through the interplay of the photograph from Glob's book that was later transformed onto the page of the poem (116).

Memory maps are creative ways to record subjective memories that fundamentally root in specific geographies. The geographer Joan Schwartz explains that 'memory maps' do not describe the real topographical contours of the land, but are 'cartographic expressions of a sense of place', mediated, reinforced, and shaped by memory.[85] Schwartz continues:

> [Memory] maps are neither detailed nor accurate. The spatial relations they communicate are more idiosyncratic than cartographic. The maps reveal more about dynamics than distances, more about the geographical imagination than topographical reality, more about identity than genealogy, more about the character of memory than the nature of land.[86]

With this description in mind, I would argue that Heaney's bog bodies – more imaginative than cartographic, more about memory than actual topographies – function also as memory maps. In 'The Grauballe Man', for instance, a relationship is documented between the collective geographical record and individual identity through a 'sense of place' that is also mediated by memory. Body maps are descriptions of the body mediated through space, history, identity, and memory. Body maps do not accurately detail the terrain of certain topographies in technical cartographic terms, but they do illuminate issues of the past through memory that directly relate to the present in a form of identity and the cultural impulse of a certain place.

In the second half of 'The Grauballe Man', Heaney raises two key questions about corpses and bodies that are related to his previous statement about bog bodies, where he proclaims, 'I am it':

> Who will say 'corpse'
> to his vivid cast?
> Who will say 'body'
> to his opaque repose? (115)

The difference between 'corpse' and 'body' in this stanza is marked between a spatial and grammatical shift from the pronoun 'I' to 'it', thereby distinguishing the change from the particular (individual) to the general (collective). Bog bodies are found, exhumed, curated, and observed by the collective and transcribed into a memory map for cultural consumption in the public sphere. Corpses, on the other hand, are the remains of humans who once had individual histories but who are no longer created and narrated through the collective archive. Corpses remain highly individualised in death; for example, tombstones mark each corpse's association with its personalised life, but bogs transform the individual corpses into collective bodies when the bodies are found and examined by the cultural collective. These differences of identity and memory in 'The Grauballe Man' become more salient when framed within the sectarian violence of Northern Ireland. To provide one critical example, Thomas Docherty views the above stanza as a question of history in terms of death and life. He asks, 'is history dead, a thing of the past; or is it alive, vivid, a present of the past?'[87] Like Docherty's nuanced view of history, bog bodies bear marks of memories that were buried, covered, and erased, but now come to exist as part of the collective memory and are divorced from specific identities. The discovering, documenting, and displaying of bog bodies reinterns them to the collective memory, and once in that realm museum curators and poets alike use methods to map the memories for various audiences that are part of the collective.

'The Grauballe Man' reveals this ambiguity about the difference between the individualised corpse and the collective body. Through the process of charting dead bodies the poem differentiates between the 'body' as an 'opaque repose' and the 'corpse' as a 'vivid caste'. The 'opaque repose' signals obscurities about the identity of the body read by the collective, whereas the 'vivid caste' gestures to a clear individual identity of a certain group, not the general collective. The corpse reference underscores the specific deaths during the Troubles, whereas the body functions as a remark on the unknowable deaths of the unknowable people who are now the bog bodies that Heaney explores in the poem. After all, both the Tollund Man and Grauballe Man are named after the places in which they were found by the collective. Corpses become bodies once they are discovered simply as bodies, stripped of specific ideologically inflected identities. The poem locates the corpse in the physical (decomposed material matter) and the body in the imaginative (memories of the body and the correlations made between the past and present). The identity of the body has been 'perfected' in the speaker's 'memory', while the corpse, 'the Dying Gaul', is 'too strictly compassed' (116). The mystery of the bog bodies is more compelling for society to decipher (through a cartographic tool of the compass even) than the corpses of sectarianism, because they are older and disconnected from contemporary politics. Heaney maps the bog body, rather than the corpse, to direct attention to the memories associated with not only the body, but also with where it is buried in the bog.

Bog bodies, similar to the corpses from the Troubles, primarily were killed through violent means: as sacrificial rituals to fertility goddesses and as punishment for alleged crimes, in one case, and for the suspected crimes connected to ethno-religious ideologies of nationalism or loyalism in the other. Heaney's Grauballe Man, for instance, was 'hooded' and then 'slashed' before being deposited into a bog (116). In turn, each hooded victim implies a specificity that is 'actual' and indeed ideological. While these lines describe the dead from the Troubles, they also appear to parallel the description of the Grauballe Man upon his own violent demise as a punishment for an unknown and alleged crime. The corpses that have become bog bodies bear evidence of death by sacrifice in the Iron Age and by execution in more recent circumstances in the process of decolonisation. Bogs have been and still are used as nameless graves for those dispatched through acts of violence. The bodies dug up in Jutland that Glob describes in *The Bog People* met their demise through acts of violence. The Tollund Man was found with a rope around his neck from a hanging and the Grauballe Man had an incision across his neck from ear to ear. In these descriptions violence is literally mapped onto their bodies to be deciphered and remembered by society, whereas corpses organically decay in the earth and remain only a memory without a corresponding map. Heaney lays this groundwork in 'Bogland' and then in 'The Tollund Man' before perfecting the poetics of mapping in 'The Grauballe Man'.

Bog bodies, therefore, show recorded memories that effectively and ambiguously chart uncertain identities that are shared and interpreted by the collective. Memory and representation directly relate to questions of identity, nationalism, power, and authority,[88] which are at the root of the ethno-religious conflict in Northern Ireland. Sectarian politics are sustained by the polarising notion that it is not *what* you say, but *who* says it. As Heaney writes in his poem 'Whatever You Say, Say Nothing', 'The famous/Northern reticence, the right gag of place' (132). The goal of sectarian violence is, in part, to eliminate traces of identity from the opposition through silencing people by transforming them into corpses (recognisable identities that have been neutralised). Corpses remain identifiable as individuals – they are 'too strictly compassed' – despite attempts at disfiguration seen in 'The Tollund Man' (116). While the 'too strictly compassed' might refer to the Dying Gaul's beliefs – he is compassed on his shield and circumscribed by it – the phrase also refers to the corpses' previous ideological identities.

Corpses quickly disappear and decay, like the ideologies attached to them, while bog bodies continue to survive in collective forms of memory; the bodies are documented in photographs, books, museums, or poems after they are discovered and unearthed from the ground. For example, the Grauballe Man exhibit at the Moesgaard Museum of Prehistory in Denmark showcases the body in a glass case for viewers to look at. Alongside the body are placards that recognise and explain the assembly of human and non-human agents involved with the discovery and subsequent preservation process. The exhibit also includes an accompaniment of texts and images as part of the museum display. All of these examples demonstrate ways to record and narrate memories of the bog body that speak to the collective.[89] Through the differences between corpses and bodies (mapped through memory), Heaney's bog bodies offer possible ways to examine violence without explicit identities attached to them. Mapping through haptic visuality and memory provokes empathy for the bodies because they evoke responses in our own bodies that are both attracted to and also repulsed by the bog bodies. Heaney's poem 'Punishment' further explains the ambiguous relationship of the object/abject body, also revealing a fusion of attractive and repulsive oppositions through a feminised bog body.

One of Heaney's most Gothic poems is perhaps 'Punishment', which exposes the bog body known as the 'Windeby Girl'. This body was deposited in a bog over 2,000 years ago and later found blindfolded with a halter around her neck; her crime was allegedly adultery or possibly even premarital relations.[90] 'Punishment' shows the symbolic and physical mapping of a bog body – but not just any body, a feminised body – and the implications involved in her death and the treatment of the body after death. In the poem, there is a clear and deliberate gendered association with women and transgressive sexuality, a recurring point in some of Heaney's other bog poems in *North* such as 'Bog Queen' and 'Strange Fruit'. Heaney has been criticised for 'Punishment', and some argue that the poem justifies the harsh punishment meted out by the nationalist community to Catholic women who consorted with British soldiers stationed in Northern Ireland.[91]

The poem indicates parallels to Catholic women who were tarred and feathered for these alleged relationships and suggests the speaker's tacit condoning of the practice (which he acknowledges while also calling into question): the speaker 'stood dumb' while the body was 'cauled in tar' (118). The woman in the bog and a contemporary Catholic woman are both 'punished' ritualistically by their communities for suspected actions related to sexual freedom and pleasure. The overlap between the past and present appears to justify contemporary violence because it safely hides behind the veneer of the past rather than confronting current practices. While the speaker may be considered voiceless and cowardly for his ability to identify with the 'tribe', connecting with the bog body's once living referent, he also appears disturbed by the simultaneous allure of and his desire for the bog body. Such a disturbance, destabilising the speaking subject itself and the audience, remains the key to understanding the feminised bog body in 'Punishment'.

This particular bog body is mapped as a Gothic 'abhuman' feminised body, charting the moral, emotional, and existential disturbances layered in the poem's chronology and corporeality. Because the body is described as abhuman – both human and non-human and yet not either – the speaker can desire it, both in spite of and because of her alleged transgressions, allowing him to project onto his present desire for and repulsion of women who are perceived to own their sexuality. Throughout the speaker's process of mapping this body, however, there remains an inherent disturbance about women's fates in the past and the present. The speaker's noticeable ambivalence is predicated on his judgement as pronounced against this feminised bog body precisely because she is mapped as abhuman, which signifies sub-human, through a mix of possessive and sensual language. Her body is safe to be desired and condemned because she has been controlled and charted in the poem. Much like the body/corpse dynamic in 'The Grauballe Man', the abhuman body in 'Punishment' loses identity and subjectivity as the speaker diagrams it as something between human and non-human, both and not quite either.

In *The Gothic Body* (2004), Hurley writes that the 'abhuman subject is a not-quite-human subject, characterised by its morphic variability, continually in danger of becoming not-itself, becoming other'.[92] Hurley's term 'abhuman' derives from Julia Kristeva's notion of abjection, but Hurley reappropriates it to demonstrate that the 'abhuman' body is a place where human identity dissolves into another form. Hurley explains that etymologically the word 'abject' means 'cast off' or 'cast away' and relates to words such as debased, degraded, humiliated, and despicable. Drawing from Kristeva's *Powers of Horror* (1982), Hurley locates the abject as 'the in-between, the ambiguous, the composite'.[93] For Kristeva, the human corpse is 'the utmost of abjection', especially when represented in a symbolic, religious society.[94] In *The Monstrous Feminine* (1993), Barbara Creed adds that Kristeva's form of abjection, as a source of horror, functions in patriarchal societies as a way of separating the human (subject) from the non-human (partial subject).[95] Creed's own take on Kristeva relates to Hurley's abhuman. Creed changes the archetypal 'female monster' to the 'monstrous feminine', as a way of emphasising patriarchy's lack of understanding (linguistically or rationally) of women and particularly through a feminised or abject body. The abject body provokes a concurrently oppositional response of both fear and fascination which has the effect of disturbing and destabilising the known order. When defining the abhuman body, Hurley concludes, 'One cannot bear to look upon it, but cannot bring oneself to look away from it either.'[96]

Hurley's definition of the abhuman, drawing on Kristeva and Creed, effectively describes the bog body in Heaney's poem because the body both repulses and attracts readers through the disturbingly preserved human remains, even though the body has been dead for thousands of years. In fact, elsewhere Heaney claims that 'in the figure of the bog body, the atrocious and the beautiful often partake of one another's reality, coexisting inextricably in the lineaments of the transformed human features'.[97] The abhuman, or the 'figure of the bog body', fruitfully conveys the oppositional qualities of the bog and the ambivalence and destabilisation Heaney emits throughout these bog poems more generally about political realities in the present. The notion of abjection is also equally ambiguous, effectively confusing subjective states. In addition to the bodies, Heaney's statement about the atrocious and beautiful seems to question the commitment to or certainty about holding a political or religious belief at any cost. This phrase repeats the opening two lines in the penultimate stanza in 'The Grauballe Man', when the speaker describes the man's fate balanced in the 'scales' with both 'beauty and atrocity' (116). The speaker's desire for the feminised body in 'Punishment' reveals a larger question about the destabilising juxtaposition between beauty and atrocity.

Some scholars have scrutinised 'Punishment' for depicting women as silent and passive objects of desire through the speaker's entrenched language of male-centred nationalist rhetoric. Patricia Coughlan's essay 'Bog Queens' remains the exemplary model of this analysis. In it, Coughlan argues that 'Punishment' portrays the bog woman as an object who is not only silenced, but who also receives the passive gaze of the speaker, an issue of objectification and disempowerment that contemporary women living in Ireland continually face.[98] Although the speaker's intent in the poem might be read as compassion and empathy for the bog woman, Coughlan maintains the result becomes a 'scopic spectacle of the girl's utter disempowerment'.[99]

Adding to this point, I want to suggest that the speaker maps his desire onto her because he views her as gendered or feminised in the poem, as a Gothic abhuman body both desired and feared. Creed makes a similar point about the abject dimension of horror: 'The subject, constructed in/through language, through a desire for meaning, is also spoken by the abject, the place of meaninglessness – thus, the subject is constantly beset by abjection which fascinates desire but which must be repelled for fear of self-annihilation.'[100] Bog bodies often evoke subjects of sexuality, sacrifice, disgust, and adultery in literature and culture because of their phenomenological and mysterious allure.[101]

However, women's bog bodies (also found in Heaney's poems 'Bog Queen' and 'Strange Fruit') are mapped differently from the men's bog bodies in 'The Grauballe Man' or 'The Tollund Man', and are portrayed as both sensationalised and monstrous through 'language' and a 'desire for meaning', going back to Creed, that emit ambiguous feelings of desire and repulsion. Mapped bog bodies in Heaney's poetry are also portrayed as a type of horror film, where visual elements parallel the imaginative, and where the feminised body is depicted as mutilated, often perceived as a form of social punishment. Despite the images of putrid bodily waste, the viewer is filled with a perverse pleasure of a both/and also terror/desire for the abjected bog body.[102] The speaker in 'Punishment' demonstrates this opposition through the 'abjected' or feminised abhuman Gothic body.

When the speaker surveys the woman's body in 'Punishment', he maps her alteration from sexualised woman to monstrous feminine by first describing her 'naked front' and 'her nipples' or 'amber beads' and then shifting to 'her shaved head' with 'exposed' brain and 'darkened combs' (117–18). His description juxtaposes repulsive aspects of the body against erotic symbolism. After such a macabre description of the body, the speaker even acknowledges, 'I almost love you' (118). While Heaney's poem calls attention to the captivating and equally horrifying commitment to nationalism and to subjective forms of identity, he also disarms the violence in the poem by mapping the contours of the woman, providing an intimate connection to the body without explicitly recognising or re-enacting sectarian violence in the present. The destabilising qualities in the poem produce a pervading sense of indeterminacy about current politics, though they still hover beneath the surface on some level, and this is reflected in the voice of the speaker who projects a similarly indeterminate outlook of desire and horror.

Although the speaker does not appear to be invested in the political situation of women – historically or presently – he is at once permitted to be disgusted by and attracted to the abhuman body. He admits that he 'would have cast' the first 'stones of silence' (118), which indicates his tacit judgement of her, as well as other transgressively sexual women in the present (118). While he can only *almost* love her, he can certainly desire her. 'Punishment' presents the dislocation of the speaking subject itself, even as the poem clearly pinpoints – through the mapping of the bog body as an abject (both cast off and wanted) – an attempt to acknowledge violence against sexually transgressive women in both the Iron Age and the Troubles. The poem's approach works in a way that may both reaffirm and reflect the inherent disempowering motives of the speaker, while also disrupting the universal persona/speaking male subject as the overarching voice.

The speaker of the poem considers himself an 'artful voyeur' (118), which reveals the act of visualising and thereby imagining how to possess or control the woman's body from a distance. As an 'artful voyeur', the speaker does mark the body as identity-less, but this description also makes clear reference to the 'art' – the poetic rendering of sight through charting and plotting. The speaker remains complicit in the violence done to the woman but also appears to be uncomfortable in that complicity. In response to her punishment, he would have cast those stones of 'silence' rather than outwardly attempt to stop it. Understanding the exactness of the tribal nature of revenge is not the same as condoning it. The speaker is himself mired in the bog, while also standing apart from it, caught in the abject experience of the bog body, a place without clear meaning. He is not a witness but a voyeur – a word twinned with sexual desire, as are his descriptions of her neck, ribs, and nipples – of the bog body, while he also produces art out of her silent suffering, at a distance.

The ambivalence and disturbance in the poem is, in no small part, about sense and perception – the speaker remains a distanced observer and this attachment makes him uncomfortable. The abhuman body heightens the audience's awareness of this voyeurism in order to call attention to the predicament of perception made about political violence and national identity. The opening two stanzas place the speaker in a seemingly empathic position, imagining the disturbance associated with what the woman might 'feel' lying in the bog. The speaker explains how he can 'feel' the 'tug' of the strap 'at the nape/of her neck', while he looks down near her 'nipples' and on to the 'frail/rigging of her ribs' (117).

The voyeuristic characteristics of these opening lines immediately create a passive body (object) for the viewer's gaze (subject). Like 'The Grauballe Man', the poem reveals a haptic map of the body that creates a multi-sensorial experience for the audience. But unlike the male bog body, 'Punishment' disempowers and exposes the woman; the body lies vulnerably face up with a descriptive plotting of her breasts, as opposed to other less revealing body parts such as the Grauballe Man's heel or chin. The description provides a sensual overtone that differs from the visual diagramming employed in the two other male bog bodies found in Tollund and Grauballe. The woman, as Coughlan points out, is silent and vulnerable while the speaker of the poem performs the scopic gaze.[103] By viewing the bog body as an abject – cast off and disposed of because of its status as in between an object and subject – the poem additionally invokes repressed desires that increase the oppositional forces of repulsion and attraction associated with the feminised abhuman bog body.

Both the anguish for her condition and the longing the speaker expresses toward her, as suggested by the body's visual description, evokes pathos in the third stanza. Like the earlier lines describing the feeling of the halter around her neck, the speaker attempts to place himself in the position of the bog body, a notable display of empathy. He can watch her 'drowned/body in the bog' (117). The speaker gazes at himself as well as the bog body in order to transfer the feelings, so that he can then continue to provide an accurately sensuous map of the body. He then contrasts this stanza with the following three, which elicit the Gothic qualities of the preserved feminised abhuman body through its demise, with her 'shaved head' resembling 'stubble of black corn' and her 'noose a ring'; she was also 'undernourished' with a 'beautiful' 'tar-black face' (117).

The three stanzas in the middle of the poem map the physical bog body not only through a 'scopic gaze', but also through the way in which they ascribe animalistic qualities to the silenced abhuman body; although framed as empathy, we are exposed to the speaker's survey of the feminised body. The 'halter', the 'scapegoat', and even the 'noose as a ring' – a wedding band image also signalling a bullring of control and power through the nose – all compare her to an animal. The feminised body is not only silent, but also controlled and attached both to the speaker in the present and to her place betrothed in history. Surprisingly, the monstrosity of her appearance and tragic demise does not repel the speaker; rather, it provokes reactions ranging from compassion and 'almost' love to fear and desire. Despite the empathetic attempts by the speaker, ultimately he furthers her state of abjection.

The abhuman body in 'Punishment' complicates the language associated with it and exposes the macabre overtones. Despite clear indications from the mapped body that the woman is dead, the language in the poem suggests the speaker yearns for her abhuman body, juxtaposing his 'love' against her anatomy: the 'brain's exposed/and darkened combs', the 'muscles' webbing', and 'numbered bones' (118). Through the invasiveness of the 'artful voyeur' – whether it is the artist, the community, or the male speaker – the body becomes a destabilised abject. The horrific circumstances of the bog body compel the voyeur and provoke the conflicting feelings of desire and repugnance.

Although this contrast might appear extreme, it is a common motif in Gothic writing. Vampires, for instance, are also considered to be abhuman bodies, evoking simultaneous feelings of desire and repulsion that support sexual feelings for an undead demon. While a vampire might be considered undead, and not the actual dead, the abhuman bog body resembles what Hurley defines as that 'not-quite-human' form with 'morphic variability'.[104] The Danish poet Palle Lauring, when commenting on the Windeby Body in 1957, similarly acknowledged this 'morphic variability' of the bog bodies: 'For 2000 years she lay, rigid in her half-brutish attempt not to die.'[105] These conflicting feelings of abhorrence and attraction evoke a tension that subtly suggests, among other experiences, the unconscious physical allure of and desire for the monstrous feminine that is also disgusting, already within the self, that threatens conscious stability in the patriarchal order.

'Punishment' raises questions about how political and religious symbolism quickly dissolve into conflicting feelings of desire and condemnation. Instead of having sympathy for women punished for alleged transgressive sexuality, the speaker focuses on ambivalent feelings of longing and judgement while surveying the abhuman body. The speaker attempts to empathise with her through his own body, but ultimately charts her predicament through pity, desire, and disgust, turning her into a feminised abhuman. Heaney may not condone the speaker's process – this is also part of the destabilising elements of the abhuman body sketched throughout – but the poem provides a glimpse of the manner in which women can be unwittingly objectified as the 'monstrous feminine', even through a grotesque and distorted body preserved in the bog for thousands of years. 'Punishment' provokes such intensity from its own disturbance of categories and selves, all of which are moral, emotional, and existential. Vendler recognises Heaney as a poet of 'undoing, of dilution, of loss', leading to 'the processes of unmaking',[106] not unlike the destabilisation of the speaking subject in 'Punishment'. Perhaps Heaney has already built in and acknowledged the repulsiveness of being that self who colludes and finds the abject body alluring, but that does not lessen the sense of disturbance throughout the poem's description of the feminised abhuman Gothic bog body. What is arguably abhuman is itself the experience of desiring the sight of the mapped bog body in the poem.

Erasing Boundaries

Heaney's major bog poems display the tenacity and scope of the bog's allure in Irish literature and culture. The poems, which yield types of literary maps through politically charged and often Gothicised bog bodies, produce many outcomes, some intentional and some unintentional. To map is an effort to reveal the unknown, even though it may be well-known to others. Mapping is also a form of exploration and exploitation. Through mapping, as in writing, we can question, consider, and explore possibilities.[107] Tally maintains that in literary cartography 'the individual writer or mapmaker is not simply making choices, selections or omissions, but is participating (perhaps even unwittingly) in larger historical and cultural processes by which these moments and places gain greater significance'.[108] Mapping, like poetry, has many unintended outcomes; the sheer act of writing/mapping makes claims and assertions, while also projecting and defining in the 'larger historical and cultural processes'. The reader also brings an interpretation, a view. The reader may be as complicit or culpable as the writer. A map is a guide, but we also read maps and interpret them. Maps also uncover, allowing for self-reflection and doubt, and show a tremendous amount of ambivalence about the ultimate product or subject being mapped or even the process by which we get to the product.

To this end, Heaney's bog poems serve as literary maps for further understanding/reading/viewing the bodies that emerge from the bogs and which exist in them in all their various manifestations. The bog bodies are both empirical (the actual bodies examined by scientists) and also imagined (the bodies conceived of by writers and viewers as cultural artefacts). Bog poems are politically, structurally, and socially unstable because they reflect the qualities of the bogs. Instability exudes from the bog and this space serves as an ideal focus for a poet discussing both volatile political circumstances and ways to avert our attention from them. Heaney's literary maps of the bog bodies do not find a solid bottom or point of origin at the centre of the bog. His form of exploratory and uncertain mapping resembles the refrain from 'Bogland' that 'the wet centre is bottomless' (42).

Deciphering his literary maps is an endlessly deep process. Heaney even admits that bog bodies 'have a double force' between reverie and intellect that 'derives from the fact that the bodies erase the boundary-line between culture and nature, between art and life, between vision and eyesight'.[109] However, the ostensible erasure of boundaries of the bog bodies provides compelling evidence to conclude that a poet like Heaney would be attracted to map them in unconventional ways because the bog bodies themselves defy logical convention. Having concluded this chapter with depictions of women in 'Punishment', Chapter 5 will discuss two woman protagonists in contemporary Irish drama who reject notions of objectification and disempowerment through their lives on the bogs.

5

Gendered Boglands

So much time was spent, in our childhoods, getting excited by the beauty of the bog. It is not a substance I could ever mention in a book: too sacred, too overworked, it will, besides, never be mine.[1]

– Anne Enright, 'At Turner Contemporary'

Capitalism, colonialism, and patriarchy, for example, are figured as a mire … Yet the pejorative use of the mire metaphor is implicated ('mired') in the capitalist, colonialist and patriarchal repudiation and vilification of wetlands.[2]

– Rod Giblett, *Postmodern Wetlands*

Women, Bogs, and Staging the Nation

The sectarian divisions in Northern Ireland, lasting from the late 1960s to the mid-1990s, overshadowed much of Irish literary and cultural production from the whole island in that period. Themes of violence, nationalism, sectarianism, economic depression, discrimination, and reactionary politics pervaded cultural critique. In the 1990s, however, change came swiftly with Mary Robinson's presidency in 1990, the Northern Ireland ceasefire in 1994, and the beginning of the Celtic Tiger economic boom also in 1994. The 'Celtic Tiger', a phenomenon of the 1990s and 2000s that ushered in a new era of alleged economic prosperity and cultural capital, can more critically be defined as a period of neocolonialism, where neoliberal economics exploit previously colonised countries, such as Ireland, to avail of lower tax rates and a cheaper, educated workforce. One of the most significant advances in Irish literary culture during the 1990s and 2000s, one typically outlying in critical approaches of Celtic Tiger culture but one magnified in this chapter, was the rise in popularity of and critical attention paid to contemporary women's writing.[3]

What follows in this chapter is an analysis of Marina Carr's *By the Bog of Cats…* (1998) and Deirdre Kinahan's *Bog Boy* (2010), two neo-Gothic plays about disenfranchised women who are pushed to the edges of Irish society and onto the bog because of their resistance to prescribed gender norms and socio-economic class expectations. Both plays demonstrate how women are denied agency in favour of economic and national development in Irish society, but both plays simultaneously reveal how the real and imagined bog provides them with a space of opportunity, power, and relative choice for their women characters. Contemporary Irish literature often employs themes related to what Eve Patten has called the 'neo-Gothic', a term used to indicate a revival of the Gothic form in a contemporary context, which 'signalled a haunted or traumatised Irish society and deep-seated disturbances in the national psyche'.[4] Carr and Kinahan, through their respective protagonists, Hester and Brigit, comment on these haunted and traumatised occurrences in Irish society by reflecting on the difficult conditions women experience during and in the aftermath of the Celtic Tiger.

Although never directly mentioned in the play, *By the Bog of Cats…* is clearly set against the backdrop of the Celtic Tiger of the 1990s. *Bog Boy*, in contrast, takes place in a post-Celtic Tiger Ireland between 2008 and 2010 (and beyond), in the aftermath of a devastated economy, culture, and national psyche. Both plays document the darker, neo-Gothic side of the Celtic Tiger period when, despite the ubiquitous narratives of progress and Irish economic independence, impoverishment and dispossession of marginalised populations increased. Each play responds to the Celtic Tiger phenomenon by locating the action on bogs at a time when economic growth, exhibited through modernisation and consumerism, was at its apex. Carr and Kinahan focus instead on a recurring theme of land and gender – part of the larger narrative of the land/gender relationship in Irish nationalism – in order to subvert and ultimately reclaim that narrative during a time when many sectors of the economy, culture, and society were flourishing. The rural bogland location would typically limit women's roles to the purely domestic, with urban spaces as the modern equivalent of opportunity and potential equity, but both plays invert this division. While the bog might be feminised, it has rarely belonged to women in the way that it does in these two plays. Instead, it serves as a space of refuge and opportunity for women who want to escape limiting domestic roles.[5]

In the introduction to *Theorizing Ireland* (2003), Claire Connolly recognises that 'Contemporary work by women writers, critics, painters and sculptors turns again and again to the interrelation between body and land, seeking to make sense, perhaps, of the embodied nature of citizenship and subjecthood'.[6] Carr and Kinahan exemplify Connolly's description of how contemporary women writers explore the relationship between subjectivity and landscape. They do so, however, in order to resist the narratives of progress and modernisation inherent in earlier nationalist discourses that merged into economic narratives of growth and development in the 1990s and 2000s. Carr and Kinahan reconsider, through their women protagonists, what it means to be a mother of the nation and embody the land. Anne McClintock has argued, 'Women are typically construed as the symbolic bearers of the nation, but are denied any direct relation to national agency.'[7] Stuck somewhere between the limited past and the limitless future, Hester and Brigit disrupt national narratives of economic progress by living on bogs.

Instead of reinforcing the nationalist stereotypes that define women's experiences in rural Ireland, Carr and Kinahan revisit and revise this highly problematic assumption. Both plays draw out the parallel between women and land as a nationalist metaphor, and then reappropriate this imagery to describe the relationship impoverished women have with spaces of patriarchal discourse so often applied to the Irish landscape. These two plays show impoverished women interacting with the bog, a space considered unprogressive and often perceived in gendered terms in Irish national mythology. Hester and Brigit do not function as prototypical rural Irish women who represent, as Patricia Coughlan warns against in connection with the nation, 'mother-figures, who are associated with unmediated naturalness'.[8] Rather, these protagonists remain uncomfortable in the stereotypical domestic sphere allocated to rural women in Ireland and resist it by locating themselves on the bog. Ultimately, then, this chapter explores these historical interventions in *By the Bog of Cats...* and *Bog Boy* and how they are overshadowed by the Celtic Tiger phenomenon, where neocolonial narratives surface in the form of economic modernisation and consumption for the nation.

The plot of *By the Bog of Cats...* retells the revenge tragedy of Euripides' *Medea* in a contemporary, Irish neo-Gothic context. The entire play is set on a bog and this space becomes integral to the actions of the characters. Setting the play on a bog also allows Carr to draw on its intrinsic oppositional characteristics, creating both a sense of fixed time in the contemporary moment and also timelessness in Irish history. Located in the Midlands of Ireland, the play stages the overlapping tensions around Irish Travellers, landscape, class, and women. *By the Bog of Cats...* is also a neo-Gothic play because it implements themes of ghosts, inheritance, and transgression, all in combination with post-nationalist undertones in contemporary Irish literature.

In the play, the audience learns that Big Josie Swane abandoned her daughter Hester Swane on the Bog of Cats at the age of seven. Hester's long-time partner and only love, Carthage Kilbride, also rejects her and decides to marry the much younger Caroline Cassidy because of her age, family connections, and willing acceptance of conventional domesticity. Tension arises because Hester and Carthage have a daughter together, Josie Kilbride, and they continue to disagree about her future – should Josie be raised in a house with Carthage and Caroline or in a caravan with Hester out on the bog? Carthage comes from a working-class family in the Midlands and Hester is an Irish 'tinker', one of the Travelling People.[9] When threatened with the potential loss of custody over Josie to Carthage and Caroline, Hester curses the whole community with vengeance. She destroys the wedding of Carthage and Caroline and then sets fire to their house and cattle, an act reminiscent of the Big House Gothic genre where writers in the nineteenth and early twentieth centuries depict nationalists burning older Anglo-Irish homes to symbolise transition and change from a colonial history to a decolonised present. The play's action quickly accelerates, and in the dénouement Hester sacrifices Josie and then kills herself in a bloody stabbing, an action asserting her resistance to allowing Josie to be raised in a domestic sphere where Josie and Hester will lose agency as women. Although the play follows a similar tragic structure to *Medea*, issues of displaced people, ethereal landscapes, and economic misfortune during Celtic Tiger Ireland dominate the play's narrative and historical context.

Previous criticism has examined the play as a tragedy and, to some extent, analysed how oppressed women overcome or succumb to the social difficulty of life in rural Ireland. Drama critics situate *By the Bog of Cats...* in the lineage of Greek tragedy, but they also tend to explore some of its commonalities with Irish mythology. Melissa Sihra recognises that the figure of Big Josie resembles Cathleen Ni Houlihan, in the eponymous play W.B. Yeats published in 1902, as a re-imagined metaphor of mother Ireland, but one who now represents the nation as a sort of anti-mother through her eroticism, cursing, and transgressions. 'Big Josie,' argues

Sihra, 'embodies the unattainability of the past and its narratives and changes that can be imposed on a nation.'[10] Hester and Josie are not just relegated to nationalist roles or figures rooted in the geographies of the past, even if these roles underscore 'the notion of otherness' ascribed to women.[11] Instead, these women's relationships with the symbolic and terrestrial space of the bog reveal their shared dispossession in neocolonial discourses of economic and social failings. While Big Josie inverts the image of Mother Ireland, Hester forgoes it altogether by reinventing the rural bog as a liberating space separate from the domestic. Rather than identifying Hester as 'the female as outlaw or deviant',[12] this chapter gives an account of Hester as a subversive figure who rejects expectations placed upon her as a woman and a Traveller living on the bog.

Critics have also commented on the liminal location of *By the Bog of Cats*.... Sihra regards the play's *mise en scène* as a 'non-place', which creates a link among 'place, identity and memory'.[13] Sihra connects Carr's non-place bog to Samuel Beckett's landscapes of material and existential nothingness in, for example, *Waiting for Godot*, through their similar presentation of unformed space. Enrica Cerquoni comparably regards the 'vividly physical image' of the play's landscape as 'a Beckettian expanse of water and mist, frozen, surreal, harsh and wild'.[14] Bernadette Bourke draws attention to the dramatic connections between the grotesque and liminal aspects of the bog, but she emphasises the qualities of the carnivalesque more than the bog. Drawing from Mikhail Bakhtin's theory of the carnivalesque, Bourke argues that the carnival qualities in the play – where order and stability succumb to an unpredictable world of chance and uncertainty – mirror the characters, historical conditions, and landscape. For Bourke, the carnivalesque 'is a strategy that allows for the blurring of boundaries between the real and the surreal, the natural and the supernatural, the past and the present, and between high and popular cultural influences'.[15] Bourke's focus largely remains on the play's 'topsy-turvydom' inherent in the carnivalesque as opposed to the landscape that it reflects. In this respect, the play's action shares similar qualities to the bog on which the scenes unfold.

Both Sihra and Bourke view the bog as a lack or absence of setting rather than a specific space through which to investigate the action in the play. Cerquoni, in contrast, explores the theatrical space in the play and how it relates to the performative qualities of the stage production. She does so by referencing various productions of *By the Bog of Cats...* and studying how individual directors construct space in the play, both

5.1 Brigit (Mary Murray) and Hughie (Steve Blount) on the bog in
Bog Boy (photo by Pat Redmond)

in terms of the bog and characters' movement on stage. For Cerquoni, the bog catalyses a broader argument about how space contributes to the visual qualities of the actual performance: 'As spectators, we are in a shifting and permeable land which moves between contrasts.'[16] Although presenting the atmosphere of the bog in technical staging terms provides a compelling angle of exploration, it does not necessarily address a central theme in the play: how the bog comforts oppressed women in a neo-Gothic framework.

Kinahan's *Bog Boy* confronts the subject of 'disappeared' bodies that were buried in bogs and stems from the sectarian violence in Northern Ireland. The historical backdrop of the play amplifies the effect of the post-Celtic Tiger collapse in Ireland, a period of Irish history beginning in 2008 that, according to the *Irish Times* journalist and author Fintan O'Toole, 'swept away the hopefulness and the sense of possibility'.[17] The sense of loss described here by O'Toole particularly affected the lower socio-economic sector, a demographic of primary focus in *Bog Boy*.

The play opens with Brigit hearing about the death of her friend Hughie. She subsequently begins to write a letter to Hughie's sister, Bernie, about a nineteen-year-old boy who Hughie was forced to bury years earlier in the bog because of an order from an IRA commander. The contents of this letter are written sporadically and woven throughout the action of the play as flashbacks. Brigit is a thirty-year-old recovering heroin addict who has been sent by her social worker, Annie, to a remote location on a bog in Co. Meath for a work/rehabilitation assignment. Brigit is also a single mother whose newborn baby, Kaylie, has been taken from her by the state because of Brigit's drug addiction. We discover that Brigit met Hughie when she moved to the town of Navan near the bog (see Fig. 5.1). The play's climactic scene takes place when Brigit and her ex-boyfriend, Darren, clash during a visit with Kaylie and Annie. Hughie shows up late as a character reference for Brigit during Annie's visit because he is seized by his own renewed fears about the authorities digging in the bog for bodies from the Troubles deposited years earlier. In addition to arriving late, Hughie is drunk, creating a problematic situation for Brigit. As the play progresses, we find out the IRA ordered Hughie to bury a body in the bog twenty years ago, and even though Hughie did not kill the boy, he remains disturbed and haunted by that event.

Since 1999, Kinahan has written several plays, such as *Be Carna* (1999), *Moment* (2012), and *Hue and Cry* (2010), all of which have been performed in smaller theatres in Ireland. Two of her recent plays were produced and performed in Dublin: *Halcyon Days* (2012) at the historic Smock Alley Theatre and *Piigs* (2013) at the Royal Court Theatre. Including *Bog Boy* as a primary work in this chapter offers a vital analysis of oppressed women and the bog; it also delivers undercurrents of hauntings and ghosts. *Bog Boy* reflects upon the aftermath of the Celtic Tiger years, and therefore effectively bookends many of the concerns raised earlier in the 1990s in *By the Bog of Cats…*. The play, as an example of a postcolonial Gothic text, examines the intersections of haunting, death, bodies, neocolonialism, and rural Ireland. Brigit's and Hughie's haunted pasts, as well as the ghostly presence of the boy buried in the bog, generate overlapping Gothic elements with contemporary themes of sectarianism and class and gender struggles. There is an important connection between the disappeared body (Gerard), a victim of sectarian violence, and the disappeared woman (Brigit), due to neocolonial circumstances in post-Celtic Tiger Ireland. Despite these relevant themes in contemporary Irish culture, *Bog Boy* has yet to be examined in Irish literary criticism.

So far, critics have offered little discussion of Hester's or Brigit's direct relationship with the bog. Carr and Kinahan juxtapose women against the backdrop of the bog because it too is an ostracised topography. Rather than existing as a 'non-place', as described by Sihra, the bog generates and mediates peoples' actions as a real and imagined space. My approach, then, shall be to demonstrate that *By the Bog of Cats…* and *Bog Boy* challenge us to imagine a new Ireland, one that can expunge some of its traumatic past, and one that also functions under different criteria than before. If one looks at the bog as a symbol of Ireland's past, which was quickly forgotten in the Celtic Tiger era, then both plays can be seen as resisting this forgetting and as a reminder that the colonial past has only transformed into a neocolonial present and future. Part of this resistance is that women in Ireland continue to face inequality. The nebulous dynamic of the bog, simultaneously stable and unstable, effectively frames the purpose of both plays: to keep the expected past and unexpected present in flux. This is why both Hester and Brigit, in connection to the bog, represent the past and challenge those in the present to reimagine an alternative future. They are characters whose role it is to signal a more generative refiguring of women's relationships with the land. The bog creates a kind of palimpsest that holds all of those past associations even while it acts as an ideal site for writers to re-inscribe new associations to it.

Before surveying each play in the following two sections, it is important to outline some of the historical circumstances contributing to the Celtic Tiger, and particularly how they underscore forms of neocolonialism in Ireland that foreground both plays. Kevin Gardiner, who was a banker in London, originally coined the term 'Celtic Tiger' in a 1994 report for Morgan Stanley.[18] The Celtic Tiger initially referred to an economic 'boom' period in the Irish Republic from 1994 to 2000, a time when GDP grew to almost 12 per cent. Between 2000 and 2008 there were visible signs that such rapid economic increases were unsustainable, but GDP still hovered around 5 per cent, considered by many to be an excellent rate compared to Ireland's economic history prior to 1994.[19]

During the 1990s Ireland became a desirable country for many multinational corporations to relocate operations. This economic phenomenon was largely due to an unprecedented influx of global capital to Ireland, where companies were offered lower corporate tax rates. Ireland also afforded companies a highly educated workforce (thanks to socialised education) that could speak English; and it had more flexible environmental laws than anywhere else in Europe. The so-called 'boom' resulted in an unthinkable transformation, from a vastly economically depressed Ireland in the 1980s to a decade of prosperity and over-abundance in the 1990s. O'Toole argues the Celtic Tiger was a period in which Ireland was trying to reinvent itself and in so doing created a 'substitute identity' from previous narratives of nationalism and Catholicism in the 1980s that were no longer working.[20] By 2008, however, the purported surplus of the Celtic Tiger years had evaporated and Ireland became the first country in the European Union to move into a recession.

Postcolonial scholars have pointed out that the Celtic Tiger name and phenomenon is loosely related to four East Asian economies called 'tigers' that were partially a result of various forms of colonisation. These include Taiwan, Hong Kong, Singapore, and South Korea.[21] A common linkage is that infrastructures in these 'tiger' economies were still recovering from previous subordinated relationships with imperial powers. The Celtic Tiger, as a cultural, social, and economic marvel, could be considered a neocolonial phenomenon, insofar as neoliberal economic practices dominated in a period of delicate national circumstances resulting from a history of colonial servitude. In other words, neocolonialism has been used as another way of explaining the power structures of globalisation and the postcolonial world within the last thirty years. Such an unprecedented global expansion of capital both fuelled and tanked the Celtic Tiger.

The social economist Ankie Hoogvelt maintains that 'Imperialism, in both the colonial and neocolonial periods, was characterised by a geographical expansion of the capitalist mode on a world scale'.[22] Neocolonialism is based upon 'geographical expansion' through economic restructuring rather than government or military occupation in more traditional forms of colonisation, and it appears where underdeveloped nations, particularly with colonial histories such as Ireland, are subjected to new forms of oppression through modernisation and progress. Proponents of neocolonial forms of modernisation continue to encourage economic expansion even though such growth polarises equitable wealth distribution, diminishes social advancement, and promotes favourable tax schemes for large investors with no stake in fostering Ireland's cultural and social vibrancy. According to the political economist Michael Barratt Brown, neocolonialism remains the 'survival of the colonial system in spite of formal recognition of political independence in the emerging countries, which became the victims of an independent and subtle form of domination by political, military, or technical [forces]'.[23] In sum, neocolonial states are characterised by struggling economies from years of colonial servitude that offer multinational corporations cheaper labour, lower corporate taxes, and fewer environmental regulations.

Postcolonial scholars have subsequently underscored the auspicious neocolonial circumstances that created the Celtic Tiger phenomenon in Ireland. In this regard, neocolonialism can be defined another way: as an attack on the social and cultural fabric of a postcolonial nation in the name of economic growth largely for wealthy investors. Or, as postcolonial critic Robert Young argues, 'Neocolonialism thus comprises not only the half-hidden narratives of colonialism's success in its continuing operations – but also the story of a West haunted by the excess of its own history.'[24] In spite of the fact that Ireland expanded its economy during the Celtic Tiger, much of the wealth aggregated in clusters at the top of the socio-economic sector. Since the 1990s, social and cultural inequalities have only increased in the face of such economic success, a situation 'haunted' by excess. Women, for example, were particularly and negatively affected by the supposed progress of Irish modernity in the Celtic Tiger years. Among other disparities compared with their male counterparts, women experienced lower wages, little job security, and lack of union protection.[25] Fortunately, culture continues to provide a space where people critically engage with economic and political oppression. Writers and artists, for instance, respond by focusing on sites of struggle where the battle of social meanings can be challenged and redefined.[26] In terms of Irish culture, some contemporary playwrights responded to the neocolonial crisis and subordination of women by critiquing these social failings.

'Independent Ireland,' according to Victor Merriman, 'is a neo-colonial state and that reality must be acknowledged in any consideration of contemporary Irish theatre.'[27] Merriman speaks more directly to this approach in theatre: 'Irish theatre is thus created as a site of public conversation on the type of social order emerging in anti-colonial nationalism. Such founding principles are uniquely available as the principled basis to interrogate the neo-colonial conditions of contemporary society, and to critique prevailing theatre practices.'[28] Over the past century, Irish theatre has regularly responded to cultural fractures and socio-political inequalities. J.M. Synge's *Playboy of the Western World* (1907), Seán O'Casey's Dublin Trilogy – *The Shadow of a Gunman* (1923), *Juno and the Paycock* (1924), and *The Plough and the Stars* (1926) – and, later, Brian Friel's *Translations* (1980) are all prominent examples of theatrical reactions to specific historical circumstances of colonisation. Notably, though, these examples, among others, exhibit a primarily male legacy in Irish theatre.

My approach in this chapter acknowledges Merriman's claim that neocolonialism must be examined in contemporary Irish theatre, but I intend to build on his assertion by advocating that neocolonial approaches must also recognise women playwrights as a significant part of these discussions. *By the Bog of Cats…* and *Bog Boy* are plays that speak to these economic instabilities at the bottom sector of the economy, but they primarily relate to women's experiences in Ireland. Merriman's larger book-length study, *'Because we are poor': Irish Theatre in the 1990s* (2011), which offers astute postcolonial/neocolonial readings of contemporary Irish drama, posits that neocolonialism as a 'recapitulation between colonial relations' actually 'sharpens the focus of critical practice in drama'.[29] Merriman identifies the links between neocolonialism and Irish theatre, but women playwrights are largely excluded in the analysis. *'Because we are poor'*, except for briefly mentioning Lady Gregory in connection with Yeats' plays, includes only one woman playwright (Carr).

Echoing earlier attempts to highlight women novelists' contributions in the 1990s and 2000s, this chapter positions two women playwrights as central to these contemporary political and social circumstances in order to avoid the historic tendency to recast nationalist discourses that appropriate gender for male hegemony. Women's writing may not register as a primary concern for many scholars, particularly some working within Irish postcolonial criticism, which has tended to propagate patriarchal forms of nationalism whether intentionally or not. Susan Cahill traces this development and comments that 'contemporary writing by Irish women challenges exclusionary constructions of Irishness and hegemonic narratives of Irish history, both underpinned by a sense of place that is conservatively bound up with representations of the female body as land'.[30] Carr and Kinahan, two playwrights revisiting previous constructions of the feminine and land, draw attention to women of the lower socio-economic sector who are mired in neocolonial dynamics in relation to a 'sense of place'. During the Celtic Tiger, the divide between urban and rural grew exponentially and provoked questions about the prevailing nationalist idea of Irishness as rooted in the land, the West, or as a tradition.[31]

By the Bog of Cats... and *Bog Boy* challenge ideas of economic modernisation in connection to rural existence for women. On one level, each play demonstrates that modernised economic policy and prosperity do not necessarily translate into progressive social change, especially for women and minority groups. In order to evolve as a society, some proponents of modernity argue, there also needs to be an invented narrative of the past as a point of reference.[32] The problem with this position is that in these 'progressive' national narratives women are relegated to the past, objectified, and, as Moynagh Sullivan contends, used to reinforce Irish 'otherness' as part of the invented postcolonial narrative.[33] This is largely why Irish feminists have been sceptical of modernising narratives in the last few decades.[34] On another level, what illuminates the concerns for women and their relationships to Ireland also relates to the space in which the plays are set – the bog – which serves as a challenge to both the future of progress and the invention of the past.

Carr's and Kinahan's plays refocus Irish drama on women's concerns, and in so doing respond to neocolonial circumstances through social and cultural forms of literature. By re-visioning the contentious women/land relationship (by way of the bog), they re-define nationalist narratives in ways that empower women rather than subjugate or erase women's identities. Victoria White makes clear that as a point of entry for women onto the Irish stage at the Abbey Theatre, *By the Bog of Cats...* has 'fearlessly put women at the centre of it'.[35] Surprisingly, *By the Bog of Cats...* was the first play written by a woman dramatist to be produced at the Abbey Theatre in many decades.[36] In *Facing Forward*, a programme

of professional development for Irish theatre artists, Annette Clancy
comments, 'As Ireland's national theatre, the Abbey's mission is to offer
world class theatre to the widest public, to help develop Irish theatre to
its full potential and to offer an artistic platform for national debate.'[37]
One might rightfully question how a national theatre can claim to support
productions that generate a robust 'national debate' when Irish women's
voices are continually underrepresented.

Unfortunately, this problem continues. The outgoing Abbey Theatre
director, Fiach MacConghail, proposed an ambitious 2016 season
entitled 'Waking the Nation', which parallels the Easter 1916 centenary
celebrations. It was evident, however, that upon the scheduled season's
release women playwrights were again largely absent, which prompted
a cultural and social protest at the Abbey on 12 November 2015,
'#WakingTheFeminists', calling women once again to action amidst
a largely male-dominated 'national' voice in Irish theatre. The event
prompted MacConghail to reconfigure the 2016 season and to include
more women playwrights in the schedule.

In addition to positioning women at the centre of the theatrical stage
in Ireland, this chapter also places women at the centre of national
representations of land. Feminist critics have previously critiqued ongoing
depictions of 'women as land' in Ireland because such portrayals reduce
women to a position of symbolic and literal fertility for nationalist
politics.[38] Historically, the British stigmatised Ireland as 'feminine' in
colonial discourses, which were partly influenced by Matthew Arnold's
mid-late nineteenth century observations that the Celtic races were
more feminised (passionate, sensual, and non-rational).[39] This is why, as
Sullivan has argued, the pejorative term 'feminine' is used, as opposed to
'woman', in both colonial and anti-colonial discourses.[40] One way to focus
on women, instead of employing objectifying notions of the feminine,
is to examine the body and discourses of embodiment. As Cahill notes,
'Irish feminism has been involved in a continued effort to question and
subvert such traditional associations between body and woman, woman
and land.'[41] Rather than follow the tendency to allegorise the female
bodies of Hester and Brigit as the land, thereby subverting their power,
this chapter examines how both characters relate to the material and
imaginative qualities associated with the bog through a shared sense of
dispossession in a neocolonial Ireland. Since women have functioned
'as an object through which Irish studies can mediate its relationship to
itself',[42] according to Sullivan, Hester and Brigit mediate themselves as

subjects through the bog as a neutral space that represents their socio-economic background and their transgressive existence as marginalised women.

It is important to note that social and political difficulties for Irish women are not exclusive to the Celtic Tiger years; they have existed for centuries. Irish women have been silenced and chastised for questioning and resisting traditional reproductive roles and matriarchal service to the nation. If the subaltern as male is subjected to silence, Gayatri Chakravorty Spivak contends that 'the subaltern as female is even more deeply in shadow'.[43] The subjected male, McClintock argues, responds to this silence through discourses of masculinised nationalism. In these constructed male nationalisms, '*gender* difference between women and men serves to symbolically define the limits of national difference and power between men'.[44] Women, in contrast, are systematically excluded from these discourses as citizens of the nation. In addition, Irish women are elevated as symbols of the nation through various constructions of gender (feminine, goddess, Mary, Mother Éire, Cathleen Ni Houlihan, Queen Maeve, land, etc.). Carr and Kinahan make this point clear through Hester and Brigit, who are disposed of and marginalised, whereas the men in both plays command and receive respect from society simply due to their gender.

Notwithstanding such disempowerment, both plays show how Hester and Brigit imagine the bog as a space of empowerment, despite the traditional associations with rural land and the feminine national mother. Hester and Brigit are not silent observers admired as prescribed cultural symbols or representatives of the domestic realm, and in many ways they resist this sort of casting. Both playwrights use voice (both characters have the most lines in each play) as a way to empowerment, sexual freedom as a way out of traditional domesticity, and the bog as a way to reappropriate women's relationships with rural Ireland and challenge previous notions of gender and geography as representing one type of cultural identity.[45]

In this dynamic, women's relationships with geography are not only relegated to ideas of homeland and nationhood as mediated by or through men, but instead they are seen through an empowering experience constructed by each woman herself. The feminist geographer Catherine Nash explains that one of the ways to achieve this aim is for Irish women to revisit cultural traditions of what Irishness and femininity can mean through themes of nature and women's bodies.[46] It is in this sense that both plays respond to the traditional paradigms in Irish literature by placing women in rural settings, but they quickly subvert the way expected representations of femininity function in relationship to a quintessential rural landscape like the bog. For Brigit and Hester, the bog triggers responses to social challenges and serves as a gendered landscape, not as a symbol or metaphor of male nationalism, but of autonomy from a neocolonial society. This chapter goes on to argue that Carr and Kinahan subvert the traditional binaries of land/bog and mother/feminine into something empowering and sustaining for women who want to own their subjecthood. Thus, the bog can serve as a place of refuge and liberation for Irish women like Hester and Brigit precisely because it is a non-domestic space not already inscribed with nationalist gender narratives of home and motherhood.

The following two sections display how Carr and Kinahan, while working in the neo-Gothic mode, challenge the perception that the land/woman binary can only stem from masculine narratives of Irish identity. They create female protagonists who are connected to the bog without becoming a prescribed nationalist allegory for it. The first section outlines the importance of location in *By the Bog of Cats...* and shows how topographies of the bog underscore Hester's doubly subjugated identity as a 'tinker' woman. I argue that Hester resists social expectations and subverts them by reappropriating myths from nationalist traditions and through her connection with the bog. In creating this character, Carr rejects notions of home, homeland, and women's places in Ireland through Gothic themes of ghosting and transgression. In the second section, I maintain that Brigit represents another type of 'disappeared' person – paralleling the literally disappeared bodies of the Troubles – resulting from the neocolonialism of the Celtic Tiger period. *Bog Boy* suggests that the bog represents a space free of judgement, and for Brigit it eschews some of the malaise and malevolence of modernity connected to the Celtic Tiger.

As uneducated but self-contained women, both characters struggle to survive in a world where geography, class, and gender continually legitimate one's social identity. And yet, by revisiting tropes of feminisation in various ways, Carr and Kinahan endow Hester and Brigit with a sense of agency that allows them to access power to some degree. The bog, with its associations with the postcolonial Gothic, and simultaneous oppositions to it, is a space that allows freedom from preconceived notions of womanhood in both plays.

'Tinker' Women on the Bogs of the Midlands

In *By the Bog of Cats...*, exploring of issues related to rural Ireland highlights the relationship between Travellers and the land. Merriman recognises: 'Although few commentators acknowledge it, *By the Bog of Cats...* is primarily a play about travellers, the land, and rural Ireland.'[47] We could expand this idea by pointing out that women's relationships with each of these three elements becomes a fourth and fundamental aspect of the play. This section explores how Hester represents the human counterpart to the bog, both through her body and through her relationship with rural Ireland as a 'tinker' woman. She connects more with ghosts than with the living and more with the uncanny bog than with society. Hester negotiates the physical and imaginative contours of the preternatural bog through her identity as a 'tinker' and from her matriarchal lineage of women who have lived on the bog. In connection with this lineage, Xavier Cassidy, who is Caroline's father and a pillar of the patriarchal community in the play, recalls:

> Let me tell ya a thing or two about your mother, big Josie Swane. I used see her outside her auld caravan on the bog and the fields covered over in stars and her half covered in an excuse for a dress and her croonin' towards Orion in a language I never heard before or since. We'd peace when she left.[48]

Bog terrains located in the Midlands underpin other representations of women 'tinkers' and rural Ireland in the play. The Irish Midlands, which consist of mostly raised bogland, are fundamental to understanding *By the Bog of Cats...* and also to Carr's entire theatrical oeuvre, as many of her other plays are set here. To understand the Midlands is to gain significant insight into Carr's characters and settings, and particularly the bog. Although the Irish Midlands have seen an exponential disappearance of bogs, they are still home to vestiges of Monaghan Bog, Clara Bog, Boora Bog, and part of the Bog of Allen, all of which contain large areas of raised bogs that once covered much of this region. Clara Bog, in Co. Offaly, remains the most significantly preserved raised bog in Ireland and it continues to receive international attention from scientific communities.[49] While Carr is purposefully ambiguous in the stage direction about the setting for *By the Bog of Cats...*, she does provide enough circumstantial evidence in the play to suggest Clara Bog is the likely location of the fictionalised 'Bog of Cats'. With only 7 per cent of Ireland's raised bogs still intact, it is particularly poignant that Carr would create such vivid settings around bogs and centre the play's action on them.[50] The play implies that bogs are cultural and biological sacrifices to the globalised economy, which also reflects the sacrifices women have to make every day in rural Ireland. In other words, it is no accident that Carr stages a play about women in this location and in these social circumstances.

Carr discusses particular elements of the Midlands in the 'Afterword' to her earlier play *Portia Coughlan* (1996), by describing the 'open spaces, the quicksand, the biting wind, the bog rosemary'.[51] Much like Anne Enright's epigraph at the beginning of this chapter, Carr retains early memories of the bog from her childhood. Unlike Enright's resistance to 'mention' bogs 'in a book' because of their 'beauty', Carr locates most of her earlier plays on or near bogs in the Midlands. Carr explains her memories of the Midlands:

> I find myself constantly there at night: lights off, head on the pillow and once again I'm in the Midlands, I'm wrestling, talking, laughing, reeling at the nocturnal traffic that place throws up. Now I think it's no accident it's called the Midlands. For me at least it has become a metaphor for the crossroads between the worlds.[52]

The bog in *By the Bog of Cats…* is commonly referred to as a liminal non-place that bridges the empirical with the mysterious. 'And Carr, the interpreter,' observes Claudia Harris, 'stands at the crossroads between these worlds, buffeted by the biting wind blowing across the Midlands bog, dispersing the mists for only a brief moment, may the scary haunting continue'.[53]

Notwithstanding the neo-Gothic elements of the bog, Carr's depiction of the contentious terrain functions as more than just a haunted setting or a nebulous liminal space. The bog fundamentally affected Carr throughout her upbringing in Co. Offaly. As a child, Carr would often create worlds outside of reality where abandoned rules and regulation submitted to what Bourke has called the 'carnival' in her Midland plays, where the carnivalesque produces a drama of subversion celebrating alternative circumstances to the ones typically prescribed to women.[54] Even though Carr attempts to create such carnivalesque moods, there is also a sense that the surrounding bog already provides and generates these moods because of its own indeterminate qualities. The bog, for instance, creates an atmosphere of subversion and ambiguity, as well as stability and predictability, which reflects the characteristics of the protagonists. The topography of the bog mirrors the mood in the play and, to a greater extent, Hester herself.

In the 'Introduction' to *The Theatre of Marina Carr* (2003), Cathy Leeney and Anna McMullan effectively contextualise Carr's work in Irish theatre as a whole and show how it specifically connects to history, gender, and space. For Leeney and McMullan, 'Carr's plays reveal a secret history on stage of this in-between space, where women are caught between inner security and outer freedom, both painfully elusive, their paradox powerfully theatrical'.[55] Even though Leeney and McMullan do not make this explicit connection, their description parallels the state of the bog as a union of opposites or an 'in-between space'. Hester's lineage of 'tinker' women, with its expansive history of discrimination, is pushed even further to the peripheries by a modernising Celtic Tiger Ireland. Indeed, Hester's comfort with the bog results in part from being marginalised as a woman, along with her ethnic status as a 'tinker', both of which are identifications that demand constant challenging and renegotiating of the rules within the social order. But the outer freedom of the bog through its disruption of order and cultivation of the supernatural does not negate Hester's 'inner security'; it expands it. Hester claims, 'I'm goin' nowhere. This here is my house [the caravan] and my garden and my stretch of the bog and no wan's runnin' me out of here' (268).

Bogs have been mistakenly, throughout a history and culture, associated with Irish rural labourers whose livelihoods have been supported by this very landform. Many prevailing stereotypes label rural people who live near bogs as 'eejits', 'bog-brained', or 'culchies', and such derogatory stereotypes have a long historical precedent, going back to the writings of Spenser, Boate, and King, among others. The archaeologist Barry Raftery explains how the pejorative label 'bog-trotters' – Irish who lived near bogs – was the ultimate confirmation of their sub-human states.[56] The expectation that each consecutive generation of rural Irish labourers would continue the legacy of living and working on the bog continues to perpetuate the stereotype and serves as an important backdrop to the play.

At the wedding of Carthage and Caroline, a young waiter remarks: 'I want to be an astronaut but me father wants me to work on the bog like him and like me grandfather. The Dunnes has always worked on the bog' (298). As though literally trapped in a bog, young Dunne cannot become an astronaut because he is from a bog. Catwoman reaffirms to the waiter, 'Oh go for the astronaut, young man' (298). It is no surprise that Catwoman – a character who is socially ostracised and considered to be insane because she too is a woman who refuses to accept prescribed gender norms in Irish society (serving as an anti-Celtic Tiger figure) – advises this young man to take a direction that traverses the margins, to make a choice of personal empowerment and fulfilment. Catwoman appears to be the character most associated with the bog. Unlike Hester, however, Catwoman's status as a woman is not in flux; instead, it is solidly in opposition to social construction. Hester, on the other hand, experiences anxiety about her ambiguous status as a 'tinker' woman, and she wants to reconcile her duties as a mother and as an empowered woman, while also refusing to submit to social constructions of domesticity.

Hester rebukes social expectation and separates herself from rural 'bog people' when she professes, 'And as for me tinker blood, I'm proud of it. It gives me an edge over all of yees around her, allows me see yees for the inbred, underbred, bog-brained shower yees are' (289). Hester initially hesitates to accept full ownership of her embodiment of the bog, which is why she stays with Carthage so long and entertains living a domestic life: 'Ya wanted me to see how normal people lived. And I went along with ya again' me better judgment. All I ever wanted was to be by the Bog of Cats' (333). She recognises the contemporary cultural label of Midlands 'bog people' as bumpkins and dolts, while also drawing on her historical identification with Irish 'tinkers', as they share a connection with the bog but are also distinct from 'bog people'. This distinction highlights a significant factor of cultural minimisation experienced by communities who have historically survived by actually living on bogs, extending even to its contemporary inhabitants. While Hester hears comments from the community about her sub-human status, she in turn provides a long-awaited voice of empowerment to women living on the bog and is 'proud of' her 'tinker blood'. In doing so, Hester separates herself as a 'tinker' from the rural Irish stereotypes.

Even though both groups use the bog, the 'tinkers' view it as synonymous with them; they are the bog and the bog is them, much like the representation of Catwoman who lives on the bog and smells like peat. As such, women, capable of producing children, become the eternal connection to the bog; it is passed through them. Women in the play resemble the bog, not in nationalist moulds of feminised land, but in a way that gives them power because the bog signifies freedom from patriarchy. Hester first rejects Carthage on personal grounds as a rural Irish man; she then embraces her ethnic and gender status in an oblique response to prevailing nationalist narratives of domestic women who serve the nation. Such resistance to disempowerment is a response to the ethnic, class, and gender codes that continually materialise in Carr's theatre throughout the Celtic Tiger years. Within Traveller circles, women can find empowerment precisely because they eschew the typical values of Celtic Tiger ideology. They resemble aspects of the bog: unyielding, resisting, transient, and vacillating between indefinable polarities within a prescribed world of consumerism and development.

Irish Travellers, or, as Carr refers to them, 'tinkers', emerge in the play as another set of marginalised people paralleling depictions of women and the bog. Carr, however, conflates both 'tinker' and woman to produce a 'doubled other', one with subjugated ethnicity and gender, thereby positioning Hester as a 'tinker' woman who embodies the bog. Central to the play is not only the theme of Irish Travellers but also the situation of women Travellers.[57] Irish 'tinkers' were historically Travelling families who roamed the land in caravans while doing traditional artisan work for money; in fact, the term 'tinkers' derives from work as tinsmiths, mending domestic and farm utensils. Irish Travellers have been historically connected to bogs because these terrains provide freedom and open space from persecution and allow mobility and transience. As a result, they have understood the limited and limitless qualities of the bog almost as a mirror to their own existence.

Some social historians have linked the origins of Irish Travellers back to the English colonial project, locating them in pre-conquest Ireland. Forms of pastoralism as a decentralised political system thrived before the imported English model of agriculture and plantation, which, in the latter case, began to encroach until it dominated during the first major phase of colonisation in the Tudor period (1485–1603). What began as a life of mobility in the twelfth century eventually became more static amidst later Tudor campaigns to 'civilise' and suppress the 'barbarism' of itinerant peoples.

As a result of the Tudor re-conquest, many Irish landowners were displaced through the system of plantation and many Catholics were replaced with Protestant settlers. Even though both Catholics and Protestants persecuted the 'tinkers', they were historically perceived as a threat to the social and political order by the colonial regime because they were more associated with Catholicism, and therefore rebellion, and because they embraced their status as transient and marginalised.[58] Accordingly, systemic racism around the 'tinkers' has deep roots in the colonial project. During the initial Norman conquest, religious status triggered discriminatory behaviour. Later in the eighteenth and nineteenth centuries, during the height of British imperialism, discriminatory ideologies were based on the notion that the Celtic race was inferior to the Anglo-Saxons.[59] Therefore, perceptions of inferiority, which carry weight even into the contemporary moment for Travelling people, emerged from social and historical issues related to race, religion, and geography.

Hester, as a 'tinker' woman, and the bog share a similar history of and resistance to oppression. Society wants Travellers to settle in the same way that it expects women to be domesticated and the bog to be productive. Centuries of drainage and other attempts to manage bogs mirror the expectations of productivity and domesticity placed on women and 'tinkers' in Irish society. For example, social demands of domesticity and nationhood extend to the other outsiders in Irish society, whether they are physical terrains or people. Carr effectively addresses such outsiders by employing a neo-Gothic mode. Subjugated outsiders, much like spectres who haunt the bog in the play, exist between real and imaginary worlds. The uneasiness about the haunted bog resembles social unease about the 'tinkers' who, as Synge observed during his travels in rural Ireland, 'have a curious reputation for witchery and unnatural powers'.[60] Xavier underscores this point when he labels Hester a 'dangerous witch' (331), which refers to both her preternatural connection with the bog and her ability, despite being a woman in rural Ireland, to own land and demonstrate self-sufficiency without a man to support her. Xavier goes so far as to suggest that Hester should be burned as a witch because she is a woman and a 'tinker', and so doubly a threat to his patriarchy. He threatens that a 'hundred year ago we'd strap ya to a stake and roast ya till your guts exploded' (331).

As a result, bogs and 'tinkers' are associated with the Irish Gothic. Bogs, much like the 'tinkers' who live on them, continually evoke unexplainable, culturally cacophonous, and subversive aspects of Irish culture. Even though it is perceived as a stationary physical topography, the shifting bog resembles the transience of the 'tinker'; they both spontaneously migrate to new locations despite logical expectation. The caravans that house the 'tinkers' often appear on these marginal lands, and the dispossessed inhabitants with different discourses, customs, beliefs, and rituals all function outside social norms. Consequently, Hester proudly wears the

5.2 Burnt-out caravan next to a bog, after the death of a Traveller, Northern Ireland (photo by Bobbie Hanvey)

mark of the 'tinker' and an independent woman, but this certainly comes at a compromising cost within her social milieu.

Hester finds refuge on the bog because it provides an unprejudiced place to camp. This is especially the case during the Celtic Tiger. Paddy Woodworth remarks that 'tinkers suffer more discrimination in our democratic Republic than they did under British rule'[61] (see Fig. 5.2). Woodworth's comment implies that the 'democratic Republic' has replicated the colonial power structure and even outdone it as an economic neo-colony. Under British rule, 'tinkers' were granted more leeway for rural caravanning without as much persecution than in contemporary Ireland during the Celtic Tiger.[62] 'Carr's protagonists,' as Bourke argues, 'live in the democratic Ireland of equal opportunities, yet find themselves trapped and marginalized.'[63]

In addition to Carr's protagonists, the bog setting functions in the play as a separate character that is also persecuted. Hester, who translates these qualities to society, connects to and identifies with the bog. Hester's inability to integrate within the rural community in the Midlands stems partly from the abandonment she experiences by her mother, father, brother, and Carthage. She tells Josie, 'Another that had your name walked away from me. Your perfect Daddy walked away from me. And you'll walk from me too. All me life people have walked away without a word of explanation' (326). By taking refuge on the bog, Hester exhibits her connection with the land and demonstrates her choice to exist on its peripheral social space. There is nowhere else she can be free. Cerquoni asserts that the 'space of the bog then is characterized by loss and longing, yet it also represents her only site of connection and survival'.[64] Adding to Cerquoni's point, the bog functions in the play as a viable home free from domesticity for those who choose, or in some cases, are forced to live disconnected from and at the fringes of society.

Hester's inability to live in a house with Carthage further demonstrates her close relationship to the marginalised boglands. It also shows that she resists gender norms by rejecting traditional Irish domesticity and the nationalist idea of home or homeland relegated to women. By doing this, Hester celebrates and relishes the freedom of the bog. Emplacement is located in the home, whereas displacement connotes the perceived absence of place or home, which could include living on a bog in a caravan.[65] Cerquoni also suggests that Carr challenges the Irish idea of domesticity by questioning the notion of homeland and revisiting it from a Traveller woman's perspective.[66] In Hester's case, displacement functions as emplacement because the idea of home is living in the caravan on the bog. For women in Ireland, typical constructions of gender around the concept of home usually equate to getting married, embracing the feminine, and producing a family, all of which support the nation. Sihra similarly acknowledges:

> In Carr's plays the family is a site of contestation, disunity, and violation where the tenacious exploration of womanhood and issues of gender and sexuality crucially resist the monological nationalist, masculinist, colonial, and postcolonial issues of identity and history that have tended to dominate Irish dramatic narratives over the last century.[67]

Building on Sihra's and Cerquoni's explanations, another way to show how Carr confronts nationalist notions of the home, homeland, and women's place in Ireland is through her employment of ghosts as a neo-Gothic element in the play.

The supernatural dimension is central to Carr's use of Gothic conventions and settings because ghosts, like the bog terrains, have no limits within social spaces. Although referring to Irish women novelists,

Anne Fogarty places the Gothic as the dominant mode of contemporary Irish writing because of its emphasis on disrupted families, haunted domestic space, and instabilities of self-identity, all of which typically focus on the mother.[68] Such a classification reinforces Patten's claim that contemporary Irish fiction often employs 'neo-Gothic' tropes of dysfunctional families, alienated children, and abused victims.[69] Ghosts, as spectres or images of the past and future, are simultaneously part of the Irish homeland and contestations of it. As discussed in Chapter 3, during the revolutionary period, writers used ghost stories (located on bogs) as a way to address the instabilities of political history in periods of national complexity and incongruity. Hester's status as existing between both real and imaginary worlds parallels similar qualities of the bog, and this connection in the play is emphasised by her associations with ghosts and the supernatural. As much as the bog exists as an indescribable place, Hester too lives between life and death, the supernatural and real, and on the fringes of the status quo.

The play opens with a conversation between Hester and the Ghost Fancier, which is a type of Grim Reaper figure who comes to take Hester away. Although the Ghost Fancier ostensibly mistakes the time of Hester's death, there is a sense that Hester might already be dead. Hester fails to adhere to any social protocol and becomes dislocated from society, and consequently dead to the nation, because she refuses to support women's function within it. Hester is also partly a ghost throughout the play because she is visible to the world but no longer has a material function in it. She is also able to see her brother Joseph, who appears as another ghost in the play, when no other characters can.

Her relation to the living is not only informed by her definition of home, but also through her matriarchal 'tinker' lineage on the bog, passed to her from Big Josie and then through her to her daughter Josie. Hester notices her pending and fluctuating state when she remarks: 'It's that hour when it could be aither dawn or dusk, the light bein' so similar' (266). This mistaken time of day reinforces the irrelevance of time for Hester, who poses as an eternal object in nature, transcending the limitations of the temporal. Even though Hester is the only person who can see the Ghost Fancier, Monica Murray, one of her only friends, assumes it has something to do with the bog. Monica remarks, 'There's no wan, but ya know this auld bog, always shiftin' and changin' and coddin' the eye' (267). It is as though anything can happen on the bog; it transcends logic or empirical judgement, while also serving as a real space of liberating potential for women like Hester in the midst of an oppressive Celtic Tiger economic and social machine.

The traditional Gothic aesthetic ascribed to the bog appears immediately in the opening stage direction when Hester drags '*the corpse of a black swan after her, leaving a trail of blood in the snow*' (265; original emphasis). This stark visual of burgundy blood splattered on the white snow of the bog contrasts with another image: Hester's dwindling essence against the cold, dead repose of the landscape. In this sense, Hester and the bog generate a similar atmosphere of death and isolation in the *mise en scène* of the play. Hester's uncompromising roots in the land indicate that she refuses to leave the bog even to save herself and Josie. Hester reflects, 'Ah, how can I lave the Bog of Cats, everythin' I'm connected to is here.' She continues, 'I'd rather die … I was born on the Bog of Cats and on the Bog of Cats I'll end me days. I've as much right to this place as any of yees, more, for it holds me to it in ways it has never held yees' (314). For Hester, dying is the ultimate act of freedom, not cowardice or disempowerment, because it is better to die free than become eradicated through the gender roles enforced by the nation.

As an embodiment of the bog, Hester asserts her position as a physical and imagined body on the precipice of death amidst the ghosts of many worlds. She is an extension of the bog on which she was born and where she will soon die. Hester's blood – signifying lineage, ethnicity, and womanhood (coming from a line of independent women) – also pours onto the external landscape of the bog when she stabs herself. But the swan ultimately represents Hester's liminal and imagined relation to society, as she negotiates the internal and external order as a woman and Irish 'tinker'. Catwoman even mentions at the beginning of the play that all the Swane women are considered swans: 'Swane means swan' (275). The swan is bleeding because Hester 'found her frozen in a bog hole last night, had to rip her from the ice. Left half of her underbelly' (266). There is even an accompanying song, 'The Black Swan', that was used during the production of the play. The last stanza of the song relates to Hester's position. Similar to the image of the swan, she is caught between two worlds:

> I wish I was a black swan
> And could fly away from here,
> But I am Josie Swane,
> Without wings, without care. (263)

Hester, too, has been ripped from the land, half of her in the physical world of the bog and the other half torn in the internal world of the unfamiliar domestic relationship with Carthage and Josie. This opening scene with the swan foreshadows Hester's ultimate act: to die free rather than live stuck in the limits placed upon her through a largely patriarchal society.

When looking to the cosmic birth order of creation, death, and rebirth, Hester represents the unnamed, dislocated generations connected to bogs, existing outside of society. By living a mythologised present, Hester defies the continual displacement of disregarded Irish 'tinkers', and consequently exists simultaneously in both the mythic past and the present. In one sense, this concept supports a nationalist reading of Hester as Mother Éire or Cathleen Ni Houlihan, both mythologised symbols of Ireland, but these depictions are creations of men and relegate women as sensationalised and fixed symbols. Elizabeth Butler Cullingford remarks:

> The personification of Ireland as a woman has served two distinct ideological purposes: as applied by Irish men it has helped to confine Irish women in a straitjacket of purity and passivity; and as applied by English cultural imperialists it has imprisoned the whole Irish race in debilitating stereotype.[70]

Rather than follow the nationalist allegory of the maternal in Irish society, Hester's role in the play emphasises her matriarchal lineage as opposed to a patriarchal world order where women are somehow subordinated and made to symbolise land for the Irish nation. Therefore, Hester's connection to the bog buttresses her own agency as part of a matriarchal line; the bog concurrently allows her to resist forms of Irish nationalism and the neocolonialism of the Celtic Tiger as depicted through characters like Xavier and Carthage. If men create the nation, then what does the nation look like for Hester?

The motherland is the bog, where Big Josie, Josie, and Hester will all return in the cycle of death and rebirth, but Carr re-appropriates the motherland to empower women rather than objectify them. Hester's last words before she dies are directed at Carthage, who epitomises the very idea of nation that she is leaving:

> Ya won't forget me now, Carthage, and when all of this is over and half remembered and you think you've almost forgotten me again,

take a walk along the Bog of Cats and wait for a purlin' wind through
your hair or a soft breath be your ear or a rustle behind ya. That'll
be me and Josie ghostin' ya. (340)

Death for the Swane women initiates rebirth as a symbol of freedom, and
the bog forms these natural ties to the cosmic cycle.

Big Josie demonstrates that the connection between the bog and their
family is ultimately tied to their lineage as women and 'tinkers', not to
Ireland as a nation. Big Josie promises Hester that she will return to the
bog of her origins; but after disappearing on the bog, Hester could only
assume this will not be in physical form. Hester reminisces to young Josie,
'Ya know the last time I saw me mother I was wearin' me Communion
dress too, down by the caravan, a beautiful summer's night and the
bog like a furnace.' She recalls, 'And I watched her walk away from me
across the Bog of Cats. And across the Bog of Cats I'll watch her return'
(297). The reminder of Big Josie's early exit from the material world as
a discriminated 'tinker' woman leaves an indelible imprint on Hester;
she alone is in control of her life, even if that means death. Instead
of expecting Big Josie to physically return to the bog someday, she is
reminded of her mother's symbolic presence every time she looks at the
bog, which triggers these opposites in Hester's vision. Hester continually
walks on the bog in the evenings and anticipates her mother's return,
while also realising that Big Josie's ghostly presence has been there all
along as a reminder of their own matriarchal history.

The play's highly tragic dénouement insinuates, comparably as we
shall see to *Bog Boy*, that killing or consuming one's child is one course of
action in opposing her growing up in a world of disempowerment. In a
final assertion of agency, Hester underscores her power as a woman and
mother to take her child's life and then her own, thwarting any patriarchal
oppression from Carthage, Xavier, or the idea of nation. Hester responds
to Carthage after he realises Josie is dead: 'Yees all thought I was just goin''
to walk away and lave her at yeer mercy. I almost did. But she's mine and
I wouldn't have her waste her life dreamin' about me an yees thwartin'
her with black stories against me' (340). As Carthage implies earlier in the
play, Hester's role is over now that he and his subordinate, Caroline, will
raise Josie – an act supporting the nation, in a house, for the greater good
of socio-economic progress.

Killing Josie is an ultimate anti-nationalist action because it rejects
the primary function of women as bearers of children, who serve as

future economic producers for the nation. Dead or erased children haunt the scenes in the play, but, as Carr's play connotes, dead children avoid the traumatic fate of living in a neocolonial world where women and Travellers still struggle to be legitimised. Emphasising this notion of the bog as the site of a cosmic/mythic cycle of rebirth somehow lessens or makes more palatable the gruesome climax of the play, which also parallels Medea's ultimate justification for killing her own children – to reassert her own agency as a woman and mother.

Within the matriarchal family lineage, strong liberatory overtones suggest that Hester insists on returning to the bog as part of a cosmogonic cycle of birth, death, and rebirth into and through the bog, and based on her own volition.[71] Hester performs her own sacrifice, as opposed to relinquishing to the narratives of goddess sacrifice propagated by nationalists to justify their subordination of women.[72] Bourke acknowledges that Carr 'reworks the folk belief in the earth as grave and womb, that "swallows up and gives birth at the same time"'.[73] This sacrificial tradition had been inherited not only because of Hester's immediate experience, but also through oral accounts handed down as part of her folk traditions. Big Josie stitched a song in this vein:

> By the Bog of Cats I dreamed a dream of wooing
> I heard your clear voice to me a-calling
> That I must go though it be my undoing.
> By the Bog of Cats I'll stay no more a-rueing –
>
> To the Bog of Cats I one day will return,
> In mortal form or in ghostly form,
> And I will find you there and there with you sojourn,
> Forever by the Bog of Cats, my darling one. (232)

The cycle of death, birth, and rebirth reinforces the continual recitation of Big Josie's song throughout the play. Passing down the matriarchal line from Big Josie to Hester to young Josie, the song indicates that the life cycles of these women are vital to the greater cosmogony of their mythologised existence on the bog. Big Josie, Hester, and Josie will not be isolated and seduced by men; instead, they will re-appropriate nationalist and imperialist images of the bog/land for their own purposes, in order to avoid being socially conditioned by these dominant narratives of sexuality and nationhood.

Hester relies upon the bog to reincarnate the memory of her remote past with the knowledge that her mother will return to her in 'mortal form or in ghostly form'; in this way, Big Josie has never left her. The bog is a living memorial to her mother and also the alternate reality experienced by women 'tinkers' living on the bog. Hester recalls, 'I made a promise, Monica, a promise to meself a long while back, all them years I was in the Industrial School I swore to meself that wan day I'm comin' back to the Bog of Cats to wait for her there and I'm never lavin' again' (324). Hester memorialises the loss of Irish 'tinker' women, which include Big Josie, Josie, and herself. She muses, 'For too long now I've imagined her comin' towards me across the Bog of Cats and she would find me here standin' strong' (336).

By the Bog of Cats… addresses both the bog and Irish culture when translating Hester's sense of abandonment to the nation itself. When we more narrowly inquire how bogs depict such unconscious emotions, we discover that their typography reveals patterns of colonial manipulation, control, and eradication. Hester confronts this neocolonial reverberation when she states, 'The truth is you want to eradicate me, make out I never existed' (315). Hester's status as a 'tinker' woman, much like the history of bogs, has been systematically eradicated through erasure in Ireland's colonial history. The bog serves as a space that provides freedom from preconceived notions of womanhood, and supports Hester's ability to break free from social expectations and domestic attachments. There is a reason Hester never escapes the bog – she embodies it and must return to it, even in death.

'Disappeared' Women in Neocolonial Ireland

Approximately a decade after Carr wrote By the Bog of Cats…, Kinahan introduced Bog Boy, a play bringing into focus many relevant social and economic issues pertaining to post-Celtic Tiger Ireland. Oristown Bog, where Kinahan sets the play, is located just north-east of Clara Bog, the assumed setting of By the Bog of Cats…. Because Clara Bog (Co. Offaly) and the smaller Oristown Bog (Co. Meath) are positioned in rural Ireland, they both deal with similar social and cultural preconceptions about the people who live on them and the places associated with them.

The remainder of the chapter explores the 'disappeared' women who are social casualties of neocolonial modernity as disenfranchised and impoverished single mothers. Although women in Ireland have continued to advance in social equality, particularly in the 1990s, class remains an issue often overshadowed by sexuality and gender.[74] Feminist analysis tends to regard economic disparities between men and women (unequal pay and opportunity for work) as an assault on all women, but even beyond one's gender, according to Sinéad Kennedy, one's class position 'mediates one's experience of oppression'.[75] Merriman argues that postcolonial critique 'seeks to demonstrate that engaging with Irish neo-colonialism as, in important respects, a recapitulation of colonial relations sharpens artists' engagement with the social contradiction of Independent Ireland'.[76] Contemporary Irish theatre responded to economic and cultural strategies propagated by the neocolonial programme that continued to support Celtic Tiger policies even after such policies had been proven to increase inequality among Irish citizens.[77] Beyond the economic dimension of these policies are cultural and social repercussions, particularly pertaining to women. Kinahan's play *Bog Boy* examines these issues in relation to women and class, and demonstrates how the bog, like in *By the Bog of Cats...*, serves as a space of liberation free from oppression.

Bog Boy begins when the protagonist Brigit is placed in Navan, Co. Meath, for a drug rehabilitation work assignment by her social worker, Annie. Brigit had previously been living on the streets in Dublin. Hughie is her neighbour in Navan and appears at first to be the classic foil to Brigit; he is stable, while being connected to the rural bogland. He initially does provide her with friendship and support, but overshadowing their relationship is a dark secret. Hughie was responsible for submerging a dead body into the Oristown Bog, near their houses, when he was part of the IRA thirty years earlier. The buried body of Gerard, the nineteen-year-old 'bog boy', becomes the secret haunting the action in this neo-Gothic play.

The stage notes for one specific scene in Act One indicates that the RTÉ News can be heard on the television in the background as Hughie sits in the café where Brigit works. The distant voice on the TV announces, 'digging is reported to have commenced at a bog near Navan, Co. Meath for the body of a nineteen-year-old boy missing from Belfast since 1972. This is the third confirmed location of a body from a group now known as "the disappeared".'[78] Gerard is one of Ireland's 'disappeared'. This identification typically refers to a group of people who were casualties of the Northern Ireland sectarian violence in the 1970s. Indeed, sixteen people have been officially classified as having been 'disappeared', with only ten bodies found.[79] In 2001, the Irish government provided amnesty to both nationalist and loyalist paramilitary groups in order to gather information about the locations of bodies who were victims of sectarian violence.[80] Brigit attempts to recall what is being said on the television for Hughie's sake because he cannot or will not listen to the broadcast. She crassly summarises, 'there's an amnesty or something, so they got a tip-off about the bog' (22). Many of the 'disappeared', like Gerard, were deposited in bogs. Gerard most likely relates to one actual case of a nineteen-year old boy from Donaghmore (Co. Tyrone) named Columba McVeigh, who has remained 'disappeared' since 1975, and whose remains are likely to be in Bragan Bog, in Co. Monaghan.

Although Hughie's connection to Gerard's disappeared body might appear to be the focus of the play, it more directly examines Brigit and her relationship to the bog. Brigit represents another category of the 'disappeared', serving as a spectre of neocolonialism that has arisen out of the Celtic Tiger era. Rather than being literally buried in the bog from sectarian violence, Brigit symbolically (as the socio-economic poor) and physically (dispossessed from Dublin and transferred to Navan) serves as the disappeared people of the Celtic Tiger. In a *New York Times* review of *Bog Boy*, Rachel Saltz claims that in 'a play about lost people, Ms. Kinahan almost lets her best creation, Brigit, get lost among the big themes of violence, guilt and complicity'.[81] The play focuses less on the larger issues of 'violence, guilt and complicity' in the social backdrop, even though Brigit is also considered 'lost'. Instead of 'lost', Brigit appears to be 'disappeared' because she represents what has been neglected, forgotten, and even erased amidst the priorities of the Celtic Tiger economy. Whereas Gerard was deposited in the material bog, Brigit remains stuck in the symbolic bog away from the urban centre.

Although it might seem that substantial increases in national wealth during the 1990s would benefit everyone in Ireland, distribution of wealth continued to remain uneven and predominantly favoured a minority of top income earners. By 2000, for instance, income of the poorest 20 per cent only rose by 1 per cent, while the income of the middle classes grew by 2–3 per cent and the top 30 per cent of earners witnessed a 4 per cent increase.[82] The Justice Commission of the Conference of Religious in Ireland (JCCRI) estimated that in 2001 the average income gap between people with money and without was as much as £IR191 per week, which was the largest disparity in the EU at that time.[83] Shawn Pogatchnik buttresses this point when referencing the director of JCCRI, Fr. Seán Healy, who said, 'Ireland has not succeeded in balancing the social with the economic. We have focused primarily on boosting the economy and failed to tackle poverty.' 'But for the first time in our nation's history,' Healy continues, 'we actually have sufficient wealth to eliminate poverty – if we have the political will.'[84]

The data indicate that economic disparities grew worse for those already economically depressed at the start of the Celtic Tiger, and socially impoverished single mothers like Brigit were the most affected. In 'Irish Women and the Celtic Tiger Economy', Kennedy concurs that the risk of poverty for a single woman during the Celtic Tiger was about 24 per cent, but if the same single woman was raising a child, then this poverty rate rose to as much as 31.7 per cent. Kennedy also maintains that the dimensions of inequality during the Celtic Tiger extend significantly beyond the realm of the economic.[85] Among many social problems, drugs were more accessible at affordable rates both during and after the Tiger. Between 2001 and 2007, according to the European Monitoring Centre for Drugs and Drug Addiction (EMCDDA), illegal drug use rose from 18 to 24 per cent. This figure had increased again to 27 per cent in 2011.[86] What is most notable is that after the economic collapse in 2008 drug use continued to rise, primarily among younger populations. These figures outline the economic disparity among classes and how they relate to drug use in Ireland from 2001 to 2011. The data make clear the social and economic malaise evident to residents and writers in Ireland at the time. As a playwright, Kinahan responds by using the character Brigit as a representative victim of post-Celtic Tiger Ireland. A single mother fighting heroin addiction, Brigit lives not only on the margins of society, she also literally relocates to the edges of the bog in an attempt to overcome her addiction.

By looking at women in the socio-economic climate of Ireland during and after the Celtic Tiger, we are able to see that neocolonial outcomes create another form of the disappeared: the living 'bodies' of those who have been forgotten in Ireland's quest to modernise at unsustainable rates. As an outspoken critic of modernity, Bruno Latour contends that 'modernization is not a movement that breaks radically with the past, but rather something that brings the past back with a vengeance in expanded scale and more entangled complexity'.[87] In this sense, spectres of the disappeared resulting from the profit-driven period of the Celtic Tiger reappear 'with a vengeance' in its aftermath – almost like the Gothic return of the repressed – because of socially moribund neocolonial policies that favour the economic oppressors. In this scenario, the disappeared women suffer most. What might initially appear to be a forgotten past in the shadows of modernity is actually a remembered past of inequality 'in expanded scale'.

Bog Boy juxtaposes Brigit against Hughie, as well as against the bog, to demonstrate a comparative reading of two types of disappeared in Ireland (see Fig. 5.3). On the one hand, Hughie provides a living memory of the disappeared from the Troubles; on the other, Brigit represents the disappeared social classes of the Celtic Tiger. Both historical events have clearly given rise to inequalities linked to different kinds of colonisation. When living near the bog, Brigit becomes more visible to herself and to those around her. When she leaves Navan the night after an incident with Darren and Kaylie, she becomes invisible, disappearing into a more modern, neocolonial Dublin. Brigit writes in her letter to Bernie: 'Took a bus back to Dublin and all that came with it. Went back on the smack. And back on the game … And I never got Kaylie, Bernie … never got nothing. I disappeared' (48).

Kinahan's concentration on socio-economic factors in the play brings with it macabre, neo-Gothic overtones of terror, both in terms of the past 'terrorism' of the sectarian violence and a form of economic 'terrorism' in the present. For example, terrorism looms in the shadows as a spectre haunting Hughie, while at the same time Brigit battles her own terror of disenfranchisement as a woman faced with abject poverty, caused partly by multinational corporate economic practices that serve only a small percentage of people in Ireland. The redress of the bog, like it also does for Hester, provides catharsis for Brigit. Brigit recalls in her letter to Gerard's sister Bernie that Gerard's killing was 'his killing in my bog' (24). Brigit's use of possessive pronouns hints at her sense of belonging in rural Ireland and to the bog.

The play informs us that the Irish state has decreed Brigit unfit to raise her own child. She has also been sent to Navan on a rehabilitation work assignment, with some intimation that such a rural community on the edges of the Oristown Bog will help her to overcome addiction and subsequent poverty. We also know that while on the bog Brigit progresses on many of these fronts; she holds down a job, stops abusing substances, and begins to integrate into the community. Initially she shows prejudice against bog culture by admitting 'the bog is fuckin' third world it is' and 'I'm used to a bit of life around me ya know … CIVILIZATION' (9; original emphasis). But she later admits to her social worker, Annie, 'I

5.3. Brigit and Hughie juxtaposed on stage (i.e. the bog) (photo by
Pat Redmond)

never thought I'd say it but I like it here in the bog, can you believe it?! I
mean it's different, real different' (25).

Brigit's use of the preposition '*in* the bog' instead of '*on* the bog'
indicates a cultural attitude that connects rather than separates her to
the terrain. 'In' suggests a relationship to or connection with the bog,
while 'on' infers hierarchy of human over non-human and a sense of
ownership. Unlike her associations with society, Brigit does not mediate
her experience through the bog; she is in it. In contrast, Hughie later talks
about the picture of Gerard that he found 'on the bog' (32). The material
photograph is on the bog, but people, particularly the bodies (living and
dead) are in the bog. By using the phrase 'in the bog', Brigit unconsciously
connects herself to other women like Hester, who are the ghosts of the

disappeared in a neocolonial Ireland, a culture that exalts investment, property development, and consumerism, while attempting to erase the marginalised groups most negatively affected by this economic structure.

Brigit has been expelled from so-called 'civilisation' as a single mother besieged by addiction. At the same time, her ex-boyfriend and the father of Kaylie, Darren, who also abused substances, retains custody of the baby and remains in Dublin. Brigit is neglected as part of the lower classes because they are not instrumental to economic progress and, as a result, witnessed very little, if any, personal improvement during the Celtic Tiger years. Women like Brigit are viewed in many cases as hindrances that need to be erased or removed; they are another type of disappeared, resembling ghosts. Although Brigit moves outside Navan to rehabilitate, she remains symbolically somewhere outside the Celtic Tiger, 'in the bog', because of her lack of apparent contributions toward economic progress and support of the nation. Brigit relocates to a space on the edges of society, or as she states, the 'fuckin' third world'. Brigit's reference to the 'Third World' presupposes that Dublin is somehow 'First World', despite the increasing poverty rates within the city during and after the Celtic Tiger. At the beginning of the Celtic Tiger period, Luke Gibbons famously stated that 'Ireland is a First World country, but with a Third World memory'.[88] Gibbons' remark underscores Brigit's impoverished position on the outskirts of the city, where desperation and subjugation are the only known currencies, in contrast to a First World economy booming in the centre of Dublin.

The notion of a 'Third World memory' might exist for some of the privileged classes enlarged by the economic boom. Nevertheless, the 'Third World' remains a reality for women like Brigit, whether she resides in rural or urban spaces. Brigit faces an almost impossible task of prospering because of her economic position; even without her drug addiction, her gender, age, and status as a single parent precludes her from social success. This scenario is unfortunately all too common for Irish women, a point Coughlan perceptively makes: 'Women are typically required, in a painful contradiction, both to sustain care and nurture at home and to meet the instrumental demands of increasingly pragmatic workplaces. The inherited cultural construction of the Irish mother still functions as a powerful background ideal, intensifying this strain.'[89] We see the same tensions surrounding constructions of mother with Hester, though in *By the Bog of Cats…* Hester's 'tinker' status and age allow her more power to rebuke these expectations. Due to this social 'strain', Brigit cannot satisfy her role as 'mother' or as caregiver and provider. In fact, her 'painful contradiction' is exacerbated because she does not have a 'pragmatic' workplace.

Although Brigit initially speaks about the Oristown Bog when she references the 'fuckin' Third World', she later comes to believe that the bog has sustained and supported her existence more than the modernised 'First World' of Dublin. When Brigit returns to Dublin, away from what she initially calls 'the middle of no-where' (9), she relapses and starts using 'smack' again, eventually living in a shelter while she medicates with methadone in an attempt to counter her addiction. When living near the bog in Navan, Brigit claims that it was different from Dublin because she 'had that hope' and 'had something ahead' (21). Less hope remains for Brigit in Dublin as an alienated woman legislated unfit to be a mother with no prospects of work. Through her gender, social class, and disability as an addict, she embodies nothing more than one of the ghostly disappeared of the Celtic Tiger. Brigit even confesses, 'I suppose I feel disappeared meself sometimes' (31).

In *Bog Boy*, the bog represents a space free of judgement. Upon first arriving in Navan, Brigit notices, 'It's a wilderness it is … a bleedin' wilderness. I mean there's not a bus!' (9). But she also recognises, 'ya never see a sinner walkin' round. No-one and nothin'. Except fuckin' cows' (9). In her own limited way Brigit admits that she feels no judgement about her past 'in the bog'. The past, recalling Latour's comment, haunts modernity with a 'vengeance'. For Brigit, the bog eschews some of the modernity connected to Dublin. Living near the bog neutralises the expectations of prescribed identity for Brigit; it provides a location where the modernity associated with Dublin, with its shelters and methadone clinics, has less impact on her life. The bog represents a living space much more real than the illusory progress of modernity in the economic system. Brigit reflects in her letter to Bernie, 'it's a beautiful place your Gerard's bog … low and brown but living if ya know what I mean' (12).

The equanimity of the bog shifts for Brigit, however, when Darren arrives with Kaylie and brings some of the entrapments of modernised Dublin. The liberatory space of the bog changes because Darren brings with him the societal expectations and definitions of what Brigit, as an Irish mother, should be in the new national economy. Upon arriving in Navan, Darren mutters, 'where the hell is this anyway?' (34). When Darren gets out of the car, the stage direction indicates that he '*stands in shite*' (34; original emphasis). He complains, 'me new runners and I just stood in shite!' (34). This is Darren's first time to set foot on the rural ground of Navan and the surrounding Oristown bog, all of which he considers to be 'shite'. With his new shoes, Darren represents the commercialisation of Dublin and his own consumer addiction. Darren's runners are contrasted against the bog as a representative symbol of shite itself. This parallel echoes Brigit's early comment, 'I'm always attracted to shite' (31).

Darren is also depicted in the play as the embodiment of the neocolonial patriarchy through his attempts to control and judge Brigit economically, socially, and personally. The narrative of the play implies that Darren has full custody of Kaylie even though it never explains the legality of the custody arrangement. This outcome occurs despite Darren's own substance issues in the past, most likely because he has more financial security because of his lower middle-class family background. In this telling scene, *Bog Boy* demonstrates how Irish males are given deference in the structure of the traditional Irish family. Darren refers to his 'Ma' on three separate occasions in front of Brigit and Annie the social worker. First, when Annie asks Darren what he has in the heavy bag, he responds, 'I dunno, me Ma packed it' (35). Second, Brigit compliments Kaylie's 'little shoes' and Darren unenthusiastically responds, 'that's me Ma, she dotes over her she does' (36). Lastly, Darren insists that they have to get back soon, even though they just arrived, because 'Ma wants us back before six' (36). In fact, there is never any mention of Darren's Da. These three examples accentuate the Oedipal partnership of Darren and his Ma, the 'couple' who are raising Kaylie. Brigit comments, 'Sure it's all they ever wanted anyway … to get me out a the picture' (37).

Beyond the Oedipal undertones that suggest a culture of entitled Irish masculinity, never fully weaned from their mothers, Darren's Ma abnegates Brigit because of her refusal to adhere to the proper woman/ mother role. In this way, the play challenges how 'proper' mothers like Darren's Ma are idealised in Irish culture. Darren's behaviour and entitlement proves to be ironic because he is actually emasculated by his mother, who packs his bags and takes care of his daughter; he also lives with her. The play subtly implies that a matriarchal system actually drives the nation, while the patriarchy holds all of the power and responsibility. Male entitlement, as seen through Darren, projects a larger issue that the play confronts through a female protagonist who has disappeared and been erased in contemporary Irish society.

In this regard, Brigit remains subjected to the entrapments of abject poverty because of her inability to fulfil the social gender norms ascribed to her as a 'mother' by patriarchy, the Catholic Church, and neocolonial economic systems at work. Brigit cannot care for Darren in the same way that his Ma can, a woman who clearly serves as a 'feminine' nationalist ideal. In contrast, society forgives Darren, the prodigal son, for his previous transgressions, which include having sex with a woman like Brigit and abusing substances. Darren, with the support of society, decides to erase Brigit from the picture because of her substance abuse and social standing. Annie, who is also part of the social structure, reminds Brigit, 'You didn't help yourself' (37). The mechanisms designed to support Brigit have actually failed her because as an unmarried mother with a child she is invisible and without a voice. The Irish state/nation ultimately sides with the child and the father, not the single mother, which we see conveyed in both *Bog Boy* and *By the Bog of Cats*…. Brigit serves as one of the many types of disappeared people who fell through the cracks in a failed economic and social policy during and after the Celtic Tiger.

One of the recurring themes in traditional Gothic works, as well as neo-Gothic ones, is that women attempt to escape from confining social spaces and expectations, such as churches, the law, or family (particularly marriage), which are most assuredly patriarchal and abusive. While men demonstrate transgression in various novels, they become the main threat to women in Gothic texts. As Punter and Byron explain, the woman in these Gothic works 'is usually depicted enjoying an idyllic and secluded life; this is followed by a period of imprisonment when she is confined to a great house or castle under the authority of a powerful male figure or his female surrogate'.[90] In *Bog Boy*, female entrapment expands to socio-economic space in addition to its traditional physical spaces (castles, houses, bogs) and imagined spaces (isolation and confinement). The men in Brigit's life – namely Darren and Hughie – both disrupt and destroy her nurturing and secluded life near the bog.

Darren represents the main threat in Brigit's life in what Punter and Byron refer to as a 'powerful male figure'. During his brief time in Brigit's house, Darren's actions are controlling, abusive, and authoritative. Upon the arrival of 'furious Darren', as Gwen Orel emphasises in her review of the play in the *Irish Examiner*, he 'destroys the peace of the bog with his anger'.[91] His abuse begins when he demands that Kaylie continue sleeping, even though this is the only time Brigit will have a chance to see her daughter during this visit (and the first time in six months). After only a few monosyllabic exchanges with Brigit, he claims, 'you're not fit to have her near ya' (36). Darren, who continues to control everyone, including

Annie, whispers to Brigit, 'Ya see I'm only humourin' these assholes. Humouring them Brigit, like me Ma said; till you fuck it up so bad the social [Annie] won't let ya near her either' (41). Darren even whispers to Brigit in private, 'Ya might have this clueless cunt [Annie] codded but I seen ya fuck it up … everytime' (37). When everything collapses for Brigit, and Darren storms out of the house with Kaylie, Brigit cries, 'I want Kaylie, I want her back … I want me life back Darren' (41). Darren responds, 'The only life you get is the one that I give ya' (41). Even Annie, although supportive of Brigit at times, ultimately sides with Darren as they leave the house. Annie functions as the male's 'female surrogate', both as an agent of control over Brigit and an agent of the patriarchal state that dictates the social worker's movements.

One important point here, and one I would argue remains a crucial undercurrent in the play, is that *Bog Boy* reveals evidence of Darren's abusive behaviour by showing his psychological and verbal violence, as well as his physical bullying when he intentionally withholds Kaylie from Brigit. In a study for the *American Journal of Public Health*, researchers found that for many women in violent and abusive relationships, where they are often sexually assaulted, forced pregnancy or pregnancy as a result of rape are common strategies applied by their abusers.[92] Research also indicates that one in five Irish women have experienced some form of violence in their relationships with men and 20 per cent of these women experience sexual assault.[93] These statistics increase for economically depressed populations, especially those involving substance abuse.

Based on this research, coupled with Darren's abusive actions and language in the play, it could be deduced in the subtext of the play that Brigit's pregnancy likely resulted from sexual assault. After all, Kaylie is the 'life' Darren claims he gave her. This is why Brigit yells back to them as they leave that she wants her 'life' back. Darren has been granted custody of Kaylie partly because Brigit, while affected by heroin addiction, tried to throw Kaylie into the Dublin canal when she was an infant. Brigit's potentially unwanted pregnancy could likely have been a result of sexual assault, a form of coercion that is all too often employed by abusive men as part of a pattern of violence and intimidating behaviour intended to control their partners. Thus, Brigit was likely driven to commit infanticide because other outlets to deal with her unwanted pregnancy, such as abortion, were not a possibility within Irish law, and she had no other option based upon her socio-economic limitations.[94] The play reveals some of the ongoing problems of domestic abuse, drug use, and unwanted pregnancies, all of which reflect social issues that have been significantly ignored amidst Ireland's economic prosperity period, as well as into the present.

The bog serves as a site of freedom for women in both *By the Bog of Cats...* and *Bog Boy* because it provides an alternative kind of narrative resisting the power structures of both economic and social policies supporting empowerment for men instead of women. When Hester kills her child and Brigit attempts to, these acts literally and symbolically empower them in each play because such actions, despite the explicit horror, give them agency over their own reproduction. In both plays, men have taken the control of reproduction from them, insomuch as the women have little choice and influence over their own bodies, lives, and children. Both plays recognise how disempowering it is for the women protagonists who are mothers to have the Irish state, or the ideological 'nation' governed by patriarchal policies, take away their children. Horrific outcomes result in a kind of death for Brigit and Hester through the separation of the mother and child. Both Brigit and Hester remain part of a larger history in Ireland, where bogs serve as macabre and unimaginable spaces for infanticide, and signal a necessary reproductive liberation for women in Irish society.

Northern Irish theatre director and film-maker Carol Moore illustrates this tragic situation that many Irish women experience in her short film *Field of Bones* (1997). It is an adaptation of Cathal Ó Searcaigh's poem '*Gort na gCnámh*'/'The Field of Bones', and relates to themes of reproduction, abuse, and infanticide resulting from patriarchy in both *By the Bog of Cats...* and *Bog Boy*. In this neo-Gothic short film, a woman flashes back to a memory of herself as a thirteen-year-old girl, a time when she watches her father beat her mother to death in the kitchen of their rural cottage. Since they were poor farmers, the young girl was expected to accept the role of 'mother' by caring for the father, working in the field, and tending the house. One night after her mother's death, the father comes into the girl's room in the middle of the night and rapes her. This sequence of incest continues over time and the girl eventually becomes pregnant. One night she goes to a part of 'the field', which is actually a bog, and births the baby by herself. She then buries the baby alive in the bog. Searcaigh captures the crude tragedy of this situation in his poem: 'My midwife was an old dog bitch, / Who lapped up my blood, chewed on afterbirth'.[95] Although bleak and ghastly, Moore's film adaptation of Searcaigh's poem demonstrates an entire history imbued with another type of disappeared people in Ireland associated with the bog: babies that have resulted from unwanted or forced pregnancies. It also employs a neo-Gothic aesthetic, as her mother appears throughout the film as a ghost and focuses on family abuse and depravity.

In this sense, then, Kinahan's example of Brigit draws from a much longer haunted history of infanticide in Ireland connected with the bog (as well as other natural spaces such as lakes or oceans), as an unfortunate solution to a form of reproductive liberation from patriarchal laws.[96] Bogs provide a clandestine space for generations of women to hide the bodies of their unwanted pregnancies from society, their families, and their husbands. The ghosts of the babies continually haunt the bog, much like the disappeared. Even though Brigit never tried to throw her baby into a bog, her story illustrates what may be a similar circumstance for the urban woman, with the Dublin canal as the closest wetland equivalent. The bog also represents a sympathetic terrain in the play, something that offers freedom through its permeability; it is a space where one can hide an unwanted baby, and for marginalised women an opportunity or a kind of agency. The important link is the bog itself, and it plays both a symbolic and physical role in the lives of each woman protagonist.

In addition to Darren, Hughie also entraps Brigit. He is the one man she trusts during her short-lived and yet empowering life near the bog until Darren and Annie bring over Kaylie. In the plan that Brigit concocts, Hughie is supposed to come over and ask for some sugar in order to demonstrate that Brigit has stability and community in her new life in Navan. Instead, he is so paralysed with fear about the authorities currently digging to find the boy in the bog that he arrives intoxicated, which only makes matters worse for her situation with Darren, Kaylie, and Annie. Darren shows even more hostility toward Hughie than he does toward Brigit, which is initially perceived as a response to Hughie's intoxication. However, Darren's resentment also contains deeper forms of discrimination related to Hughie's connection to the rural bogland. From Darren's perspective, Hughie is a 'culchie', a derogatory name for people who live in rural areas. Darren mutters, 'you're not passin' me daughter to that' (30). 'That', of course, refers to Hughie. Darren sees Hughie as a new 'man' for Brigit and therefore a threat to his position as father figure and patriarchal leader of the (broken) household. Despite the fact that Hughie arrives at her house drunk on an important day for Brigit, she still forgives him: 'It wasn't your fault … fuckin' nothing new in it' (42).

Hughie resembles all of the other destructive men in Brigit's life when he insists on foisting his own buried secret on her. He tells Brigit the story about when he thought he was only burying guns in the bog for the IRA, only to then see them shoot 'a rat' who could not, ostensibly, keep his 'gob shut' (45). For thirty years Hughie has repressed this secret at the cost of his own psychological and physical health. After dumping the secret onto a very resistant Brigit, he then requests she inform the police that they are digging in the wrong spot of the bog because he cannot bring himself to do it. Hughie insists, 'I've tried all week but I can't. I've not had the courage for thirty years Brigit and I don't have it now' (46). Hughie's lack of courage pertains more to abandoning Brigit than confronting his past. He even attempts to displace his own imprisonment onto Brigit, which she describes as 'Using me to do your dirt' (47).

Brigit's own response to patriarchy – in the form of Darren, the state worker Annie, neocolonialism of the Celtic Tiger, and Hughie – builds to this climax at the end of the play. Before leaving Hughie to stew in his own paralysing memories, while also refusing to contact the police on his behalf, Brigit delivers the climactic lines of the play:

> And I thought you were different … I thought you were … for once … just for once … someone … someone good … someone decent. Someone who didn't want shit from me but you're just as bad … no, you're worse … worse than Darren, worse than me Da … worse than any of them usin' me. (47; original ellipses)

Bog Boy's dénouement underscores the dispossession and oppression women feel in neocolonial Ireland. For Brigit, the bog is a stable, idyllic place for a short period of time in her life, even though she had to overcome her own prejudices about rural Ireland as the 'Third World' in order to experience such a feeling. According to Brigit, Hughie is 'worse than Darren, worse than me Da' because she trusted him. But the bog, with its 'big bog holes seeping' (12), provides a space of hope, stability, and the potential of freedom, even if only for a brief moment. She writes in her letter to Bernie, 'Seeping like this is the place [bog] where the world opens up, opens up and sighs' (12). For a moment Brigit was free of her urban confinement, when she eventually 'opens up and sighs', only to then return to Dublin as one of the disappeared women in the neocolonial state of post-Celtic Tiger Ireland.

The Celtic Tiger Hangover

Both Marina Carr and Deirdre Kinahan offer an implicit link between the marginalisation of the bog and women in Ireland, but they do so by reinscribing previous perceptions of the women/land association. Carr and Kinahan resist the neocolonialism of the Celtic Tiger era by challenging traditional representations of domesticity through the cultural practice of theatre. This chapter has explored how Hester and Brigit are outcasts in a society that does not provide support or freedom in the same way that the bog does. The bog challenges neocolonialism, which during the Celtic Tiger years insisted that modernity, in the form of consumerism and development, was the only way to shirk the colonial past. The disenfranchised classes, and particularly women in this socio-economic register who were not the focus of modernised policies, suffered the most. Analysing the bog in *By the Bog of Cats...* and *Bog Boy* brings to the fore social issues during the Celtic Tiger, drawing on neo-Gothic conventions, and allows the audience to witness social repercussions from another angle.

By using the traditional rural settings of the bog, Kinahan and Carr promote the idea that women can redefine their role in contemporary Ireland from mothers of the nation to mothers of self-liberation. Women, in both plays, find liberation in these marginalised terrains. While living on the bog, Brigit stays clean and sober, but when she moves back into the 'civilisation' of Dublin, she relapses. Embracing modernity in a technological and cosmopolitan future rather than in 'a form of perpetual hesitancy', according to Killeen, 'may not be altogether possible in Celtic Tiger Ireland since it appears that the Irish have finally made a choice and reflected the hyphenated mind of the past'.[97] Such a 'hyphenated mind' in contemporary Ireland is not only about hybridisation between modernity and the past, but also about modernity and the future. Brigit's return to 'civilisation' as opposed to continuing to 'live in the bog' challenges the notion that the only way forward for her, and symbolically for Ireland, is to ignore the Gothicised past of the bog and embrace a modernised future. The play suggests that in the bog and its collective memory resides hope for the present, particularly for those 'disappeared' by modernisation and post-nationalist neocolonial patriarchy. As Kinahan intimates through her protagonist Brigit, Ireland must face the hangover left by the years of Celtic Tiger over-indulgence – a future of debt and imposed austerity that is not too dissimilar from recovery or substance abuse.

Reflecting back to the 1890s, by way of another *fin de siècle* in Stoker's *The Snake's Pass* (as seen in Chapter 2), the bog again functions as a space where writers return in order to counter some of the narratives of modernisation that permeate the status quo. By bringing the past to challenge the present to promote a better future, the bog is used to address some of the temporal, social, and cultural issues that remain indeterminate in an otherwise unstable history. The bog is again used in literature as a way to reclaim the social order. The next and final chapter discusses some of these current and future directions that writers may explore to conceptualise the role of the bog in Irish culture.

6

Bog Gothic, Bog Noir, and Eco-bog Writing

A bog is its own diary; its mode of being is preservation of its past.[1]

– Tim Robinson, *Connemara: Listening to the Wind*

The last four chapters have explored how, for certain writers from 1890 to the present, the indeterminate bog elicits both postcolonial and Gothic associations and provides a fruitful way to examine national histories through literature and culture. This chapter identifies three sub- 'modes', 'forms', or 'genres' that have taken shape and continue to develop in contemporary literature about bogs in Ireland. First, it investigates Gothic literature that loosely associates with the bog, creating an 'affect' known as 'Bog Gothic', particularly as it links to Patrick McCabe's novel *The Butcher Boy* (1992). Next, I will examine Irish crime writing that relies on a genre called 'Bog Noir', in Patrick McGinley's novel *Bogmail* (1978), as well as in a few brief overviews of Erin Hart's crime-novel series set in Ireland. This chapter ends by looking at writing that confronts ecological threats to bogs, or 'Eco-bog Writing', in the topographical writings and activism of Tim Robinson. All three sub-approaches within literary culture about bogs address some gaps in previous chapters, while they also offer directions for future enquiry that might prove to be rewarding for further critical exploration of bogs. Each sub-genre of bog literature contains elements of the postcolonial Gothic, a critical paradigm applicable to most forms of Irish literature about bogs, where the residues of colonisation continue to exist in various forms and are accompanied by various Gothic conventions involving dead bodies, psychological trauma, and hauntings, among other effects. Moving away from a specific geo-historical approach employed in the last four chapters focusing on particular periods of colonial tension, this chapter provides a broader rendering of contemporary works that have and continue to define the direction of bog literature and culture in Ireland.

Bog Gothic

Various critics and scholars have labelled the work of contemporary novelist Patrick McCabe as 'Bog Gothic', because its style and scope conjure metaphors of a regressive and supernatural rural Ireland that aligns with stereotypes of boglands going back hundreds of years. This label can be seen in reviews, encyclopaedia entries, articles, and book chapters. John O'Mahony writes in a 2003 article in *The Guardian*, 'King of the Bog Gothic', that McCabe 'has single-handedly coined his own genre, the affectionately termed "Bog Gothic".'[2] One problem with O'Mahony's description is that it assumes there are of other forms of the Bog Gothic mode to be 'King' of in existence elsewhere. Another problem is that he claims McCabe's literary style to be self-titled, when in actuality it was O'Mahony who regarded McCabe's work as Bog Gothic. Kilfeather briefly notes that McCabe adopts this term 'to characterise his own reformulation of the genre', particularly 'in opposition to the "big house" Gothic which has continued to surface in the past fifty years'.[3] In an entry on McCabe in the *Encyclopedia of the Gothic* (2013), Ellen McWilliams also refers to McCabe's work as 'Bog Gothic', but astutely problematises this phrase a bit further. She maintains that this association is largely due to the 'gruesome content of his novels and his preferred setting of small town, rural Ireland'. McWilliams goes on to draw more links between the Gothic and McCabe's fiction: 'Most of McCabe's narrators are maniacal outsiders cut off and excluded from mainstream society. The overriding narrative voice of McCabe's fiction is that of the madman whose stories of life in Ireland, north and south of the border, take the form of Gothic fairy tales.'[4] In another short article, Ellen Scheible writes about McCabe's brand of Gothic literature, comparing it to early forms of vampire fiction, with mind/body dualism as a metaphor for the 'inherent paradox underlying national identity'.[5] The moniker Bog Gothic has only been extended to other Irish literature that engages with the bog to a smaller extent. In a review of a performance of Carr's *By the Bog of Cats...* at the Abbey Theatre in 2015, Padraic Killeen discusses Carr's connection to 'Greek myths and Irish bog gothic'.[6] While the descriptor could in theory extend beyond McCabe's work, Bog Gothic as a particular sub-genre, mode, or form of the Irish Gothic, depending upon how it might be used and defined, still remains almost exclusively associated with McCabe's fiction.

In these primary examples, each critic and scholar recognises and draws on the usage of the term Bog Gothic but without too much attention devoted to the specific form and purpose. The term seems easy to now apply to McCabe, with a combination of satire, seriousness, and macabre, all of which capture the essence of his fiction. It could even be categorised in what Tracy Fahey has called '*Irish vernacular Gothic*', which offers a limited sense of 'otherness' deriving from collective Irish cultural and folk memories involving rites, stories, and rituals that contain specific meaning for 'peoples of the same community', and some of which might include 'living Gothic' (collective folk memory) or 'Bog Gothic' (folklore and ghost stories).[7] The otherness of an Irish vernacular Gothic described here by Fahey aligns with other modes of the postcolonial Gothic discussed throughout this book and resonates more convincingly as a literary sub-genre with social and political import. The very idea of a Bog Gothic style or sub-genre has been associated with the 'otherness' in collective Irish memory, but it is much less about the actual or real topography of the bog. In a 2013 interview, McCabe admits that the term never originated from him: 'The Bog Gothic was a journalistic thing … a catchall journalistic term.' Indeed, McCabe did not agree with the usage of Bog Gothic initially because he 'thought it was inaccurate'. He goes on to suggest, 'Probably *Winterwood* is a Gothic book, but it's pretty open in many ways anyway: a lot of it is in the city, the bog world is not even there.'[8]

An analysis of McCabe's fiction and adapted drama reveals that the bog as a material or physical space is rarely in the frame, even though some sense of it looms in the background. For example, the essence of the bog floats over the stories as a miasma, conjuring pasts while also challenging current reality. Rather than focus on the bog as a central concern, McCabe's fiction euphemistically represents the marginalised consciousness of those pejoratively associated with rural Ireland, which, as has been examined throughout this book, is often applied to bog culture. This effect also appears somewhat in his more recent novel *The Stray Sod Country* (2010), which, like his other works, depicts a dislocated rural Ireland in the 1950s, serving as a liminal space often invoking misery as well as banality. The bog is invoked almost like a ghost haunting the characters, but the apparition is seldom seen or recognised in the pages of the text; it is primarily etched in our imagination and sense of being because of the 'affect' it has created, drawing on a history of Irish literature incorporating bogs.

Contentious Terrains in many ways troubles the link between the physical bog and what we might call the 'bog affect' in Irish literature and culture. The expression Bog Gothic identifies a potentially problematic association between the bog and culture, one that has previously provoked pejorative and at times racist stereotypes from earlier English writers like Spenser, Boate, and King. As I have pointed out, many twentieth-century Irish writers later challenge and deviate from such negative labels, re-appropriating the bog as a complex space in Irish culture, not merely a wasteland to be drained. It seems, then, that using a term like Bog Gothic, which was intended to be somewhat glib and satirical, appropriates older forms of colonial racism and discrimination toward the rural Irish who live on or near bogs, and whose families depended upon them for fuel to survive over the centuries.[9] This sentiment still lingers today with socially scornful terms like 'culchie', drawing on previous terms like 'bog trotter'.

For this reason, and along with reading McCabe's own thoughts on the genesis of the term – that it was a 'journalistic term' for dramatic effect – I ultimately refrain from using Bog Gothic as a way to frame McCabe's fiction. Instead, I want to suggest that McCabe's fiction produces a bog affect in Irish Gothic literature more than it does a specific form of Bog Gothic. The notion of a bog affect has a multifaceted meaning. First, it is simply a literal example of the physical and cultural effects of the bog, as experienced by the characters in the work or even the reading audience. Second, McCabe's fiction can itself be multifarious, serving as a unity of opposites among realism, fairy tale, and social history (as in the social fantastic), leaving the reader with a sense of confusion and uncertainty. Finally, the bog, like the style of McCabe's fiction, produces an 'affective' experience through the notion of 'affect' – an emotional relationship to the human body generated by external forces (non-human 'bodies').

Affect is admittedly a slippery term and remains difficult to define because of what the cultural geographer Nigel Thrift has called its 'non-representational' status as a 'non-object'.[10] Due to its non-representational and hybridised state, it also takes many shapes depending upon how it is used and who is using it. Regardless, affect is a useful way in which we can try to measure the body's 'immersion in and among the world's obstinacies and rhythms', arising out of the '*in-between-ness*' of action and being acted upon.[11] According to Gregory Seigworth and Melissa Gregg,

'Affect is found in those intensities that pass body-to-body (human, non-human, part-body, and otherwise), in those resonances that circulate about, between, and sometimes stick to bodies and worlds, and in the very passages or variations between these intensities and resonances themselves.'[12] In addition to the body-to-body function of affect, there also exists a human to non-human exchange that creates an *in-between-ness* of both action and being acted upon. The simultaneity of affect – both in and out of/affect or being affected by – produces an analysis of the body in relation to its physical surroundings. This process eschews ubiquitous Cartesian dualism in an attempt to achieve a non-binary model, which brings us back to the concept of Thirdspace as a simultaneity of opposites drawing on both/and also logic. I have already defined and deconstructed the bog throughout the last four chapters, so this section on McCabe seeks to define and demonstrate the bog affect as it applies specifically to arguably his most critically acclaimed novel, *The Butcher Boy*, through one of the few scenes located on a bog.

The novel follows the story of Francie Brady, who is dealing with mental health issues. The novel blends elements of rural realist fiction depicting a small town in a socially repressive and economically depressive early 1960s' Ireland with Gothic fantasy and imaginative fiction. Francie struggles to separate the fantasy he reads in comic books from the harsh reality that surrounds him while living in poverty with an abusive father. It also reaches fantastical extremes with layers of the macabre and phantasmagorical. Francie's mental condition moves from unstable to psychopathic toward the end of the novel. In the dénouement, for example, he gruesomely murders Mrs Nugent (a local middle-class woman and mother to one of Francie's classmates, Phillip) in her home. He then disassembles her body, symbolically like one of the pigs in the factory where he works, and writes 'PIG' on the walls with her blood. Mrs Nugent, who holds traditional cultural values that combine the residues of prosperity of colonial Ireland with the extant class structure, represents a 'contrapuntal' situation for Francie. Said refers to the contrapuntal as an approach that considers perspectives of the colonised (they are Irish) and coloniser (they strive to be English), thereby seeing two opposing identities simultaneously.[13] For Francie, Mrs Nugent serves as both the coloniser and colonised, a confusion that vexes him throughout the novel and that leads him to Mrs Nugent's brutal murder.

The style of the novel largely reflects the condition of Francie, which is unstable and unreliable. McCabe creates a first-person narration that resembles a form of stream of consciousness, where grammar and syntax succumb to the inner machinations of Francie's volatile psyche. This literary effect mirrors the instability of the surrounding rural atmosphere, while it also resembles the abusive environment in which Francie is raised (his alcoholic father, Benny, verbally and physically abuses both his wife and Francie). Francie is a victim of poverty and abuse as much as he is a progenitor of violence and chaos. McCabe even termed the novel's setting 'a limbo land', reflecting the tensions within a small Irish town slowly and often reluctantly transitioning into a modern world.[14]

The Butcher Boy is not only an ideal example of the bog affect in Irish Gothic literature, but it could also be considered a form of 'social fantastic' literature, which deviates from previous efforts as social realism in his earlier novel *Carn* (1989). Largely associated with the work of Pierre Mac Orlan in the 1920s and 1930s, the social fantastic is a cinematic art term describing the modern condition of social spaces mixed with the fear and consciousness of realism depicted through multi-generic forms of literary, graphic, and visual cultures.

The rare appearance of the bog in physical form (in any of McCabe's novels, not just *The Butcher Boy*) occurs during Francie's stay at the 'industrial school'. Run by priests, this school holds residents who are interned and forced to work on the bog. Francie recalls, 'Every day after that off we'd tramp to the bogs with Bubble [Francie's name for one of the priests] at the head throwing big cheery smiles at the people of the town standing there gawping after us.'[15] During the work days, women of the town would whisper to each other 'there they go the poor orphans' (74). The interned residents, who are either orphans or in some disciplinary situation like Francie, associate the bog with punishment, as well as their own rural identity. In the novel Francie refers to the 'bogmen' with their 'boney arses' and 'boggy faces' (75). Francie's constant disapproving reiteration of bogmen throughout the novel underscores the dinge and smells of rural existence that connect to bogs, as well as Francie's experience in rural Ireland. For Francie, the 'bogmen' are ultimately 'dirty bog-trotters!' (75). Francie also understands on some level how his status is the same as the 'bog-trotters' he so often mocks. Such a sentiment later turns Francie against Mrs Nugent because she thinks Francie's family is filthy like pigs, much like Francie considers the bog people to be.

The physical space of the bog only receives a small amount of attention in McCabe's work and this scene in particular conjures up the pejorative affect of the bog through the novel. The physical space offers an *in-between-ness*, serving as both action and being acted upon. Francie becomes quite aggressive and resentful when working on the bog for the priests because he largely believes himself to be above such work. Upon hearing the women lament about the boys' orphan status, for instance, Francie thought: 'I had a mind to turn round and shout hey fuckface I'm no orphan' (74). At this point Francie is not technically an orphan, but this scene clearly foreshadows that eventuality later in the novel.

However, all of the boys working in the bog serve as symbolic orphans in a postcolonial Ireland, still suffering the economic effects of decolonisation, both as actors in the new nation and being acted upon as victims of economic and social instability. They represent the 'Other for the community' without a stable nation. Some of this recent history of decolonisation emerges through story while working on the bogs.[16] Francie recalls:

> We'd dig all day long and Bubble would tell us stories about the old days when he was young and the English were killing everybody and the old people used to tell stories around the fire and you were lucky if you got one slice of soda bread to feed the whole family. (74)

It is not only the children who are orphans; the priests and most of these rural communities are stranded without much guidance, or what Tim Gauthier calls a 'self-loathing' that would 'mirror the country's neocolonial condition … calling into question both notions of nationhood and cultural hybridity'.[17] Their orphaned status not only represents a lack of biological parents, but also an absent unified nation and confused identity, pointing to the historical spectre of poverty and neglect. After all, the novel is set ambiguously in an area of the Republic on the Northern Ireland border, a political space implicitly referred to throughout the novel that signals the symbolic border between coloniser and colonised, containing a confused hybrid identity.

Contrasting the hybridised 'other' of the orphan in this scene, functioning as an outsider of society as well as the nation, there also exists an affective relationship with the bodies of the workers and the body of the bog. In one of his many delusions, Francie talks to the bogs about Bubble: 'Yes, said the bogs, he's my favourite priest in the whole school. Then off they'd go trying to get up to the front to talk to him' (74). Here we see another example of the bog affect, which as Seigworth and Gregg previously explain, moves from human to non-human, or body-to-body, conjuring intensities and resonances of *in-between-ness*. Francie is both acting and being acted upon in this sequence, which generates his most supernatural and mystical experience on the bog.

While at the school, Francie begins to take long walks alone down on the bogs. It is at this point he begins to hear 'holy voices'. As it turns out, Francie believes he hears Our Lady speaking to him. Francie recollects:

> I read that in a book about this holy Italian boy. He was out in a field looking after the sheep next thing what does he hear only this soft voice coming out of nowhere you are my chosen messenger the world is going to end and all this. One minute he's an Italian bogman with nothing on him only one of his father's coats the next he's a famous priest going round the world writing books and being carried around in a sedan chair saying the Queen of Angels chose me. Well I thought – you've had your turn Father Italian Sheep man so fuck off now about your business here comes Francie Brady hello Our Lady I said. (77)

This passage presents an example of the first person stream of consciousness style that pervades McCabe's novel, but it also represents one of the only scenes set on the physical bog, a place where ghosts appear even in the form of Our Lady for both Francie and the Italian boy in the story. Francie's physical proximity to the bog, like the Italian boy, conjures the apparition of Our Lady, thereby creating simultaneity of affect, both in and out of or being affected by the body's relationship to its physical environment. After telling Father Sullivan about his experience, Father Sullivan assures Francie that he had 'unlocked something very precious' (78). Rather than show incredulity, the 'bogmen' and the priests, all who have a body-to-body relationship with the bog, believe Francie's story. They also praise him for it. Francie proudly thought, 'Father Sull loved to hear it was my stories of the saints in the low field [bog]' (78).

In this way, McCabe's depiction of the physical bog produces a type of bog affect, which accentuates a simultaneity of opposites in how it captures both an essence of bog culture and the feelings of being on or experiencing a bog. Bog Gothic is understandably more of a provocative way to refer to literature representing bogs with political and Gothic undertones. However, McCabe's fiction, along with other writings in this book, ultimately resists this sort of totalisation or over-determination of the bog and instead highlights the nuances of it in Irish culture.

Bog Noir

Another emerging sub-genre or mode is called Bog Noir, or how crime and justice often relate to bogs in Irish literature and culture. Bogs are terrains where historical events disclose physical objects and imagined memories, whether they are relics like the treasure of gold or the jewelled crown in *The Snake's Pass*, Iron Age bog bodies in Heaney's poetry, corpses from sectarianism in O'Connor's 'Guests of the Nation', or decayed relics of memory in O'Faolain's 'A Meeting'. Although not a focus of each chapter, forms of unlawful activity exist in many of the works already discussed in this book. In *The Snake's Pass*, Black Murdock swindles land from Phelim Joyce – while attempting to murder Bat Moynahan on the bog – and for his own profit Arthur attempts to destroy an entire bog that supports the region. In 'Guests of the Nation', Bonaparte and Noble assist with the murder of two innocent British soldiers on the bog; neither soldier had committed any crime other than holding an opposing national identity. In 'A Meeting', the narrator recalls and even revels in some of the heinous crimes that he and Sally committed during the revolutionary period. Heaney's bog poems partly concentrate on the bodies of people who were killed for alleged criminal activity or societal transgressions both in the Iron Age and during sectarian conflicts in Northern Ireland. In *By the Bog of Cats...*, Hester sacrifices her own daughter and then kills herself. These horrific events follow crimes of arson on Carthage's land. Finally, Kinahan's *Bog Boy* discusses some of 'the disappeared' who were indiscriminately killed and furtively buried in bogs during the Troubles. As these examples suggest, perpetrators of these 'illegal' activities naturally gravitate to the bog because of the terrain's extraordinary traits of concealment, mystery, fear, and preservation.

Some scholars have already acknowledged that Gothic literature is an important precursor to modern and contemporary crime writing (or detective fiction), coupling the similarities between detective fiction and the ghost story, and because of the underlying conventions of suspense.[18] As David Punter succinctly claimed in his presentation at the International Gothic Association conference in Vancouver (2015), 'Where would Gothic be without crime?'[19] Edgar Allan Poe's 'The Murders in the Rue Morgue' (1841), Joseph Sheridan Le Fanu's *In a Glass Darkly* (1872), and Stoker's *Dracula* (1897) are all largely structured as supernatural detective stories firmly rooted in the Gothic genre. Sheridan Le Fanu's psychic detective Dr Hesselius later influenced the construction of Conan Doyle's Sherlock

Holmes, the consulting detective, in addition to Algernon Blackwood's John Silence, the scientific investigator, in *John Silence: Physician Extraordinary* (1908),[20] and William Hope Hodgson's Thomas Carnacki, ghost-finder detective, who first appeared in the *Idler Magazine* in 1910.[21] All of these investigators explore metaphysical 'crimes' related to the uncanny. Even if they are out to prove scientific or rational explanations related to these events (Holmes), many of these stories are part of Gothic literature. There is a tenuous line in both Gothic and crime writing between the real and imaginary, rational and irrational, and law and disorder ('laws' being both scientific and social). Exploration and detection often lead to complicated truths about haunted pasts that are not easily explained through modern systems of justice.

Writers have challenged the questionable demarcation between crime and justice in postcolonial contexts where two sets of laws, those of the colonised and of the coloniser, often work in contrast to one another and remain in constant tension and conflict. Notions of 'justice' and 'truth' become relative in multifaceted histories and geographies, where colonial politics have developed into national and then later transnational concerns. Amitav Ghosh's novel *The Calcutta Chromosome* (1995), for example, is about an Indian investigator named Murugan who is now settled in New York but who also must work within imperialist histories between his Indian and American pasts. In addition, Doyle's imagined crimes in many of his Sherlock Holmes stories originate in India or elsewhere in the British Empire, like Australia, only to then collide with the imperial centre back in London, thereby complicating vastly different legal systems and traditions.[22] Using conventions of crime fiction in postcolonial and/ or transnational contexts exposes the problems of law and ethics within communities that have already faced issues with discriminatory legal systems and domestic policing that simultaneously support imperial rule of law and corrupt legal systems. This mode of literary exploration uncovers the epistemological and ideological tensions in postcolonial contexts.[23] Andrew Pepper has also argued that the detective is already a 'liminal, contrary figure' and that the form itself is 'riven with ambiguities and contradictions … satiated in a logic that is simultaneously reactionary and progressive'.[24]

If bogs are inherently a simultaneity of opposites functioning as an alternative space, then how do Irish writers address the relationship between crime and justice and the ways this dynamic relates to bogs? Does the bog help demarcate the vague line separating crime from justice? Because bogs both conceal and preserve, as well as function as repositories for both real objects and imagined symbols, they are often used as locations for depositing bodies, guns, drugs, food, or even memories. The dangerous and menacing qualities of bogs tend to thwart people from investigating them too closely, including anyone attempting to enforce the law. The limited and limitless qualities of bogs challenge the limits and limitlessness of the law, and as a result bogs and notions of justice defy clearly defined social codes.

Irish crime or detective fiction offers a rich narrative resource for current and future critical studies of bogs represented in literature and culture. What is referred to as 'Emerald Noir', 'Dublin Noir', or 'Hibernian Homicide', Irish crime writing has become recognised as a cultural study of representation and identity, as well as a general social commentary.[25] Over the last two decades during the rise and fall of the Celtic Tiger – amidst Catholic Church scandals, the Good Friday Agreement in Northern Ireland, political cronyism leading to EU bailouts, and inequitable austerity measures – Irish Noir continues to perform as a cultural mirror and moral compass, charting definitions of criminality and social space. Irish crime fiction has quickly become one of the leading cultural responses to Ireland's post-Celtic Tiger crisis because it serves as an exemplary mode of popular writing accessible to large audiences where crimes, such as the displacement of families, environmental degradation, xenophobia towards immigrants, gender inequality, and moribund development projects (such as the 'ghost estates'), have been identified and confronted. Crime/detective fiction located in Ireland, from writers like Patrick McGinley, Erin Hart, Tana French, John Galvin, Ken Bruen, and Brian McGilloway, has loosely highlighted the bog as a space where the contours of crime and justice blur together, and I suspect future works of crime writing will continue to draw on the multidimensional and contentious bog terrain as the sub-genre develops in the twenty-first century.

Patrick McGinley's *Bogmail* offers one notable example of crime fiction worth discussing here because it draws upon the image of the bog through the Gothic convention of the macabre layered with absurdist humour surrounding an equally bizarre murder. Even the book's title – a combination of a crime (blackmail) and the location in which it occurs (on a bog) – indicates a specific sub-genre of bog crime fiction, one we might call 'Bog Noir'. But *Bogmail* has also been recognised as a well-written novel, not only a thriller or mystery novel relegated to the cultural status of 'pop fiction', but a work that could be considered a literary achievement. Indeed, Nancy Knowles affirms that *Bogmail* functions as a 'pseudo-detective novel' that 'operates on a level other than popular fiction'.[26] Originally published in 1978, *Bogmail* has been largely overlooked, despite the BBC series made about it in 1991 titled 'Murder in Eden'. The novel was reissued in 2013 and released into an Irish reading market voracious for more crime fiction. In this sense, *Bogmail* has only recently reappeared in the literary consciousness, as both a compelling detective novel and piece of writing.

The rather absurdist plot follows Roarty, who is a widower and publican in the fictionalised village of Glenkeel in Co. Donegal. Roarty's barman Eamonn Eales, known for his 'lecherous' exploits, becomes interested in Roarty's daughter.[27] On a somewhat quotidian impulse, Roarty decides to kill Eales one day by hitting him on the back of the head with the spine of a large encyclopaedia. He then proceeds to hide the body in the nearby bog. Everything seems to be resolved for Roarty until he receives a letter from what is humorously called a 'bogmailer', demanding weekly cash payments of £30 placed into a Dublin bank account in exchange for ongoing silence about the murdered body buried in the bog. Rather than capitulate to the bogmailer, Roarty assumes the role of amateur detective and attempts to decipher who might be bogmailing him amongst the colourful and all equally culpable residents of the village of Glenkeel; the group includes Crubog (a land-hungry patron of the pub), Rory Rua (fisher), Sergeant McGing (local cop), the Englishman Potter (employed with an American mining company), Gim Gillespie (journalist), and Mogaill Maloney (village intellectual and pseudo-Marxist).

Bogmail demonstrates how the physical and symbolic bog performs as a place of crime, intrigue, and uncertainty, while the novel also deploys Gothic conventions of paganism and the supernatural in contrast to a claustrophobic and conservative Catholic village in the remote regions of Co. Donegal. Like many of the writers before him, McGinley recognises how the qualities of the bog creatively support settings for writing about them. When contemplating where to place the body, Roarty thinks, 'Bogs were noted for their powers of preservation. Five hundred years from now some slow-thinking turf-cutter would unearth him with his slane, a time capsule preserved by tannin' (27). Roarty also notes the bog 'was quiet, the sky low and opaque, and the air heavy and clammy' (29). The Gothic elements again emerge when Roarty goes out on the bog to bury the body and hide evidence of the crime he had just committed. Resembling similar ghostly accounts in O'Connor's 'Guests of the Nation', the narration in *Bogmail* states that Roarty 'strained his ear to listen but neither animal nor insect stirred. Yet he did not feel alone. It seemed to him that a thousand invisible eyes were staring at him out of the darkness' (29). Walking from his car out to the middle of the bog, Roarty also notices 'a ragged splotch of ghostly light' (30).

Rather than serving as a mere background or a clandestine container in which to hold the body, the bog remains a central theme in *Bogmail*. It exists as a central character, while it also produces a bog affect on the overall story, summoning an air of intrigue and confusion. In addition, the bog catalyses the criminal element in the novel through its abilities to conceal that which should not be known, but in so doing the bog also reveals these secrets at inopportune times. As Roarty predicts, a turf-cutter will eventually unearth the body, a body that would remain identifiably preserved in the anaerobic bog. After depositing the body in the bog, Roarty 'visualized the darkness over the bog being rent by bluish light … expunging footprints, swelling the surface of the sod, burying his secret deeper and rendering a fathom unfathomable' (34).

McGinley's novel additionally features the both/and also spatio-temporal logic associated with the bog. After returning home from dumping Eales' corpse in the bog, Roarty wanted to 'sleep and forget' and so he plays Schumann's cello concerto on the gramophone while he sips whiskey (31). The description of the music, with its immediate melancholy evoked in the first movement, reflects the qualities he experiences while out on the bog, 'with eerie insight' into 'the entangled state of his thoughts' (32). Roarty believes that 'Schumann was the composer *par excellence*' for this occasion, particularly the cello concerto, because it depicts the 'struggle between light and dark, between conscious and unconscious', but rather than 'expressed as a struggle', it is 'a fusion of opposites that tantalized the mind' (32). McGinley embeds this scene with Schumann's cello concerto in the chapter most focused on the bog as a reflection of the fusion of opposites that both the bog and concerto share. This brief overview shows that *Bogmail* depicts the ways in which bogs open creative possibilities for writers, through their oppositional, political, and Gothic qualities. *Bogmail*, published in the late 1970s, serves as a pioneering example of Irish crime fiction, a genre that did not gain popularity until the mid- to late 2000s.

Erin Hart's archaeological crime novels provide another case to survey here because they serve as the most contemporary example of crime fiction focused on bogs in Ireland. Hart has significantly expanded upon what *Bogmail* achieved, and in some ways is currently the representative writer of the Bog Noir sub-genre in detective fiction. In the first of Hart's Nora Gavin and Cormac Maguire detective novel series (there are now four), Hart acutely re-familiarises audiences to the world of bog bodies in *Haunted Ground* (2005). The novel aptly opens by immediately sinking the reader, along with a slane, directly into a bog: 'With a sodden rasp, Brendan McGann's turf spade sliced into the bank of earth below his feet.'[28] After two turf-cutters in the west of Ireland find a perfectly preserved severed head of a young woman in the bog, Gavin (American pathologist) and Maguire (Irish archaeologist) are contacted to investigate. The theme of bog bodies that Heaney popularised so poignantly in the Irish literary imagination becomes the focus in *Haunted Ground*, as well as in Hart's subsequent novels, but her book provides a unique combination of archaeology and forensic science used as tools for detection.

In Hart's second book, *Lake of Sorrows* (2007), another bog body is found in Loughnabrone Bog, which is described as a holy place shrouded in legend and sorrow. Gavin and Maguire are again called in to investigate this preserved Iron Age bog body found in the Midlands (Co. Offaly). Quickly upon arriving, a fresh body is found in the bog, one that prompts Gavin and Maguire to begin a contemporary investigation about pagan ritual amidst the traditional histories and folklores of rural Ireland. *Lake of Sorrows* begins similarly to *Haunted Ground*, and quickly establishes the bog as not only the leading motif in the novel but also as a material and symbolic terrain with overtones of death, horror, and the unexplainable: 'The moment he pushed into the frigid water at the bottom of the bog hole, his eyes fluttered open, and his mind grasped the fact that he would certainly die here.' The narrator goes on to explain in the same passage that the bog 'was a mysterious, holy place, home to spirits and strange mists, a place of transformation and danger'.[29]

While the third book, *False Mermaid* (2010), pushes the pause button on bogs and instead explores the haunted case of a seal-maiden (selkies – seals that can shed skins and become human), Gavin and Maguire are back to the bog in *The Book of Killowen* (2013), the fourth book about a ninth-century body found in the boot of a car that was buried in the bog. Similarly to *Haunted Ground* and *Lake of Sorrows*, *The Book of Killowen* opens with bodies found in bogs: one is contemporary and one is centuries old. The book opens on the Killowen Bog in 877 BCE before transporting the audience back to the present, where Gavin and McGuire are called upon to investigate another body that somehow relates to the body from the ninth century.

As in the first two novels, turf-cutters unearth a body. Roarty's early comment in *Bogmail* describes the situation that seems to begin all of Hart's bog body novels: 'Five hundred years from now some slow-thinking turf-cutter would unearth him with his slane, a time capsule preserved by tannin.' In this case, it is a labourer named Kevin Donegan who finds the body while digging holes for 'gas lines' or foundations for 'excavation'. Hart captures the familiar atmosphere of the bog: 'It was early enough that mist still covered the lowest parts of the bog, an eerie presence that muffled the sharp cries of birds, the unearthly keening of a hare.'[30] Throughout the four novels, and perhaps perfected in *The Book of Killowen*, Hart creates a historical and archaeological crime series that accentuates the timelessness and intangible qualities, as well as the more obvious concrete and tangible ones, of bogs in Irish culture. *The Book of Killowen* treats the bog as a porthole, almost like a time machine, where Gavin and McGuire can investigate two crimes thousands of years apart through a physical terrain.

What Hart's crime novels accomplish, other than a sustained focus on bogs, is that they display a prolonged and serialised crime series about an archaeologist who specialises in bog bodies within a political and Gothicised atmosphere, conjuring ghosts of colonisation and pre-historic trauma. Siobhan Dowd's book of young adult (YA) fiction, *Bog Child* (2008), follows a theme similar to Hart's, using the central motif wherein the protagonist finds a prehistoric murdered girl, later named 'Mel', buried in the bog near the Northern Ireland border in 1981. *Bog Child* is, however, less of a detective novel (even though it is framed as a 'mystery'), and instead a book about young adults finding maturity within themselves and the 'nation' as a society at a time of political upheaval and uncertainty during the sectarian conflicts. This political and social bildungsroman combines the history of the Troubles, particularly the hunger strikes in 1981, with prehistoric trauma depicted through the actual bog body and the haunting dreams which are triggered by it for the protagonist Fergus McCann.[31] In this way, *Bog Child* essentially sketches a retelling of Heaney's bog poems in novel form for young adults instead of relying on conventional detective fiction devices like Hart's series of books do.

While we have already seen a detective series about a pathologist disinterring buried secrets in Ireland's past (for example, Benjamin Black's character Quirke in 1950s Dublin), we have yet to see attention drawn to the mysterious and complex occurrences around the Irish bog, particularly through the eyes of an archaeological expert like McGuire. These archaeo-crime based novels offer the most prolonged look to date (and in serial form) at how boglands remain sites of interest for writers because they serve as cultural, scientific, supernatural, and social spaces to stage literary works. Other writers in this study have previously explored many of the themes that both Hart and McGinley dig up in the Irish bog. Hart's novels do, however, demonstrate a growing connection between crime writing and bogs in literature and culture, and offer an exemplary genre of Bog Noir.

Eco-Bog Writing

The final form to be explored in this section is ecologically informed non-fiction writing about bogs, specifically the work and activism of Tim Robinson. If bogs continue to rapidly disappear through urban development and fuel production, how will they influence Irish writers or culture in the future? While I explore this topic to some extent in Chapter 2, it is through the lens of the postcolonial Gothic in the late nineteenth century, and perhaps not quite as germane to writings in the late twentieth and early twenty-first centuries.

In addition to their political and supernatural associations, bogs currently remain the most endangered ecosystem in Ireland. Over 92 per cent of them have been used for fuel or damaged through commercial development and industrialisation. Boglands contain rich and vibrant flora and fauna, which signals their high degree of biodiversity, a measure of the variety and health of organisms in a particular ecosystem. Evaluating biodiversity is an important way to maintain a healthy environment for not only non-human organisms, but also humans around the globe, and particularly in areas where organisms are being destroyed at unsustainable rates. In addition to biodiversity, bog restoration also helps to curb flooding in various parts of Ireland. Flooding has been a major issue in Ireland in recent years, damaging farmland, homes, and infrastructures of cities. Drainage of bogs for agriculture, peat extraction, or even forestry raises water tables elsewhere. During heavy rain for prolonged periods, water tables overflow without an abundance of bogs to serve as natural rain containers or sponges. The future of bog writing may well be dependent upon how or if bogs can be protected and conserved in the next few decades. But with the increasing elimination of bogs, might there be more Eco-bog writings that address these concerns directly?

As discussed in Chapter 1, one major threat to bogs continues to be fuel production through the process of turf cutting. The semi-state body *Bord na Móna* (Peat Production Corporation), was established in Ireland in 1946 to promote industrialised peat extraction for commercial use. At this point, it was estimated that over half of the large Midland raised bogs recorded since 1814 had been cut away for fuel. This amount equalled an astonishing million tonnes of turf, or 800 hectares a year.[32] Exploiting bogs for fuel continued up until the 1970s during which some surveys were conducted and later written about by R.F. Hammond in *The Peatlands of Ireland* (1979), where he classified bogs into major ecological types.[33] Paralleling other movements worldwide, national consciousness increased about ecological damage and environmental justice.

After many public events were held over several years, a panel of experts formed the National Peatland Conservation Committee (now called the Irish Peatland Conservation Council, IPCC) during 'Bog Conservation Week' in 1982. The IPCC remains vigilant in educating the public about boglands and through research. Despite the evidence of environmental degradation to bogs, controversy remains in Ireland over cutting in protected areas. In fact, the Irish government breached EU environmental regulations because twenty-one out of thirty-one protected bogs designated as 'Special Areas of Conservation' suffered damage through cutting, burning, or draining in 2011 alone.[34] Turf cutting for fuel remains the primary danger because it destroys the irreplaceable habitat of bogs that has taken thousands of years to develop. Foss and O'Connell, among others, have predicted that with 92 per cent of raised and 82 per cent of blanket bogs already lost, all unprotected bogs will become extinct in the twenty-first century.[35]

Conserving boglands is not only important for maintaining cultural identity and ecological biodiversity in Ireland; bogs also contribute to fighting climate change, the most significant environmental (and perhaps planetary) danger facing the globe in the twenty-first century. Bogs present scientists with records of over ten thousand years of changing climates and environments in Ireland,[36] and for the last five millennia bog ecosystems have even stored sequestered carbon.[37] In this way, bogs act as natural carbon sequestration units (or 'sinks'), places where carbon dioxide (CO_2) is captured from the atmosphere.

The process of Carbon Capture and Storage (CCS) remains a stopgap measure for containing the increasing levels of carbon in the atmosphere partly responsible for global warming. There are two ways to accomplish CCS: manually or naturally. For manual methods, CO_2 is extracted from exhaust gases of a power station and then injected into boreholes deep underground. Lasting for thousands of years, according to researchers, this CO_2 retention is aided by geochemical reactions that ultimately lead to the formation of solid, immobile, and carbonate minerals. The problems with this manual method of CCS are numerous but two significant ones are cost and transport, the latter of which requires pipelines to be built to move CO_2 over long distances for eventual injection into the boreholes.[38] One of the main 'natural' methods of CCS, other than simply reducing the world's carbon output, comes from global wetlands. Researchers have shown that 20 per cent of the world's current terrestrial carbon is captured and stored in bogs located in the northern hemisphere.[39] But in Ireland, bogs hold half of the carbon stored in the earth.[40] In addition to their cultural connections, bogs are ecosystems that help to reduce greenhouse gases. This is why the destruction of bogs, and even to a larger extent reclamation and fuel production of all wetlands around the globe, accelerates climate change by releasing CO_2 back into the atmosphere. Bogland ecosystems are an essential aspect of a healthy biosphere because they maintain global carbon balance and biodiversity, as well as provide continual educational and cultural value.

Chapter 2 identified some of the environmental threats to bogs at the end of the nineteenth century as well as some of the literary and cultural responses to them. These risks were largely based upon theories of commercialising natural resources that would provide economic sovereignty for Ireland and thus political separation from the British Empire. The reality remains that the legacy of the colonial project is neocolonial commercialisation and resource development from both national and multi-national corporations that most threaten the existence of bogs in Ireland. In this sense, very little has changed over the last 125 years. Bogs remain an energy source for local populations, but are mainly exploited by larger industrial campaigns. They continue to disappear through practices of economic domination not unlike forms of what the historian Alfred W. Crosby calls 'ecological imperialism', or a process by which Europeans changed ecosystems in the colonies by destroying local ecologies with European forms of development and agricultural practices (for example, by introducing invasive species).[41] Contemporary Irish writers, to a large extent, have yet to respond to how these narratives of economic exploitation specifically relate to the environmental hazards of bogs.

One exception is Robinson, who is an award-winning non-fiction landscape writer and cartographer, and who has already been referenced at various points throughout this book. Originally from Yorkshire, England, Robinson moved to the Aran Islands in 1972 and eventually settled in Roundstone, Co. Galway. Robinson wrote the encyclopaedic *Connemara* trilogy – *Listening to the Wind* (2006), *Last Pool of Darkness* (2008) and *A Little Gaelic Kingdom* (2011) – among other important books and essays about the culture and natural histories surrounding the landscapes and topographies of western Ireland.[42] The trilogy, taking over thirty years to complete through both maps and writings, is considered to be the most extensive ecological study since the Praeger's detailed catalogue of botanist writings and collected natural histories.

Robinson's form of landscape or 'topographical' writing attempts to *map* the material as well as cultural and historical-cultural terrains of specific topographies through prose. Rather that act as a celebration of 'nature', as in 'nature writing', topographical writing explores the deeper layers of culture and geology, history and botany, the imagination and deep time. Robert Macfarlane, also a landscape/topographical writer in the United Kingdom who published the highly acclaimed books *Mountains of the Mind* (2003), *The Wild Places* (2007), and *The Old Ways* (2012), maintains that Robinson's writings are 'one of the most sustained, intensive and imaginative studies of a landscape that has ever been carried out'.[43] But what makes Robinson worthy of discussion is how he has written about and publicly championed the ecological and cultural importance of bogs in Ireland.

In his semi-autobiographical collection of essays *My Time in Space* (2001), Robinson explains how the Roundstone Bog is 'an occasion, a locus, of wild speculation' that must be defended 'against the great wrecking-machine of commerce'. Robinson goes on to admit in the same passage that 'the State is not likely to declare it [the bog] a Place of Philosophical Importance', though he and others clearly do.[44] At the peak of the Celtic Tiger in the mid-1990s, a business association in Clifden (Co. Galway) proposed building an airport on Roundstone Bog to increase tourism and provide faster business travel between Dublin and Clifden (and Connemara more generally). Robinson wrote many pieces defending the Roundstone Bog from this development proposal – rife

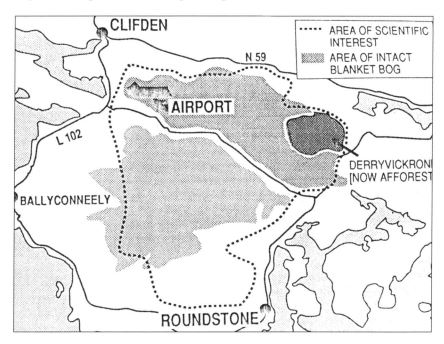

CLIFDEN

····· AREA OF SCIENTIFIC
INTEREST

▓▓▓ AREA OF INTACT
BLANKET BOG

N 59

AIRPORT

L 102

BALLYCONNEELY

DERRYVICKRON
[NOW AFFOREST

ROUNDSTONE

6.1 Map of proposed airport in Roundstone Bog (from Tim Robinson
Archive, Hardiman Library, NUI, Galway)

with 'job creating' rhetoric – that sought to build what many believed was
an unnecessary airport (see Fig. 6.1). The debates lasted for over a dozen
years, throughout which Robinson would on many occasions be asked by
the 'Save Roundstone Bog (SRB)' group, which he was also a part of, to
explain to the public why it was important to conserve Roundstone Bog.

In response to the SRB's appeals to the public, many critics claimed,
'It's only a bit of old bog', to which Robinson replied:

> as if there were no distinctions to be noted between upland bog and
> the rarer oceanic lowland blanket bog, between bog that has been
> ruined by machine turf cutting and bog that is still miraculously
> intact, and above all between all other bogs and Roundstone Bog
> itself, which has no parallels anywhere on the Earth![45]

The pro-airport lobby also argued that thirteen acres is not that much to
give up, considering there was much more bog in the area. They appealed,
'Aren't the people of Connemara worth thirteen acres of bog?'[46] In a
letter published in the *Connacht Tribune*, Robinson provided this response:

Beyond that the bog spreads wide, golden or purple or grey according to the seasons, flowing up and over a low rise into a labyrinth of streams with a hundred lakes, as far as Errisbeg Hill, which arches its back like an angry cat against the southern sky. Such sights are good for the soul! Clifden holds something in trust here for the human spirit, for ever.[47]

The assumption by the pro-airport group was that a slice of bog could be removed without any environmental or cultural effect in their own backyard of Clifden. After all, would not an airport have greater benefit to the people than 'a bit of old bog'?

The bog's existence provides not only cultural and historical associations, ones that Robinson painstakingly outlines in certain parts of his *Connemara* trilogy, it also serves as a sensitive ecosystem that captures carbon and houses millions of organisms that remain essential to a rich and vigorous place for humans to live as well. Ecology is a scientific study that underscores the interconnectedness and interactions of all organisms and their environments, which extends to both humans and non-humans. In order to exist, all organisms must interact and co-exist. The bog itself provides a microcosmic look at the entire macrocosm of a region's ecosystems for hundreds of thousands of years. Robinson invites audiences to see 'ecosystems flowing across the land like cloud shadows on a breezy day' over the Roundstone Bog. He continues to describe what can be found in a sample extracted deep within the bog:

> first, the raw stony desert left by the Ice Age; next, the tundra following on the heels of the retreating glaciers, and its colonization by birch and dwarf willow; then lakes with beds of trees, invaded by sphagnum and filling up with peat to form a bog; a birch wood taking over the bog surface as it dries out, and becoming a pine forest; finally bog again, overwhelming the pines and preserving their roots.[48] (see Fig. 6.2)

The 'series of epochal transformations condensed into a few metres of dirt', as outlined by Robinson above, furthers the argument that bogs serve as scientific and cultural history books which simply cannot be removed for the short-term economic gain of commercial development for a handful of people. The bog must instead be preserved for the long-term benefit of many humans and non-humans.

6.2 Layers of history in a 'Turf Bank' (painting by Angie Shanahan)

The Roundstone Bog has historically served as a laboratory for peat bog research by many notable international ecologists and botanists before Robinson, some of whom include Knud Jessen, Harry Godwin, Hugo Osvald, and Frank Mitchell, not to mention Praeger, who called the Roundstone Bog that 'great bogland behind Urrisbeg'.[49] Praeger spearheaded this research team on the Roundstone Bog in 1935, capturing the eternal essence of this landform in geologic time. He discusses the experience in his book *The Way that I Went* (1937):

> We stood in a ring in that shelterless expanse while discussion raged on the application of the terms soligenous, topogenous and ombrogenous … The only pause in the flow of argument was when Jessen or Osvald, in an endeavour to solve the question of the origin of the peat, would chew some of the mud brought up by the boring tool from the bottom of the bog, to test the presence or absence of gritty material … But out of such occasions does knowledge come, and I think that the aqueous discussion has borne and will bear fruit. For the bogs and what they can teach us of the past history of our country are yet to a great extent a sealed book, though they will not remain so much longer.[50]

The literary elements of the bog ring true in Praeger's account, offering a narrative of history through corporeal processes of experience in our imagination.

Robinson's epic work largely about boglands, *Listening to the Wind*, is part homage to Praeger and others, part autobiography, and part repository of stories. It underscores the vital status of the Roundstone

Bog in Ireland, while also serving as a reference to global ecologies. Robinson reads the pages of the bog's history once more before it disappears forever. The pro-airport lobby fronted the moment that Praeger warned about: the exploitation of the bog and its educational aptitude for shortsighted commercial gains, which are mere nanoseconds in geologic time. Robinson continues this lineage of ecological writing, but does so through more literary means, functioning as a landscape or topographical writer who focuses more on the essence of place, the extracted meanings of culture and history of the landscape, rather than the harder science motivated by those before him. Robinson serves as a literary non-fictive example of Eco-bog writing, hence the reason for his inclusion in this book, as opposed to other scientific writers such as Jessen, Osvald, Mitchell, or Praeger.

The battle between commerce and preservation in the Roundstone Bog airport debate notwithstanding, what Robinson highlights are the essential qualities of bogs to this region in Connemara, as well as throughout Ireland (see Fig. 6.3). Writers often confront such social struggles, whether through the politics of colonisation in Heaney, or through the politics of environmental degradation of bogs through forms of neocolonisation in Carr. Eco-bog writings – underscoring the ecological approaches to bogs – continue to have impact. The proposed airport on Roundstone Bog was eventually blocked from being built, but, as Robinson warns, 'no permanent institution has emerged from the campaign, to research, educate about and protect the Bog, which will always be under threat'.[51] Robinson's writings, however, do create a literary 'institution' that educates readers about the ecological and cultural importance of bogs in Ireland. Robinson deduces, 'If a writer has a function in the community it is to try and think things out for himself or herself, and not just in a tiny local and short-term context either.'[52] For many writers, their function in the community (even on a national or international level) is to partly address various forms of social injustice. Each writer discussed in the last four chapters of this book confronts injustices, but they 'think things out' through representations of the bog.

Robinson's other bog writings found in *Listening to the Wind* recognise the Gothic or ghostly elements that both attract and repel audiences. Thus, one way to view Robinson's writings could be through the lens of the 'Eco-Gothic': ecological approaches to Gothic literature and culture where the natural environment can be investigated through fear and anxiety, as well as the sublime and the supernatural. Many of Robinson's

6.3 Atlantic blanket bog in Connemara, Co. Galway (from Pat Collins' film *Tim Robinson: Connemara*, photo by Colm Hogan)

bog writings incorporate ecological topics with faint but recognisable Gothic undercurrents. Another common way to approach the Eco-Gothic is through catastrophic horror narratives of destruction and annihilation, with the concept that fear generates this particular impulse. The notion of ecophobia, which is derived from a psychological understanding of an irrational and unexplainable aversion to or fear of the natural world, provides another way of considering the Eco-Gothic.[53]

Looking at Robinson's writings, he speaks of bogs as spaces where people continually see ghosts, the dead of the past and the stories of the future. 'The bog is not for me an emblem of memory,' he writes, 'but a network of precarious traverses, of lives swallowed up and forgotten. I plan to revisit every part of it and rescue all its stories.'[54] Stories themselves are as timeless and seductive as bogs. Ever the consummate storyteller himself, Robinson reveals to the reader that the 'bog-lore I get from Roundstone people, and which I will lend to this tree, consists of stories that drift over Roundstone Bog like patches of mist'. Such stories involve a father's 'ghost crossing the bog once', stories about family members 'who could cross the bog in incredibly short times', and a story about 'a witch living in Murvey who used to fly into Roundstone on two sods of turf'.[55] The narrative of the bog, like a piece of writing or story, is continually read against memories of supernatural occurrences that both entice and frighten.

While Robinson does not engage in fear narratives, his debates with the pro-airport lobby in Clifden might reveal some issues with ecophobia on their end, a condition that Robinson attempted to assuage through explanations of both the aesthetic and communal qualities of Roundstone Bog. A contemporary writer like Robinson, who partly engages with both neocolonial threats of commercialising the bog and contemporary Gothic stories about it, appreciates and warns against the ongoing environmental risks facing bogs in the future. If a 'bog is its own diary', as he claims, then writers must read the pages of it, like a literary history of lives forgotten or misremembered, before it completely vanishes.[56]

This final chapter explores more broadly where literary representations of bogs have and could continue to develop, calling into question the fate of Irish bogs as a way of transitioning into prescient twenty-first-century concerns related to politics, writing, and culture. If the last few hundred years provide any sort of guide, it seems inevitable that Irish writers will continue to engage with the uncanny qualities of bogs and promote the way they illumine issues of unexplainable phenomena and political and social ruptures. But as Killeen astutely points out:

> The challenge for contemporary Irish Gothic is to move away from a now tired attack on the mid-twentieth century as a site of horror and repression, a view which suggests a contrast with the supposedly liberal and progressive Celtic Tiger of the new millennium, and to find a way to deal with the new realities through a Gothic story set firmly in the present.[57]

The question remains: in what ways will writers respond and through what forms, whether Bog Gothic, Bog Noir, or Eco-Bog modes of writing? In the short term, then, Irish writers could turn to the bog by way of the neo-Gothic, as writers before them did, to address political disturbances in the twenty-first century – not as a psychological 'repressed' state of horror looking back at a regressive past, but as an *in situ* realist mode of literary activism. Writers could also seize upon interpretations of the Eco-Gothic, confronting the legacy of ecological attacks of bogs, based upon fear and ignorance, through Gothic conventions. Does ecophobia, as exhibited in the Eco-Gothic, provide a contemporary critical approach to address the environmental threat to bogs? Will there perhaps be a genre of environmental detective fiction that explores ecological crimes committed on bogs? Based upon substantial evidence of environmental scientists, bogs will continue to decrease in size and virtually disappear except where preserved. How then will exploitative economic policies continue to affect the ecologies of bogs? Will there be an exclusively twenty-first-century examination of bogs in literature and culture? If so, have contemporary writers invested in bogs the same way writers did in the nineteenth and twentieth centuries?

Uncertain Futures

For the bogs and what they can teach us of the past history of our country are yet to a great extent a sealed book, though they will not remain so much longer.[1]

– Robert Lloyd Praeger, *The Way that I Went*

The geographer Yi-Fu Tuan underscores how topographies demonstrate 'the affective bond between people and place or setting'.[2] The 'affective bond' of the bog draws writers to its deep and muddy waters and in so doing writers are able to highlight anomalous circumstances in history and culture by adopting the bog as both a real setting and powerful metaphor. Geography itself is a kind of writing, what Derek Gregory and others have called a literal 'earth-writing'.[3] Such an approach in geography also suffuses literary narratives with specific topographies or landforms that combine both physical characteristics and cultural associations. This spatio-temporal logic surrounds the bog and writings about it, creating otherwise disparate associations. These disorientating affects of the bog provide what Sanders calls a 'nocturnal obscurity', where a person can 'get lost', where 'time is eerily suspended', and where 'things can disappear as if gulped down by strange forces and reappear as if "frozen in time"'.[4] Geographical histories, like literary ones, tend to be highly political, provoking unresolved issues in culture and society 'frozen' in deep time only to surface as half realities, half dreams.

While this book's approach is primarily literary, it must also address the inherent issues that emerge from the main subject about boglands, that is, how political and geographical histories underscore the writers' motives, responses, and interactions to and with bog culture. This book began by demonstrating that bogs are more than a ubiquitous terrain found over many parts of Ireland, and that their literary reflection is much broader than what could be reduced to the archives of scientific studies. Instead, it subsequently overviews how the indeterminate qualities of bogs – simultaneously contradictory and complementary, stable and unstable – allow Irish writers to continually shape and reshape the symbolic meanings and physical qualities of the bog in literary works while also using Gothic conventions. This book is ultimately an intervention in a number of different fields in Irish Studies, such as Gothic, postcolonial, geographical, and environmental studies, and does so through a landform that allows for such a variety of critical approaches that inspect the 'nocturnal obscurity' where 'time is eerily suspended' within space.

This conclusion offers a few thoughts about the uncertain future of bogs and their effect on Irish society. One future entails the environmental or ecological outcome, one that might seem depressingly short and potentially tragic. Bogs can be perceived as wilderness areas, which, like the impenetrable density of some rainforests, contain a deep and vast network of ecologies and cultures within the peat. According to Tim Pearce, the conservation officer for the Ulster Wildlife Trust, 'We must prepare ourselves to campaign and lobby for the retention of our peatland heritage; its historical significance, the evidence of ages past buried in its depths and the peculiar sense of space, the wilderness that is our bogland.'[5] One way of campaigning for Ireland's remaining wilderness is to engage with both the physical and imaginative qualities of the bog by supporting literary culture and its penchant for illuminating these topographies. Indeed, the notional 'wilderness' conjures cultural associations, what would be called 'protected' areas in conservational terminology. Protected areas of bogland already exist, but framing them as one of Ireland's last wilderness areas – admitting a social construction and inherent responsibility within this notion – might be one way to interconnect their intrinsic cultural and scientific presence in Ireland.

Bog culture might expand more into Irish society as its own field of exploration, one that has already been termed 'bogology' by two scientists in the UK. On their website, 'Bogology', the scientists Dr Matt Amesbury (University of Exeter) and Dr Tom Roland (University of Southampton) have sketched an open-access space for people to read about, view, and understand the complexity of peatland networks. Their blog – punned as a PeatBlog – contains articles by many guest contributors, while other elements of the site are purely educational and celebrate the tremendously nuanced environment of bogs around the world. One can even post a question in the 'ask a bogologist' section. The stated aim of bogology is to examine 'the science of peatlands and past climate change', but the website also offers information on anything related to the science and culture of peatlands.[6] Bogs are unfortunate victims of climate change, but they are also simultaneously preventers of it. The uncertain future of bogs parallels the equally uncertain future of the earth. Can the living organisms in the world, human and non-human, sustain a continual rise in global temperature?

Ecology, as discussed in Robinson's writings (Chapter 6), is the study of organisms interacting with their environments. While ecology is not synonymous with environmentalism, it is often used in combination with it to accentuate the importance of a healthy or sustainable environment, which would contain high levels of biodiversity and generative interaction between all organisms. Hence, the term 'sustainability' was developed in the late 1970s and early 1980s by social, environmental, and economic theorists to identify beneficial ways society might grow and progress without destroying the world around it.[7] We can, however, extrapolate the definition of ecologies from the sciences and think of it in terms of society and culture. How do humans function in social registers? Are we governed by the same rules of existence as other non-human organisms in the larger ecology of the planet and the environments in which we exist? Can humans separate themselves from the ecological systems they attempt to control? These questions remain relevant through both historical and contemporary concerns about how we relate to bogs, represent them in culture, and value them in the social sphere. Anthropogenic (human-caused) climate change breaks ecological stability or 'sustainability' through largely unjustifiable forms of destruction and disunity. The essence of climate change is a break-up or disruption of ecology – a purposeful interference of organisms (i.e. humans and non-humans) interacting harmoniously for greater health and diversity within a particular ecosystem.

Therefore, the notion of bogology also serves as a way to think about bogs on a 'both/and also logic' cultural and scientific scale. By examining the literary representations of bogs, this book has opened up new perspectives on the multifarious ways in which bogs function in the world. Pushing research about bogology a bit further, I want to suggest that climate change does not only disturb the ecologies of bogs; it also affects the ecologies of culture and society associated with bogs, opening another way to consider the uncertain futures of bogs. Even if bogs completely disappear from the earth, the imaginative bog affect will continually remain, perhaps in the pages of literary works conjuring topographical ghosts. Bogs, after all, distort the living and the dead, prolonging geologic time through imaginary and cultural histories.

Climate change equates to cultural change as much as to ecological change because of the social and cultural networks of writers and artists responding to and producing forms of art about the ways in which the imagined and material spaces around us continue to change. In this way, bogology is both an essential scientific and a cultural study of bogs. This book performs a type of 'literary bogology' analysis in its attempt to show how writers continue to be attracted to and seduced by the uncanny bog and then use it as a way to address – sometimes overtly and sometimes obliquely – political narratives and social ruptures in Ireland from 1890 to the present. Framing a study about bogs through the postcolonial Gothic serves as a useful method of enquiry because it elucidates how culture and politics related to colonisation also appear unstable and haunted. What all of the writers (both analysed or briefly mentioned) in this book have in common is the way in which they adopt both a literal and symbolic sense of the bog, preventing us from limiting our own perception to any single perspective, thereby challenging over-determined concepts about history and nation, land and identity, ambiguity and certainty, gender and agency, crime and justice, and ecology and society, all of which relate to Ireland's sustainable future as a social and civic space.

As we see in Chapter 1, there is a history of writings that have commonly misunderstood the bog terrain and used it to promote socio-political agendas that largely disenfranchised parts of the Irish population. The bog is then re-appropriated by Irish writers in the modern and contemporary periods to creatively excavate equally volatile and contentious topics. The opposition between industrially exploiting and preserving the bog in Stoker's *The Snake's Pass*, outlined in Chapter 2, begins the literary analysis and in some ways also ends it. The dilemma Stoker poses in the novel – whether to exploit the bog for greater economic and national independence or to conserve its environmental integrity as part of Irish identity – continues to dominate discussions into the twenty-first century (as we see with Robinson and the Roundstone Bog). Nationalism and haunting, to which I turn in Chapter 3, similarly reveal some of the instabilities around literary narratives that focus on the bog, allowing a space of uncertainty and flux to characterise and guide a conversation about the otherwise difficult subject of nationalism during an influential revolutionary period in the early 1920s. O'Connor and O'Faolain underscore the importance of ghosts in Irish history as a way to redress the past and allow generative futures of imaginative spaces rather than focus on decaying histories. In turn, mapping Gothic bog bodies presents a way for Heaney to explore the political struggles in Northern Ireland in the 1960s and 1970s, as well as general issues of violence, history, and memory in his poetry and non-fiction prose. Heaney's bog poems – through the bodies that emerge from the bog – provide a literary map of ambiguously real and imagined spaces in order to explore notions of commitment and identity to the nation, religion, collective communities, and individual people.

In Chapter 5 the theme of re-appropriating gender and land appears in two contemporary plays about bogs, each with women protagonists and written by female playwrights. Kinahan and Carr challenge the notion of gendered boglands, decoupling the female as land from nationalist symbolism in order to then promote women's autonomy within a neocolonial and modernised Celtic Tiger period. The bog serves as a space of refuge and opportunity for women in both plays, despite its usual correlation with waste, lethargy, and stagnation. According to Fintan O'Toole, at the end of the Celtic Tiger period an 'uneasy feeling of going back to the past' developed because the past no longer contained any comfort for Irish society.[8] Carr and Kinahan both presciently use the bog not as a way to return to the past, but rather to reinvent national narratives in the present and future about women and domesticity within socio-economic circumstances. Chapter 6 outlines some of the varieties and forms of writing that address the bog in contemporary literature. Bog Gothic, used as a satirical term to describe McCabe's fiction, contains connotations that bring us back to Spenser, Boate, and King, unnecessarily casting the bog as a damaged and controversial space. Instead, McCabe's fiction produces a bog affect, an expression of the bog that challenges pejorative associations with it. Bog Noir, situated as a form of detective fiction and one of the more popular modes of writing in Ireland, confronts crime and inequities in contemporary Irish society. Eco-bog writing, bringing us back to Stoker at the beginning, opens discussions about how we might consider boglands in Irish society as both cultural and protected 'wilderness' spaces.

The literary works throughout this book all contribute to the project of literary bogologies, the literary study of bogs as cultural and scientific spaces. Bogs remain relevant in Ireland in the twenty-first century, but, like the country after the economic collapse of the Celtic Tiger, they too face significant challenges and uncertain futures, prompting studies like this one to demonstrate the important part bogologies play in Ireland and elsewhere. Bogs have retained an increasing international importance both aesthetically and scientifically because of significant depletion around the globe.[9] Similar to how this book begins, it ends with the understanding that representations of boglands in literature and culture ultimately raise more questions than can be answered. And so I have concluded here by offering a few thoughts and open-ended questions about the uncertain futures of bogs in the midst of immense changes to our climate systems, and the ways in which they have affected society and culture.

The goal of this book was to highlight some of the ways in which we can approach and analyse the role of bogs in Irish literature and culture. It shows that Irish writers, along with environmental scientists and concerned citizens, may continue to examine through literature and culture the social issues that are as unstable and contentious as the terrain of the bog. Robinson observes that the bog 'is a stage, in both senses: people enter it and exit again, and their time in it is an interval between two periods of social existence. They are solitaries, paths of mist, almost ghost already.'[10] Although *Contentious Terrains* only offers a slice of an immeasurable amount of geologic time in the existence of the bog, a single page from its own 'diary', my task here has been to display some of the many ways the bog shimmers in the literary and cultural imagination for modern and contemporary Irish writers. If the bog is a 'stage' and provides a way to witness the interval between two periods of social existence, where does this leave us in the time ahead? At what stage of the bog's cultural and biological history will writers enter it in the future or revisit it in the past? What will materialise out of these 'paths of mist' emanating from this widely used terrain in Irish writing? We have entered and exited the bog at many stages, and witnessed the way its nebulous and powerfully seductive qualities illuminate key moments in Ireland's colonial history. Histories, like ghosts, transform over time. Histories and memories are like mists that confuse and disorientate moments of the past while at the same time offer reflection and clarity for the future.

Endnotes

Introduction

1   Tim Robinson, *Connemara: Listening to the Wind* (Dublin: Penguin, 2006), p. 5.
2   Catherine Wynne, *The Colonial Conan Doyle: British Imperialism, Irish Nationalism, and the Gothic* (Westport, CT: Praeger, 2002), p. 77.
3   Bryony Coles and John Coles, *People of the Wetlands: Bogs, Bodies and Lake-Dwellers* (London: Thames and Hudson, 1989), p. 151.
4   Karin Sanders, *Bodies in the Bog and the Archeological Imagination* (Chicago: University of Chicago Press, 2009), p. 6.
5   Fred Botting, *Gothic* (London: Routledge, 1996), p. 2.
6   Lizabeth Paravisini-Gebert, 'Colonial and Postcolonial Gothic: The Caribbean', in Jerrold E. Hogle (ed.), *The Cambridge Companion to Gothic Fiction* (Cambridge: Cambridge University Press, 2002), p. 229.
7   Wetland is a term that was created in 1956 and therefore might appear anachronistic to use when discussing the nineteenth century. Wetland landscapes were generally (and pejoratively) referred to as swamps or bogs until a conceptual shift in environmental consciousness occurred in the mid-twentieth century. See Jeremy Caradonna, *Sustainability: A History* (New York: Oxford University Press, 2014), pp. 90–91. As I argue in Chapter 2, however, some of this environmental consciousness shifted at the end of the nineteenth century in Ireland. In order to avoid confusion, I will refer to bogs as wetlands even before 1956, despite the possibly anachronistic dimensions of the term.
8   There are many uses of the Gothic uncanny, some of which I will address more fully in Chapter 2 through Freud's essay 'Uncanny'. When used as a general term, I refer to the Oxford English Dictionary definition: weird, mysterious, unexplainable, and supernatural. The uncanny is also considered a combination of opposing qualities, such as attraction and repulsion. For a comprehensive study, see Nicholas Royle, *The Uncanny* (Manchester: Manchester University Press, 2003).
9   Jarlath Killeen, 'Irish Gothic: A Theoretical Introduction', *The Irish Journal of Gothic and Horror Studies* 1 (Fall 2006), n.p., web, accessed 3 Sept. 2011, http://irishgothichorrorjournal.homestead.com/jarlath.html.
10   Dianne Meredith, 'Hazards in the Bog – Real and Imagined', *The Geographical Review* 92.3 (July 2002), p. 319.
11   Sanders, *Bodies in the Bog*, p. 12.
12   Kelly Hurley, 'Abject and Grotesque', in Catherine Spooner and Emma McEvoy (eds), *The Routledge Companion to Gothic* (London: Routledge, 2007), p. 139.
13   Edward Soja, *Thirdspace: Journeys to Los Angeles and Other Real-and-Imagined Places* (Malden, MA: Blackwell, 1996), p. 2.
14   ibid., p. 7.
15   ibid., p. 3.

16 ibid., p. 5.
17 ibid., p. 3.
18 Verena Andermatt Conley, *Spatial Ecologies: Urban Sites, State and World-Space in French Cultural Theory* (Liverpool: Liverpool University Press, 2012), pp. 4–5.
19 The postcolonial theorist Homi Bhabha also discusses a concept of 'third space' that is quite different from Soja's 'Thirdspace'. Bhabha's third space connects to his other theories of hybridity and liminality, which all theorise alternative 'locations' in cultures affected by colonisation. In *Location and Culture* (London: Routledge, 1994), Bhabha conceptualises third space as an alternative linguistic (based upon Lacanian theory) and cultural space of 'otherness'. Bhabha's third space functions as a linguistic and temporal dimension in culture, focused on the 'temporal space of enunciation' when two cultures overlap (55), whereas Soja's Thirdspace remains linked to physical spaces or geographies. In this sense, Soja's theory of Thirdspace serves as a more effective introductory remark for imagining the bog's unusual geographical and cultural characteristics. Hereafter, I will refer to my own notion of how the bog functions as a physical/symbolic space, as a union/simultaneity/fusion of opposites.
20 See Yi-Fu Tuan, *Topophilia: A Study of Environmental Perception, Attitudes, and Values* (New York: Columbia University Press, 1974).
21 Yi-Fu Tuan, *Landscapes of Fear* [1979] (Minneapolis: University of Minneapolis Press, 2013), p. 3.
22 ibid., p. 6.
23 John Wylie, *Landscape* (London: Routledge, 2007), p. 1.
24 ibid., pp. 1–2.
25 Stuart McLean, 'BLACK GOO: Forceful Encounters with Matter in Europe's Muddy Margins', *Cultural Anthropology* 26.4 (2011), p. 592.
26 Gaston Bachelard, in trans. Edith R. Farrell, *Water and Dreams: An Essay on the Imagination of Matter* (Dallas, TX: The Pegasus Foundation, 1983), p. 104. Originally published in French as *L'Eau et les rêves, essai sur l'imagination de la matière* (Paris: Librairie José Corti, 1942).
27 Tuan, *Landscapes of Fear*, p. 5.
28 ibid., p. 6.
29 This slightly differs from notions of the 'sublime', which since the eighteenth century paired feelings of nature and fear as an aesthetic experience akin to beauty, and largely remains imaginative in practice. From a Burkean perspective, the sublime creates a feeling of insignificance in the face of grandeur, such as with a mountain range, producing both fear/awe and beauty. It implies distance rather than proximity because of the immensity of the subject, whether it is thinking about landscapes or about the idea that material world is more powerful than we can imagine. However, bogs in many ways create the opposite effect by producing an underwhelming feeling of insignificance because of their smaller scale to the naked eye, but are deceptive because of the immensity of their depths and pluralistic qualities. The fear of bogs has become cultural because of how they are represented in literature, for example. Although earlier authors of eighteenth-century Gothic novels relied on the sublime as a literary dimension, the term underscores a two- rather than three-dimensionality, and therefore will not be addressed in any detail here. For more, see Edmund Burke, *A Philosophical Enquiry: Into the Origin of our Ideas of the Sublime and Beautiful* [1757] (Oxford: Oxford University Press, 1990).
30 Edward Said, *Culture and Imperialism* (New York: Vintage, 1993), p. 226.

31 Derek Gregory, 'Edward Said's Imaginative Geographies', in Michael Crang and Nigel Thrift (eds), *Thinking Space* (London: Routledge, 2000), p. 303.
32 ibid., p. 305.
33 Wynne, *Colonial Conan Doyle*, p. 77.
34 ibid., p. 70.
35 Terry Eagleton, *The Truth About the Irish* (Dublin: New Island Books, 2002), p. 31.
36 Sanders, *Bodies in the Bog*, p. 7. Original emphasis.
37 See, for example, David Bellamy, *The Wild Boglands* (Dublin: Country House, 1986); Peter Foss and Catherine O'Connell, 'Bogland: Study and Utilization', in John Wilson Foster (ed.), *Nature in Ireland: A Scientific and Cultural History* (Montreal: McGill-Queen's University Press, 1997), pp. 184–98; Barry Raftery, 'The Archaeology of Irish Bogs', in Marinus L. Otte (ed.), *Wetlands of Ireland: Distribution, Ecology, and Uses and Economic Value* (Dublin: University College Dublin Press, 2003), pp. 202–209; Stuart McLean, '"To Dream Profoundly": Irish Boglands and the Imagination of Matter', *Irish Journal of Anthropology* 10.2 (2007), pp. 61–69; as well as Sanders' *Bodies in the Bog* and Meredith's 'Hazards in the Bog'.
38 Jarlath Killeen, *The Emergence of Irish Gothic Fiction: History, Texts, Theories* (Edinburgh: University of Edinburgh Press, 2014), p. 23.
39 Two notable examples of literary representations of bogs in the 1950s would be Walter Macken, *The Bogman* [1952] (London: Pan Books, 1972) and Máirtín Ó Cadhain, 'The Edge of the Bog' / *Ciumhais an Chriathraigh*, in *Two Stories* / *Dhá Scéal* [1953], trans. Louis de Paor, Mike McCormack, and Lochlainn Ó Tuairisg (Galway: Arlen House, 2006). Ó Cadhain's story, which is briefly discussed in Chapter 1, also speaks to a tradition of Irish language writings about bogs that could be more developed in future studies. In addition, John McGahern's *Memoir* (London: Faber and Faber, 2005), as well as *That They May Face the Rising Sun* (London: Faber and Faber, 2002), contain scenes about bogs. Indeed, there are other notable works containing bogs that simply could not be included in the scope of this study.
40 William Hughes and Andrew Smith, 'Introduction: Defining the Relationships between Gothic and the Postcolonial', *Gothic Studies* 5.2 (2003), p. 1.
41 Botting, *Gothic*, p. 3.
42 Julian Moynahan, *Anglo-Irish: The Literary Imagination of a Hyphenated Culture* (Princeton, NJ: Princeton University Press, 1994), p. 111.
43 Andrew Smith, *Gothic Literature* (Edinburgh: Edinburgh University Press, 2007), p. 8.
44 Hughes and Smith, 'Defining the Relationships', p. 2.
45 Anthony Vidler, *The Architectural Uncanny: Essays in the Modern Unhomely* (Cambridge, MA: MIT Press, 1992), p. 11.
46 Chris Baldick, 'Introduction', in Chris Baldick (ed.), *The Oxford Book of Gothic Tales* (Oxford: Oxford University Press, 2009), p. xix.
47 ibid., p. xx.
48 Siobhán Kilfeather, 'The Gothic Novel', in John Wilson Foster (ed.), *Cambridge Companion to the Irish Novel* (Cambridge: Cambridge University Press, 2006), p. 83.
49 James Watt, *Contesting the Gothic: Fiction, Genre & Cultural Conflict, 1764–1832* (Cambridge: Cambridge University Press, 1999), p. 6.
50 Yael Shapira, 'Where the Bodies are Hidden: Anne Radcliff's "Delicate" Gothic', *Eighteenth-Century Fiction* 18.4 (2006), p. 463.
51 Cited in Smith, *Gothic Literature*, p. 3.
52 See Patrick Brantlinger, *Rule of Darkness: British Literature and Imperialism, 1830–1914* (Ithaca: Cornell University Press, 1988).

53   Julie Newman, *The Ballistic Bard: Postcolonial Fictions* (London: Arnold, 1995), p. 70.
54   Andrew Smith and William Hughes, 'Introduction: The Enlightenment Gothic and Postcolonialism', in Andrew Smith and William Hughes (eds.), *Empire and the Gothic: The Politics of Genre* (Gordonsville, VA: Palgrave Macmillan, 2003), p. 12. In addition to Smith and Hughes, see also Paravisini-Gebert, 'Colonial and Postcolonial Gothic: The Caribbean', published in 2002.
55   David Punter and Glennis Byron, *The Gothic* (Oxford: Blackwell Publishing, 2004), p. 54.
56   Hughes and Smith, 'Defining the Relationships', p. 1. Original emphasis.
57   ibid., p. 1.
58   James Procter and Angela Smith, 'Gothic and Empire', in Catherine Spooner and Emma McEvoy (eds), The Routledge Companion to Gothic (London: Routledge, 2007), p. 96.
59   Luke Gibbons, *Transformations in Irish Culture* (Cork: Cork University Press, 1996), p. 15.
60   Margot Gayle Backus, *The Gothic Family Romance: Heterosexuality, Child Sacrifice, and the Anglo-Irish Colonial Order* (Durham: Duke University Press, 1999), p. 15.
61   For more on Cronin's label of the Irish Gothic, see Vera Kreilkamp, *The Anglo-Irish Novel and the Big House* (Syracuse, NY: Syracuse University Press, 1998), p. 118.
62   John Paul Riquelme, 'Introduction: Dark Modernity from Mary Shelly to Samuel Beckett: Gothic History, the Gothic Tradition, and Modernism', in John Paul Riquelme (ed.), *Gothic and Modernism* (Baltimore: Johns Hopkins University Press, 2008), p. 5.
63   Catherine Spooner, 'Gothic in the Twentieth Century', in Catherine Spooner and Emma McEvoy (eds), *The Routledge Companion to Gothic* (London: Routledge, 2007), p. 38.
64   Seamus Deane, 'Production of Cultural Space in Irish Writing', *Boundary 2* 21.3 (Fall 1994), p. 133.
65   See Killeen, *Irish Gothic Fiction* and Jarlath Killeen, *Gothic Ireland: Horror and the Irish Anglican Imagination in the Long Eighteenth Century* (Dublin: Four Courts Press, 2005).
66   Christina Morin and Niall Gillespie, 'Introduction: De-Limiting the Irish Gothic', in Christina Morin and Niall Gillespie (eds), *Irish Gothics: Genres, Forms, Modes, and Traditions, 1760–1890* (London: Palgrave Macmillan, 2014), p. 2.
67   Killeen, *Irish Gothic Fiction*, p. 13.
68   ibid., p. 17.
69   ibid., p. 13.
70   ibid., p. 17.
71   There are three shorter essays related to the Irish postcolonial Gothic that I have been able to locate. Enda Duffy concludes a chapter about race discourse in the British Empire with a section entitled 'Postcolonial Gothic', although the term is not used in the actual section. Duffy briefly traces this lineage through the Big House Gothic via Elizabeth Bowen and James Joyce, in part, and ends with John McGahern and Patrick McCabe. However, Duffy offers more of a survey of this mode of Irish Gothic rather than any sort of theorisation of the approach. See Enda Duffy, '"As White As Ours": Africa, Ireland, Imperial Panic, and the Effects of British Race Discourse', in Graham MacPhee and Prem Poddar (eds), *Empire and After: Englishness in Postcolonial Perspective* (New York: Berghahn Books, 2007), pp. 25–56. In another short essay, Eóin Flannery briefly outlines the importance of the postcolonial Gothic, but largely draws on previous critical explanations of it that are already mentioned in my Introduction. For more, see Flannery, '"A Land Poisoned": Eugene McCabe

and Irish Postcolonial Gothic', *Literature & History* 22.2 (Autumn 2013), pp. 91–112. Lastly, Calvin Keogh revisits Stoker's *Dracula* through a 'postcolonial Irish Gothic' lens. Although the article provides a history of revisionist debates in Irish postcolonial studies, it does not as clearly outline the link to the Gothic beyond the reading of *Dracula* as a Gothic novel. See Calvin W. Keogh, 'The Critics' Count: Revisions of *Dracula* and the Postcolonial Irish Gothic', *The Cambridge Journal of Postcolonial Literary Inquiry* 1.2 (2014), pp. 189–206. All of these examples are worth noting here but they do not theorise the approach as much as Hansen or Valente in the book-length form.

72   Jim Hansen, *Terror and Irish Modernism: The Gothic Tradition from Burke to Beckett* (Albany: SUNY Press, 2009), p. 11.

73   ibid., p. 8.

74   Stephen D. Arata, 'The Occidental Tourist: *Dracula* and the Anxiety of Reverse Colonization', *Victorian Studies* 33.4 (1990), p. 625.

75   Joseph Valente, *Dracula's Crypt: Bram Stoker, Irishness, and the Question of Blood* (Urbana: University of Illinois Press, 2002), p. 3. For another look at *Dracula* as a postcolonial Gothic novel in Irish Studies, see also Seamus Deane, 'Land & Soil: A Territorial Rhetoric', *History Ireland* 2.1 (Spring 1994), pp 31–34.

76   Backus, *Gothic Family*, pp. 2 and 3.

77   Luke Gibbons, *Gaelic Gothic: Race, Colonialism and Irish Culture* (Galway: Centre for Irish Studies, 2004).

78   Killeen, *Gothic Ireland*, p. 18.

79   Killeen, 'Irish Gothic'.

80   The spelling of O'Faolain's name is the English version from the Cambridge University Press published *Dictionary of Irish Biography*. Some prefer to use the Irish spelling, Seán Ó Faoláin, though the English version remains the most common usage and for consistency will be employed throughout this book.

81   Robinson, *Connemara*, p. 16.

82   Derek Gregory, *Geographical Imaginations* (Oxford: Blackwell, 1994), p. 45.

1. The Protean Nature of Bogs

1   Raftery, 'The Archaeology', p. 202.

2   David Bellamy, *The Wild Boglands* (Dublin: Country House, 1986), p. 17.

3   Tadhg Foley, review of Catherine Wynne, *The Colonial Conan Doyle: British Imperialism, Irish Nationalism, and the Gothic* (Westport, CT: Greenwood Press) in *Irish Studies Review* 11.3 (2003), p. 361.

4   Foss and O'Connell, 'Bogland', p. 184.

5   Dan Charman, *Peatlands and Environmental Change* (New York: John Wiley and Sons, 2002), p. ix.

6   McLean, 'To Dream', p. 61.

7   Robinson, *Listening*, p. 30.

8   Gerard Doyle and Colmán Ó Críodáin, 'Peatlands – Fens and Bogs', in Marinus L. Otte (ed.), *Wetlands of Ireland: Distribution, Ecology, and Uses and Economic Value* (Dublin: University College Dublin Press, 2003), p. 79.

9   John Feehan, 'Bogs', in F.H.A. Aalen, Kevin Whelan, and Matthew Stout (eds), *Atlas of the Irish Rural Landscape* (Cork: Cork University Press, 2011), p. 168.

10   Feehan, 'Bogs', p. 170.

11   Doyle and Ó Críodáin, 'Peatlands', pp. 79–80.

12   Counties in Ireland will be abbreviated as 'Co' throughout this book.

13   Doyle and Ó Críodáin, 'Peatlands', p. 79.

14 Foss and O'Connell, 'Bogland', p. 184. The nature in which bodies are preserved in bogs extends beyond the process of anaerobic submersion. The substance sphagnan aids in preservation because it contains a polysaccharide (sugar) in the cell walls of the sphagnum (bog moss) that grows on the surface of the bog. Once the moss dies and seeps into the bog, it is converted into a brownish humic acid. It is the combination of the humic acid, sphagnan, and several other compounds that bind with calcium and nitrogen released from the body. The calcium thwarts the growth of bacteria that would otherwise cause decay. This process also results in the body's skin colour, appearing as a brownish or tanned appearance resembling leather. Most organic matter can survive in the bog, such as skin, fingernails, hair, and wool, except for substances made from plant fibres. See Wijnand Van der Sanden, *Through Nature to Eternity: The Bog Bodies of Northwest Europe* (Amsterdam: Batavian Lion International, 1996), p. 18.

15 Bellamy, *The Wild Boglands*, p. 19.

16 Foss and O'Connell, 'Bogland', p. 186.

17 Sanders, *Bodies in the Bog*, p. 9.

18 Raftery, 'The Archaeology', p. 202

19 Doyle and Ó Críodáin, 'Peatlands', pp. 97–98 and Robinson, *Connemara*, pp. 60–63. I am especially grateful to Robinson's chapter on turf for explaining the process and providing the Irish terms.

20 Marc Lallanilla, 'Turf Wars: Irish Fighting Ban on Peat Harvesting', *livescience*, July 29, 2013, web accessed on 5 January 2016, www.livescience.com/38498-ban-on-turf-cutting-peat.html

21 Foss and O'Connell, 'Bogland', p. 191.

22 Rachel Giese, *The Donegal Pictures* (Winston-Salem, NC: Wake Forest University Press, 1987). Rachel now uses the surname Brown and has requested that her photos be referenced as 'by Rachel Giese Brown'. For more information on Rachel Brown's photography and biography, visit her website at www.rachelbrownphoto.com.

23 Michael Viney, 'Woodcock for a Farthing: The Irish Experience of Nature', *The Irish Review*, 1 (1986), p. 63.

24 Roland Barthes, 'The Rhetoric of the Image', in Alan Trachtenberg (ed.), *Classic Essays on Photography* (New Haven, CT: Leete's Island Books, 1980), p. 269.

25 W.J.T. Mitchell, 'Introduction', in W.J.T. Mitchell (ed.), *Landscape and Power* (Chicago and London: The University of Chicago Press, 1994), p. 1.

26 For more on turf-cutting and visual culture, see Christine Cusick, 'Moments of Story: Rachel Giese's *The Donegal Pictures*', in Eóin Flannery and Michael Griffin (eds), *Ireland in Focus: Film, Photography and Popular Culture* (Syracuse: Syracuse University Press, 2009), pp. 86–106, and Derek Gladwin, 'Eco-Haptic Photography: Visualizing Bogland in Rachel Giese's *The Donegal Pictures*', *Photography and Culture* 6.2 (2013), pp. 157–174.

27 McLean, 'To Dream', p. 63.

28 Bellamy, *The Wild Boglands*, p. 19.

29 ibid., p. 20.

30 Foss and O'Connell, 'Bogland', p. 185.

31 Feehan, 'Bogs', p. 168.

32 Sanders, *Bodies in the Bog*, p. 17.

33 John Wilson Foster, 'Encountering Traditions', in John Wilson Foster (ed.), *Nature in Ireland: A Scientific and Cultural History* (Montreal and Kingston: McGill-Queen's University Press, 1997), p. 38.

34 Giraldus Cambrensis, in Thomas Wright (ed.), trans. by Thomas Forester, *Topographia Hibernica / The Topography of Ireland* [1188] (Cambridge, Ontario: Parentheses Publications Medieval Latin Series, 2000), Chapter XXXVIII.

35 Julia Reinhard Lupton, 'Mapping Mutability, or Spenser's Irish Plot', in Brendan Bradshaw, Andrew Hadfield, and Willy Maley (eds.), *Representing Ireland: Literature and the Origins of Conflict, 1534–1660* (Cambridge: Cambridge University Press, 2010), p. 98.

36 Edmund Spenser, *A View of the Present State of Ireland* [1596], *Renascene Editions* (University of Oregon, 1997), p. 13, Web, accessed 8 Jan. 2016, https://scholarsbank. uoregon.edu/xmlui/bitstream/handle/1794/825/ireland.pdf?sequence=1

37 Foster, 'Encountering Traditions', p. 28.

38 ibid., p. 26.

39 ibid., p. 30.

40 ibid., p. 29.

41 Gerard Boate, *Irelands Naturall History: Being a True Description of its Situation, Greatness, Shape and Nature* (London: Samuel Hartlib, 1652), pp. 108 and 106.

42 ibid., p. 106.

43 ibid., p. 114.

44 Robert Lloyd Praeger made this observation in 1949 based upon his own research on the bogs of Ireland. See Foss and O'Connell, 'Bogland', p. 187.

45 Liam Heneghan, 'The Epistemology of Hatred: A Case Study of Irish Bogs', *3 Quarks Daily*, 17 June 2013, web, accessed 7 Jan. 2016, www.3quarksdaily.com/ 3quarksdaily/2013/06/the-epistemology-of-hatred-a-case-study-of-irish-bogs.html

46 William King, 'Of the Bogs, and Loughs of Ireland', *Philosophical Transactions of the Dublin Philosophical Society* 15 (1685), p. 955.

47 King, 'Of the Bogs', p. 554.

48 ibid., pp. 948 and 949. Italics original emphasis.

49 ibid., p. 953. Italics original emphasis.

50 ibid. Italics original emphasis.

51 Killeen, 'Irish Gothic'.

52 King, 'Of the Bogs', p. 948.

53 There are other scientific studies about boglands in the nineteenth century, in addition to the more well-known *Report* mentioned here. See Alexander Nimmo, *Fourth Report on the Bogs in That Part of the Country of Galway to the West of Lough Corrib* (Ordered by the House of Commons, 1814) [Nimmo also worked as an engineer on the *Report*]; Henry Coulter, *The West of Ireland: Its Existing Condition, and Prospects* (Dublin: Hodges and Smith, 1862); and George Preston White, *A Tour in Connemara, with Remarks on Its Great Physical Capabilities* (Dublin: James McGlashan, 1851). Thanks to Lisabeth C. Buchelt for this detailed note in her edited critical edition of *The Snake's Pass* (Syracuse: Syracuse University Press, 2015), p. 57 n.4. It is worth noting, however, that all of these accounts were funded largely to further draining and cultivating bogs for economic purposes.

54 Foss and O'Connell, 'Bogland', p. 188.

55 Katie Trumpener, *Bardic Nationalism: The Romantic Novel and the British Empire* (Princeton: Princeton University Press, 1997), p. 46.

56 Maria Edgeworth, *Castle Rackrent, An Hibernian Tale taken from facts and from the manners of the Irish squires before the year 1782* [1800] (Oxford: University of Oxford Press, 2008), p. 27.

57 ibid., pp. 16–17.

58 Maria Edgeworth's father, Richard Lovell Edgeworth, was employed by the 1809 Bogs Commission to estimate possible drainage schemes across Ireland. See Claire Connolly, *A Cultural History of the Irish Novel, 1790–1829* (Cambridge: Cambridge University Press, 2011), p. 213, n. 82.

59 Trumpener, *Bardic Nationalism*, p. 46.

60 James Joyce, in Robert Scholes and A. Walton Litz (eds), *Dubliners: Text, Criticism, and Notes* (New York: Viking, 1969), p. 233. There is an excellent section about bogs in Joyce's 'The Dead' in James Fairhall's forthcoming essay in *James Joyce Quarterly*, 'The Bog of Allen, the Tiber River, and the Pontine Marshes: An Ecocritical Background of "The Dead"'.

61 Qtd. in Bellamy, *The Wild Boglands*, p. 11.

62 McLean, 'To Dream', p. 63.

63 Seamus Heaney, *Opened Ground: Poems 1966–1996* (London: Faber and Faber, 1998), p. 123.

64 Qtd. in McLean, 'To Dream', p. 61.

65 McLean, 'To Dream', p. 61.

66 *Bogland Symposium Exhibition* (Ireland: Crescent Art Centre, 1990), p. 12.

67 ibid.

68 Eagleton, *The Truth*, p. 31.

69 ibid.

70 Luke Gibbons, '"Some Hysterical Hatred": History, Hysteria, and the Literary Revival', *Irish University Review* 27:1 (Spring/Summer 1997), p. 15.

71 Morin and Gillespie, 'Introduction', p. 1.

72 Louis de Paor, 'Introduction: Introducing Máirtín Ó Cadhain', *The Canadian Journal of Irish Studies* 34.1 (Spring 2008), p. 13.

73 Máirtín Ó Cadhain, 'The Edge of the Bog/Ciumhais an Chriathraigh', in Louis de Paor, Mike McCormack, and Lochlainn Ó Tuairisg (eds and trans.), *Two Stories/Dhá Scéal* (Galway: Arlen House, 2006), p. 43.

74 ibid.

75 Heaney, *Opened Ground*, pp. 41–42.

2. Environments of Empire

1 Catherine Wynne, 'The Bog as Colonial Topography in Nineteenth-Century Irish Fiction', in Terrence McDonough (ed.), *Was Ireland a Colony?* (Dublin: Irish Academic Press, 2005), p. 323.

2 Albert Memmi, *The Colonizer and the Colonized* [1965] (Boston: Beacon Press, 1991), p. 9.

3 Deane, 'Production', p. 119.

4 Roy Foster, *Paddy and Mr. Punch: Connections in Irish and English History* (London: Penguin, 1995), p. 263. Although parts of *The Snake's Pass* first appeared serialised in *The People* in 1890, it attempted to capture the problems in 1870s and 1880s' Ireland

5 Terry Eagleton, *Heathcliff and the Great Hunger: Studies in Irish Culture* (London: Verso, 1995), p. 4.

6 Thomas Bartlett, *Ireland: A History* (Cambridge: Cambridge University Press, 2010), p. 320.

7 Nicholas Daly, *Modernism, Romance, and the Fin de Siècle: Popular Fiction and British Culture, 1880–1914* (Cambridge: Cambridge University Press, 1999), pp. 68–69.

8 Ruth Dudley Edwards, *An Atlas of Irish History* (London: Routledge, 2005), p. 168.

9 Daly, *Modernism*, p. 69.

10   Bram Stoker, *The Snake's Pass in The Collected Supernatural & Weird Fiction of Bram Stoker,*
     Vol. 5 (London: Leonaur Publishing, 2009), p. 11. For the remainder of this chapter,
     all references to this work will be placed in the text. A critical edition of *The Snake's*
     Pass, edited by Lisabeth C. Buchelt, was published in 2015 (well after this chapter
     was completed). This version is currently the best edition of Stoker's novel. See Bram
     Stoker, *The Snake's Pass: A Critical Edition,* Lisabeth C. Buchelt (ed.) (Syracuse: Syracuse
     University Press, 2015).

11   Eagleton, *Heathcliff,* p. 31.

12   1995 was something of a watershed year for publications about *The Snake's Pass,*
     starting with Nicholas Daly, 'Irish Roots: The Romance of History in Bram Stoker's
     "The Snake's Pass"', *Literature and History,* 3:4:2 (Autumn: 1995), pp. 42–70, which
     was later expanded into a chapter in his book *Modernism, Romance, and the Fin de*
     Siècle. The same year, Christopher Morash published '"Ever under some unnatural
     condition": Bram Stoker and the Colonial Fantastic', in Brian Cosgrove (ed.),
     Literature and the Supernatural: Essays for the Maynooth Bicentenary (Dublin: Columba Press,
     1995). Morash's essay examines Stoker's political identity, which partly draws from
     The Snake's Pass as a place where soil, drawing from Deane's analysis of Dracula in
     'Production', is 'a locus on anxiety' (110), and where Stoker explores this idea of the
     literary fantastic through the bog. One could argue that both essays initiated critical
     discussions in the 1990s about *The Snake's Pass,* but Daly's critical treatment of the
     novel focuses entirely on *The Snake's Pass* and colonial spaces, one which the bog
     occupies, whereas Morash's essay uses *The Snake's Pass* as only a part of his analysis to
     support his position about Stoker's deployment of the 'literary fantastic'.

13   Daly, *Modernism,* p. 55.

14   ibid., p. 54.

15   See, Gibbons, '"Some Hysterical Hatred"', pp. 7–23.

16   Gibbons, '"Some Hysterical Hatred"', p. 14.

17   William Hughes, '"For Ireland's Good": The Reconstruction of Rural Ireland in
     Bram Stoker's "*The Snake's Pass*"', *Irish Studies Review* 3:12 (2008), p. 17.

18   ibid.

19   Wynne, 'The Bog', p. 310.

20   ibid., p. 311.

21   Two other noteworthy essays focused on *The Snake's Pass* were published in the last
     few years. Lisabeth C. Buchelt writes about Stoker's narrative technique and the
     dinnseanchas tradition (stories about placenames) in the novel. Jarlath Killeen writes
     about masculinity in *The Snake's Pass,* specifically through nationalist portrayals of
     men associated with the Land Wars and the Gaelic Athletic Association (GAA).
     Killeen demonstrates that their cultural influence on Stoker (along with his own body
     history) affected the characters developed in the novel. However, neither Killeen's
     nor Buchelt's essays add any new perspectives about the bog not already addressed
     by Morash, Daly, Hughes, Gibbons, or Wynne. See Lisabeth C. Buchelt, '"Delicate
     Fantasy" and "Vulgar Reality": Undermining Romance and Complicating Identity
     in Bram Stoker's *The Snake's Pass*', *New Hibernia Review* 16.1 (2012), pp. 113–33, and
     Jarlath Killeen, 'Bram Stoker and Irish Masculinity in *The Snake's Pass*', in *Irish Gothics:*
     Genres, Forms, Modes, and Traditions, 1760–1890 (New York: Palgrave Macmillan, 2014),
     pp. 168–87. In addition, I also published an essay on the bog in *The Snake's Pass,*
     which was a much earlier and rather different version of this chapter, but it focused
     on the 'Eco-Gothic'. See Gladwin, 'The Bog Gothic: Bram Stoker's "Carpet of
     Death" and Ireland's Horrible Beauty', *Gothic Studies* 16.1 (2014), pp. 39–54.

22   Trumpener, *Bardic Nationalism,* p. 54.

23   ibid., p. 52.

24   ibid., pp. 46–47.

25   Stuart McLean, *The Event and its Terrors: Ireland, Famine, Modernity* (Palo Alto: Stanford University Press, 2004), pp. 41–42.

26   Daly, *Modernism*, p. 75.

27   Hughes, "'Ireland's Good'", p. 18.

28   Donal Clarke, 'Brief History of the Peat Industry in Ireland', in *Irish Peat Society Seminar Proceedings* (Dublin, 2006), p. 7.

29   George Moore, *Parnell and His Island* (London: Swan Sonnenschein, Lowrey, 1887), p. 99

30   Smith and Hughes, 'Introduction', p. 3.

31   Trumpener, *Bardic Nationalism*, p. 52.

32   Daly, *Modernism*, p. 75.

33   Declan Kiberd, *Irish Classics* (Cambridge, MA: Harvard University Press, 2001), p. 386.

34   Andrew Smith, 'Demonising the Americans: Bram Stoker's Postcolonial Gothic', *Gothic Studies* 5.2 (Fall 2003), p. 23.

35   Valente, *Dracula's Crypt*, p. 16.

36   ibid., p. 18. Stoker's identity remains a debated subject. For example, Morash argues that Stoker's ancestry is English, whereas David Glover links Stoker to the Ascendancy Anglo-Irish. See Morash, "'Even Under'", pp. 102–03, and David Glover, *Vampires, Mummies and Liberals: Bram Stoker and the Politics of Popular Fiction* (Durham, NC: Duke University Press, 1996), p. 9. Valente's analysis remains the most comprehensive and convincing because it clearly traces Stoker's family lineage, challenging the notion that Stoker is Anglo-Irish.

37   Valente, *Dracula's Crypt*, p. 22. Gibbons, "'Some Hysterical Hatred'", p. 15, also pinpoints Stoker as a 'philosophical Home Ruler'. In addition, Morash documents that Stoker's wife acknowledged John Dillon, the militant Irish nationalist, to be a family friend in a letter she wrote. See, Morash, "'Even Under'", p. 112. Stoker also befriended one of the prime motivators of the Irish cultural revival, Standish O'Grady, who encouraged him to submit some of his short fiction to Sampson Low. See Valente, p. 22.

38   Glover, *Vampires*, p. 31.

39   Valente, *Dracula's Crypt*, p. 22. Valente goes on to point out that Stoker repeatedly voted against the dissolution of British imperial rule in the Trinity College Historical Society debates, but, at the same time, Stoker praised nationalist Catholic figures like Daniel O'Connell. He also voted for abolition of the Irish viceroyalty.

40   Barbara Belford, *Bram Stoker: A Biography of the Author of "Dracula"* (London: Weidenfeld and Nicholson, 1996), p. 77.

41   Carol A. Senf, *Science and Social Science in Bram Stoker's Fiction* (Westport, CT: Greenwood Press, 2002), p. 134.

42   Paul Murray, *From the Shadow of Dracula: A Life of Bram Stoker* (London: Jonathan Cape, 2004), pp. 2–3.

43   Aidan O'Sullivan, 'Crannógs: Places of Resistance in the Contested Landscapes of Early Modern Ireland', in Barbara Bender and Margot Winer (eds), *Contested Landscapes: Movement, Exile and Place* (Oxford: Berg, 2001), p. 89.

44   Trumpener, *Bardic Nationalism*, pp. 42–43.

45   Another possible literary reference would be that of Lord Byron's narrative poem *Mezeppa* (1819), which, as one of the earliest treatments of vampires, would have other suggestive connections to Stoker's Gothic underpinnings in *The Snake's Pass*.

46   Smith, *Gothic Literature*, p. 6.
47   Trumpener, *Bardic Nationalism*, p. 37.
48   Clarke, 'Brief History', p. 7.
49   Boate, *Irelands Naturall History*, pp. 114 and 117.
50   Gibbons, '"Some Hysterical Hatred"', p. 14.
51   ibid., p. 15.
52   Botting, *Gothic*, p. 9.
53   Hughes, '"Ireland's Good"', p. 19.
54   ibid., p. 20.
55   ibid.
56   Freud, 'The Uncanny' [1919], *The Uncanny* (New York: Penguin, 2003), p. 124.
57   ibid., p. 125.
58   Punter and Byron, *The Gothic*, p. 293.
59   Derek Gladwin, 'Ecocriticism', in Eugene O'Brien (ed.), *Oxford Bibliographies in Literary and Cultural Theory* (New York: Oxford University Press, 2016), n.p., web, accessed 3 Jan. 2016, www.oxfordbibliographies.com/obo/page/literary-and-critical-theory.
60   Serenella Iovino and Serpil Oppermann, 'Material Ecocriticism: Materiality, Agency, and Models of Narrativity', *Ecozone@* 3.1 (2012), p. 79.
61   Thomas Hardy, *The Return of the Native* [1878] (New York: Penguin, 1979), p. 55.
62   Iovino and Oppermann, 'Material Ecocriticism', p. 79.
63   Bram Stoker, 'The Great White Fair in Dublin: How There Has Arisen on the Site of the Old Donnybrook Fair a Great Exhibition as Typical of the New Ireland as the Former Festival was of the Ireland of the Past', *The World's Work* IX 54 (May 1907), p. 573.
64   Iovino and Oppermann, 'Material Ecocriticism', p. 84.
65   ibid., p. 82.
66   Botting, *Gothic*, p. 8.
67   ibid., p. 6.
68   ibid., p. 7.
69   ibid.
70   Graham Huggan and Helen Tiffin, *Postcolonial Ecocriticism: Literature, Animals, Environment* (London: Routledge, 2010), p. 8. Original emphasis.
71   Smith, 'Demonising', p. 20.
72   Botting, *Gothic*, p. 12.
73   Daly, *Modernism*, p. 55, and Valente, *Dracula's Crypt*, p. 17.
74   See, for example, Julian Moynahan's *Anglo-Irish* and Jarlath Killen's *Gothic Ireland*.
75   Said, *Culture and Imperialism*, p. 225.
76   Gibbons, '"Some Hysterical Hatred"', p. 14.

3. Special Histories of Nationalism

1   Avery Gordon, *Ghostly Matters: Haunting and the Sociological Imagination* (Minneapolis: University of Minnesota Press, 2008), p. xvi.
2   María del Pilar Blanco and Esther Peeren, 'Introduction: Conceptualizing Spectralities', in María del Pilar Blanco and Esther Peeren (eds), *The Spectralities Reader: Ghosts and Haunting in Contemporary Cultural Theory* (London: Bloomsbury, 2013), p. 2.
3   Simon Gikandi, 'Postcolonial Theory and the Specter of Nationalism', *Clio* 36.1 (2006), p. 80.
4   Gordon, *Ghostly Matters*, p. xvi.

5   ibid.
6   The 'spectral turn' in theory is typically marked by the publication of Jacques Derrida's *Specters of Marx* (London: Routledge, 1994). After this publication, ghosts have been increasingly examined through critical vocabularies of Marxism and capitalism, particularly in light of Derrida's notion of hauntology and Franco Moretti's analysis of vampirism as a metaphor for the capitalist system in *Signs Taken For Wonders* (London: Verso, 1983). In terms of spectral theory and nationalism, Pheng Cheah published *Spectral Nationality: Passages of Freedom from Kant to Postcolonial Literature of Liberation* (New York: Columbia University Press, 2003) and 'Spectral Nationality: The Living-on of the Postcolonial Nation in Neocolonial Globalization', *Boundary 2* 26.3 (Fall 1999), pp. 225–52, both of which address a range of issues related to spectres in Marxist, capitalist, and postcolonial works. Despite this critical spectral history, I mainly draw from Gordon in this chapter because her study more explicitly examines ghosts and hauntings in the social sphere.
7   This chapter uses the terms 'ghosts', 'spectres', and 'revenants' interchangeably, as they relate to anything with a spirited, energetic, or even imagined presence that haunts. María del Pilar Blanco and Esther Peeren also define ghosts quite generally as 'appearing as anything from figments of the imagination, divine messengers, benign or exacting ancestors, and pesky otherworldly creatures populating particular loci to disturbing figures returned from the dead bent on exacting revenge, revealing hidden crimes, continuing a love affair or simply searching for a way to pass on'. See 'Introduction', p. 1. Gordon similarly maintains that the 'ghost is a crucible for political mediation and historical memory'. See *Ghostly Matters*, p. 18.
8   Gordon, *Ghostly Matters*, p. xvi.
9   Smith, *Gothic Literature*, pp. 122–23.
10   See, for example, Caoilfhionn Ní Bheacháin, 'Seeing Ghosts: Gothic Discourses and State Formation, *Éire-Ireland* 47.3/4 (Fall/Winter 2012), pp. 37–53.
11   Seamus Deane, *Celtic Revivals: Essays in Modern Irish Literature* (London: Faber and Faber, 1985), p. 14.
12   Richard Kearney, *Postnationalist Ireland: Politics, Culture, Philosophy* (London: Routledge, 1997), p. 11.
13   Gikandi, 'Specter of Nationalism', p. 77.
14   Kearney, *Postnationalist Ireland*, p. 8.
15   Benedict Anderson, *Imagined Communities: Reflections on the Origin and Spread of Nationalism* [1983] (London: Verso, 2006), pp. 3–6.
16   For more on the history of the Easter Rising, see Charles Townshend, *Easter 1916: The Irish Rebellion* (New York: Penguin, 2005) and Fearghal McGarry, *The Rising: Ireland, Easter 1916* (Oxford: Oxford University Press, 2011).
17   Deane, *Celtic Revivals*, p. 14.
18   Gikandi, 'Specter of Nationalism', p. 76.
19   David Lloyd, *Ireland After History* (Cork: Cork University Press, 1999), p. 24.
20   O'Connor was in the IRA and O'Faolain was in the Irish Volunteers.
21   Joe Cleary, *Outrageous Fortune: Capital and Culture in Modern Ireland* (Dublin: Field Day Publications, 2007), p. 144.
22   Joyce largely rejected the ideas of the Revivalists but he is nevertheless often associated with them. In his later book *The Irish* [1947] (London: Penguin, 1969), O'Faolain frames the style of the Revivalists as Romantic (pp. 142–43). According to Cleary, Joyce was, for O'Faolain, the 'exemplary realist and the tutelary figure for all later twentieth-century Irish writing'. See Cleary, *Outrageous*, p. 147.

23   Cleary, *Outrageous*, p. 176.
24   Michael Neary, 'Whispered Presences in Sean O'Faolain's Stories', *Studies in Short Fiction* 32 (1995), p. 11.
25   Ní Bheacháin, 'Seeing Ghosts', pp. 44–45.
26   ibid., p. 45.
27   Moretti, *Signs*, p. 83. Original emphasis.
28   Frank O'Connor, 'Guests of the Nation' [1931], *Frank O'Connor Collected Stories* (New York: Vintage Books, 1982), p. 8. For the remainder of this chapter, all references to this story will be placed in the text.
29   Brian Cleeve, *A Dictionary of Irish Writers* (Cork: Mercier Press, 1967), p. 101. There have been many notable adaptations of 'Guests of the Nation' since its publication, namely Denis Johnston's silent adaptation *Guests of the Nation* (1935), Brendan Behan's Irish language play *An Ghiall/The Hostage* (1957), Neil Jordan's critically acclaimed film *The Crying Game* (1992), and Daniel Speers' most recent film adaptation *Guests of a Nation* (2012). In fact, O'Connor's story had been adapted so often that he once commented to Yeats that he was not aware it had been adapted by a specific person since it had already been used so often by the collective. See O'Connor, *An Only Child and My Father's Son: An Autobiography* (London: Pan Books, 1988), p. 216.
30   Stanley Renner, 'The Theme of Hidden Powers: Fate vs. Human Responsibility', *Studies in Short Fiction* 27 (1990), p. 375.
31   Qtd. in Michael Storey, 'The Guests of Frank O'Connor and Albert Camus', *Comparative Literature Studies* 23.3 (1986), pp. 250–51.
32   Eugene O'Brien, 'Guests of the Nation: Geists of the Nation', *New Hibernia Review / Iris Éireannach Nua* 11.3 (2007), p. 116.
33   ibid., pp. 116–117.
34   Although my analysis briefly references Derrida's notions of haunting on a couple of occasions (mainly here in the endnotes), this chapter does not provide a Derridian analysis of hauntology for two reasons. First, Derrida has become the main source for spectral readings of literary texts and I want to offer a new analysis. Second, Gordon's approach to spectral theory charts a clearer direction for my own argument about social and national connections between the characters and the bog.
35   Sean O'Faolain, 'A Meeting', *Midsummer Night Madness: Collected Short Stories*, Vol. 1 [1932] (New York: Penguin Books, 1982), p. 273. For the remainder of this chapter, all references to this story will be placed in the text.
36   Neary, 'Whispered Presences', p. 11. O'Faolain is equally known in Irish Studies for his criticism and editorial stewardship of the journal *The Bell* (founded in 1940), as he is for his ability to superbly craft a short story.
37   In addition to dozens of essays, there are, although now quite dated, several substantial book-length studies of O'Faolain's literary output. See, for example, Paul A. Doyle, *Sean O'Faolain* (New York: Twayne Publishers, 1968); Joseph Storey Rippier, *The Short Stories of Sean O'Faolain* (New York: Barnes & Noble Books, 1976); Richard Bonaccorso, *Sean O'Faolain's Irish Vision* (Albany: State University of New York Press, 1987) and Pierce Butler, *Sean O'Faolain: A Study of Short Fiction* (New York: Twayne Publishers, 1993). The most recent study is Paul Delaney, *Seán O'Faoláin: Literature, Inheritance and the 1930s* (Dublin: Irish Academic Press, 2015). Despite the volume of critical writings about O'Faolain, 'A Meeting' has only received a cursory glance.
38   Katherine Hanley, 'The Short Stories of Sean O'Faolain', *Eire-Ireland: A Journal of Irish Studies* 6.3 (1971), p. 6.
39   ibid.

40   Anderson, *Imagined Communities*, p. 4.
41   Punter and Byron, *The Gothic*, p. 55.
42   Brian Graham, 'The Imagining of Place: Representation and Identity in Contemporary Ireland', in Brian Graham (ed.), *In Search of Ireland: A Cultural Geography* (London: Routledge, 1997), p. 195.
43   Killeen, *Gothic Literature*, p. 28.
44   Cheah, *Spectral Nationality*, p. 1.
45   Anderson, *Imaginary Communities*, p. 25.
46   ibid.
47   Hanley, 'The Short Stories', pp. 10–11.
48   Cheah, *Spectral Nationality*, p. 1.
49   Bonaccorso, *Sean O'Faolain*, p. 51.
50   Sean O'Faolain, 'This Is Your Magazine', *The Bell* 1 (1940), p. 5.
51   Qtd. in Kiberd, *Irish Classics*, p. 482.
52   Donal McCartney, 'Sean O'Faolain: A Nationalist Right Enough', *Irish University Review* 6.1 (Spring 1976), p. 79.
53   Gordon, *Ghostly Matters*, p. 17.
54   Boreens are small, unpaved rural roads, often winding through bogs.
55   Cheah, *Spectral Nationality*, p. 1.
56   Gordon, *Ghostly Matters*, p. 125.
57   Bhabha, 'Narrating the Nation', p. 5.
58   Gordon, *Ghostly Matters*, p. 63.
59   ibid.
60   ibid., p. xvi. Beyond the Irish context, there is a larger commentary about abusive systems of power with regard to capitalist and community themes at work in the story, specifically in connection with the First World War where financial capital and power overarched the Gothicised and liminal battlefields in France. If this argument were to be examined further, which is beyond the range of this chapter, then Derrida's *Specters of Marx* would be a helpful critical lens.
61   Smith, *Gothic Literature*, p. 87.
62   Bhabha, 'Narrating the Nation', p. 3.
63   McCartney, 'Sean O'Faolain', p. 86.
64   Qtd. in Bonaccorso, *Sean O'Faolain*, p. 49.
65   Bonaccorso, *Sean O'Faolain*, pp. 48–50.
66   Daniel Corkery, *Synge & Anglo-Irish Literature* (Cork: Mercier Press, 1931), p. 14.
67   ibid., p. 19.
68   Bonaccorso, *Sean O'Faolain*, p. 51.
69   Bryan Fanning, 'Hidden Ireland, Silent Irelands: Sean O'Faolain and Frank O'Connor Versus Daniel Corkery', *Studies: An Irish Quarterly Review* 95.379 (Autumn 2006), pp. 252–53.
70   David Pierce, *Light, Freedom, and Song: A Cultural History of Modern Irish Writing* (New Haven: Yale University Press, 2005), p. 96.
71   Kearney, *Postnationalist Ireland*, p. 9.
72   Hansen, *Terror and Irish Modernism*, p. 11.
73   Storey, 'The Guests', p. 257.
74   David Lloyd, *Anomalous States: Irish Writing and the Post-Colonial Moment* (Durham: Duke University Press, 1993), p. 6.
75   ibid., p. 6.
76   Bartlett, *Ireland*, p. 258.

77 O'Brien, 'The Guests', p. 122.
78 Richard Ellmann, 'Introduction', *Frank O'Connor: Collected Stories* (New York: Vintage, 1981), p. viii.
79 Neary, 'Whispered Presences', p. 12.
80 ibid., p. 11.
81 O'Brien, 'The Guests', p. 121.
82 Neary, 'Whispered Presences', p. 11.
83 Bonaccorso, *Sean O'Faolain*, p. 51.
84 Gordon, *Ghostly Matters*, p. 8.
85 Neary, 'Whispered Presences', p. 15. Original emphasis.
86 Gordon, *Ghostly Matters*, p. 8.

4. Mapping Gothic Bog Bodies

1   I have adapted this quote for contemporary usage and changed 'man' to 'person'.
2   Robert T. Tally Jr., *Spatiality* (New York: Routledge, 2013), p. 45.
3   Although there is no clear consensus on the subject, Heaney's 'bog poems' generally include the following: from *Death of a Naturalist* (1966): 'Digging'; from *Door in the Dark* (1969): 'Bogland'; from *Wintering Out* (1972): 'The Tollund Man', 'Bog Oak', and 'Nerthus'; from *North* (1975): 'Come to the Bower', 'Belderg', 'Bog Queen', 'The Grauballe Man', 'Punishment', 'Kinship', 'Strange Fruit', and 'Act of Union'. In addition to these poems, I draw from Heaney's first collection of non-fiction prose, *Preoccupations: Selected Prose, 1968–1978* (New York: Farrar, Straus, Giroux, 1980), various interviews, and lectures, where in all cases Heaney frequently describes his relationship with the bog. All direct quotes from these works by Heaney follow fair use guidelines.
4   For more comprehensive histories of the Troubles in Northern Ireland, see J. Bowyer Bell, *The Irish Troubles: A Generation of Violence, 1967–1992* (Dublin: Gill and Macmillan, 1993) and Tim Pat Coogan, *The Troubles: Ireland's Ordeal 1966–1996 and the Search for Peace* (London: Hutchinson, 1995).
5   David Kennedy, '"Tell-tale skins" and "Repeatable Codes": Historical Bodies and Mythic Readings in Seamus Heaney's "Bog Poems"', *English* 54.208 (Spring 2005), p. 39.
6   Hurley, 'Abject', p. 138
7   Kennedy, '"Tell-tale skins"', p. 39.
8   ibid., p. 39.
9   Peter Turchi, *Maps of the Imagination: The Writer and Cartographer* (San Antonio, TX: Trinity University Press, 2004), p. 11.
10 Lloyd, *Anomalous*, p. 18.
11 Despite the controversial placename differentiation between Londonderry and Derry, I will be referring to this city as Derry based upon Heaney's own usage. In pre-Christian times Derry was known as *Daire-Calgaich*, or the 'oak wood of Calgach'. During the reign of James I, particularly while under a charter granted to London companies in 1613, the name Derry was changed to Londonderry, in order to reflect British occupation. Because of this contested colonial history, the divide between using Londonderry or Derry still exists. See Gerry Smyth, *Space and the Irish Cultural Imagination* (Basingstoke: Palgrave Macmillan, 2001), pp. 136–137.
12 Diarmaid Ferriter, *The Transformation of Ireland* (Woodstock, NY: Overlook Press, 2004), p. 626.
13 Michael Longley, a Protestant poet from Northern Ireland, similarly responds to the Troubles through what he calls '[m]y nature writing', which, he goes on to say, 'is my

most political'. Qtd. in Pierce, *Light*, p. 271. Other writers and poets use geographical metaphors to represent the Troubles, but Heaney remains the focus here because of his devotion to the bog.

14 A few dozen full-length studies on Heaney are in circulation and the number of articles and conference papers devoted to him far exceeds that of any other contemporary Irish writer. With this in mind, I limit my critical overview to the scholars who have engaged solely with Heaney's treatment of the bogs and bog bodies.

15 See in this order, Edna Longley 'North: "Inner Emigré" or "Artful Voyeur"?', in Edna Longley (ed.), *Poetry in the Wars* (Newcastle: Bloodaxe Books, 1986), p. 154; Deane, *Celtic*, p. 175; Patricia Coughlan, '"Bog Queens": The Representation of Women in the Poetry of John Montague and Seamus Heaney', in Claire Connolly (ed.), *Theorizing Ireland* (London: Palgrave, 2003), p. 42; Lloyd, *Anomalous*, p. 17; and Helen Vendler, *Seamus Heaney* (Cambridge, MA: Harvard University Press, 1998), pp. 38–39.

16 O'Brien, *Heaney*, p. 5.

17 ibid.

18 Vendler, *Heaney*, p. 48

19 ibid., p. 47.

20 ibid., p. 55.

21 John Wilson Foster, *Colonial Consequences: Essays in Irish Literature and Culture* (Dublin: Lilliput, 1991), p. 177.

22 Punter and Byron, *The Gothic*, p. xix.

23 Heaney, *Preoccupations*, p. 18.

24 Heaney, *Opened Ground*, p. 95. All subsequent quotes from Heaney's poetry in this chapter, regardless of the volume, come from this collection and are placed in the text.

25 Dianne Meredith, 'Landscape or Mindscape? Seamus Heaney's Bogs', *Irish Geography* 32.2 (1999), p. 127.

26 Stuart McLean, 'Bodies from the Bog: Metamorphosis, Non-human Agency and the Making of "Collective" Memory', *Trames* 12.62/57 (2008), p. 306.

27 Sanders, *Bodies in the Bog*, p. 84.

28 ibid., p. 47.

29 ibid., p. 85.

30 Lloyd, *Anomalous*, p. 24.

31 ibid., p. 13.

32 ibid., p. 27.

33 Deane, *Celtic Revivals*, p. 174.

34 Graham Huggan, *Territorial Disputes: Maps and Mapping Strategies in Contemporary Canadian and Australian Fiction* (Toronto: University of Toronto Press, 1994), p. 4.

35 Tally, *Spatiality*, p. 46.

36 Moynagh Sullivan, 'The Treachery of Wetness: Irish Studies, Seamus Heaney and the Politics of Parturition', *Irish Studies Review* 13.4 (2005), p. 454.

37 Heaney, *Preoccupations*, p. 54.

38 Qtd. in Meredith, 'Landscape', pp. 127–128.

39 Seamus Heaney, 'The Man and the Bog', in Bryony Coles and John M. Coles (eds), *Bog Bodies, Sacred Sites and Wetland Archaeology* (Exeter: University of Exeter and National Museum of Denmark, WARP, 1999), p. 3.

40 Foster, *Colonial*, p. 82.

41 Heaney, *Preoccupations*, p. 42.

42 Due to fair use guidelines, there is a limit, depending upon overall length, to how much a poem can be quoted. This is the reason that most of the bog poems in this chapter have been cited briefly. For more clarity, especially to new readers of Heaney's bog poems, please follow along with a full version of each poem.

43 Huggan, *Territorial Disputes*, p. 4 and p. 27.

44 Lloyd, *Anomalous*, p. 21.

45 Paul Rodaway, *Sensuous Geographies: Body, Sense and Place* (London: Routledge, 1994), p. 133.

46 Edward Broadbridge, 'Radio Interview with Seamus Heaney', in Edward Broadbridge (ed.), *Seamus Heaney Skoleradioen* (Copenhagen: Danmarks Radio, 1977), p. 39.

47 Rodaway, *Sensuous Geographies*, p. 31.

48 James Randall, 'An Interview with Seamus Heaney', *Ploughshares* 5.3 (1979), pp. 17–18.

49 Heaney, 'The Man', p. 3

50 Heaney, *Preoccupations*, p. 19.

51 ibid., p. 52.

52 Jay Parini, 'The Ground Possessed', in Harold Bloom (ed.), *Modern Critical Views: Seamus Heaney* (New York: Chelsea House, 1986), p. 106.

53 Heaney, 'The Man', p. 3.

54 Although Glob's book focuses on two of the most well-known preserved bog bodies found in Denmark in the 1950s, the first recorded bog body was found in Ireland in 1781 in Co. Down. Heaney's poem 'Bog Queen' is about this particular bog body.

55 Heaney, 'The Man', p. 3.

56 ibid., p. 4.

57 ibid., p. 3.

58 Sanders, *Bodies in the Bog*, p. 8.

59 Peter Vilhelm Glob, *The Bog People: Iron-Age Man Preserved*, trans. R.L.S. Bruce-Mitford (Ithaca, NY: Cornell University Press, 1969), p. 45.

60 McLean, 'Bodies', p. 303.

61 Vendler, *Heaney*, pp. 43–44.

62 Elmer Andrews, *The Poetry of Seamus Heaney: All the Realms of Whisper* (London: Macmillan, 1988), pp. 65–66.

63 Kennedy, '"Tell-tale skins"', p. 40.

64 Heaney, 'The Man', p. 3.

65 Glob, *Bog People*, pp. 56–57.

66 ibid., pp. 48–49.

67 Neil Corcoran, *Seamus Heaney* (London: Faber and Faber, 1998), p. 35.

68 Huggan, *Territorial Disputes*, p. 4.

69 O'Brien, *Heaney*, p. 25.

70 Vendler, *Heaney*, p. 45.

71 ibid.

72 Anthony Purdy, 'The Bog Body as Mnemotype: Nationalist Archaeologies in Heaney and Tournier', *Style* 36.1 (Spring 2002), p. 97.

73 Sanders, *Bodies*, p. 87.

74 Lloyd, *Anomalous*, p. 27.

75 O'Brien, *Heaney*, p. 35.

76 Laura Marks, *The Skin of Film: Intercultural Cinema, Embodiment, and the Senses* (Durham, NC: Duke University Press, 2000), p. 162.

77 Marks, *The Skin*, p. 151.

78 Vendler, *Heaney*, p. 44.

79 McLean, 'Bodies', p. 305.

80 Heaney, *Preoccupations*, pp. 57–58.

81 Purdy, 'Bog Body', p. 94.

82 Qtd. in Broadbridge, 'Radio Interview', p. 10.

83 Heaney, 'The Man', p. 4.

84 Anthony Purdy, 'Memory Maps: Mnemotopic Motifs in Creates, Poulin, and Robin', *Essays on Canadian Writing* 80 (2003), p. 262.

85 Joan Schwartz, 'Constituting Places of Presence: Landscape, Identity and the Geographical Imagination', in Marlene Creates, *Places of Presence: Newfoundland Kin and Ancestral Land, Newfoundland 1989–1991* (St Johns, NL: Killick Press, 1991), p. 13. The term 'memory maps' was initially introduced by Marlene Creates to describe her attempt at mapping people's experiences with the land through art.

86 Schwartz, 'Constituting Places', p. 11.

87 Thomas Docherty, 'Ana-; or Postmodernism, Landscape, Seamus Heaney', in Anthony Easthope and John O. Thompson (eds), *Contemporary Poetry Meets Modern Theory* (Hemel Hempstead: Harvester Wheatsheaf, 1991), p. 70.

88 Edward Said, 'Invention, Memory, and Place', *Critical Inquiry* 26 (2000), p. 176.

89 McLean, 'Bodies', p. 307. This exhibit is part of a larger project titled *The Mysterious Bog People*, which toured Europe and Canada between 2004 and 2005, in addition to having a permanent home in Denmark. This exhibit further supports the idea that bog bodies are sites of collective memory that have been mapped by archaeologists and poets alike.

90 After extensive DNA testing, the Canadian anthropologist Heather Gill-Robinson concluded that the 'Windeby Girl' excavated in Northern Germany (in 1952) is actually a boy. The body was fourteen years old at the point of death. See Sanders, *Bodies*, p. 115. Given this information, I will refer to the body as a 'feminised' body to reflect both the incongruity of the body's sex, now known to be male, but also the speaker's gendering and feminisation of the body in the poem as female. The variance in gender further complicates the poem's meaning and prompts arguments about the speaker's desire for the body. The abhuman descriptor serves another important purpose: it de-genders the body. The abject body in 'Punishment' now appears also as a queer body, void of gendered identity and yet also evoking erotic attraction despite the unknown gender. Rather than pursue this other line of inquiry – the abhuman queer body – I instead focus on the feminised body since it relates more to the speaker's disturbance in 'Punishment'.

91 O'Brien, *Heaney*, p. 38.

92 Kelly Hurley, *The Gothic Body: Sexuality, Materialism, and Degeneration at the Fin de Siècle* (Cambridge: Cambridge University Press, 2004), p. 3.

93 Hurley, 'Abject', p. 138.

94 Qtd. in Hurley, 'Abject', p. 144.

95 Barbara Creed, *The Monstrous Feminine: Film, Feminism, Psychoanalysis* (London: Routledge, 1993), p. 68.

96 Hurley, 'Abject', p. 138.

97 Heaney, 'The Man', p. 4.

98 For two other influential feminist readings of Heaney's bog poems, see Elizabeth Butler Cullingford, '"Thinking of Her … as … Ireland": Yeats, Pearse and Heaney', *Textual Practice* 4.1 (1990), pp. 1–21 and Sullivan, 'The Treachery of Wetness'.

99   Coughlan, '"Bog Queens"', p. 55.
100 Creed, *Monstrous Feminine*, pp. 70–71.
101 Sanders, *Bodies*, p. 121.
102 Creed, *Monstrous Feminine*, p. 71.
103 Coughlan, '"Bog Queens"', p. 55.
104 Hurley, *Gothic Body*, p. 3.
105 Qtd. in Christine Finn, '"Words from kept bodies": The Bog Body as Literary Inspiration', in Bryony Coles and John M. Coles (eds), *Bog Bodies, Sacred Sites and Wetland Archaeology* (Exeter: University of Exeter and National Museum of Denmark, WARP, 1999), p. 80.
106 Vendler, *Heaney*, p. 47.
107 Turchi, *Maps*, p. 11.
108 Tally, *Spatiality*, p. 58.
109 Heaney, 'The Man', p. 4.

5. Gendered Boglands

1   Anne Enright, 'At Turner Contemporary', *London Review of Books* 35.24, 19 Dec. 2013, web, accessed 23 March 2014, www.lrb.co.uk/v35/n24/anne-enright/at-turner-contemporary.
2   Giblett, Postmodern Wetlands, p. 9.
3   For a comprehensive outline of women's writing in this period, see Susan Cahill, *Irish Literature in the Celtic Tiger Years 1990–2008: Gender, Bodies, Memory* (New York: Continuum, 2011).
4   Eve Patten, 'Contemporary Irish Fiction', in John Wilson Foster (ed.), *The Cambridge Companion to the Irish Novel* (Cambridge: Cambridge University Press, 2006), p. 259. Patten's use of the term indicates a revival of the Gothic form for many contemporary Irish fiction writers. The term was originally used to explain the revival of the Gothic in the nineteenth century. In fact, the neo-Gothic more commonly refers to architecture than literature in the nineteenth century. However, the terms neo-Gothic and Gothic, as contemporary markers of the form, are almost interchangeable. Throughout this chapter I will refer to the neo-Gothic when specifically addressing Carr's and Kinahan's plays and Gothic when referring to the form more generally, to stay consistent with previous chapters.
5   There have been other dramatic works with bogs as a background setting in Irish literature, such as John B. Keane's *Sive* (1983), where a young woman being forced into marriage drowns in a bog. However, this theme would contain an opposite narrative to the one addressed in this chapter. Rather than become empowered through the bog, it destroys the woman within an extant patriarchal society. In addition, this chapter examines women playwrights focused on the contemporary Midlands; *Sive* is set in rural County Kerry in the 1950s.
6   Claire Connolly, 'Introduction: Ireland in Theory', in Claire Connolly (ed.), *Theorizing Ireland* (London: Palgrave, 2003), p. 3.
7   Anne McClintock, 'Family Feuds: Gender, Nationalism and the Family', *Feminist Review* 44 (Summer 1993), p. 62.
8   Coughlan, 'Bog Queens', p. 42.
9   The term Irish 'tinker' (not capitalised) will be used throughout this chapter when referring to *By the Bog of Cats...* because of its congruency with Carr's own usage in the play. The terms 'tinker' and 'itinerant' were once dominant nomenclatures, but these names are now considered to be discriminatory terms in Ireland. I will,

however, use the preferred title 'Irish Travelling People', or 'Travellers' for short, when discussing this ethnic group outside of my direct analysis of *By the Bog of Cats*.... Using the term 'tinker' triggers a longer, racial history that will not be addressed in depth here because it is beyond the scope of this chapter. In short, the Irish Travelling People are currently a recognised ethnic group in Ireland. Mary Burke contends, 'The Travellers, or to most Irish sedentary people before the 1960s, the "tinkers", are members of a historically nomadic minority community defined by anthropologists as an ethnic group that has existed on the margins of Irish society for perhaps centuries' (2). For a compressive literary and cultural history, see Burke's excellent introduction in '*Tinkers': Synge and the Cultural History of the Irish Traveller* (Oxford: Oxford University Press, 2009). For another racial and ethnic analysis, see Jane Helleiner, 'Gypsies, Celts, and Tinkers: Colonial Antecedents of Anti-Traveller Racism in Ireland', *Ethnic and Racial Studies* 18.3 (1995), pp. 532–553.

10 Melissa Sihra, 'A Cautionary Tale: Marina Carr's *By the Bog of Cats*', in John P. Harrington (ed.), *Modern and Contemporary Irish Drama* (New York: W.W. Norton, 2009), pp. 582–583.

11 ibid., p. 583.

12 ibid., p. 584.

13 ibid., p. 586.

14 Enrica Cerquoni, '"One bog, many bogs": Theatrical Space, Visual Image and Meaning in Some Productions of Marina Carr's *By the Bog of Cats...*', in Cathy Leeney and Anna McMullan (eds), *The Theatre of Marina Carr: 'before rules was made'* (Dublin: Carysfort Press, 2003), p. 178.

15 Bernadette Bourke, 'Carr's "cut-throats and gargiyles": Grotesque and Carnivalesque Elements in *By the Bog of Cats...*', in Cathy Leeney and Anna McMullan (eds), *The Theatre of Marina Carr: 'before rules was made'* (Dublin: Carysfort Press, 2003), p. 129.

16 Cerquoni, '"One bog"', p. 179.

17 Fintan O'Toole, *Enough is Enough: How to Build a New Republic* (London: Faber and Faber, 2010), p. 4.

18 Cahill, *Celtic Tiger*, p. 4.

19 Alan Barrett, Ide Kearney, and Jean Goggin, 'Research Bulletin', *Quarterly Economic Commentary* 9.1 (Spring 2009), p. 1.

20 O'Toole, *Enough*, p. 3.

21 Cleary, *Outrageous*, p. 46.

22 Ankie Hoogvelt, *Globalization and the Postcolonial World: The New Political Economy of Development* (Baltimore: Johns Hopkins University Press, 2001), p. 47.

23 Michael Barratt Brown, *Economics of Imperialism* (London: Penguin Books, 1974), p. 256.

24 Robert J.C. Young, 'Neocolonial Times', *Oxford Literary Review* 13 (1991), p. 3.

25 Patricia Coughlan, 'Irish Literature and Feminism in Postmodernity', *Hungarian Journal of English and American Studies* 10.1/2 (Spring/Fall, 2004), p. 178.

26 Peadar Kirby, Luke Gibbons, and Michael Cronin, 'Introduction', in Peadar Kirby, Luke Gibbons, and Michael Cronin (eds), *Reinventing Ireland: Culture, Society, and the Global Economy* (London: Pluto, 2002), p. 4

27 Victor Merriman, '"Poetry shite": Towards a Postcolonial Reading of Portia Coughlan and Hester Swane', in Cathy Leeney and Anna McMullan (eds), *The Theatre of Marina Carr: 'before rules was made'* (Dublin: Carysfort Press, 2003), p. 147.

28 ibid., p. 149.

29 Merriman, '*Because we are poor': Irish Theatre in the 1990s* (Dublin: Carysfort Press, 2011), p. 6.

30   Cahill, *Celtic Tiger*, p. 14.

31   Coughlan, 'Feminism in Postmodernity', p. 178.

32   As I discuss in Chapter 3, O'Connor and O'Faolain resisted similar national narratives in the post-revolutionary period and attempted to challenge them through representations of the bog.

33   Moynagh Sullivan, 'Feminism, Postmodernism and the Subjects of Irish and Women's Studies', in P.J. Matthews (ed.), *New Voices in Irish Criticism* (Dublin: Four Courts Press, 2000), pp. 249–250.

34   Coughlan, 'Feminism and Postmodernity', p. 178.

35   Victoria White, 'Women Writers Finally Take Centre Stage', *The Irish Times*, 15 Oct. 1998, p. 16, accessed 11 Nov. 2013, www.irishtimes.com/culture/women-writers-finally-take-centre-stage-1.203857.

36   Cerquoni, '"One bog"', p. 176.

37   Qtd. in Victor Merriman, 'A Responsibility to Dream: Decolonising Independent Ireland', *Third Text* 19.5 (Fall 2005), p. 493.

38   See, for example, Eavan Boland, *A Kind of Scar: The Woman Poet in a National Tradition* (Dublin: Attic Press, 1989), Elizabeth Bulter Cullingford, '"Thinking of Her ... as ... Ireland": Yeats, Pearse and Heaney', and Catherine Nash, 'Embodied Irishness: Gender, Sexuality, and Irish Identities', in Brian Graham (ed.), *In Search of Ireland: A Cultural Geography* (London: Routledge, 1997), pp. 108–127.

39   Matthew Arnold, *On the Study of Celtic Literature and Other Essays* [1910] (London: Everyman's Library, 1976), pp. 80–81.

40   Sullivan, 'Feminism', p. 249.

41   Cahill, *Celtic Tiger*, p. 16.

42   Sullivan, 'Feminism', p. 250.

43   See 'Can the Subaltern Speak?', in Cary Nelson and Lawrence Grossberg (eds), *Marxism and the Interpretation of Culture* (Urbana: University of Illinois Press, 1988), p. 287.

44   See 'Family Feuds', p. 62, original emphasis.

45   Nash, 'Embodied', p. 117.

46   ibid., p. 120.

47   Merriman, '"Poetry shite"', p. 154.

48   Marina Carr, *By the Bog of Cats…. Marina Carr: Plays 1* (London: Faber and Faber, 1999), p. 294. All subsequent quotes from *By the Bog of Cats…* are placed in the text. All quotes from Carr and Kinahan in this chapter follow fair use guidelines.

49   Patrick Crushell, Andrew Connolly, Matthijs Schouten, and Faser J.G. Mitchell, 'The Changing Landscape of Clara Bog: The History of an Irish Raised Bog', *Irish Geography* 41.1 (March 2008), p. 89.

50   Crushell et al., 'Clara Bog', p. 89.

51   Qtd. in Claudia Harris, 'Rising Out of the Miasmal Mists: Marina Carr's Ireland', in Cathy Leeney and Anna McMullan (eds), *The Theatre of Marina Carr: 'before rules was made'* (Dublin: Carysfort Press, 2003), p. 217.

52   Qtd. in ibid., p. 217.

53   ibid., p. 232.

54   Bourke, '"cut-throats and gargiyles"', p. 128.

55   Cathy Leeney and Anna McMullan, 'Introduction', in Cathy Leeney and Anna McMullan (eds), *The Theatre of Marina Carr: 'before rules was made'* (Dublin: Carysfort Press, 2003), p. xvii.

56   Raftery, 'The Archaeology', p. 12.

57   For example, in both Frank McGuinness' and Victoria White's reviews of the play, neither critic mentions Hester's identity as a Traveller. See Merriman, "'Poetry shite'", p. 156.

58   Helleiner, 'Gypsies', pp. 535–536.

59   ibid., p. 540.

60   J.M. Synge, *Travels in Wicklow, West Kerry and Connemara* [1910] (London: Serif, 2005), p. 20.

61   Paddy Woodworth, 'Foreword', in J.M. Synge, *Travels in Wicklow, West Kerry and Connemara* [1910] (London: Serif, 2005), p. 12.

62   ibid.

63   Bourke, "'cut-throats and gargiyles'", p. 133.

64   Cerquoni, "'One bog'", p. 183.

65   Una Chaudhuri, *Staging Place: The Geography of Modern Drama* (Ann Arbor: University of Michigan Press, 1995), p. 182.

66   Cerquoni, "'One bog'", p. 175.

67   Melissa Sihra, 'Nature Noble or Ignoble: Woman, Family, and Home in the Theatre of Marina Carr', *Hungarian Journal of English and American Studies (HJEAS)* 11.2 (Fall 2005), p. 134.

68   Cited in Cahill, *Celtic Tiger*, p. 21.

69   Patten, 'Contemporary', p. 259.

70   Cullingford, "'Thinking of Her'", p. 1.

71   When Hester burns Carthage's house and cattle as her ultimate Medean act of revenge, she fulfils a destruction myth in the cosmogonic cycle, which usually results in either a flood or fire. Hester seeks to purge history of abuse and abandonment through the trial of fire rather than floodwater. The latter would recall her adoption of the watery nature of the bog with its sunken memories that, once unravelled, arouse pain and trauma. Flood myths align with the human psyche, identified with the 'Great Mother', and represent the symbol of new life born of the cosmic waters of the Great Mother. Fire myths, with exceptions such as Ragnorak in the Icelandic myth *Prose Edda*, signify total annihilation – an absolute destruction of the old world order. Through fire Hester reifies the traditional form of destruction against the patriarchal order as represented by Carthage and Xavier. For more on destruction myths, see David Adams Leeming, *The World of Myth* (Oxford: Oxford University Press, 1990), p. 43.

72   Cullingford, "'Thinking of Her'", p. 1.

73   Bourke, "'cut-throats and gargiyles'", p. 132.

74   This period of advanced equality began with Mary Robinson becoming the first woman president of Ireland in 1990, an appointment that ignited changes in contraception legislation, homosexual law reform, and divorce laws by 1993. In 2010, a Civil Partnership Bill passed, which increased rights for unmarried couples, same-sex relationships, and children of civil union partners. See Cahill, *Celtic Tiger*, p. 5.

75   Sinéad Kennedy, 'Irish Women and the Celtic Tiger Economy', in Colin Coulter and Steve Coleman (eds), *End of Irish History? Critical Approaches to the Celtic Tiger* (Manchester: Manchester University Press, 2003), p. 95.

76   Merriman, 'A Responsibility', p. 496.

77   ibid.

78   Deirdre Kinahan, *Bog Boy* (unpublished, 2010), p. 21. Since *Bog Boy* is an unpublished play, all quotes in this chapter are from the June 2011 New York and Irish tour script that Kinahan sent to me. As a result, the page numbers following each citation in parentheses will be different from any subsequent versions of the play if published.

79   See the website of the Independent Commission for the Location of Victims Remains/An Coimisiún Neamhspleách um Aimsiú Taisí Íospartach, accessed 12 March 2016, http://www.iclvr.ie.

80   The Provisional IRA were largely responsible for bodies buried in the Republic of Ireland during the Troubles in the 1970s and 1980s, but loyalist paramilitary groups, such as the Ulster Defence Force (UDF) and Ulster Volunteer Force (UVF), were also involved in this act of removing evidence.

81   Rachel Saltz, 'A Lost Girl of Ireland, Dealing With its Lost Boys', rev. of *Bog Boy*, dir. Deirdre Kinahan, *The New York Times*, 16 Sept. 2011, n.p.

82   Gerry Smyth, 'National Identity After the Celtic Tiger', *Estudios Irlandeses* 7 (2012), p. 133.

83   Kennedy, 'Irish Women', p. 98.

84   Qtd. in Shawn Pogatchnik, 'Celtic Tiger Economy Increasingly Makes Ireland Land of Princes and Paupers: UN', *The Canadian Press*, 16 July 2004, n.p.

85   Kennedy, 'Irish Women', p. 65 and p. 95.

86   European Monitoring Centre for Drugs and Drug Addiction (EMCDDA), 'Country Overview: Ireland', web, accessed 12 Dec. 2013, www.emcdda.europa.eu/countries/ireland.

87   Bruno Latour, 'Politics of Nature: East and West Perspectives', *Ethics & Global Politics* 4.1 (2011), p. 4.

88   Gibbons, *Transformations*, p. 3.

89   Coughlan, 'Feminism in Postmodernity', p. 177.

90   Punter and Byron, *The Gothic*, pp. 278–279.

91   Gwen Orel, 'Bogboy's Beauty Makes The Disappeared Real', rev. of *Bog Boy*, dir. Deirdre Kinahan, *Irish Examiner*, 13 Sept. 2011, Arts Examiner, sec.12.

92   Hortensia Amaro, Lise E. Fried, Howard Cabral, and Barry Zuckerman, 'Violence During Pregnancy and Substance Use', *American Journal of Public Health* 80.5 (1990), p. 575.

93   Patricia Kelleher and Monica O'Connor, *'Making the Links': Towards an Integrated Strategy Towards the Elimination of Violence Against Women in Intimate Relationships with Men* (Dublin: Women's Aid, 1995), p. 3.

94   Since abortion is outlawed in Ireland, even in instances of rape and incest, Brigit would have had little or no choice other than to have the child regardless of the circumstances of her conception. And due to her poverty, she does not even have the option to go abroad for an abortion. Because of these financial and social limitations, working- or lower-class women often continue with pregnancies against their will and in spite of the abusive circumstances in which they often occur, which then continues to worsen their economic circumstances. See Kennedy, 'Irish Women', p. 103 and p. 105.

95   Cathal Ó Searcaigh and Denise Blake, 'Gort na gCnámh / The Field of Bones', *The Poetry Review* 73 (Summer 2002), p. 99.

96   A well-known example is the Kerry Babies Tribunal where a local woman was blamed for a newborn baby that was found stabbed to death on White Strand beach at Cahirciveen, Co. Kerry. A tribunal of inquiry followed where a team of forty-three men, including lawyers, police officers, doctors, and psychiatrists, probed the accused woman in court. As the Irish journalist Nell McCafferty notes, much of the tribunal focused more on the woman's sexual history than on connecting her to the dead newborn. Indeed, the murder investigation was clearly obfuscated by religious morality and patriarchy, in that the woman was on trial for all of the women of Ireland battling for social progress. The Kerry Babies Tribunal also reminded the

Irish public that infanticide still exists for socially dispossessed women. See Nell McCafferty, *A Woman to Blame: The Kerry Babies Case* (Dublin: Attic Press, 1985). Heaney's poem 'Limbo', in *Wintering Out* (1972), also addresses a woman in the west of Ireland who decides to drown her illegitimate son. Similar themes about abortion and infanticide are also explored in Margo Harkin's film *Hush-a-Bye Baby* (London: Channel 4 Television, 1989). However, these three other examples do not occur on bogs.

97 Killeen, 'Irish Gothic'.

6. Bog Gothic, Bog Noir, and Eco-bog Writing

1   Robinson, *Connemara: Listening to the Wind*, p. 47. All quotes from Robinson, McCabe, McGinley, and Hart in this chapter follow fair use guidelines.

2   John O'Mahony, 'King of Bog Gothic', *The Guardian*, 30 August 2003, n.p., web, accessed 10 October 2015, www.theguardian.com/books/2003/aug/30/fiction. patrickmccabe.

3   Kilfeather, 'The Gothic Novel', p. 94.

4   Ellen McWilliams, 'Patrick McCabe', in William Hughes and Andrew Smith (eds), *The Encyclopedia of the Gothic* (Oxford: Blackwell Publishing, 2013), web, accessed 20 October 2015, www.blackwellreference.com/public/uid=860/tocnode?id=g978140 5182904_chunk_g978140518290415_ss1-10.

5   Ellen Scheible, 'Reanimating the Nation: Patrick McCabe, Neil Jordan, and the Bog Gothic', *Bridewater Review* 31.1 (2012), p. 5.

6   Padraic Killeen, 'Greek myths and Irish bog gothic make for potent mix at the Abbey', *Irish Examiner*, 17 August 2015, web, accessed 11 November 2015, www. irishexaminer.com/lifestyle/artsfilmtv/greek-myths-and-irish-bog-gothic-make-for-potent-mix-at-the-abby-348469.html. I also published an essay about the relationship of bogs and Gothic literature, but it did not address McCabe. See Gladwin, 'The Bog Gothic', as well as note 9.

7   Tracy Fahey, 'A Dark Domesticity: Echoes of Folklore in Irish Contemporary Gothic', in Lorna Piattie-Farnell and Maria Beville (eds), *The Gothic and Everyday: Living Gothic* (Basingstoke: Palgrave Macmillan, 2014), p. 154. Italics original emphasis.

8   All quotes are from Mathias Lebargy, 'Draining out the Colours: An Interview with Patrick McCabe', *Estudios Irlandeses* 8 (2013), p. 141.

9   In my own aforementioned article 'The Bog Gothic', my intent was to use the term as a way of explaining the links between the bog and 'Eco-Gothic' literature rather than draw on a term associated with McCabe. However, I have since revisited my position on this term and prefer the idea of the 'bog affect' that can be applied to various forms of literature loosely or directly associated with the bog, which is what I explain here in this chapter.

10 Nigel Thrift, *Non-representational Theory: Space/Politics/Affect* (London: Routledge, 2008), pp. 5–6.

11 Gregory J. Seigworth and Melissa Gregg, 'An Inventory of Shimmers', in Gregory J. Seighworth and Melissa Gregg (eds), *Affect Theory Reader* (Durham, NC: Duke University Press, 2010), p. 1. Original emphasis.

12 ibid.

13 Said, *Culture and Imperialism*, p. 51.

14 O'Mahony, 'Bog Gothic', n.p.

15 Patrick McCabe, *The Butcher Boy* (London: Picador, 1992), p. 74. Hereafter page number will remain in the text.

16   Tim Gauthier, 'Identity, Self-Loathing and the Neocolonial Condition in Patrick
     McCabe's *The Butcher Boy*', *Critique: Studies in Contemporary Fiction* 44.2 (2003), p. 197.
17   ibid., 196.
18   Ian Campbell Ross, 'Introduction', in Declan Burke (ed.), *Down These Green Streets: Irish
     Crime Writing in the 21st Century* (Dublin: Liberty Press, 2011), p. 21, and Michael Cook,
     Detective Fiction and the Ghost Story: The Haunted Text (London: Palgrave Macmillan),
     p. 1. See also Maurizio Ascari, *A Counter-History of Crime Fiction: Supernatural, Gothic,
     Sensational* (London: Palgrave Macmillan, 2009) and Catherine Spooner, 'Crime and
     the Gothic', in Charles J. Rzepka and Lee Horsley (eds), *A Companion to Crime Fiction*
     (Oxford: Wiley-Blackwell Publishing, 2010), pp. 245–257.
19   David Punter, 'Crimes of the Future', International Gothic Association 12th Biennial
     Conference, Vancouver, Canada, 30 July 2015.
20   Smith, *Gothic Literature*, p. 125. Smith credits the point about comparing Le Fanu's Dr
     Hesselius with Blackwood's scientific investigator to E.F. Bleiler in his 'Introduction'
     to *Best Ghost Stories of Algernon Blackwood* (New York: Dover, 1973), p. viii.
21   Although from America, Edgar Allan Poe's detective C. Auguste Dupin should
     rightfully be considered the forerunner to this supernatural detective genre in the
     mid-nineteenth century. Like Holmes, however, Dupin does not strictly investigate
     supernatural phenomena.
22   Such stories would include *The Sign of Four* (1890), 'The Adventure of Wisteria Lodge'
     (1908), and 'The Adventure of the Speckled Band (1892), just to name a few.
23   Marc Singer and Nels Pearson, 'Introduction', in Marc Singer and Nels Pearson
     (eds), *Detective Fiction in a Postcolonial and Transnational World* (London: Ashgate, 2010), p.
     10. For the first general study on the subject, see Ed Christian (ed.), *The Post-Colonial
     Detective* (Houndmills: Palgrave, 2001). For studies on the nineteenth century, see also
     Pablo Upamanyu Mukherjee, *Crime and Empire: The Colony in Nineteenth-Century Fictions
     of Crime* (Oxford: Oxford University Press, 2003), Caroline Reitz, *Detecting the Nation:
     Fictions of Detection and the Imperial Venture* (Columbus: Ohio State University Press,
     2004).
24   Andrew Pepper, *The Contemporary American Crime Novel: Race, Ethnicity, Gender, Class*
     (Edinburgh: Edinburgh University Press, 2000), p. 34.
25   See, for example, Burke's edited collection *Down These Green Streets*. In addition, see
     the special issue Ian Campbell Ross and William Meier (eds), 'Irish Crime Since
     1921', *Éire-Ireland: An Interdisciplinary Journal of Irish Studies* 49.1–2 (Spring/Summer
     2014).
26   Nancy Knowles, 'Empty Rhetoric: Argument by Credibility in Patrick McGinley's
     Bogmail', *English Language Notes* 39.3 (March 2002), p. 79. In fact, a few scholars have
     already noted the critical significance of *Bogmail* in contemporary Irish literature and
     culture; however, any analysis of the bog remains largely absent in these critical essays.
     See also Thomas F. Shea, 'More Matter with More Art: Typescript Emendations in
     Patrick McGinley's Bogmail', *The Canadian Journal of Irish Studies* 23.2 (Dec. 1997),
     pp. 23–37, and Moira Casey, '"The Harmless Deceptions of Male Companionship":
     Sexuality and Male Homosocial Desire in Patrick McGinley's *Bogmail*', *Colby Quarterly*
     35.3 (Sept. 1999), pp. 184–97.
27   Patrick McGinley, *Bogmail* [1978] (Dublin: New Island Books, 2013), p. 1. Hereafter,
     all citations will be placed in the text.
28   Erin Hart, *Haunted Ground* (New York: Scribner, 2005), p. 3.
29   Erin Hart, *Lake of Sorrows* (New York: Scribner, 2007), p. 3.
30   Erin Hart, *The Book of Killowen* (New York: Scribner, 2013), p. 13.

31 See Siobhan Dowd, *Bog Child* (Oxford: David Fickling Books, 2008).
32 Feehan, 'Bogs', p. 173
33 Foss and O'Connell, 'Bogland', p. 193. See also R.F. Hammond, *The Peatlands of Ireland* (Dublin: An Foras Taluntais Soil Survey Bulletin, 1979).
34 Roy Tomlinson, 'Blanket Bogs', in F.H.A. Aalen, Kevin Whelan, and Matthew Stout (eds), *Atlas of the Irish Rural Landscape* (Cork: Cork University Press, 2011), p. 185.
35 Foss and O'Connell, 'Bogland', p. 195. See also P.J. Foss and C.A. O'Connell, *Irish Peatland Conservation Plan 2000* (Dublin: Irish Peatland Conservation Council, 1996).
36 Raftery, 'The Archaeology', p. 202.
37 Feehan, 'Bogs', p. 185.
38 Paul L. Younger, *Energy: All that Matters* (London: John Murray Learning, 2014), p. 37.
39 'Climate Change: Mitigation – Carbon Capture and Storage', *Earthwatch Educational Resources, Climate Change* 5 (2007), p. 3.
40 Feehan, 'Bogs', p. 185.
41 See Alfred W. Crosby, *Ecological Imperialism: The Biological Expansion of Europe, 900–1900* (Cambridge: Cambridge University Press, 1986).
42 For a complete study of Robinson's work, see Christine Cusick and Derek Gladwin (eds), *Unfolding Irish Landscapes: Tim Robinson, Culture, and Environment* (Manchester: Manchester University Press, 2016).
43 Robert Macfarlane, 'Rock of Ages', *The Guardian*, 14 May 2005, n.p., web, accessed 9 Sept. 2014, www.theguardian.com/books/2005/may/14/featuresreviews.guardian review34.
44 Tim Robinson, *My Time in Space* (Dublin: Lilliput Press, 2001), p. 185.
45 ibid., p. 189.
46 ibid., p. 190.
47 ibid., p. 191.
48 Robinson, *Connemara*, p. 51.
49 ibid., pp. 47–50.
50 Qtd. in Foss and O'Connell, 'Bogland', p. 189. See also Robert Lloyd Praeger, *The Way That I Went* (Dublin: Hodges Figgis & Company, 1937).
51 Robinson, *My Time*, p. 194. Ironically, the Galway airport closed down in 2010, which indicates that had the Roundstone airport been built, it too would have closed during the economic recession following the 2008 collapse.
52 Robinson, *My Time*, p. 190.
53 Simon Estok, 'Theorizing in a Space of Ambivalent Openness: Ecocriticism and Ecophobia', *Interdisciplinary Studies in Literature and the Environment* 16.2 (2009), p. 208. For a more compressive analysis of the Eco-Gothic, see Andrew Smith and William Hughes (eds), *EcoGothic* (Manchester: Manchester University Press, 2013).
54 Robinson, *Connemara*, p. 20.
55 ibid., p. 16 and p. 61.
56 ibid., p. 47.
57 Killeen, *Irish Gothic*, p. 207.

Conclusion

1 Qtd. in Foss and O'Connell, 'Bogland', p. 189.
2 Tuan, *Topophilia*, p. 136.
3 Gregory, 'Said', p. 305.
4 Sanders, *Bodies in the Bog*, p. 7.
5 *Bogland Symposium*, n.p.

6   See bogology.org.
7   Caradonna, *Sustainability*, p. 1.
8   O'Toole, *Enough is Enough*, p. 4.
9   Feenan, 'Bogs', p. 168.
10   Robinson, *Listening to the Wind*, p. 20.

Bibliography

Amaro, Hortensia, Lise E. Fried, Howard Cabral, and Barry Zuckerman, 'Violence During Pregnancy and Substance Use', *American Journal of Public Health* 80.5 (1990), pp. 575–579

Anderson, Benedict, *Imagined Communities: Reflections on the Origin and Spread of Nationalism* [1983] (London: Verso, 2006)

Andrews, Elmer, *The Poetry of Seamus Heaney: All the Realms of Whisper* (London: Macmillan, 1988)

Arata, Stephen, 'The Occidental Tourist: *Dracula* and the Anxiety of Reverse Colonization', *Victorian Studies* 33 (Summer 1990), pp. 621–645

Arnold, Matthew, *On the Study of Celtic Literature and Other Essays* [1910] (London: Everyman's Library, 1976)

Ascari, Maurizio, *A Counter-History of Crime Fiction: Supernatural, Gothic, Sensational* (London: Palgrave Macmillan, 2009)

Bachelard, Gaston, in trans. Edith R. Farrell, *Water and Dreams: An Essay on the Imagination of Matter* (Dallas, TX: The Pegasus Foundation, 1983)

Backus, Margot Gayle, *The Gothic Family Romance: Heterosexuality, Child Sacrifice, and the Anglo-Irish Colonial Order* (Durham, NC: Duke University Press, 1999)

Baldick, Chris, 'Introduction', in Chris Baldick (ed.), *The Oxford Book of Gothic Tales* (Oxford: Oxford University Press), pp. xi–xxiii

Barrett, Alan, Ide Kearney, and Jean Goggin, 'Research Bulletin', *Quarterly Economic Commentary* 9.1 (Spring 2009), pp. 1–4

Barthes, Roland, 'The Rhetoric of the Image', in Alan Trachtenberg (ed.), *Classic Essays on Photography* (New Haven, CT: Leete's Island Books, 1980), pp. 269–285

Bartlett, Thomas, *Ireland: A History* (Cambridge: Cambridge University Press, 2010)

Belford, Barbara, *Bram Stoker: A Biography of the Author of 'Dracula'* (London: Weidenfeld and Nicholson, 1996)

Bell, J. Bowyer, *The Irish Troubles: A Generation of Violence, 1967–1992* (Dublin: Gill and Macmillan, 1993)

Bellamy, David, *The Wild Boglands* (Dublin: Country House, 1986)

Bennett, Andrew and Nicholas Royle, *Introduction to Literature, Criticism and Theory* 2nd Ed (London: Prentice-Hill, 1999)

Bhabha, Homi K., 'Introduction: Narrating the Nation', in Homi K. Bhabha (ed.), *Nation and Narration* (London: Routledge, 1990), pp. 1–7

—. *The Location of Culture* (London: Routledge, 1994)

Bleiler, E.F., 'Introduction', *Best Ghost Stories of Algernon Blackwood* (New York: Dover, 1973), pp. v–x

Boate, Gerard, *Irelands Naturall History: Being a True Description of its Situation, Greatness, Shape and Nature* (London: Samuel Hartlib, 1652)

Bogland Symposium Exhibition (Ireland: Crescent Art Centre, 1990)

Boland, Eavan, *A Kind of Scar: The Woman Poet in a National Tradition* (Dublin: Attic Press, 1989)

Bonaccorso, Richard, *Sean O'Faolain's Irish Vision* (Albany: State University of New York Press, 1987)

Botting, Fred, *Gothic* (London: Routledge, 1996)

Bourke, Bernadette, 'Carr's "cut-throats and gargiyles": Grotesque and Carnivalesque Elements in *By the Bog of Cats…*', in Cathy Leeney and Anna McMullan (eds), *The Theater of Marina Carr: 'before rules was made'* (Dublin: Carysfort Press, 2003), pp. 128–144

Brantlinger, Patrick, *Rule of Darkness: British Literature and Imperialism, 1830–1914* (Ithaca: Cornell University Press, 1988)

Broadbridge, Edward, 'Radio Interview with Seamus Heaney', in Edward Broadbridge (ed.), *Seamus Heaney Skoleradioen* (Copenhagen: Danmarks Radio)

Brown, Michael Barratt, *Economics of Imperialism* (London: Penguin Books, 1974)

Burke, Edmund, *A Philosophical Enquiry: into the Origin of our Ideas of the Sublime and Beautiful* [1757] (Oxford: Oxford University Press, 1990)

Burke, Mary, *'Tinkers': Synge and the Cultural History of the Irish Traveller* (New York: Oxford University Press, 2009)

Buchelt, Lisabeth C., '"Delicate Fantasy" and "Vulgar Reality": Undermining Romance and Complicating Identity in Bram Stoker's *The Snake's Pass*', *New Hibernia Review* 16.1 (2012), pp. 113–133

Butler, Pierce, *Sean O'Faolain: A Study of the Short Fiction* (New York: Twayne Publishers, 1993)

Cahill, Susan, *Irish Literature in the Celtic Tiger Years 1990–2008: Gender, Bodies, Memory* (New York: Continuum, 2011)

Caradonna, Jeremy, *Sustainability: A History* (New York: Oxford University Press, 2014)

Carr, Marina, *By the Bog of Cats…* in *Marina Carr: Plays 1* (London: Faber and Faber, 1999)

Carrigan, Anthony, *Postcolonial Tourism: Literature, Culture, and Environment* (London: Routledge, 2011)

Casey, Moira, '"The Harmless Deceptions of Male Companionship": Sexuality and Male Homosocial Desire in Patrick McGinley's *Bogmail*', *Colby Quarterly* 35.3 (Sept. 1999), pp. 184–97

Cerqoni, Enrica, '"One bog, many bogs": Theatrical Space, Visual Image and Meaning in Some Productions of Marina Carr's *By the Bog of Cats…*', in Cathy Leeney and Anna McMullan (eds), *The Theater of Marina Carr: "before rules was made'* (Dublin: Carysfort Press, 2003), pp. 172–199

Chaudhuri, Una, *Staging Place: The Geography of Modern Drama* (Ann Arbor: University of Michigan Press, 1995)

Cheah, Pheng, 'Spectral Nationality: The Living-on of the Postcolonial Nation in Neocolonial Globalization', *Boundary 2* 26.3 (Fall 1999), pp. 225–252

—. *Spectral Nationality: Passages of Freedom from Kant to Postcolonial Literatures of Liberation* (New York: Columbia University Press, 2003)

Christian, Ed (ed.), *The Post-Colonial Detective* (Houndmills: Palgrave, 2001)

Charman, Dan, *Peatlands and Environmental Change* (New York: John Wiley and Sons, 2002)

Clarke, Donal, 'Brief History of the Peat Industry in Ireland', *Irish Peat Society Seminar Proceedings* (Gorey: Newton House, 2006), pp. 6–12

Cleary, Joe, *Outrageous Fortune: Capital and Culture in Modern Ireland* (Dublin: Field Day Publications, 2007)

Cleeve, Brian, *A Dictionary of Irish Writers* (Cork: Mercier Press, 1967)

'Climate Change: Mitigation – Carbon Capture and Storage', *Earthwatch Educational Resources, Climate Change* 5 (2007), pp. 1–8, web, accessed 23 Oct. 2012

Coles, Bryony and John Coles, *People of the Wetlands: Bogs, Bodies and Lake-Dwellers* (London: Thames and Hudson, 1989)

Concoran, Neil, *Seamus Heaney* (London: Faber and Faber, 1998)

Connolly, Claire, *A Cultural History of the Irish Novel, 1790–1829* (Cambridge: Cambridge University Press, 2011)

—. 'Introduction: Ireland in Theory', in Claire Connolly (ed.), *Theorizing Ireland* (London: Palgrave, 2003), pp. 1–13

Connolly, Seán J., 'Culture, Identity and Tradition: Changing Definitions of Irishness', in Brian Graham (ed.), *In Search of Ireland: A Cultural Geography* (London: Routledge, 1997), pp. 43–63

Cook, Michael, *Detective Fiction and the Ghost Story: The Haunted Text* (London: Palgrave Macmillan, 2014)

Coogan, Tim Pat, *The Troubles: Ireland's Ordeal 1966–1996 and the Search for Peace* (London: Hutchinson, 1995)

Corkery, Daniel, *Synge and Anglo-Irish Literature* [1931] (Cork: Mercier Press, 1966)

Coughlan, Patricia, '"Bog Queens": The Representation of Women in the Poetry of John Montague and Seamus Heaney', in Claire Connolly (ed.), *Theorizing Ireland* (London: Palgrave, 2003), pp. 41–60

—. 'Irish Literature and Feminism in Postmodernity', *Hungarian Journal of English and American Studies* 10.1/2 (Spring/Fall, 2004), pp. 175–202

Creed, Barbara, *The Monstrous Feminine: Film, Feminism, Psychoanalysis* (London: Routledge, 1993)

Crosby, Alfred W., *Ecological Imperialism: The Biological Expansion of Europe, 900–1900* (Cambridge: Cambridge University Press, 1986)

Crushell, Patrick, Andrew Connolly, Matthijs Schouten, and Faser J.G. Mitchell, 'The Changing Landscape of Clara Bog: The History of an Irish Raised Bog', *Irish Geography* 41.1 (March 2008), pp. 89–111

Cullingford, Elizabeth Butler, *Ireland's Others: Gender and Ethnicity in Irish Literature and Popular Culture* (Cork: Cork University Press, 2001)

—. '"Thinking of Her … as … Ireland": Yeats, Pearse and Heaney', *Textual Practice* 4.1 (1990), pp. 1–21

Cusick, Christine, 'Moments of Story: Rachel Giese's *The Donegal Pictures*', in Eóin Flannery and Michael Griffin (eds), *Ireland in Focus: Film, Photography and Popular Culture* (Syracuse: Syracuse University Press, 2009), pp. 86–106

Daly, Nicholas, 'Irish Roots: The Romance of History in Bram Stoker's "The Snake's Pass"', *Literature and History* 3.4/2 (1995), pp. 42–70

—. *Modernism, Romance, and the Fin de Siècle: Popular Fiction and British Culture, 1880–1914* (Cambridge: Cambridge University Press, 1999)

de Paor, Louis, 'Introduction: Introducing Máirtín Ó Cadhain', *The Canadian Journal of Irish Studies* 34.1 (Spring 2008), pp. 10–17

Deane, Seamus, *Celtic Revivals: Essays in Modern Irish Literature* (London: Faber and Faber, 1985)

—. 'Land and Soil: A Territorial Rhetoric', *History Ireland* 2.1 (1994), pp. 31–34

—. 'Production of Cultural Space in Irish Writing', *Boundary 2* 21.3 (Fall 1994), pp. 117–144

del Pilar Blanco, María and Esther Peeren, 'Introduction: Conceptualizing Spectralities', in Maria del Pilar Blanco and Esther Peeren (eds), *The Spectralities Reader: Ghosts and Haunting in Contemporary Cultural Theory* (London: Bloomsbury, 2013), pp. 1–28

Delaney, Paul, *Seán O'Faoláin: Literature, Inheritance and the 1930s* (Dublin: Irish Academic Press, 2015)

Derrida, Jacques, *Spectres of Marx: The State of Debt, the Work of Mourning and the New International* [1994] (London: Routledge, 2006)

Docherty, Thomas, 'Ana-; or Postmodernism, Landscape, Seamus Heaney', in Anthony Easthope and John O. Thompson (eds), *Contemporary Poetry Meets Modern Theory* (Hemel Hempstead: Harvester Wheatsheaf, 1991), pp. 68–80

Dowd, Siobhan, *Bog Child* (Oxford: David Fickling Books, 2008)

Doyle, Gerard and Colmán Ó Críodáin, 'Peatlands – Fens and Bogs', in Marinus L. Otte (ed.), *Wetlands of Ireland: Distribution, Ecology, and Uses and Economic Value* (Dublin: University College Dublin Press, 2003), pp. 79–108

Doyle, Paul A., *Sean O'Faolain* (New York: Twayne Publishers, 1968)

Dudley Edwards, Ruth, *An Atlas of Irish History* (London: Routledge, 2005)

Duffy, Enda, '"As White As Ours": Africa, Ireland, Imperial Panic, and the Effects of British Race Discourse', in Graham MacPhee and Prem Poddar (eds), *Empire and After: Englishness in Postcolonial Perspective* (New York: Berghahn Books, 2007), pp. 25–56

Eagleton, Terry, *Heathcliff and the Great Hunger: Studies in Irish Culture* (London: Verso, 1995)

—. *The Truth About the Irish* (Dublin: New Island Books, 2002)

Edgeworth, Maria, *Castle Rackrent: An Hibernian Tale taken from facts and from the manners of the Irish squires before the year 1782* [1800] (Oxford: University of Oxford Press, 2008)

Ellmann, Richard, 'Introduction', in Richard Ellmann (ed.), *Frank O'Connor: Collected Stories* (New York: Vintage, 1981), pp. vii–xiii

Enright, Anne, 'At Turner Contemporary', *London Review of Books* 35.24, 19 December 2013

Estok, Simon, 'Theorizing in a Space of Ambivalent Openness: Ecocriticism and Ecophobia', *Interdisciplinary Studies in Literature and the Environment* 16.2 (2009), pp. 203–25

European Monitoring Centre for Drugs and Drug Addiction, 'Country Overview: Ireland', web, accessed 25 October 2012, http://www.emcdda. europa.eu/countries/ireland

Fahey, Tracy, 'A Dark Domesticity: Echoes of Folklore in Irish Contemporary Gothic', in Lorna Piattie-Farnell and Maria Beville (eds), *The Gothic and Everyday: Living Gothic* (Basingstoke: Palgrave Macmillan, 2014), pp. 152–169

Fanning, Bryan, 'Hidden Ireland, Silent Irelands: Sean O'Faolain and Frank O'Connor Versus Daniel Corkery', *Studies: An Irish Quarterly Review* 95.379 (Autumn 2006), pp. 251–259.

Feehan, John, 'Bogs', in F.H.A. Aalen, Kevin Whelan, and Matthew Stout (eds), *Atlas of the Irish Rural Landscape* (Cork: Cork University Press, 2011), pp. 168–174

Ferris, Ina, *The Romantic National Tale and the Question of Ireland* (Cambridge: Cambridge University Press, 2002)

Ferriter, Diarmaid, *The Transformation of Ireland* (Woodstock, NY: Overlook Press, 2004)

Field of Bones, dir. Carol Moore (Belfast: Straight Forward Productions, 1997)

Finn, Christine, '"Words from kept bodies": The Bog Body as Literary Inspiration', in Bryony Coles and John M. Coles (eds), *Bog Bodies, Sacred Sites and Wetland Archaeology* (Exeter: University of Exeter and National Museum of Denmark, WARP, 1999), pp. 79–83

Flannery, Eóin, '"A Land Poisoned": Eugene McCabe and Irish Postcolonial Gothic', *Literature & History* 22.2 (Autumn 2013), pp. 91–112

Foley, Tadhg, rev. of Catherine Wynne, *The Colonial Conan Doyle: British Imperialism, Irish Nationalism, and the Gothic* (Westport, CT: Greenwood Press) in *Irish Studies Review* 11.3 (2003), pp. 360–362

Foss, Peter and Catherine O'Connell, 'Bogland: Study and Utilization', in John Wilson Foster (ed.), *Nature in Ireland: A Scientific and Cultural History* (Montreal: McGill-Queen's University Press, 1997), pp. 184–198

—. *Irish Peatland Conservation Plan 2000* (Dublin: Irish Peatland Conservation Council, 1996)

Foster, John Wilson, *Colonial Consequences: Essays in Irish Literature and Culture* (Dublin: Lilliput, 1991)

—. 'Encountering Traditions', in John Wilson Foster (ed.), *Nature in Ireland: A Scientific and Cultural History* (Montreal and Kingston: McGill-Queen's University Press, 1997), pp. 23–70

Foster, Roy, *Paddy and Mr. Punch: Connections in Irish and English History* (London: Penguin, 1995)

Freud, Sigmund, 'The Uncanny' [1919], in Adam Phillips (ed.), *The Uncanny*, trans. David Mclintock (New York: Penguin, 2003)

Gauthier, Tim, 'Identity, Self-Loathing and the Neocolonial Condition in Patrick McCabe's *The Butcher Boy*', *Critique: Studies in Contemporary Fiction* 44.2 (2003), pp. 196–212

Giblett, Rod, *Postmodern Wetlands: Culture, History, Ecology* (Edinburgh: Edinburgh University Press, 1996)

Gibbons, Luke, *Gaelic Gothic: Race, Colonialism and Irish Culture* (Galway: Centre for Irish Studies, 2004)

—. '"Some Hysterical Hatred": History, Hysteria, and the Literary Revival', *Irish University Review* 27:1 (Spring/Summer 1997), pp. 7–23

—. *Transformations in Irish Culture* (Cork: Cork University Press, 1996)

Giese, Rachel, *The Donegal Pictures* (Winston-Salem, NC: Wake Forest University Press, 1987)

Gikandi, Simon, 'Postcolonial Theory and the Specter of Nationalism', *Clio* 36.1 (2006), pp. 69–84

Giraldus Cambrensis, in Thomas Wright (ed.) and Thomas Forester (trans.), *Topographic Hibernica / The Topography of Ireland* [1188] (Cambridge, ON: Parentheses Publications Medieval Latin Series, 2000), Ch. XXXVIII

Gladwin, Derek, 'Ecocriticism', in Eugene O'Brien (ed.), *Oxford Bibliographies in Literary and Cultural Theory* (New York: Oxford University Press, 2016), n.p., web, accessed 3 Jan. 2016, www.oxfordbibliographies.com/obo/page/literary-and-critical-theory

—. 'Eco-Haptic Photography: Visualizing Bogland in Rachel Giese's *The Donegal Pictures*', *Photography and Culture* 6.2 (2013), pp. 157–174

—. 'The Bog Gothic: Bram Stoker's "Carpet of Death" and Ireland's Horrible Beauty', *Gothic Studies* 16.1 (2014), pp. 39–54

Gladwin, Derek and Christine Cusick (eds), *Unfolding Irish Landscapes: Tim Robinson, Culture, and Environment* (Manchester: Manchester University Press, 2016)

Glob, Peter Vilhelm, *The Bog People: Iron-Age Man Preserved*, trans. R.L.S. Bruce-Mitford (Ithaca, NY: Cornell University Press, 1969)

Glover, David, *Vampires, Mummies and Liberals: Bram Stoker and the Politics of Popular Fiction* (Durham, NC: Duke University Press, 1996)

Gordon, Avery, *Ghostly Matters: Haunting and the Sociological Imagination* (Minneapolis: University of Minnesota Press, 2008)

Graham, Brian, 'The Imagining of Place: Representation and Identity in Contemporary Ireland', in Brian Graham (ed.), *In Search of Ireland: A Cultural Geography* (London: Routledge, 1997), pp. 192–212

Gregory, Derek, 'Edward Said's Imaginative Geographies', in Michael Crang and Nigel Thrift (eds), *Thinking Space* (London: Routledge, 2000), pp. 302–348

—. *Geographical Imaginations* (Oxford: Blackwell, 1994)

Hammond, R.F., *The Pealands of Ireland* (Dublin: An Foras Taluntais Soil Survey Bulletin, 1979)

Hanley, Katherine, 'The Short Stories of Sean O'Faolain', *Éire-Ireland: A Journal of Irish Studies* 6.3 (1971), pp. 3–11

Hansen, Jim, *Terror and Irish Modernism: The Gothic Tradition from Burke to Beckett* (Albany: SUNY Press, 2009)

Hardy, Thomas, *The Return of the Native* [1878] (New York: Penguin, 1979)

Harris, Claudia W., 'Rising Out of the Miasmal Mists: Marina Carr's Ireland', in Cathy Leeney and Anna McMullan (eds), *The Theatre of Marina Carr: 'before rules was made'* (Dublin: Carysfort Press, 2003), pp. 216–232

Hart, Erin, *The Book of Killowen* (New York: Scribner, 2013)

—. *False Mermaid* (New York: Scribner, 2010)

—. *Haunted Ground* (New York: Scribner, 2005)

—. *Lake of Sorrows* (New York: Scribner, 2007)

Heaney, Seamus, 'The Man and the Bog', in Bryony Coles and John M. Coles (eds), *Bog Bodies, Sacred Sites and Wetland Archaeology* (Exeter: University of Exeter and National Museum of Denmark, WARP, 1999), pp. 3–6

—. *Opened Ground: Poems 1966–1996* (London: Faber and Faber, 1998)

—. *Preoccupations: Selected Prose, 1968–1978* (New York: Farrar, Straus, Giroux, 1980)

Helleiner, Jane, 'Gypsies, Celts, and Tinkers: Colonial Antecedents of Anti-Traveller Racism in Ireland', *Ethnic and Racial Studies* 18.3 (Summer 1995), pp. 532–553

Heneghan, Liam, 'The Epistemology of Hatred: A Case Study of Irish Bogs', *3 Quarks Daily*, 17 June 2013, web, accessed 7 Jan. 2016, www.3quarksdaily.com/3quarksdaily/2013/06/the-epistemology-of-hatred-a-case-study-of-irish-bogs.html

Hoogvelt, Ankie, *Globalization and the Postcolonial World: The New Political Economy of Development* (Baltimore: Johns Hopkins University Press, 2001)

Huggan, Graham, *Territorial Disputes: Maps and Mapping Strategies in Contemporary Canadian and Australian Fiction* (Toronto: University of Toronto Press, 1994)

Huggan, Graham, and Helen Tiffin, *Postcolonial Ecocriticism: Literature, Animals, Environment* (London: Routledge, 2010)

Hughes, William, '"For Ireland's Good": The Reconstruction of Rural Ireland in Bram Stoker's "The Snake's Pass"', *Irish Studies Review* 3.12 (2008), pp. 17–21

Hughes, William and Andrew Smith, 'Introduction: Defining the Relationships between Gothic and the Postcolonial', *Gothic Studies* 5.2 (2003), pp. 1–6

Hurley, Kelly, 'Abject and Grotesque', in Catherine Spooner and Emma McEvoy (eds), *The Routledge Companion to Gothic* (London: Routledge, 2007), pp. 137–146

—. *The Gothic Body: Sexuality, Materialism, and Degeneration at the Fin de Siècle* (Cambridge: Cambridge University Press, 2004)

Hush-a-Bye Baby, dir. Margo Harkin (London: Channel 4 Television, 1989)

Iovino, Serenella and Serpil Oppermann, 'Material Ecocriticism: Materiality, Agency, and Models of Narrativity', *Ecozone@* 3.1 (2012), pp. 75–91

Joyce, James, in Robert Scholes and A. Walton Litz (eds), *Dubliners* [1914]*: Text, Criticism, and Notes* (New York: Viking, 1996)

Kearney, Richard, *Postnationalist Ireland: Politics, Culture, Philosophy* (London: Routledge, 1997)

Kelleher, Patricia and Monica O'Connor, '*Making the Links': Towards an Integrated Strategy Towards the Elimination of Violence Against Women in Intimate Relationships with Men* (Dublin: Women's Aid, 1995)

Kennedy, David, '"Tell-tale skins" and "Repeatable Codes": Historical Bodies and Mythic Readings in Seamus Heaney's "Bog Poems"', *English* 54.208 (Spring 2005), pp. 35–47

Kennedy, Sinéad, 'Irish Women and the Celtic Tiger Economy', in Colin Coulter and Steve Coleman (eds), *End of Irish History? Critical Approaches to the Celtic Tiger* (Manchester: Manchester University Press, 2003), pp. 95–109

Keogh, Calvin W., 'The Critics' Count: Revisions of *Dracula* and the Postcolonial Irish Gothic', *The Cambridge Journal of Postcolonial Literary Inquiry* 1.2 (2014), pp. 189–206

Kiberd, Declan, *Irish Classics* (Cambridge, MA: Harvard University Press, 2001)

Kilfeather, Siobhán, 'The Gothic Novel', in John Wilson Foster (ed.), *Cambridge Companion to the Irish Novel* (Cambridge: Cambridge University Press, 2006), pp. 78–96

Killeen, Jarlath, 'Bram Stoker and Irish Masculinity in *The Snake's Pass*', in *Irish Gothics: Genres, Forms, Modes, and Traditions, 1760–1890* (New York: Palgrave Macmillan, 2014), pp. 168–187

—. *The Emergence of Irish Gothic Fiction: History, Texts, Theories* (Edinburgh: Edinburgh University Press, 2014)

—. *Gothic Ireland: Horror and the Anglican Imagination in the Long Eighteenth Century* (Dublin: Four Courts Press, 2005)

—. 'Irish Gothic: A Theoretical Introduction', *The Irish Journal of Gothic and Horror Studies* 1 (Fall 2006), n.p., web., accessed 3 Sept. 2011, http://irishgothichorrorjournal.homestead.com/jarlath.html

Killeen, Padraic, 'Greek myths and Irish bog gothic make for potent mix at the Abbey', *Irish Examiner*, 17 August 2015, web, accessed 11 November 2015, www.irishexaminer.com/lifestyle/artsfilmtv/greek-myths-and-irish-bog-gothic-make-for-potent-mix-at-the-abby-348469.html

Kinahan, Deirdre, *Bog Boy* (Unpublished, 2010)

King, William, 'Of the Bogs, and Loughs of Ireland', *Philosophical Transactions of the Dublin Philosophical Society* 15 (1685), pp. 948–960

Kirby, Peadar, Luke Gibbons, and Michael Cronin, 'Introduction', in Peadar Kirby, Luke Gibbons, and Michael Cronin (eds), *Reinventing Ireland: Culture, Society, and the Global Economy* (London: Pluto, 2002), pp. 1–20

Knowles, Nancy, 'Empty Rhetoric: Argument by Credibility in Patrick McGinley's *Bogmail*', *English Language Notes* 39.3 (March 2002), pp. 79–87

Kreilkamp, Vera, *The Anglo-Irish Novel and the Big House* (Syracuse, NY: Syracuse University Press, 1998)

Lallanilla, Marc, 'Turf Wars: Irish Fighting Ban on Peat Harvesting', *livescience*, 29 July 2013, web, accessed 5 January 2016, www.livescience.com/38498-ban-on-turf-cuttingpeat.html

Latour, Bruno, 'Politics of Nature: East and West Perspectives', *Ethics & Global Politics* 4.1 (2011), pp. 1–10

Lebargy, Mathias, 'Draining out the Colours: An Interview with Patrick McCabe', *Estudios Irlandeses* 8 (2013), pp. 134–142

Leeming, David Adams, *The World of Myth* (Oxford: Oxford University Press, 1990)

Leeney, Cathy and Anna McMullan, 'Introduction', in Cathy Leeney and Anna McMullan (eds), *The Theatre of Marina Carr: 'before rules was made'* (Dublin: Carysfort Press, 2003), pp. xv–xxvii

Lloyd, David, *Anomalous States: Irish Writing and the Post-Colonial Moment* (Durham NC: Duke University Press, 1993)

—. *Irish Times: Temporalities of Modernity* (Dublin: Field Day Publications, 2008)

Longley, Edna, 'North: "Inner Emigré" or "Artful Voyeur"?', in Edna Longley (ed.), *Poetry in the Wars* (Newcastle: Bloodaxe Books, 1986), pp. 140–169

Lupton, Julia Reinhard, 'Mapping Mutability, or Spenser's Irish Plot', in Brendan Bradshaw, Andrew Hadfield, and Willy Maley (eds), *Representing Ireland: Literature and the Origins of Conflict, 1534–1660* (Cambridge: Cambridge University Press, 2010), pp. 93–115

Macfarlane, Robert, 'Rock of Ages', *The Guardian*, 14 May 2005, web, accessed 9 Sept. 2014, www.theguardian.com/books/2005/may/14/featuresreviews.guardianreview34

Macken, Walter, *The Bogman* [1952] (London: Pan Books, 1972)

Marks, Laura, *The Skin of Film: Intercultural Cinema, Embodiment, and the Senses* (Durham, NC: Duke University Press, 2000)

McCafferty, Nell, *A Woman to Blame: The Kerry Babies Case* (Dublin: Attic Press, 1985)

McCartney, Donal, 'Sean O'Faolain: A Nationalist Right Enough', *Irish University Review* 6.1 (Spring 1976), pp. 73–86

McClintock, Anne, 'Family Feuds: Gender, Nationalism and the Family', *Feminist Review* 44 (Summer 1993), pp. 61–80

McCormack, W.J., 'Introduction to Irish Gothic and after 1820–1945', in Seamus Deane (ed.), *The Field Day Anthology of Irish Writing* Vol. II (Derry: Field Day Publications, 1991), pp. 831–53

McGahern, John, *Memoir* (London: Faber and Faber, 2005)

—. *That They May Face the Rising Sun* (London: Faber and Faber, 2002)

McGarry, Fearghal, *The Rising: Ireland – Easter 1916* (Oxford: Oxford University Press, 2011)

McGinley, Patrick, *Bogmail* [1978] (Dublin: New Island, 2013)

McLean, Stuart, 'BLACK GOO: Forceful Encounters with Matter in Europe's Muddy Margins', *Cultural Anthropology* 26.4 (2011), pp. 589–619

—. 'Bodies from the Bog: Metamorphosis, Non-human Agency and the Making of "Collective" Memory', *Trames* 12.62/57 (2008), pp. 299–308

—. *The Event and Its Terrors: Ireland, Famine, Modernity* (Palo Alto: Stanford University Press, 2004)

—. '"To Dream Profoundly": Irish Boglands and the Imagination of Matter', *Irish Journal of Anthropology* 10.2 (2007), pp. 61–69

McWilliams, Ellen, 'Patrick McCabe', in William Hughes and Andrew Smith (eds), *The Encyclopedia of the Gothic* (Oxford: Blackwell Publishing, 2013), web, accessed 20 October 2015, www.blackwellreference.com/public/uid=860/tocnode?id=g9781405182904_chunk_g978140518290415_ss1-10

Memmi, Albert, *The Colonizer and the Colonized* [1965] (Boston: Beacon Press, 1991)

Meredith, Dianne, 'Hazards in the Bog – Real and Imagined', *The Geographical Review* 92.3 (July 2002), pp. 319–332

—. 'Landscape or Mindscape? Seamus Heaney's Bogs', *Irish Geography* 32.2 (1999), pp. 126–134

Merriman, Victor, *'Because We Are Poor': Irish Theatre in the 1990s* (Dublin: Carysfort Press, 2011)

—. '"Poetry Shite": Towards a Postcolonial Reading of Portia Coughlan and Hester Swane', in Cathy Leeney and Anna McMullan (eds), *The Theater of Marina Carr: 'before rules was made'* (Dublin: Carysfort Press, 2003), pp. 145–159

—. 'A Responsibility to Dream: Decolonising Independent Ireland', *Third Text* 19.5 (Fall 2005), pp. 487–497

Mitchell, W.J.T., 'Introduction', in W.J.T. Mitchell (ed.), *Landscape and Power* (Chicago and London: The University of Chicago Press, 1994), pp. 5–34

Moore, George, *Parnell and His Island* (London: Swan Sonnenschein, Lowrey, 1887)

Morash, Christopher, '"Ever Under Some Unnatural Condition": Bram Stoker and the Colonial Fantastic', in Brian Cosgrove (ed.), *Literature and the Supernatural* (Dublin: Columba Press, 1995), pp. 95–118

Moretti, Franco, *Signs Taken for Wonders* [1983] (London: Verso, 2005)

Morin, Christina, and Niall Gillespie, 'Introduction: De-Limiting the Irish Gothic', in Christina Morin and Niall Gillespie (eds), *Irish Gothics: Genres, Forms, Modes, and Traditions, 1760–1890* (London: Palgrave Macmillan, 2014), pp. 1–12

Moynahan, Julian, *Anglo-Irish: The Literary Imagination of a Hyphenated Culture* (Princeton, NJ: Princeton University Press, 1994)

Mukherjee, Pablo Upamanyu, *Crime and Empire: The Colony in Nineteenth-Century Fictions of Crime* (Oxford: Oxford University Press, 2003)

Murray, Paul, *From the Shadow of Dracula: A Life of Bram Stoker* (London: Jonathan Cape, 2004)

Nash, Catherine, 'Embodied Irishness: Gender, Sexuality, and Irish Identities', in Brian Graham (ed.), *In Search of Ireland: A Cultural Geography* (London: Routledge, 1997), pp. 108–127

Neary, Michael, 'Whispered Presences in Seán O'Faolain's Stories', *Studies in Short Fiction* 32 (1995), pp. 11–19

Newman, Julie, *The Ballistic Bard: Postcolonial Fictions* (London: Arnold, 1995)

Ní Bheacháin, Caoilfhionn, 'Seeing Ghosts: Gothic Discourses and State Formation', *Éire-Ireland* 47.3/4 (Fall/Winter 2012), pp. 37–53

O'Brien, Eugene, 'Guests of the Nation: *Geists* of the Nation', *New Hibernia Review / Iris Éireannach Nua* 11.3 (2007), pp. 114–130

—. *Seamus Heaney: Creating Irelands of the Mind* (Dublin: Liffey Press, 2002)

Ó Cadhain, Máirtín, 'The Edge of the Bog / *Ciumhais an Chriathraigh*', in Louis de Paor, Mike McCormack, and Lochlainn Ó Tuairisg (trans. and eds), *Two Stories / Dhá Scéal* [1953] (Galway: Arlen House, 2006), pp. 9–58

O'Connor, Frank, 'Guests of the Nation' [1931], in Richard Ellmann (ed.), *Frank O'Connor Collected Stories* (New York: Vintage Books, 1982)

—. *An Only Child and My Father's Son: An Autobiography* (London: Pan Books, 1988)

O'Faolain, Sean, *The Irish* [1947] (London: Penguin, 1969)

—. 'This Is Your Magazine', *The Bell* 1 (1940), pp. 5–9

—. 'A Meeting' [1932], *Midsummer Night Madness: Collected Short Stories* Vol. 1 (New York: Penguin Books, 1982)

O'Mahony, John, 'King of Bog Gothic', *The Guardian*, 30 August 2003, n.p., web, accessed 10 October 2015, www.theguardian.com/books/2003/aug/30/fiction.patrickmccabe

Orel, Gwen, 'Bogboy's Beauty Makes the Disappeared Real', rev. of *Bog Boy*, dir. Deirdre Kinahan, *Irish Examiner*, 13 Sept. 2011, Arts Examiner: sec. 12

Ó Searcaigh, Cathal, and Denise Blake, 'Gort na gCnámh / The Field of Bones', *The Poetry Review* 73 (Summer 2002), pp. 95–99

O'Sullivan, Aidan, 'Crannogs: Places of Resistance in the Contested Landscapes of Early Modern Ireland', in Barbara Bender and Margot Winer (eds), *Contested Landscapes: Movement, Exile and Place* (Oxford: Berg, 2001), pp. 87–101

O'Toole, Fintan, *Enough is Enough: How to Build a New Republic* (London: Faber and Faber, 2010)

Paravisini-Gebert, Lizabeth, 'Colonial and Postcolonial Gothic: the Caribbean', in Jerrold E. Hogle (ed.), *The Cambridge Companion to Gothic Fiction* (Cambridge: Cambridge University Press, 2002), pp. 229–257

Parini, Jay, 'The Ground Possessed', in Harold Bloom (ed.), *Modern Critical Views: Seamus Heaney* (New York: Chelsea House, 1986), pp. 97–119

Patten, Eve, 'Contemporary Irish Fiction', in John Wilson Foster (ed.), *The Cambridge Companion to the Irish Novel* (Cambridge: Cambridge University Press, 2006), pp. 259–75

Pepper, Andrew, *The Contemporary American Crime Novel: Race, Ethnicity, Gender, Class* (Edinburgh: Edinburgh University Press, 2000)

Pierce, David, *Light, Freedom, and Song: A Cultural History of Modern Irish Writing* (New Haven: University of Yale Press, 2005)

Pogatchnik, Shawn, 'Celtic Tiger Economy Increasingly Makes Ireland Land of Princes and Paupers: UN', *The Canadian Press* 16 July 2004, n.p., web, accessed 5 May 2013

Praeger, Robert Lloyd, *The Way That I Went* (Dublin: Hodges Figgis & Company, 1937)

Procter, James, and Angela Smith, 'Gothic and Empire', in Catherine Spooner and Emma McEvoy (eds), *The Routledge Companion to Gothic* (London: Routledge, 2007), pp. 95–104

Punter, David and Glennis Byron, *The Gothic* (Oxford: Blackwell Publishing, 2004)

Purdy, Anthony, 'The Bog Body as Mnemotype: Nationalist Archaeologies in Heaney and Tournier', *Style* 36.1 (Spring 2002), pp. 93–110

—. 'Memory Maps: Mnemotopic Motifs in Creates, Poulin, and Robin', *Essays on Canadian Writing* 80 (2003), pp. 261–281

—. 'Unearthing the Past: the Archaeology of Bog Bodies in Glob, Atwood, Hebert and Drabble', *Textual Practice* 16.3 (2002), pp. 443–458

Raftery, Barry, 'The Archaeology of Irish Bogs', in Marinus L. Otte (ed.), *Wetlands of Ireland: Distribution, Ecology, and Uses and Economic Value* (Dublin: University College Dublin Press, 2003), pp. 202–209

Randall, James, 'An Interview with Seamus Heaney', *Ploughshares* 5.3 (1979), pp. 7–22

Reitz, Caroline, *Detecting the Nation: Fictions of Detection and the Imperial Venture* (Columbus: Ohio State University Press, 2004)

Renner, Stanley, 'The Theme of Hidden Powers: Fate vs. Human Responsibility', *Studies in Short Fiction* 27 (1990), pp. 371–377

Riquelme, John Paul, 'Toward a History of Gothic and Modernism: Dark Modernity from Bram Stoker to Samuel Beckett', *Modern Fiction Studies* 46.3 (2000), pp. 585–605

Rippier, Joseph Storey, *The Short Stories of Sean O'Faolain: A Study in Descriptive Techniques* (New York: Barnes & Noble Books, 1976)

Robinson, Tim, *Connemara: Listening to the Wind* (London: Penguin, 2006)

—. *My Time in Space* (Dublin: Lilliput Press, 2001)

Rodaway, Paul, *Sensuous Geographies: Body, Sense and Place* (London: Routledge, 1994)

Ross, Ian Campbell, 'Introduction', in Declan Burke (ed.), *Down These Green Streets: Irish Crime Writing in the 21ˢᵗ Century* (Dublin: Liberty Press, 2011), pp. 14–38

Royles, Nicholas, *The Uncanny* (Manchester: Manchester University Press, 2003)

Said, Edward, *Culture and Imperialism* (New York: Vintage, 1993)

—. 'Invention, Memory, and Place', *Critical Inquiry* 26 (2000), pp. 175–192

Saltz, Rachel, 'A Lost Girl of Ireland, Dealing With Its Lost Boys', rev. of *Bog Boy*, dir. Deirdre Kinahan, *The New York Times*, 16 Sept. 2011, n.p. web, accessed 5 Dec. 2013, www.nytimes.com/2011/09/17/theater/reviews/deirdre-kinahans-bogboy-review.html

Sanders, Karin, *Bodies in the Bog and the Archeological Imagination* (Chicago: University of Chicago Press, 2009)

Scheible, Ellen, 'Reanimating the Nation: Patrick McCabe, Neil Jordan, and the Bog Gothic', *Bridewater Review* 31.1 (2012), pp. 5–6

Schwartz, Joan, 'Constituting Places of Presence: Landscape, Identity and the Geographical Imagination', in Marlene Creates, *Places of Presence: Newfoundland Kin and Ancestral Land, Newfoundland 1989–1991* (St Johns, NL: Killick Press, 1991)

Senf, Carol A., *Science and Social Science in Bram Stoker's Fiction* (Westport, CT: Greenwood Press, 2002)

Seigworth, Gregory J., and Melissa Gregg, 'An Inventory of Shimmers', in Gregory Seigworth and Melissa Gregg (eds), *Affect Theory Reader* (Durham, NC: Duke University Press, 2010), pp. 1–25

Shapira, Yael, 'Where the Bodies Are Hidden: Anne Radcliff's "Delicate" Gothic', *Eighteenth-Century Fiction* 18.4 (2006), pp. 453–476

Shea, Thomas F., 'More Matter with More Art: Typescript Emendations in Patrick McGinley's Bogmail', *The Canadian Journal of Irish Studies* 23.2 (Dec. 1997), pp. 23–37

Sihra, Melissa, 'A Cautionary Tale: Marina Carr's *By the Bog of Cats*', in John P. Harrington (ed.), *Modern and Contemporary Irish Drama* (New York: W.W. Norton, 2009), pp. 382–386

—. '"Nature Noble or Ignoble": Woman, Family, and Home in the Theatre of Marina Carr', *Hungarian Journal of English and American Studies* 11.2 (Fall 2005), pp. 133–147

Singer, Marc, and Nels Pearson, 'Introduction', in Marc Singer and Nels Pearson (eds), *Detective Fiction in a Postcolonial and Transnational World* (London: Ashgate, 2010), pp. 1–14

Smith, Andrew, 'Demonising the Americans: Bram Stoker's Postcolonial Gothic', *Gothic Studies* 5.2 (Fall 2003), pp. 20–31

—. *Gothic Literature* (Edinburgh: Edinburgh University Press, 2007)

Smith, Andrew and William Hughes (eds), *EcoGothic* (Manchester: Manchester University Press, 2013)

—. 'Introduction: Defining the Relationships Between Gothic and the Postcolonial', *Gothic Studies* 5.2 (Fall 2003), pp. 1–6

—. 'Introduction: The Enlightenment Gothic and Postcolonialism', in Andrew Smith and William Hughes (eds), *Empire and the Gothic: The Politics of Genre* (Gordonsville, VA: Palgrave Macmillan, 2003), pp. 1–12

Smyth, Gerry, 'National Identity After the Celtic Tiger', *Estudios Irlandeses* 7 (2012), pp. 132–137

—. *Space and the Irish Cultural Imagination* (Basingstoke: Palgrave Macmillan, 2001)

Soja, Edward, *Thirdspace: Journeys to Los Angeles and Other Real-and-Imagined Places* (Malden, MA: Blackwell, 1996)

Spenser, Edmund, *A View of the Present State of Ireland* [1596], Renascene Editions (University of Oregon, 1997), p. 13, web, accessed 8 Jan. 2016, https://

scholarsbank.uoregon.edu/xmlui/bitstream/handle/1794/825/ireland. pdf?sequence=1

Spivak, Gayatri, 'Can the Subaltern Speak?', in Cary Nelson and Lawrence Grossberg (eds), *Marxism and the Interpretation of Culture* (Urbana: University of Illinois Press, 1988), pp. 271–313

Spooner, Catherine, 'Crime and the Gothic', in Charles J. Rzepka and Lee Horsley (eds), *A Companion to Crime Fiction* (Oxford: Wiley-Blackwell Publishing, 2010), pp. 245–257

—. 'Gothic in the Twentieth Century', in Catherine Spooner and Emma McEvoy (eds), *The Routledge Companion to Gothic* (London: Routledge, 2007), pp. 38–48.

Storey, Michael, 'The Guests of Frank O'Connor and Albert Camus', *Comparative Literature Studies* 23.3 (1986), pp. 250–262

Stoker, Bram, 'The Great White Fair in Dublin: How There Has Arisen on the Site of the Old Donnybrook Fair a Great Exhibition as Typical of the New Ireland as the Former Festival was of the Ireland of the Past', *The World's Work* IX 54 (May 1907), p. 573

—. *The Snake's Pass* [1890] in *The Collected Supernatural & Weird Fiction of Bram Stoker* Vol. 5 (Leonaur Publishing, 2009)

—. *The Snake's Pass: A Critical Edition*, Lisabeth C. Buchelt (ed.) (Syracuse: Syracuse University Press, 2015)

Sullivan, Moynagh, 'Feminism, Postmodernism and the Subjects of Irish and Women's Studies', in P. J. Matthews (ed.), *New Voices in Irish Criticism* (Dublin: Four Courts Press, 2000), pp. 243–251

—. 'The Treachery of Wetness: Irish Studies, Seamus Heaney and the Politics of Parturition', *Irish Studies Review* 13.4 (2005), pp. 451–468

Synge, J.M., *Travels in Wicklow, West Kerry and Connemara* [1910] (London: Serif, 2005)

Tally Jr., Robert T., *Spatiality* (New York: Routledge, 2013)

Thrift, Nigel, *Non-representational Theory: Space/Politics/Affect* (London: Routledge, 2008)

Tomlinson, Roy, 'Blanket Bogs', in F.H.A. Aalen, Kevin Whelan, and Matthew Stout (eds), *Atlas of the Irish Rural Landscape* (Cork: Cork University Press, 2011), pp. 180–185

Townshend, Charles, *Easter 1916: The Irish Rebellion* (New York: Penguin, 2005)

Trumpener, Katie, *Bardic Nationalism: The Romantic Novel and the British Empire* (Princeton: Princeton University Press, 1997)

Tuan, Yi-Fu, *Topophilia: A Study of Environmental Perception, Attitudes, and Values* (New York: Columbia University Press, 1974)

Turchi, Peter, *Maps of the Imagination: The Writer and Cartographer* (San Antonio, TX: Trinity University Press, 2004)

Valente, Joseph, *Dracula's Crypt: Bram Stoker, Irishness, and the Question of Blood* (Urbana: University of Illinois Press, 2002)

Van der Sanden, Wijnand, *Through Nature to Eternity: The Bog Bodies of Northwest Europe* (Amsterdam: Batavian Lion International, 1996)

Vendler, Helen, *Seamus Heaney* (Cambridge, MA: Harvard University Press, 1998)

Vidler, Anthony, *The Architectural Uncanny: Essays in the Modern Unhomely* (Cambridge, MA: MIT Press, 1992)

Viney, Michael, 'Woodcock for a Farthing: The Irish Experience of Nature', *The Irish Review* 1 (1986), pp. 58–64

Watt, James, *Contesting the Gothic: Fiction, Genre & Cultural Conflict, 1764–1832* (Cambridge: Cambridge University Press, 1999)

White, Victoria, 'Women Writers Finally Take Centre Stage', *The Irish Times* 15 October 1998, n.p., web, accessed 11 Nov. 2013, www.irishtimes.com/culture/women-writers-finally-take-centre-stage-1.203857

Woodworth, Paddy, 'Forward', in J.M. Synge, *Travels in Wicklow, West Kerry and Connemara* [1910] (London: Serif, 2005), pp. 7–15

Wylie, John, *Landscape* (London: Routledge, 2007)

Wynne, Catherine, 'The Bog as Colonial Topography in Nineteenth-Century Irish Fiction', in Terrence McDonough (ed.), *Was Ireland a Colony?* (Dublin: Irish Academic Press, 2005), pp. 309–25

—. *The Colonial Conan Doyle: British Imperialism, Irish Nationalism, and the Gothic* (Westport, CT: Praeger, 2002)

Young, Arthur, in Arthur Wollaston Hutton (ed.), *Tour of Ireland (1776–1779)* [1780] (London: Bell, 1892)

Young, Robert J.C., 'Neocolonial Times', *Oxford Literary Review* 13 (1991), pp. 1–3

Younger, Paul L., *Energy: All that Matters* (London: John Murray Learning, 2014)

Index

Note: illustrations are indicated by page numbers in **bold**.